CHILDREN AT RISK

CHILDREN AT RISK

Edited by

JOAN M. LAKEBRINK, PH.D.

DePaul University
Chicago, Illinois

With a Foreword by

Marvin J. Fruth, PH.D.

Professor
University of Wisconsin—Madison

CHARLES C THOMAS • PUBLISHER
Springfield • Illinois • U.S.A.

Published and Distributed Throughout the World by

CHARLES C THOMAS • PUBLISHER
2600 South First Street
Springfield, Illinois 62794-9265

©*1989 by* CHARLES C THOMAS • PUBLISHER

ISBN 0-398-05534-3

Library of Congress Catalog Card Number: 88-24886

With THOMAS BOOKS *careful attention is given to all details of manufacturing
and design. It is the Publisher's desire to present books that are satisfactory as to their
physical qualities and artistic possibilities and appropriate for their particular use.*
THOMAS BOOKS *will be true to those laws of quality that assure a good name
and good will.*

Printed in the United States of America
SC-R-3

Library of Congress Cataloging-in-Publication Data

Children at risk/edited by Joan M. Lakebrink: with a foreword by
  Marvin J. Fruth.
    p.   cm.
  Bibliography: p.
  ISBN 0-398-05534-3
  1. School attendance—United States. 2. Dropouts—United States.
3. Education and state—United States. 4. Socially handicapped
children—Education—United States. I. Lakebrink, Joan M.
LC131.C55 1989
371.2′913′0973—dc19
                                         88-24886
                                            CIP

CONTRIBUTORS

VAN DOUGHERTY, B.A.
Education Commission of the States
Denver, Colorado

JUDY EBY, PH.D.
DePaul University
Chicago, Illinois

NANCY A. EVERS, PH.D.
University of Cincinnati
Cincinnati, Ohio

GERALD WM. FOSTER, PH.D.
DePaul University
Chicago, Illinois

SHARON R. GUTHRIE, PH.D.
DePaul University
Chicago, Illinois

FLOYD M. HAMMACK, PH.D.
New York University
New York, New York

JULIA JAMES, M.ED.
Northbrook School District 28
Northbrook, Illinois

JOAN M. LAKEBRINK, PH.D.
DePaul University
Chicago, Illinois

JOHN J. LANE, PH.D.
DePaul University
Chicago, Illinois

MARGARET ANN LEONARD, Ph.D.
Counseling Psychologist
Lockport, Illinois

EILEEN MCGUIRE, M.Ed.
Chicago Public Schools
Chicago, Illinois

ANGELA PEREZ MILLER, Ph.D. CANDIDATE
Chicago Public Schools
Chicago, Illinois

SANDRA PELLENS-MEINHARD, Ph.D. CANDIDATE
Oregon State Department of Education
Salem, Oregon

PEDRO REYES, Ph.D.
University of Wisconsin — Madison
Madison, Wisconsin

SHEILA C. RIBORDY, Ph.D.
DePaul University
Chicago, Illinois

SR. FRANCES RYAN, Ph.D.
DePaul University
Chicago, Illinois

EDITH R. SIMS, M.S.
Chicago Public Schools
Chicago, Illinois

SUZANNE WEGENER SOLED, Ph.D.
University of Cincinnati
Cincinnati, Ohio

JOYCE SWEEN, Ph.D.
DePaul University
Chicago, Illinois

JOHN R. TACCARINO, Ph.D.
DePaul University
Chicago, Illinois

JULIE UNDERWOOD, J.D., Ph.D.
University of Wisconsin — Madison
Madison, Wisconsin

GARY G. WEHLAGE, Ed.D.
University of Wisconsin — Madison
Madison, Wisconsin

KATHRYN C. WIGGINS, Ph.D.
DePaul University
Chicago, Illinois

NANCY S. WILLIAMS, Ph.D.
DePaul University
Chicago, Illinois

J. HARRY WRAY, Ph.D.
DePaul University
Chicago, Illinois

Next in importance to freedom and justice is popular education, without which neither freedom nor justice can be permanently maintained.
              — President James A. Garfield

For my parents, Sylvester and Viola Lakebrink, who understood this

                    and

                Adrienne
                Michael
                Sylvia
                Elizabeth
                Susan
                Mary
                Timothy
                John
                Jerome
                Rebecca
                Mark

FOREWORD

Historically, as conditions have changed, the American educational enterprise has adapted its programs to meet the needs of divergent student populations. Although in each generation some didn't quite "make it," there was a "living" to be made and opportunities for self expression, even for those of limited academic ability. Today a rapidly changing world and especially international competition pose immense threats to our future well-being while at the same time changing demographics increasingly entrust the future of the republic to a greater proportion of individuals who prematurely terminate their formal education.

While education, more than any other enterprise, will determine the well-being of the nation and its place in the 21st century, of equal importance will be its impact on the individual. Education will increasingly expand or limit individual opportunities to achieve the American dream. As early as 1960, the President's Commission on National Goals proclaimed:

> The goal of any generation of the United States is to guard the rights of the individual, to insure his [or her] development and to enlarge his [or her] opportunities.

As in the past, education will continue to provide a bedrock for self-expression and development. However, projected demographic trends show an increasing number of children who, for a variety of reasons, are at risk of dropping out. These projections will have tragic consequences not only for these children themselves but for each of us and the nation as well.

Professor Joan Lakebrink has assembled a knowledgeable group of academics and practitioners who, from a variety of perspectives, address the conditions that put children at risk of dropping out. More importantly, they offer many ideas and practical suggestions to educators and policy makers on how to meet the needs of these children, as well as how to improve education for all children. This is a timely book and worthy of careful perusal.

INTRODUCTION

When Thomas Jefferson asserted in another age, "If a nation expects to be ignorant and free, in a state of civilization, it expects what never was and never will be," he did not indicate education for every citizen. It is clear, however, that the survival of the nation is indeed dependent upon the full development of every person. The National Commission on Excellence in Education, in its noted report *A Nation at Risk*, (1983) recognized that it was not sufficient to educate a few exceptional students.

We have done better in education as we have progressed as a nation. By 1900 the average American received about seven years of schooling and 20 percent never went to high school at all. By mid-century about half the population graduated from high school. Today nearly everyone attends school and more than half go on to some form of higher education. Still many do not receive an adequate education. We have cause to worry about our free state of civilization.

This book examines why many do not receive an appropriate education. The authors do not make recommendations as to the number of years subjects should be required by all students. Nor do they suggest longer school days or school years. They do not even demand competency testing. Indeed, several view these simplistic devices which may, in reality, work against education for all because the manner of education has far greater impact on the lives of children than these quantitative measures.

This book, rather, examines policies, practices and circumstances that place students at risk of not being educated. The authors also identify groups of children who are at risk because of these circumstances. They further offer insights to help alleviate the situations which place students at risk.

The authors bring a rich background to examine the question. All are careful researchers and practitioners in some area of education. The authors from public school districts represent teachers, principals, special educators, and central office/field supervisors. The persons affiliated with universities represent a wide spectrum of teacher education, physical education, educational foundations, educational administration, psychology, sociology, law and political science. Further, there is a perspective offered from state departments of education and the Education Commission of the States.

The authors have attempted to look at students as persons who learn, feel and grow in specific ways. The development of children as learners is examined from the perspective of their various environments. These may be the media bombardment, poverty background exasceerbated by low teacher expectations, language and ethnic heritage foreign to the school establishment, stress caused by trauma or loss of parent, drug or alcohol use, or inappropriate placement or teaching.

The spectrum of students considered is a broad one, from so-called slow learners to learning disabled to gifted with special emphasis given to development of the individual through good teaching. Practices which enhance the engagement of students in their own education are emphasized. Several chapters address specific teaching-learning issues such as teacher expectations of student potential, developing thinking skills in all students, sensitivity to learning approaches, and imaginative programming to engage students.

Several authors focus on specific policy issues which may place students at risk. Their analyses emerge, in part, from studies of youth who have dropped out of school. Terminology is carefully provided, trends noted and, most importantly, recommendations offered for improving the school practices designed to provide education in a way that students learn. Consideration is given to children of minority race or language background. Specific observations and suggestions are made for school officials and the larger community.

Finally, arguments are made by all the authors as to what we owe the children. Specific legislation already in place is examined for its effects on children, but the public will is challenged further. It is simply unconscionable that a society not do all that is necessary to educate its children.

A particularly high-risk group of children are the poor. Poor children have fewer resources to support their formal schooling and they attend schools in areas unattractive to many talented teachers and administrators. Furthermore, because they are isolated from children of middle and upper class, they have no power to effect changes in their lives. The power brokers neglect them and thereby remove the one tool that America claims is their chance to advance themselves—education. It is as if the poor children do not matter. "They don't show appreciation for schooling; their teachers aren't any good, so why try to help them? They must reform first and then we will help" seems to be the rhetoric.

The Alice in Wonderland logic seems obvious. Can America afford to ignore its poor children even if it does not recognize them as inherently worthy of its attention? (This is a difficult question to ask because of its enormous moral implications.) The National Commission asserts that "Citizens know intuitively what some of the best economists have shown in their research, that education is one of the chief engines of a society's material well-being. . . . Citizens also know in their bones that the safety of the United States depends principally on the wit, skill, and spirit of a self-confident people, today and tomorrow" (1983, 17). The number of children in poverty continues to rise. Our failure to educate them not only deprives the country of social and economic benefits but incurs grave costs in terms of long term social services.

Education is not an isolated phenomenon. Education is related to economic, political, and cultural conflicts within the nation. It is partially formed by them and contributes in some measure to their resolution. If the nation is to be strong in its democratic resolve, it must resolve that every child receive a real chance to develop his or her powers of mind, body, and spirit. Only then can the individual achieve skills and judgment needed to live responsibly and contribute to the common good. A child at risk is a nation at risk.

CONTENTS

CHILDREN AT RISK

Chapter 1

YOUTH AT RISK: THE NEED FOR INFORMATION

VAN DOUGHERTY

INTRODUCTION

During the past few years an increased dialogue on education in this country has paved the way for a wide range of programs, policies and reforms dealing with schools, students, and teachers. These initiatives have, by and large, focused on raising teacher salaries, increasing course requirements for students and making the high school curriculum more rigorous. The most recent conversations about education center on students who are not completing their high school education or who are in danger of not doing so. Although these students are not a recent phenomenon, they are now receiving increased attention.

According to numerous studies, polls, surveys and data bases, a sizeable number of youth are not successfully participating in the educational process. The term "at-risk youth" is now commonplace among researchers, policy makers and educators. These young people are at risk not only of not getting a diploma, but also of graduating with inadequate academic competencies, of not pursuing additional educational experiences, of not becoming successfully employed and of not making a successful transition to adulthood and becoming productive members of society.

The reasons these youth are at risk are many. Substance abuse, delinquency, pregnancy, poverty, and low educational achievement are all familiar indicators of the plight of many young people. Statistics on each underscore the magnitude of the problem. About 22 percent of children live in poverty; drug and alcohol abuse have risen 60-fold since 1960; teenage homicide is up 200 percent for whites since 1950; teenage arrests doubled from 1960 to 1980; teenage unemployment is up 35 percent for whites and 60 percent for non-whites since 1961. Although

3

any one of these indicators is cause for alarm, the fact that many youth fall into multiple categories is even more troubling.

Why the rising concern about dropouts in particular, the most obvious case of being "at risk," and about at-risk youth in general? First, few of the education reforms enacted in the early 1980s have addressed the needs of students who may see these new, stricter policies as the final push out the schoolroom door (MDC, 1985). There is also concern that more rigorous academic standards may increase the dropout rate (Natriello, Pallas, 1986).

Second, minority populations, who traditionally have not performed as well in school and have had higher dropout rates than their white counterparts, are making up an increasing proportion of public school enrollments (Hodgkinson, 1985; Levin, 1985). This combination portends that even larger numbers of minority students may not complete high school, a failing that will follow these students the rest of their lives. The U.S. Department of Commerce estimates that students with only one or two years of high school will earn 25 percent less over their lifetime than high school graduates, a loss to society in terms of tax revenues as well as to the individual.

Heightened interest in competitiveness in the world marketplace is a third reason for concern. Studies show that U.S. business and industry will experience shortages of entry-level workers within the next decade and that many jobs will require higher skills than today's typical high school graduates possess (National Commission on Excellence in Education, 1983; ECS, 1983). Large numbers of high school students at risk of school failure is economically unacceptable.

Fourth, it costs society more to provide for a population dependent on welfare and other state and federal subsidies than to educate and assist students in becoming participating members of society. One researcher estimated that society loses $200,000 per dropout through loss of tax revenues and increased welfare, unemployment and crime costs (Catterall, 1985). This adds up to $200 billion for each school class across the nation. Even if those figures are substantially reduced to allow for weak labor markets and other factors, the losses still add up to $26,000 per dropout and more than $20 billion per class cohort, he found.

Harold Hodgkinson of the Institute for Educational Leadership has pointed out that the costs to the nation reach even further. In 1950, every American retiree had 17 workers paying his or her Social Security benefits. In 1992, that figure will drop to three, one of them minority, he said.

State and local policy makers are looking for solutions to this increasing population of youth at risk. They want to know where to put the effort, where to put the money, how much it will cost and what kinds of policies and programs will help solve the problem. But, they are getting different messages about who is at risk, what kinds of information they should collect and what are the best ways to use that information.

Gathering information about youth at risk should not be an obstacle to action, but the lack of accurate, meaningful information has made it difficult for educators and policy makers to get a true picture of the scope and nature of the problem. This chapter looks at the information commonly available to policy makers and explores some of the issues in collecting, understanding and using this information.

THE PROBLEMS

Data and statistics serve some important functions. They show how many people are or are not affected by a particular policy/issue. Data describe characteristics of students and groups of students who are at risk. They help policy makers determine, and illustrate, whether schools, organizations, programs and policies are successful. They help them understand whether a problem is increasing or decreasing, what resources are needed and how they should be distributed.

Organizations, federal, state and local governments, and schools collect a wealth of information. Nationally, the National Assessment of Educational Progress focuses on trends in achievement. The Scholastic Aptitude Test and American College Testing programs try to predict future achievement in postsecondary education.

Data sets from the federal *High School and Beyond* data base have been analyzed to determine how achievement and attitudes differ among students who drop out of school and those who stay. (The most frequently cited studies from that data base analyze the school experiences of 1980 high school sophomores from 1980 to 1982). Other data from the federal government and national organizations supply information on poverty, unemployment and teen pregnancy. Evaluation data from Chapter 1 and Head Start programs describe the impact of early intervention on the later education success of children. Organizations such as the Council of Chief State School Officers collect data across states on the

ʋuth who drop out of school. State departments of education
ʌi school districts collect student-related statistics such as test
ʌores, attendance patterns and grade-point averages. State and local
youth-serving organizations gather data on the clients they serve.

Lack of data is not the issue. Given the extent of data collection, it
should be easy to determine exactly who is at risk of failing the education process. Why, then, is it so difficult to do so? There are several
reasons. (1) The definitions of youth at risk are diverse and conflicting.
"There are at least as many definitions of a dropout," for example, "as
there are school districts recording dropouts," according to Phi Delta
Kappa's Center for Evaluation, Development and Research. The three
major sources of national data—the Census Bureau, the National Center
for Education Statistics and the *High School and Beyond* survey—use
different definitions, and come up with dropout rates ranging from 14 to
28 percent. (2) Information is not available to the right people, such as
teachers who are the ones working directly with students. (3) Educators
and policy makers do not use, know how to use or understand the information that is available. Most likely, it is a combination of all of these.

The collection, interpretation and use of data and information about
high-risk youth raise a number of issues at both the state and local levels.
The following section discusses indicators that help tell who is at risk.
Subsequent sections discuss problems in managing large quantities of
data and ways policy makers can use information to inform and make
better policy.

INDICATORS OF RISK

How does one judge who is at risk? Traditionally, risks have been
calculated in terms of background characteristics and conditions (e.g.,
poverty and ethnicity). Descriptions of risk also focus on family characteristics, such as living in single-parent households, or on specific
problems such as pregnancy or substance abuse.

This chapter is principally concerned with youth who may be at risk
in the educational sense, students who, for a variety of reasons, do not
perform well in school and who are likely to drop out. The school career
of these students is characterized by low achievement, poor self-esteem,
frequent absences and behavior problems. If such risk factors can be
identified, they can be used to tailor policies and programs that will keep
an "at-risk" student in school.

While much of the research has focused on characteristics of you.... .
an attempt to find out why some drop out of school or to identify
students who are likely to, researchers are increasingly looking at school
factors that contribute to the problem, such as tracking policies, inconsistent treatment of discipline problems or disinterested teachers (Fine,
1985; Wehlage and Rutter, 1986). Any discussion about future data needs
should include the characteristics of schools that may have a negative
impact on students.

Student Indicators

Using national, state, and locally generated data, some states and
districts are attempting to devise profiles of high-risk students by finding out why students dropped out. Most of the profiles are based on
self-reports by dropouts and the *High School and Beyond* study. Often
used by researchers to understand why a student left school, the latter
cites reasons such as "did not like school," "could not get along with
teachers" or "had to help to support family."

The belief is that profiles of dropouts will provide schools with a
better estimate of the problems and the potential demands that will be
placed on the schools. However, many studies of dropouts simply list the
reasons that students give for dropping out. Unfortunately, they don't
provide much insight into what preceded that decision. Methods to
identify students at risk of dropping out need to provide more than
simply a checklist of variables.

Discussions with teachers, principals, counselors, and other education
personnel indicate that a wide range of indicators can and should be
used to identify at-risk youth. Among them are low attendance, poor
school performance (as evidenced by both low grades and standardized
test scores) and grade retention. These data generally are collected by
all schools.

Other, more qualitative indicators are less likely to be systematically
recorded by schools, yet teachers say that many of these signal that a
student may be having difficulties both inside and outside school. Passive or disruptive behavior in classrooms, health, or emotional problems
are frequently mentioned. Teachers also say that students who have no
connection to the school outside the classroom—who do not belong to
clubs or participate in organized sports or extracurricular activities—are

students who show signs of disconnection to school and may be at risk of dropping out.

Some school districts are trying to link quantitative and qualitative information to provide school personnel with a more complete picture of students. A North Carolina district uses a "Potential School Dropout Form" developed by the North Carolina Department of Education. Student information provided by teachers, counselors, administrators, and parents is included on the form. The collected information ranges from basic student data such as attendance, grade retention, basic skills, subjects failed and family history to "observed data" such as school performance, behavior, study/work habits, participation in extracurricular activities, self-concept, types of friends, substance abuse, physical and/or mental health problems.

In Florida, researchers at Florida Atlantic University based the following observations on research into the use of profiles and applying profile characteristics.

1. Profiles consisting of a list of variables or criteria often do not provide adequate direction to policy makers and educators because they fail to: (a) identify which are the most important factors in a student's decision to drop out, (b) specify the combinations of variables that may predict a future dropout or (c) identify the critical times at which certain factors or events adversely affect a student.

2. Some identification systems are based on "catalyst variables"—events that immediately precede the decision to drop out. Profiles relying strictly on these often result in a student's problems being identified too late or in factors that led to the decision being ignored.

3. The most accurate identification methods frequently use data not readily available in student records, such as teacher observations and interviews.

4. Many profiles identify factors that cannot be addressed by existing school services or programs.

5. Many profiles ignore school factors such as unfair or inconsistent discipline policies that contribute to a student's decision to drop out.

6. Variables such as socioeconomic status, sex and racial/ethnic background are fairly useless predictors when the majority of a school's

student population is associated with them (Florida Department of Education, 1986).

However, as the Florida researchers observed, the importance of the fifth and sixth observations listed above must be stressed. Policy makers must recognize that schools with few "at-risk youth" may differ drastically from large urban schools whose populations are increasingly comprised of many students who, for a variety of reasons, may choose to prematurely end their educational career. The current structure of public schools may not be capable of educating a majority population of at-risk youth. Schools with many high-risk youth may not have the capacity to work with students individually. They may not have sufficient resources, in terms of time, money, staff or expertise, to provide the multitude of educational and other services needed to reach a large population of youth at risk. This is not to say that urban systems are doomed to failure, only that solutions beyond attempting to identify at-risk youth by a checklist of student characteristics must be pursued. If states get into the business of indicators and profiles of high-risk youth, this distinction must be taken into consideration.

Nonetheless, the criteria for designing profiles hold some promise for developing a framework for some schools to use as they address the needs of youth at risk. As it stands now, much of the information about youth at risk, especially qualitative observations, is not always gathered in a systematic way, is not provided to school staff in ways they can use and is not linked to an appropriate and timely intervention.

School Indicators

Because many background characteristics and situations of students are unalterable, one must also examine the experiences students have in school. Studies of the schooling process indicate that schools must change some of their policies and practices to achieve greater success with some students. In an analysis of the *High School and Beyond* data that looked primarily at administrative practices and school policies, researchers found that certain characteristics of schools negatively affect students and increase their disconnection to school (Wehlage & Rutter, 1986). Their findings indicate that (1) perceived lack of teacher interest in students, (2) ineffective and unfair discipline systems and (3) the allowance of widespread truancy "form a pattern that cannot be easily dismissed because they reflect a fundamental problem with the perceived legitimacy of the institution." They further state that these problems have implications not only for dropouts but also for the degree of involvement by those who choose to stay. Other researchers agree, saying that structural factors, such as tracking and sorting students or suspension and expulsion policies, often force students out of school (Fine, 1986).

If the school is to blame, at least in part, for the disengagement of students, then educators need to know how students perceive schools and teachers, and how teachers perceive students and the schools in which they teach. Data on the interactions between the school, student and teacher and on the perceptions of students and teachers should be used to identify areas for improvement.

Several instruments are available to help gather this information: Educational Quality Assessment, Quality of School Life, Effective Schools Battery, and Wisconsin Youth Survey. These instruments are designed with high-risk youth as the focus. They seek information about student expectations, perceptions about rules and regulations, attitudes toward the school and teachers. They also include questions about teacher expectations, student interest and involvement in school and school climate.

A key concern for state and local policy makers is how to use profiles or indicators and, at the same time, avoid negative labels, stigmas and self-fulfilling prophesies. Identifying students as being at risk could potentially do more harm than good if efforts are not made to ensure that such students are not subjected to situations that increase their disconnection to school and their education.

DATA MANAGEMENT

The day-to-day management of large quantities of information is no small task. Teachers remark that they know quite a bit about the students they come in contact with, but have little time to share that information with other teachers and staff. Many schools do not provide a formal structure by which teachers can record their observations and consult with each other on the best ways to work with individual students.

Computers hold much promise because they make it possible for greater amounts of student information to be shared among all school personnel. A carefully designed software package that allows for a variety of student information to be recorded could provide useful information on an ongoing basis. Information could be categorized not only by students, but also by class, grade and teacher. Analyses of the data could indicate, for example, which students took certain classes, how much absenteeism there was in a given class or grade, behavior patterns and other variables. A computerized student record system also could yield information on how successful or unsuccessful certain efforts have been with individual students. Such data could be the basis for attempts to improve programs, policies and services (ECS, 1985).

For such a system to work, however, it must be easily accessible to those personnel who have the most contact with students—the teachers. Unfortunately, teachers remark that computers are not commonly available to them. As one teacher said: "I go into a first-grade classroom and students have access to computers, while the teacher is busy drawing lines on a sheet of paper to record attendance in the class."

A Colorado school district is currently developing such a computerized system to identify at-risk students. In cooperation with the Human Resources Department and other agencies such as social services, Head Start, juvenile justice and mental health, the district drew up a list of seven indicators related to dropping out of school: attendance, mobility/transiency, family status, ethnicity, suspension, gender and achievement. A district committee composed of counselors, social workers and psychologists will match student information to the indicators to rank students from high to low risk. A team of educators and agency personnel will identify the needs of high-risk students and develop an alternative education program and/or recommend other strategies. Community agencies will provide information on students who are receiving their services, although specific details will not be part of the computerized student record. The philosophy behind this system is to monitor the progress of high-risk youth inside and outside the school to spot problems before they develop. This program was piloted in the 1987–88school year in four elementary, two middle, and two high schools.

However, computerized individual student profiles that contain more personal information on a student and his/her experiences, both inside and outside the classroom, raise several important issues. One is access. Another is the legal question of privacy. Who will have access to the information? Will the information create unfair prejudices about certain students? What kinds of information are and are not necessary for educators to have?

CURRENT DATA NEEDS

After the data are collected, how should policy makers use what they find out?

To Learn About the Magnitude of the Problem

Before sound policy can be formulated, local and state policy makers must understand how big the problem is—how many young people are at risk? Where are they? Are their numbers increasing or decreasing? What particular problems do they have?

To begin, states should define who should be considered a drop out and require all school districts to use that definition. This would provide a state with comparable and accurate information about the number of drop outs in every district and school. However, while a statewide definition is necessary to eliminate technical and political problems that hamper more accurate and reliable collection of data, it will not answer all the data needs at the local level.

What it will do is help states collect the base data they need to evaluate the impact of services for at-risk youth and to spot and monitor trends. A trend toward more teenage pregnancies, for instance, can help determine policy and program responses. Trends can be used as evidence to develop financial support for education and create and continue public awareness of the problem.

Monitoring statewide trends can also yield information about future needs of the student population. For example, in Colorado, entering first graders are tested on a variety of skills, including listening, word analysis, vocabulary, reading, language skills and mathematics. The lack of such skills indicates these students are likely to need additional help as they progress through school. The first graders also are categorized by those who have had preschool and/or kindergarten experience. The Department of Education is finding that blacks and Hispanics enter school with far fewer skills than Anglo students. Information such as this has been used to develop support for a new task force, First Impressions, which will study and develop policy strategies for early childhood education in Colorado.

Another indicator of how widespread a certain problem might be is the demographic breakdown of a community or state. Researchers know that dropouts, for example, tend to be disproportionately from minority and low-income families. As states look at causes of and strategies to prevent dropping out, they need to know the characteristics of their population and how it's changing. For example, studies show that in certain areas of the country, the white majority is being replaced by blacks and Hispanics (Hodgkinson, 1985). Other studies show that the dropout rate is not remaining constant among groups of students. The Census Bureau has indicated that dropout rates for blacks and for white females have decreased, while the figures for white and Hispanic males have increased (U.S. Department of Commerce, 1982).

Baseline information also is necessary to understand where concentrations of high-risk youth are. Across large districts, as well as within states, schools may vary widely in the make-up of their student population and the school's capacity to provide comprehensive services to students at risk. This distinction must be kept in mind when developing policy and programs.

In summary, at the state level, better documentation and understanding of the magnitude of the problem assists policy makers in marshalling the resources needed to address the issues of youth at risk. As long as data are perceived to be inaccurate and unreliable, it will be difficult, at best, to convince policy makers, legislators and educators that there really is a problem and that they should provide the necessary resources, whether dollars or human capital, and to encourage leaders at both the state and local level.

To Evaluate the Effectiveness of Programs and Policies

Policy makers and educators should also have data to develop and evaluate programs and to change or implement new policies. Systematic evaluations of programs and services depend on data to determine whether or not a particular strategy has produced the desired results. Due to the recent increase in the number of programs to high-risk youth and dropouts, we have a clearer picture of how many youth are being served, through which programs and interventions. What is now needed is a clearer picture of what works with which students or groups of students, at which age level and by which strategy or combination of strategies.

However, few programs are systematically assessed. The Consortium on Dropout Prevention (a group of nine school districts across the country formed to gather and share information about dropout prevention practices) surveyed 564 middle and high schools in member districts during 1985 to look at, among other things, evaluation of programs initiated to prevent dropouts. It found that 13 percent of the programs were being formally evaluated; 26 percent had data of some kind, such as attendance, retention, graduation rates, but 61 percent were unable to provide any data about student progress due to participation in the program. The researchers noted that "without a reasonable data base, changes caused by program interventions cannot be validly or consistently measured" (Consortium on Dropout Prevention, 1986).

Evaluation data also help policy makers determine a program's costs versus benefits. This information can be used in two ways: (1) cost benefit studies can determine if a program's costs exceed the benefits and (2) cost effectiveness studies can determine whether one program is more effective in terms of cost than another program. Evidence suggests that successful interventions may be expensive—lower class size, new curriculum, staff training. Given the fiscal picture in many schools, it will be necessary to determine if a given program is worth the cost (Rumberger, 1986).

As schools and districts try to identify exemplary programs and strategies to adapt or develop in their systems, they need reliable evidence that: (1) certain programs are more effective when compared to regular school programs, (2) certain program components can be attributed to a reduction in dropout rates or increased student achievement and (3) costs of programs are reasonable in light of measured outcomes (Consortium on Dropout Prevention, 1986).

CONCLUSION

Although policy makers have some broad-based data about youth at risk, they seldom have all the information they need to make critical education policy decisions. The place to start when making state policy is to understand the magnitude of the problem—how many youth drop out of school, why did they leave, how many other youth are at risk of leaving? Data are also necessary to determine the scope of the problem. Is the state's at-risk population primarily confined to a small number of students in a few schools or districts? Does it encompass certain groups of students? Is it a problem that is confined to high school or does it extend to the early grades? These and other questions must be answered prior to developing policies to address the needs of these youth.

At the local level, better information is needed about the progress of students through school and about what types of interventions have been tried. More qualitative information, such as study habits, parental support or health problems can help schools better understand and serve their students. Documenting the magnitude of the problem is important, but improving education for youth at risk requires new types of information.

Research is just beginning to unravel the complexities of the at-risk youth population—what works with which students and why. Program evaluations should look not only at students who do and do not successfully complete programs, who graduate from high school or drop out, who have fewer absences, etc., but also at student and staff attitudes, expectations, changes in student behavior, self-esteem, feelings of self-worth and future goals. School policies and practices should be examined to determine what structures contribute to student disconnection from school.

Information of this kind is a starting point for looking at how schools educate all children, not just those who are deemed "at risk." Data on students, schools and programs are the foundation upon which policy can be made. Information is obtainable; however, it is just beginning to be used in ways that increase understanding of why students leave school and why some schools are more successful with certain students than others.

REFERENCES

Brown, R. "State Responsibility for At-Risk Youth," *Metropolitan Education.* Fall 1986.

Carnegie Forum on Education and the Economy. *A Nation Prepared: Teachers for the 21st Century.* Washington, D.C.: CFEE, 1986.

Casserly, M. Council of the Great City Schools. "Preliminary Technical Analyses of Dropout Statistics in Selected Great City Schools." Washington, D.C.: CSG, January 1986.

Catterall, J. *On the Social Costs of Dropping Out.* Palo Alto, California: School of Education, Stanford University, December 1985.

Cibulka, J. "State Level Policy Options for Dropout Prevention," *Metropolitan Education,* Fall 1986.

Identifying School-Based Dropout Prevention Strategies: A Survey of High School and Middle School Programs in Nine Cooperating Districts." Paper delivered at the annual meeting of the American Educational Research Association, San Francisco. New York: Consortium on Dropout Prevention, April 1986.

Council of Chief State School Officers. *Collecting National Dropout Statistics.* Washington, D.C.: State Education Assessment Center, September 1986.

Education Commission of the States. *Reconnecting Youth,* Denver: ECS, October 1985.

Ekstrom, R. et al. "Who Drops Out of High School and Why? Findings from a National Study," *Teachers College Record,* vol. 87, spring 1986.

Fine, M. "Why Urban Adolescents Drop Into and Out of Public High School," *Teachers College Record,* vol. 87, spring 1986.

Florida Department of Education and the Florida Center for Dropout Prevention. *Dropout Prevention: A Manual for Developing Comprehensive Plans.* Tallahassee, Fla., September 1986.

Hammack, F. "Large School Systems' Dropout Reports: An Analysis of Definitions, Procedures and Findings," *Teachers College Record,* vol. 87, spring 1986.

Hess, F. and D. Lauber. *Dropouts for the Chicago Public Schools.* Chicago: Chicago Panel on Public School Finances, May 1986.

Hodgkinson, H. *All One System: Demographics of Education, Kindergarten Through Graduate School,* Washington, D.C.: Institute for Educational Leadership, Inc., 1985.

Levin, H. "The Educationally Disadvantaged: A National Crisis," working paper No. 6. Philadelphia: Public/Private Ventures, 1985.

MDC, Inc. *The States' Excellence in Education Commissions: Who's Looking Out for At-Risk Youth.* Chapel Hill, N.C.: 1985.

National Commission on Excellence in Education. *A Nation At Risk: The Imperative for Educational Reform.* Washington, D.C.: U.S. Government Printing Office, 1983.

Natriello, G. et al. "Taking Stock: Renewing Our Research Agenda on the Causes and Consequences of Dropping Out," *Teachers College Record,* vol. 87, spring 1986.

North Carolina Department of Public Instruction. *Joining Hands: The Report of the Model Programs for Dropout Prevention* Raleigh, N.C.: December 1986.

Pallas, A. "The Determinants of High School Dropout", Report No. 364 Baltimore: Center for Social Organization of Schools, Johns Hopkins University, October 1986.

Pennsylvania Department of Education. *Achieving Success With More Students: Addressing the Problem of Students At Risk.* Harrisburg, Pa.: March 1987.

Rumberger, R. "High School Dropouts: A Problem for Research, Policy and Practice." Palo Alto, Cal.: Stanford Education Policy Institute, September 1986.

Stern, D. "Dropout Prevention and Recovery in California," prepared for the California State Department of Education. Berkeley, Calif.: University of California School of Education, February 1986.

Stern, D. et al. "Reducing the High School Dropout Rate in California: Why We Should and How We May," report to the California Policy Seminar. Berkeley, Calif: University of California School of Education, February 1985.

U.S. Department of Commerce, Bureau of the Census. "School Enrollment: Social and Economic Characteristics of Students," *Current Population Reports,* Series P20. Washington, D.C.: U.S. Government Printing Office, 1982.

Wehlage, G. and R. Rutter. "Dropping Out: How Much Do Schools Contribute to the Problem?" *Teachers College Record,* vol. 87, spring 1986.

Chapter 2

FACTORS THAT AFFECT THE COMMITMENT
OF CHILDREN AT RISK TO STAY IN SCHOOL

Pedro Reyes

INTRODUCTION

As early as 1852 the Massachusetts legislature enacted a compulsory school attendance law to make sure that the underprivileged would become "literate and moral" and be of benefit rather than danger to society (Hunt and Clawson, 1975). Twenty-seven states had compulsory attendance laws by 1890 and by 1918 every state had enacted such a legislation. Only two states, South Carolina and Mississippi, have repealed their laws. South Carolina, however, has reinstated the act after a trial period (Children's Defense Fund, 1974). Today all states have enacted compulsory school attendance laws, including Mississippi.

Although the original intent of such legislation still is alive in today's school attendance laws, the well-being of society is not its only concern. The laws include children's right to schooling and their right to be protected from labor exploitation. Today's free public education also has been extended to all children, including the physically handicapped, the emotionally disturbed, mentally retarded, the blind and the deaf. Education has become not only a necessity but also a right of every child.

Despite these laws many children who enter the public education system never complete high school. There are many reasons why they drop out or never graduate from high school. This chapter will include an outline of the personal and school factors that play significant roles in the student's decision to stay in or drop out of school. It will deal primarily with minority students because they are the ones most likely to drop out before graduation. The chapter is divided into four sections: (1) general statistics on children at risk, (2) the family's role in the child's decision to stay in or drop out of school, (3) the school's role in the child's decision to stay in or drop out of school, and (4) potential solutions to reduce dropout behavior.

GENERAL STATISTICS OF DROPOUTS

Definition

Current research indicates that the strongest predictors of the tendency to drop out are academic failure, school and social isolation, and a lack of support for academic achievement on the part of close relatives and peers. The same research strongly indicates that dropping out is related to socioeconomic class. Lower socioeconomic youth are more likely to experience isolation in school and have more exposure to others who have failed in school. Other research gives strong support for the proposition that frustration and alienation resulting from academic failure is the single most important reason why children leave school prior to completion. Besides tending to come from low income families, the dropouts tend to exhibit discipline problems in school, have a high rate of truancy, underachieve academically, not read at grade level, and feel rejected by, and reject, the school.

Dropouts are defined as "persons of a given cohort who are not enrolled in school in October of the year in question and have not received a high school diploma or an equivalent high school certificate (GED)" (U.S. Government Accounting Office, 1986). This definition has been criticized by Rumberger (1987) as being too narrow. For instance, he raised questions about how subsequent enrollments are accounted for and how dropout rates were calculated, implying that dropout rates are not precise and thus difficult to assess accurately the problem.

Although there is no consistent definition of a school dropout, several studies have attempted to estimate dropout rates. Estimates indicate that in 1900 about 90 percent of all males did not receive a high school diploma. By 1920, that percentage did not change dramatically. It dropped to 80 percent. During the 1950s, however, the completion rate was over 50 percent. By 1960s the graduation rate reached its peak; the overall dropout rate was 40 percent. By 1965, however, the dropout rate was reduced to 25 percent. It was also reported that by 1980 that 60 percent had dropped to less than 16 percent (U.S. Bureau of the Census, 1985).

On the other hand, Rumberger (1987) reported that with the cohort of 18–19 year-olds the dropout rate differs. For instance, in 1980 the dropout rate for white, black, and hispanic males was 16.1, 22.7 and 43.1 percent respectively. The same study reported that in 1984 the dropout rate for whites and blacks remained fairly constant while for hispanics the dropout rate dropped to 26.2 percent for that particular cohort. For females in the same cohort the dropout rate for whites in 1980 was 13.8 and has slightly increased to 14.0 in 1984. For black females 19.8 percent dropped out of school in 1980; in 1984 nonetheless the 19.8 percent was reduced to a 14.5 percent. On the other hand, the dropout rate for hispanic females was 34.6 in 1980, while in 1984 the dropout rate declined to 26.2 percent.

These figures, however, only reflect national averages and do not show the dropout problems encountered in inner-city schools. For instance, Aspira (1983) reported dropout rates for tenth grade through graduation for ethnic groups in New York State. The figures show that the dropout rate for hispanic students in New York ranges from 73.2 percent to 27 percent, while for blacks the range is from 67.2 to 32.7 percent. Table 2-1 presents these dropout figures. Obviously, the problem of student dropout is severe for these particular groups; and even if the statistics are divided into two geographic areas in the State of New York, the dropout rates for hispanics and blacks change very little. For example, in upstate New York the dropout rate for hispanics is 29.3, while for blacks the percentage is 38.8. In New York City, however, the overall dropout rate is alarming; 72 percent of the black student population does not complete high school, while 79.7 percent was reported to be the dropout rate for hispanics.

Recently, the Task Force on the New York State Dropout Problem (1987) indicated that the dropout figures in New York have not changed. The task force presented the following dropout figures: Latinos 62 percent, African Americans 53 percent, and Native Americans 43 percent. Furthermore, the New York Times (1986) reported a dropout rate of more than 75 percent at Thomas Jefferson High School in Brooklyn where the student body is predominantly African American and Latino.

The figures are also staggering as we review the dropout rates for the City of Chicago. For example, Kyle (1984) reported that the attrition rate for Chicago Public Schools has been very consistent for the last 10 years at 50 percent. However, when he calculated the dropout rate for a Chicago school district, he discovered that 74 percent of a fresh-

Table 2-1.
Dropout Rates for Racial and Ethnic Groups For Tenth Grade
For 1978-79 and 1979-80 Through Graduation in 1981-82

Geographic Area	Dropout Rates	
	Hispanics	Blacks
New York State	61.9	53.9
Upstate New York	27.0	32.7
New York City	66.7	61.1
Bronx County	70.2	67.2
Kings County	68.8	64.9
New York County	73.2	58.6

Source: Aspira Dropout Study.

man class of 1,363 did not graduate with their cohort.

In California, dropout studies show a median dropout rate of approximately 36.8 percent yearly in grades nine through twelve (California State Department of Education, 1986). The percentage of dropouts, however, does not show the figures exhibited by Chicago or New York. Nevertheless, California is among the first 10 states with the highest dropout percentages (National Center for Statistics, 1986).

A longitudinal study conducted in Philadelphia with a cohort of 505 male and female Puerto Rican tenth graders, found that more than one-third (34.7) of youngsters entering the tenth grade had left school by their senior year. The same study found that fewer than 8 percent of public school youngsters who dropped out returned to school to complete their education (Gutierrez and Montalvo, 1984). Finally, the Dade County of Florida has also reported dropout figures that range between 15 to 20 percent and 40 to 50 percent among school districts in the county. Other major cities have reported similar figures.

In sum, the problem of student dropout, whether they be from small or inner-city schools, is a serious indictment against the public school system. If we assume that a high school education is a minimum necessity to survive in this society, the exorbitant number of youth who leave school without the skills needed for life is intolerable. Why are minority students most affected by the dropout phenomenon? The current research has looked into two possible answers: personal and school factors.

Personal Factors

Personal influences comprise a broad range of factors, including, socioeconomic, sociopsychological and academic preference. Research shows that socioeconomic status is correlated with dropout rates. For instance, Combs and Cooley (1968) studied 440,000 ninth graders from public and private schools for several years. They found that half of the boys and 50 percent of the girls who dropped out of school were from the lowest quartile of the socioeconomic scale. Bachman, Green and Wirtanen (1971) also found that socioeconomic status was strongly correlated with school dropout. Furthermore, Rumberger (1983) suggested that social class is a potent variable in predicting who will drop out. Similarly, Peng (1985) showed that 1,980 sophomores from the bottom socioeconomic quintile had a dropout rate at 17 percent; while students from the top socioeconomic quintile had a dropout rate of only 5 percent. Sherraden's (1985) study showed that the percentage of white 14–17 year olds from poor families (income under $10,000) who were not enrolled in school was nearly twice as high for all black students. Furthermore, Hoffer (1986) suggested that economic constraints influence dropout behavior. For instance, some students may drop out of school because of the immediate need to generate income for their family or for themselves. Students may also forego school for work because they perceive that in the long run they benefit more from work than from school.

In addition to socioeconomic influences, several sociopsychological variables have been found to influence dropout behavior. For example, students' expectations of educational achievement is a powerful predictor of dropping out (Kim, 1985; Wehlage and Rutter, 1986). Research shows that those students who expect to attend college have a higher probability of finishing high school than those who do not plan to go on to college. Rumberger (1983) also found that aspects of family background such as education of parents, family structure and size and geographical location influence dropout behavior. Ekstron et al. (1986) concluded that the mother's educational aspiration for the student, the number of study aids in the home, parental involvement, and nonschool learning opportunities were found important. For example, lack of parental involvement in the education of their children increased the likelihood of dropping out. Gadwa and Griggs' (1985) study proved that the lack of parental support was one of the major reasons for dropping out. Also, parents' level of educational achievement is related to early exit from school. Howell and Frese (1982) found that the higher the parents' educational achievement, the lower the chances that their children would drop out of school. Conversely, low level of parents' academic achievement is also related to dropout behavior. Wagner (1984) concluded that one of the major reasons poor children quit school is a lack of parental emphasis on the value of education.

Studies have also shown that family stability and the quality of parent-child relationships affect the dropping out behavior (Pallas, 1984). Students who come from families with domestic problems such as family breakup may have little energy to cope with school demands. Mahan and Johnson's (1983) study of suburban Chicago dropouts reported that divorce, separation and death often were present in the families of dropouts they surveyed. Rumberger (1983) suggested that students who have two parents are more likely to continue their schooling than those from single-parent homes. Research indicates that having only one parent may result in lack of adequate parental supervision, increased family demands, or both (Fine, 1986).

The community's peer group norms also affect dropout behavior. For example, Kyle (1984) showed that gangs in inner-city high schools in Chicago were a major concern of dropouts. These students perceived their lives to be in danger because of the many crimes committed by gang members in high schools.

Finally, students' academic failure is one of the major factors contributing to dropping out. It is clear that those students who do not do well in the academic subjects are more prone to dropout problems than those students who do well in the academic subjects. Howard and Anderson (1978), however, have pointed out that poor academic performance leads to additional negative influences encouraging students to drop out. For example, sagging student interest results in lower grades and skipping classes. Also, parental involvement increases the student's negative and defensive attitude, leading eventually to the decision to drop out.

Several authors correlate poor academic performance and problem behavior contributors to dropout rates. For instance, Ekstron et al. (1986) suggested that acting-out and negative behavior is as critical as academic performance in contributing to the ultimate decision to drop out. Gadwa and Griggs (1985) also concluded that truancy, poor attendance and suspension were factors that explained dropout behavior. Naranjo (1978), on the other hand, reported that school problems such as boredom and inability to get along with classmates and teachers were cited by dropouts as reasons for leaving school. Other studies have reported low self-esteem and alienation (Sewall et al., 1981; Mahen and Johnson, 1983) as behaviors that also contribute to dropout behavior.

One point that is clear in the literature is that lower intelligence is not the cause of dropping out. In fact, Fine and Rosenberg (1983) have shown that many dropouts have academic ability above the mean, and are self-motivated. If Fine and Rosenberg are correct in their assertions, why is it that many students, especially minorities, leave school earlier than the majority? Could it be that the school as an organization also contributes to dropout behavior? Research concerning schools and their effect on student dropout behavior is reviewed in the next section.

School Factors

Wehlage and Rutter (1986) have argued that most of the quantitative and longitudinal studies on high school dropouts look at the causes, correlates, or motives underlying the actions of dropouts, and that little or no research has been conducted on the school itself. They argue that the school itself may contribute to negative experiences that lead to dropout. For instance, Wehlage and Rutter reported that more than 60 percent of the dropouts rated the effectiveness of their school's discipline as poor or fair. Moreover, the same group of dropouts rated "teacher interest in students" 50–60 percent fair to poor, and 64 percent of the dropouts rated the fairness of their school discipline as poor or fair. What is even more striking in their findings was that 48 percent of the white college-bound students gave poor or fair ratings to the schools in discipline fairness.

Other studies also report that school dropouts have higher correlations with school variables than with their minority/ethnic group status. Sexton (1985), for example, reported that schools with above average suspension rates had higher dropout rates than schools with average suspension rates. Another important school-variable closely associated with dropping out is school delay (being over-age compared to one's cohort), curriculum program placement, attendance and discipline problems (Ekstron, Goertz, Pollack, & Rock, 1986; Pallas, 1984). School delay carries with it a stigma because students are held back and are not with their peer group. Hoffer (1986) also indicated that delay may be indicative of other difficulties, for example, learning disorders or a lack of English language proficiency.

Further, some research shows that program placement reduces the probability of dropping out. Mertens, Seitz and Cox (1982) suggested that vocational enrollment reduces the likelihood of student dropout. Attendance and discipline problems also contribute to dropping out. For example, Berla (1986) reported that at least two types of punishment play a major role in dropping out. First, when students are given long suspensions, they are not likely to be successful in completing the academic work required for graduation or for credit for the current semester or term. Second, the use of grade reduction and withholding credit as a punishment for tardiness, absence, or other school offense may result in the student's becoming discouraged about being able to finish high school.

Wehlage and Rutter (1986) suggested that another major problem related to dropout is the inability of schools to respond to the different needs of their students. They suggested that a need exists to hold "educators responsible for those students who are not ideal academic performers as well as for those who are talented" (p. 390). They also called for the evaluation of the school's authority system and for a redefinition of the school work. Accordingly, school work is narrowly defined to serve only those who are bound for higher education. Poor students may view the school's curriculum as irrelevant to their needs and may drop out of school. Wagner (1984) argued that this is certainly the case with poor students.

Another potential contributor to dropout behavior is the student-teacher interaction. Felice (1984) showed that, although black dropouts had higher IQs (but lower grade point averages) than nondropouts, teachers rated the dropouts lower in academic ability and motivation than nondropouts. Steinberg et al. (1984) argued that a teacher pays less frequent attention to a language minority youth than to other children. When attention is paid, it is more likely to be negative. This negative interaction is another factor that contributes to dropout rates among language minority students. Many other studies cited that teachers who do not care or help contribute to the students' dropout decision. Wehlage and Rutter (1986) characterized the high school as a place where teachers are not interested in students.

Finally, the current push for newer and tougher educational standards is another source of conflict between the student and the school. Students who are struggling to get through may find new obstacles impossible to overcome. For some students raising standards may be encouraging; but for other students these new demands may be a source of frustration and failure. In fact, McDill, Natriello and Pallas (1985) suggested that these new demands may lead to higher dropout rates, especially among the poor and disadvantaged.

In sum, there is a problem of serious magnitude that needs immediate attention—dropouts. To blame the student for having a single parent, being from a lower socioeconomic scale, or not having the "proper" middle-class values is an irresponsible, short-sighted, and an illogical solution. The child is in such conditions not because of his/her choice, but because society in general has contributed to such a state of being. Therefore, to blame the dropout is to blame society. Similarly, to blame the school for the dropout problems is also not the solution to the problem. What educators need to do is to analyze critically the problem and act swiftly. Talk alone doesn't help and forestalling action only complicates matters more. Schools do not need modifications; schools need changes—changes that would eradicate the dropout problem. It is unconscionable, in a democratic society to allow a great number of children to go on in life without a high school education. What can be done about it? The next section includes some ideas and programs that may help diminish dropout behavior.

Potential Solutions

As discussed earlier, one of the key elements contributing to dropout behavior is the students' expectation of educational attainment (Wehlage & Rutter, 1986). Those students who expected to finish did so; those who did not have such an expectation did not finish. Therefore, it would be a good school policy to foster the students' expectations of educational attainment, especially for those students who exhibit characteristics that predict dropping out.

Another school policy that may be changed to help diminish school dropout is grade promotion. It is clear in the research that those students who have repeated one or more years are more prone to dropout. It is also clear that keeping the student behind his/her peer group is counter-productive. The research shows that remediation may be a better alternative than not promoting the student. Thus, a sound school policy would consider remediation as opposed to grade retention.

The school discipline system has been identified also as a possible contributor to dropout behavior (Wehlage & Rutter, 1986). This study showed that dropouts as well as college-bound kids rated the school discipline system from fair to poor. A fair and equitable school discipline policy would help keep some students from leaving school early. This finding has implications to understand reasons for dropping out. If a potential dropout student perceives that he/she is mistreated, that student would be more likely to drop out of school.

The school effectiveness literature has also identified several characteristics that make schools effective. For example, researchers cite that an orderly school climate, strong principal leadership, expectations for achievement, good communication between school and home, and a fair and consistent discipline system are strong elements that characterize effective schools. School administrators should carefully analyze their schools and look for these elements that make schools effective. Strong efforts should be made by administrators to establish those characteristics of effective schools where they are not present.

In addition to these ideas, there are some in-school programs that help reduce the dropout problem in schools. One such program is an early identification of potential dropouts. Most schools experiencing severe dropout problems have some kind of early identification program. Some schools try to help students who need assistance, while others try to identify potential dropouts, but help only those students most likely to respond to their efforts. Some criteria used by schools to identify dropouts include the following:

irregular attendance patterns
over-age in grade
parents divorced or separated
family moves frequently
poor grades
lacks basic skills (using standardized measures)
limited proficiency in English
alcohol/drug abuse
educational level of parents
peers are not school-oriented
health problems (mental or physical)

A successful early identification program would consider all of these characteristics to identify potential dropouts.

Another in-school program used to prevent school dropout is the counseling and mentorship program. This program assumes that students are provided adequate counseling. Once counselors identify potential dropouts, they engage the students' parents in assisting them to develop post-high school options for dropouts. A major role of the counselor is to be the mentor for students. If the school decides to use this program, the counselor/student ratio should be adequate to have a successful counseling/mentorship program.

Research has also identified that many students, especially minority females, drop out of school because of pregnancy. While preventing teen pregnancy is not the solution to dropping out, a school policy or strategy to help prevent pregnancies would definitely aid in reducing dropout rates. For instance, a school-based health clinic that provides medical services has been successful in reducing teen pregnancies in some states around the country. It has been also documented that the dropout rate has decreased in those pilot-schools which use health clinics.

Another program that has been used in Atlanta is the full-time schools program. In this program, students spend all year round in school. A major objective of this program is to keep poor teenagers free of pressures such as drugs, alcohol, fights or crimes. Research has demonstrated that the summer break has had a negative effect among poor teenagers and that the full-time school concept has shown positive results.

School-business collaboration is another strategy that has been used to reduce dropout rates. Involving the business community in partnerships helped potential dropouts develop the necessary skills to stay in school and become productive members of society. Boston has had a high degree of success in forming these partnerships. Several firms have signed agreements with public schools; since these agreements were signed, the student attendance has increased and reading and math scores have also gone up.

A modified academic curriculum is a common method to reduce dropout rates. The essence of this approach is to bring together all potential dropouts in a single group and provide remediation. Students are brought up to grade level and then encouraged to complete high school with their peers. Students are moved together from class to class with the idea to make school less threatening and a better experience for potential dropouts. These programs are similar to special education classes that pull students out of the mainstream classes to give them special attention and remedial assistance. Joliet, Illinois schools have been successful with this program. Their school statistics show that at least 80 percent of the students have returned to the regular classroom.

Vocational education, perhaps, is the most prevalent program used to prevent dropping out of schools. Schools try to prepare students for the world of work, through career exploration and teaching them some kind of vocation. In Wisconsin some high schools use job placement programs to shape the behavior of students. For example, if the student has bad habits such as drug use, poor class attendance, and the like, the school would not place the student in the job; he/she must break away from those habits before placement. In California, some high schools operate occupational training programs for potential dropouts. These programs have been fairly successful in reducing dropout rates.

Finally, there are some larger city districts such as Dallas that use incentive programs to reduce dropout rates. Selected schools have a system of rewards to encourage students to stay in school. The incentives range from monetary rewards to exemption of term papers and exams. For instance, the Dallas School District has a fund to help students in need; poor students who do not have the means to buy school supplies are provided with that money. In Colorado, students who do not skip a single day during the semester are exempt from final exams. Another example of this approach is the incentive of accelerated grade advancement. Some Boston public schools offer such an incentive; the student must complete a set of goals set forth in a contract at the beginning of the year. The student may be promoted to the next grade level without having to wait the full year.

In summary, this chapter has reviewed some of the reasons why students do not complete high school education, including personal and school factors that contribute to dropout behavior. In addition some ideas to help reduce the dropout problems and some of the most successful in-school programs to help decrease dropout rates were reviewed. The problem at hand needs short- and long-term solutions. A learned society can no longer tolerate the current dropout rates, especially from ethnic groups who are growing exponentially.

REFERENCES

Aspira of New York. (1983). Racial and ethnic high school dropout rates in NYC: Summary report. New York, NY.

Bachman, J. G., Green, S., and Wirtanen, I. D. (1971). Dropping out: Problem or symptom? Ann Arbor: University of Michigan, Institute for Social Research.

Berla, N. (1986). Some discipline policies lead to student dropouts. *Network*. Columbia, MD: National Committee for Citizens in Education.

California State Department of Education. (1986). California dropouts: A status report. Sacramento, CA.

Carnegie Council on Policy Studies in Higher Education (1979). Giving youth a better chance. San Francisco: Jossey-Bass.

Children Out of School in America. A Report by the Children's Defense Fund of the Washington Research Project. (1974, October). Cambridge, MA.

Combs, J., and Cooley, W. W. (1969). Dropouts: In high school and after school. *American Educational Research Journal, 5,* 343–363.

Ekstron, R., et al. (1986). Who drops out of high school and why? *Teachers College Record, 87,* 356–373.

Felice, L. G. (1984). Black student dropout behavior: Disengagement from school, rejection, and racial discrimination. *The Journal of Negro Education, 50,* 415–424.

Fine, M. (1986). Why urban adolescents drop into and out of public high school. *Teachers College Record, 87,* 393–409.

Fine, M., and Rosenberg, P. (1983). Dropping out of high school: The ideology of school and work. *Journal of Education, 165,* 257–272.

Gadwa, K., and Griggs, S. A. (1985). The school dropout: Implications for counselors. *The School Counselor, 33,* 9–17.

Gutierrez, M. J., and Montalvo, B. (1984). Dropping out and delinquency among Puerto Rican youths: A longitudinal study. Aspira Inc. of Pennsylvania.

Hoffer, T. B. (1986). *High school retention of Hispanic-American youth.* Paper presented at the Tomas Rivera Center for Policy Studies, Claremont, CA.

Howard, M. A. P., and Anderson, R. J. (1978). Early identification of potential school dropouts: A literature review. *Child Welfare, 57,* 221–230.

Howell, F. M., and Frese, W. (1982). Early transition into adult roles: Some antecedents and outcomes. *American Educational Research Journal, 19,* 51–73.

Hunt, T. C., and Clawson, E. V. (1975). Dropouts then and now. *High School Journal,* LVIII.

Kim, Seak-Kim. (1985). *Oppositional practices among high school boys: Their expression, determinants, and consequences.* Unpublished doctoral dissertation, University of Wisconsin-Madison.

Kyle, C. L. (1984). The Aspira Chicago Drop-out Study. Research Report for Aspira Inc. of Illinois, Chicago, IL.

Mahan, G., and Johnson, C. (1983). Dealing with academic, social, and emotional problems. *NASSP Bulletin, 6,* 80–83.

McDill, E., et al. (1985). Raising standards and retaining students: The impact of the reform recommendations on potential dropouts. *Review of Educational Research, 55,* 415–433.

Mertens, D. M., et al. (1982). Vocational education and the high school dropout. Columbus, OH: The National Center for Education Statistics.

Naranjo, T. (1978). Nineteen Pueblo Dropout Study. Albuquerque, NM: Bureau of Indian Affairs, Department of Interior. *The New York Times.* (1986, June 17).

Pallas, A. M. (1984). *The determinants of high school dropout.* Unpublished doctoral dissertation, Johns Hopkins University.

Peng, S. S. (1985). High school dropouts: A national concern. Washington, DC: National Center for Education Statistics, U.S. Department of Education.

Rumberger, R. W. (1983). Dropping out of high school: The influence of race, sex, and family background. *American Educational Research Journal, 20,* 199–220.

Rumberger, R. W. (1987). High school dropouts: A review of issues and evidence. *Review of Educational Research, 57,* 101–121.

Sewell, R., et al. (1981). High school dropout: Psychological, academic, and vocational factors. *Urban Education, 16,* 65–78.

Sexton, P. W. (1985). Trying to make it real compared to what? Implications of high school dropout statistics. *Journal of Educational Equity and Leadership, 5,* 92–106.

Sherraden, M. W. (1985). School dropouts in perspective. Washington, D.C.: Education Commission of the States.

Steinberg, L., et al. (1984). Dropping out among language minority youth. *Review of Educational Research, 54,* 113–132.

The Task Force on the New York State Dropout Problem. (1987). Dropping out of school in New York State: The invisible people of color. A report commissioned by the New York State African Institute of the State University of New York.

U.S. Bureau of the Census (1985). Statistical abstract of the United States, 1986, (196th ed.). Washington, D.C.: U.S. Government Printing Office.

U.S. Government Accounting Office (1986). School dropouts: The extent and nature of the problem. Washington, D.C.: U.S. Printing Office.

Wagner, H. (1984). Why poor kids quit attending school. *Education, 105,* 185–188.

Wehlage, G., and Rutter, R. (1986). Dropping out: How much do schools contribute to the problem? *Teachers College Record, 87,* 374–392.

Chapter 3

THE TIMING OF DROPPING OUT, THE POSSIBILITY OF EARLY IDENTIFICATION, AND THE NEED FOR INTERVENTION BEFORE HIGH SCHOOL

JOYCE A. SWEEN

INTRODUCTION

In the past 10–15 years, there has been an ever increasing awareness of the serious nature of the problem of high school dropout in this country. The problem is of a near disastrous order of magnitude, running as high as 45 percent of the high school freshman enrollment in such cities as Chicago and New York. Various agencies, including federal, state and local governments, as well as private organizations and corporate charitable trusts have invested large sums of money and effort both to study and find remedies for the problem.

The situation has also been of great concern to educators at all levels. The latter group, over the years, has directed much of its effort to curriculum changes, student testing programs, remedial educational programs, bilingual education, teacher-student interaction, reviewing the role of the school principal or administrator, and development and modifications in academic standards.

Studies of the dropout problem and of possible intervention programs have been directed in two primary areas: (1) The first has been the identification of common characteristics of the "at-risk" students as well as of their dropout pattern. (2) The second has been to evaluate and test various dropout prevention or student retention programs, both within and outside of the school system. These programs fall into several broad categories: including tutoring; remedial education classes; student and family counseling to increase parental support and limit external disruptive factors such as gangs, etc.; the involvement of community organizations and support services; as well as major undertakings in revision of school curricula, and the inclusion of bilingual education and alternative schools.

In the past 5 years, the author has devoted a good deal of effort in the areas of dropout intervention program evaluation, and characterization of the dropout. This chapter will present certain data, and conclusions based on those data, dealing with the timing of high school dropout, and the apparent need for undertaking intervention and/or remedial steps before entry of those students into high school.

PRIMARY CONCLUSIONS

(1) **Early Predictability of Potential Dropout is a Clear Possibility.** It is self-evident, and referenced by numerous investigators, that the dropout act is seldom an instantaneous decision, rather it is a protracted process based on many factors, both within and without the school system. There are certain "warning signals" indicating a potential problem with a particular student. Reading, mathematics and science scores, while not in themselves a definition of the cause of the problem, do generally signal the presence of a problem. Our data indicate that these signals are apparent and surprisingly consistent even at very early levels. While the extensive statistical data referenced in this paper only go as low as 6th grade reading scores, other researchers have reported indications of dropout warnings as early as 3rd, and even 1st grade (e.g., Lloyd, 1978).

Early warning signals provide the opportunity for early intervention, or the taking of other corrective measures in the educational process, to address the student's needs and deficiencies.

(2) **The Majority of High School Dropout Activity is an Accomplished Fact by Grade 11.** Our calculations, based on an extensive data base characterizing the dropout problem in the Chicago Public High School system, clearly show that 66 percent of the total dropouts will have left high school by the 11th grade. This indicates that intervention programs at the high school Junior and Senior grade levels, *while important to those students still remaining in school,* will have missed serving the majority of the dropouts.

Again, this finding stresses the need for early intervention, preferably at the elementary or, at the very latest, at the junior high school levels.

It should also be noted that a somewhat misleading conclusion is frequently drawn relating the dropout rates for freshmen and sophomores.

By definition, a student in Illinois, for example, may not withdraw from school as a formal dropout until age sixteen. Thus, a number of Freshmen below that age category do not classify as dropouts until after their 16th birthday. At that time many of them will also be classified as Sophomores. These factors can lead to a frequent misanalysis by investigators who draw the conclusion that the dropout rate for the Freshman year is low and that dropping out takes place *after* the first year of high school, when in actuality, it may have taken place in the Freshman year.

An additional source of error is based on a focus on *high school* dropout numbers which overlook those students who *never* even enroll in secondary school, but are lost in the process between junior high and high school (or even earlier in junior high or elementary grades). Our own data presented here do not include that group of students, but recognizes and acknowledges this omission. This means that the actual overall "school" dropout rate is probably substantially higher than reported for high school only.

(3) **Despite the Need for Early Intervention, There Still Remains a Need for High School Junior and Senior Class Level Intervention Efforts.** While the writer very strongly urges, both in this and other papers, that intervention be undertaken as early as possible, it must also be recognized that there is a need for intervention programs at the upper high school levels. There are some problems which are more indigenous to older age groups and can only be addressed as they develop. Quite obviously, for example, there is a higher effect from pregnancy rate at the high school level. Similarly, there is more pressure towards gang activity and drug use, as well as other extra-school pressures on the older students.

The type of intervention directed to these students will by necessity need to be much more intensive and personalized than at lower grade levels; frequently addressing not only academic efforts and achievements but also the myriad of other problems potentially interfering with that student's academic participation.

Since two-thirds of the high school dropouts will be gone by the Junior year, the group of remaining "at-risk" students requiring these intensive support structures will also be smaller.

(4) **The Type of School Attended Appears to Have a Pronounced Effect on the Dropout Rate.** Our data clearly demonstrate that there is a dramatic difference, by a factor of 3:1, in the dropout rates between the four different types of high schools in the 62-school Chicago Public High School system. While the Nonselective high schools represent approxi-

mately 80 percent of the total high school student enrollment, the enrollment in the Selective Academic and Vocational high schools was sufficiently large to draw definitive conclusions. The dramatic difference in dropout rates between the Selective and Nonselective high schools indicates an area requiring further study to determine whether the better record is due to the schools or to the "selected" nature of the students.

A further interesting observation, discussed in greater detail below, is the fact that the Reading Score "warning signal" does not appear to apply to the same degree in the Selective *Vocational* high schools (where students have both lower reading scores *and* lower dropout rates) as compared to the Nonselective schools.

DATA INTERPRETATION AND RESULTS

The above conclusions regarding the predictability and the timing of the dropout process are based on extensive data extrapolated from the computer files of the Chicago Board of Education.[1] The availability of such a data base presented an opportunity for longitudinal study of a large, well-documented student body in the 62 schools of the Chicago Public High School system.

The sample itself consisted of three cohorts of entering Freshmen composed of some 96,000 students, including one cohort of approximately 30,000 students for which we were able to obtain the 6th grade Reading and Mathematics scores. All cohorts were followed over the four-year high school period.

In this study, students were identified as dropouts through the computerized tracing of their identification numbers over their high school years. Dropouts were defined as students who, entering high school in 9th grade, were 16 years of age and were not in school, not graduated, not transferred, or not deceased. This procedure somewhat underestimates the true dropout rate due to the classification of unverified transfers as nondropouts. Students still in school 5 years after entering high school were also classified as nondropouts for the purposes of this study.

For all three cohorts, the 8th grade Minimum Competency Test scores and the 9th grade Reading and Mathematics test scores were available. It is important to recognize that while Reading or Mathematics scores present excellent measures of academic achievement, they do not necessarily indicate the cause of academic failure and/or subsequent dropout.

Thus, a student with major family problems, language difficulties, learning or other handicaps, or drug, gang and other personal or peer problems may exhibit low reading scores. A remedial effort addressing only reading or other academic areas may, or may not, resolve the above mentioned problems.

Nevertheless, the analyses presented here show that low *reading* scores in the elementary grades are a primary indicator of strong dropout potential in high school and, furthermore, an indicator which is readily detectable to pinpoint the need for some form of early dropout prevention intervention. Our analyses also showed that low *mathematics* or *minimum competency* scores can also serve as similar warning signals, but for reasons of space limitation those data are not presented in this chapter.

The following tables and figures take into consideration such diverse factors as type of high school, 6th and 9th grade reading scores, and high school-year of dropout as they relate to the overall dropout rates. When presented in these forms, some interesting and heretofore unsuspected or undocumented relationships become apparent. For example, the reading score, which under almost all circumstances has proven to be a bell-weather of academic problems, appears to play a much lesser role in predicting dropout rates in Chicago's Selective *Vocational* high schools. The specific results are presented and discussed in relation to Tables 3-1, 3-2, and 3-3 and Figure 3-1 below.

Table 3-1 presents an overview of Chicago's public high schools from the 1982–83 to the 1985–86 school years in terms of student membership, grade 12 reading achievement and dropout rate based on the Freshman to Senior year student loss. The columns in Table 3-1 represent all high school students and students enrolled in the four different types of Chicago Public High Schools, namely, (1) Nonselective Segregated, (2) Nonselective Integrated, (3) Selective Vocational and (4) Selective Academic.

Segregated schools are defined by more than 70 percent minority enrollment and represent some 55 percent of the total Chicago public high school student body. Integrated schools are defined as 30 percent nonminority, and represent approximately 26 percent of the total city high school student body, while the Vocational and Academic high schools, where students are selected by application, together represent 19 percent of the citywide high school student body.

The rows of Table 3-1 represent (a) the total approximate high school membership for school years 1982–83 to 1985–86, (b) the Median Percen-

Table 3-1.
Chicago Public High Schools: Student Membership, Median Grade 12
Reading Percentiles, and High School (4-year)
Drop-out Rates by Type of High School for School Years
1982–83 to 1985–86.

		Type of High School			
	All	*Non selective Segregated*	*Non selective Integrated*	*Selective Vocational*	*Selective Academic*
A. *Total Student Membership* (a)					
1982–83	114,132	—	—	—	—
1983–84	108,128	60,761	27,597	10,859	8,911
1984–85	110,004	61,070	28,566	11,106	9,272
1985–86	104,234	52,537	31,421	11,347	8,909
B. *Median Reading Percentile for Grade 12* (b)					
1982–83	32.0	21.4	39.6	34.0	62.0
1983–84	34.0	23.3	40.1	37.4	69.0
1984–85	34.0	24.8	37.6	36.8	73.0
1985–86	34.0	25.2	39.3	35.4	72.3
C. *Freshman (4-year) Dropout Rate* (c)					
1982–83	41.6	50.8	33.7	26.0	17.9
1983–84	39.5	48.3	34.3	25.7	14.0
1984–85	44.9	50.7	40.5	32.1	17.2
1985–86	48.1(d)	—	—	—	—

a. As reported in "Chicago Public Schools: Fall Test Scores and Selected Characteristics," Board of Education, City of Chicago.

b. The "Tests of Achievement and Proficiency" (TAP) are given to Chicago Public High School students in the Fall of each year. The TAP consists of six subtests: Reading, Using Sources of Information, Social Studies, Written Expression, Mathematics and Science. Only the Reading subtest medians are presented here. Medians for other subtests follow similar patterns for the four types of schools.

c. Based on number of freshmen entering in the Fall *four years prior* and not graduating, transferring, dying or continuing in school in June of the listed school year, e.g. the 1982–83 dropout rate is based on those freshmen entering in the Fall of 1979. Figures for types of high schools are averages based on dropout rates for individual schools. Figures may differ slightly from those reported elsewhere due to methods of calculation.

d. Dropout rates by type of school were not available for 1985–86, however, the Illinois State Board of Education's "School Year Report Card Summary 1985–86" reported an overall high school graduation rate for Chicago of 51.9 percent.

tile Reading scores for Grade 12 by school year, and (c) the dropout rate
for the entering Freshman cohorts of 1979 to 1982 (that is, those Freshmen
due to graduate in June of years 1983 to 1986, respectively).

In interpreting this Table, it is important to recognize that the Median
Grade 12 Reading Percentile is based on a national Median Percentile of
50.0 and that, furthermore, the dropout of students prior to their Senior
year has most likely *already eliminated* a major portion of the academically poorest students before the 12th grade reading tests were ever
given. Thus, the *true* reading level at Grade 12 (had all Freshmen
remained) is certainly even lower than presented.

This point is particularly tragic for the Nonselective Segregated High
Schools. These schools enroll over 50 percent of Chicago's public high
school students and lose, on the average, half of their entering freshmen
over the four-year high school period. And these schools have, for their
remaining students, a Median Reading Percentile for Grade 12 at or
below the first quartile of 25.0 (Table 3-1).

Figure 3-1 portrays the timing and percentage of Chicago's public high
school dropouts in graphic form over a four-year period (Freshman to Senior years) for the four types of Chicago Public High Schools. The raw data
supporting Table 3-1 had demonstrated that there was a consistency in
Freshman cohorts, thus, Figure 3-1 shows the Freshman cohorts of 1978,
1979, and 1980 combined; N = 96,245 students. (There are approximately
33,000 students entering 9th grade each year in the Chicago Public
High Schools.)

Careful examination of Figure 3-1 presents some rather unique conclusions.

The graph is based on three (not four) separate dropout rates across
the four years of high school. This was done since the dropout rate by the
end of the Freshman year is somewhat ambiguous. A number of the
students are under 16 years of age and, thus, not eligible for "officially"
being classified as dropping out of school. Consequently, the first dropout point represented in Figure 3-1 (June of the Sophomore year) totals
the Freshman and Sophomore years.

For the Vocational and Academic high schools, these first two school
years represent dropout rates of 3.5 percent and 5.7 percent, respectively;
whereas, the Segregated high schools already show a higher dropout
rate of 16.1 percent in the same time period. The Integrated high
schools fall in between, with a dropout rate of 9.3 percent by the
Sophomore year.

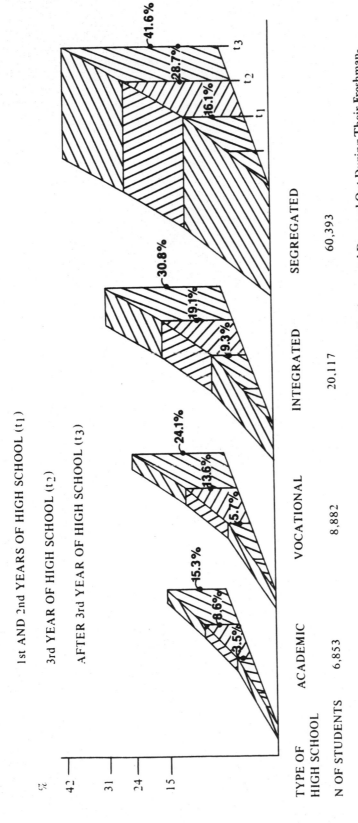

CUMULATIVE PERCENT DROPOUT BY:

1st AND 2nd YEARS OF HIGH SCHOOL (t_1)

3rd YEAR OF HIGH SCHOOL (t_2)

AFTER 3rd YEAR OF HIGH SCHOOL (t_3)

TYPE OF HIGH SCHOOL	ACADEMIC	VOCATIONAL	INTEGRATED	SEGREGATED
N OF STUDENTS	6,853	8,882	20,117	60,393

Figure 3-1. Cumulative Percent of Students Who Entered Chicago Public High Schools as Freshmen and Dropped Out During Their Freshman-Sophomore (1st–2nd) Years, Junior (3rd) Year or Senior (4th) Year by Type of High School: Freshmen of 1978, 1979 and 1980 Combined.

Table 3-2.
Percent of the Chicago Public High School Student Dropouts Who Dropped Out During Their Freshman-Sophomore (1st-2nd) Years, Junior (3rd) Year or Senior (4th) Year by Type of High School: Freshmen of 1978, 1979 and 1980 combined.

	Type of High School				
	All	*Non selective Segregated*	*Non selective Integrated*	*Selective Vocational*	*Selective Academic*
Time of Dropping Out					
t_1: Freshman and Sophomore Years	35.7	38.6	30.2	24.0	22.8
t_2: Junior Year	30.1	29.4	32.1	32.9	29.5
t_3: Senior Year	34.2	32.0	37.7	43.1	47.7
Total N Dropouts (a)	34,501	25,119	6,192	2,143	1,047

(a) Based on those students entering as Freshmen in the Fall of 1978, 1979, and 1980 in Chicago's Public High Schools who dropped out of high school by the end of their senior (4th) year, i.e., June of 1982, 1983, and 1984, respectively.

At the end of the four high school years, the Academic, Vocational, Integrated and Segregated high schools showed dropout rates of 15.3 percent, 24.1 percent, 30.8 percent and 41.6 percent, respectively.

In examining the time-frame of dropping out, one can consider the percentage of total entering students who remain, or, more interestingly, the percent of the total dropouts who have dropped out *at any one point.* Thus, by the end of the Sophomore year, 22.8 percent of the Freshman students who will drop out of the Academic high schools will have done so. However, nearly double, or 38.5 percent, of the Freshmen who will drop out will have done so by the end of the Sophomore year in the Segregated high schools. These data are shown in Table 3-2.

Significantly, just over two-thirds (69 percent) of the total dropouts in the Segregated high schools will already be gone by the end of their Junior year. Thus, Senior-year intervention programs will be limited to addressing less than one-third of the total dropouts in these high schools. This clearly illustrates the need for early dropout intervention. In these high schools, retention programs must begin in the Freshman year (or earlier, in the elementary feeder schools).

Table 3-3 compares the 6th grade and 9th grade reading scores and subsequent high school dropout rate for one cohort, the Class of 1984 (entering Freshmen in 1980). For this cohort longitudinal data were

Table 3-3.
High School Dropout Rates by Sixth and Ninth Grade Reading Achievement:
Chicago Public High School Class of 1984
(Entering Freshmen of 1980) by Type of High School.

		Type of High School			
	All	Non selective Segregated	Non selective Integrated	Selective Vocational	Selective Academic
Freshman (4-year) Dropout Rate for Students:					
1. *Reading Below Grade Level*					
—in 6th grade	37.1(a)	39.8	33.8	24.2	20.2
—in 9th grade	38.2	40.1	35.6	26.1	17.7
2. *Reading Above Grade Level*					
—in 6th grade	19.0	22.8	21.4	19.6	10.3
—in 9th grade	17.9	20.8	20.6	19.8	7.2

(a) Percent of students entering Chicago Public High School as Freshmen in 1980, with the indicated Reading level, who dropped out of High School within four years. Only students for whom Reading scores were available are included in the Table. For 6th grade Reading scores, 6,476 freshman students were at or above level and 17,248 were below level; the respective N's for the four types of High Schools are: 2,234, 12,531; 1,734, 2,932; 1,011, 1,548; 1,497, 237. For 9th grade Reading scores, 8,466 freshman students were at or above level and 16,254 were below level; the N's for the four types of High Schools are: 3,061, 12,197; 2,227, 2,816; 1,518, 1,124; 1,660, 117. While not presented in this Table, 6th and 9th grade Mathematics scores and 8th grade Minimum Competency scores are similarly related to subsequent dropout rates. Reading scores are based on *Iowa Tests of Basic Skills* given in the Spring of the sixth grade and on the *Tests of Achievement and Proficiency* given in the Fall of ninth grade.

available over the *seven year* span from Fall of 6th grade to Spring of 12th grade.

The longitudinal data in this table clearly demonstrate that in the Segregated, Integrated and Academic high schools, the dropout rate for those students reading *below* grade level in either 6th or 9th grade, warns of an almost two-fold greater risk of high school dropout.

There is little difference between those showing below-grade reading scores, in 6th and 9th grade, and their subsequent dropout rate. Thus, poor reading performance *as early as the 6th grade* is a significant "warning signal" for potential high school dropout.

A further serious consideration for the above cited entering class of 1980 Freshmen is the fact that close to three-fourths (72.7 percent) of the 23,724 students for whom 6th grade reading scores were available in Table 3-3 were reading below grade level in 6th grade. For that majority of the cohort which entered Chicago's Segregated high schools, *85 percent* were reading below grade level *in 6th grade.*

An interesting observation can be made from Table 3-3 with respect to the Vocational high schools. While those reading below grade-level in the 6th grade had a 4.6 percent higher dropout rate in these high schools, the difference was significantly less than for the other three types of high schools. This would indicate that low reading achievement does not play as significant a role in the dropout from vocational high school as it does in the general or academically-oriented high schools.

While lower dropout rates are common to the selective high schools, vocational schools seem to *equally retain* those students with low reading achievements and those reading above grade level. This is probably due to the overall lower opportunity for academic achievement courses in vocational schools. Gamoran (1987), for example, finds vocational track students to have lower math and reading achievement even when prior achievement and other background variables are controlled.

That vocational schooling may limit academic achievement needs to be balanced with the potentially higher "holding power" of vocational curricula for students with lower academic achievement levels.

SUMMARY

In this section of the book, the author has attempted to present several conclusions reached during her research, supported by actual data from that research.

In the preparation of the manuscript, the works by numerous other researchers in this general area were reviewed. Much of their work indicates results which tend to corroborate those presented here.

In some instances, such as Lloyd, 1978, identification of problem students were reported as low as third grade. Other authors stressed the importance of nonschool pressures and factors as causative factors. The works of some of these other authors are referenced at the end of this chapter.

The overall summative conclusion reached by this writer, and expressed by other authors in different words is that: the dropout problem is a serious, complex, multifaceted, and protracted process; frequently starting early in the educational process. Early experiences and failures compound to additional failures, inspiring lower self-image and/or lower educational aspirations, and frequently culminating in withdrawal and/or dropping out. Thus, the actual act of dropping out is only a final step.

Furthermore, this downhill process appears to take place at an ever-accelerating pace. Thus, the earlier that an intervention and/or other corrective measure can take place in the process, the better are the possibilities of success.

Endnote

[1] The author is indebted to Dr. Irving Brauer and, particularly, Dr. William Rice of the Office of Research and Evaluation, Chicago Board of Education for making the longitudinal analyses presented here possible.

REFERENCES

Bock, Darrel R. and Elsie G.J. Moore. *Advantage and Disadvantage.* Erlbaum: Hillsdale, N.J., 1986.

Casserly, M. and F. Stevens. *Dropouts from the Great City Schools.* Washington, D.C.: Council of the Great City Schools, 1986.

Cervantes, L. *The Dropout: Causes and Cures.* The University of Michigan Press: Ann Arbor, MI, 1965.

Fine, M. and P. Rosenberg. "Dropping Out of High School: The Ideology of School and Work." *Journal of Education.* Vol. 165 (3), 1983, 257–272.

Fitzsimmons, S.J., J. Cheever, E. Leonard, and D. Macunovich. "School Failure: Now and Tomorrow." *Developmental Psychology.* 1969: 1, pp. 134–146.

Gamoran, Adam. "The Stratification of High School Learning Opportunities." *Sociology of Education.* 1987, Vol. 60: pp. 135–155.

Howard, M. and R. Anderson. "Early Identification of Potential School Dropouts: A Literature Review." *Child Welfare,* 57 (4) pp. 221–230, 1978.

Jencks, C.L., M. Smith, H. Acland, M.J. Bane, D.K. Cohen, H. Gintis, B. Heyns and S. Michaelson. *Inequality: A Reassessment of the Effects of Family and Schooling in America.* New York: Basic Books, 1972.

Lee, Valerie E. and Anthony S. Bryk. Curriculum Tracking as Mediating the Social Distribution of High School Achievement. *Sociology of Education,* Vol. 61 (April), 1988, 78–94.

Lindgren, H. *Educational Psychology in the Classroom.* New York: Oxford University Press, 1980.

Lloyd, Norman Dee. "Prediction of School Failure from Third Grade Data. *Educational and Psychological Measurement.* 1978: pp. 1193–1200.

Peng, Samuel S. "High School Dropouts: Descriptive Information from High School and Beyond." Bulletin 83-2216, pp. 1–9, National Center for Education Statistics, November, 1983.

Rosenbaum, J.E. 1976. Inequality: The Hidden Curriculum of High School Tracking. New York: John Wiley and Sons.

Rumberger, R.W. "Dropping Out of High School: The Influences of Race, Sex and Family Background." *American Educational Research Journal.* 1983, Vol. 20, 199–220.

Weber, J.M. "The Role of Vocational Education in Decreasing the Dropout Rate." Washington, D.C.: Office of Vocational and Adult Education, 1986.

————, *The Urban School Reform Initiative,* U.S. Department of Health, Education and Welfare. September, 1979.

Chapter 4

PRINCIPAL PERCEPTIONS OF THE AT-RISK CHILD

John J. Lane

No one knows exactly why children drop out of school. We do know that after nearly forty years of decline recent short-term dropout trends have begun to increase. Worse, incidence of dropping out among poor minorities is now about 40 percent. The dropout rate in Chicago approaches 50 percent with some Chicago high schools experiencing a dropout rate of nearly 70 percent.

As in all big-city school systems, a constellation of social, economic, psychological, and educational factors contribute to high dropout rates. In order to begin to sort out these factors, a group of researchers associated with the Chicago Area Studies Center of DePaul University undertook the analysis of data on more than 94,000 students. The data had been gathered, in large part, for a 1985 study of Chicago dropouts directed by the Chicago Panel on Public School Finance. (It was the Panel that discovered that, despite an "official" dropout rate of 8 percent, a figure derived from a complex leave code system, the real dropout rate approached 44 percent.) Part of the DePaul study included a principal survey on the at-risk child. Highlights of that report form the basis for this chapter.

When complete and accurate data are unavailable as was the case in this study, perceptions about a problem take on added importance. Under any circumstances, perceptions of principals are especially valuable, because of the way principals perceive a problem greatly influences how that problem will be addressed and whether or not it will become a priority matter for the school.

In that light, we attempted to survey all the Chicago high school principals asking them to identify the major forces that contribute to students' dropping out of school and to share their wisdom about how to handle the dropout problem. The principals' response was most positive. Nearly all of the 67 principals of nonspecial schools responded in some way or other. The report here, however, is based on the response of 65 principals.

Two other points need to be clarified. First, for the purposes of our study, a dropout was defined as a student who enters the ninth grade and after five years is either not in school, not graduated, or not transferred. Second, following other recent research reports on Chicago schools, our data were presented by type of school. Chicago has four major types of schools: selective academic, selective vocational, nonselected integrated, and nonselective segregated. Selective academic accept about 7 percent of entering freshmen. Graduates of these schools are generally college-bound. Selective vocational schools also focus on preparing students for postsecondary work. Obviously, they also emphasize preparation in manual and technical arts and engineering. Nonselective integrated high schools are general neighborhood high schools with no specific selection criteria. Often these schools are located in predominately white neighborhoods with an enrollment predominantly white. Nonselective segregated schools are also general high schools with no specific entrance criteria. Enrollment is composed almost entirely of minority students.

Based on both a review of the literature relating to dropouts and truancy and on interviews with administrators in the Pupil Personnel Office, ten factors were identified as contributing significantly to dropping out of school: course failures, pregnancy, fear of gangs in the neighborhood, fear of gangs in the schools, irrelevant curriculum, peer pressure, teacher absenteeism, student class cuts, truancy, and student language problems. Principals were also invited to list any additional factors which they believe contribute to dropping out. Principals responded to all questions considering only their own schools, not the entire school system.

According to the Chicago Public High School principals, the number one factor contributing to students' dropping out of school is course failures. This perception supports the qualitative research findings of several researchers who have found that many students do not appear to understand the cumulative effect of course failures. That is, many students find themselves at the end of the sophomore year, with several failures. Apparently, only then do they come to understand that graduation is not two but at least three years away. Discouraged, they leave school.

Course Failures

TYPE	MOST	VERY	IMPORTANT	SOMEWHAT	LEAST
Selective Academic	33.3	33.3	33.3	0	0
Selective Vocational	33.3	0	33.3	33.3	0
Non-Selective Vocational	33.3	40.0	20.0	0	6.7
Non-Selective Segregated	37.1	34.3	17.1	8.6	2.9
Non-Typical	12.5	25.0	25.0	0	37.5

Figure 4-1.

Course failures may be explained in part also by the principals' observation that the second and third most important contributors to dropping out are truancy and class cuts. Here the logic is simple. If the students do not attend class, it is difficult, if not impossible, to pass a course. While there is no official policy about automatic failure for students who do not attend class, interviews with various district personnel reveal that students who miss twenty sessions of a course in fact fail that course.

Surprisingly, despite the great number of students with multiple course failures, principals found little fault with the relevancy of the present high school curriculum. Only two principals viewed "irrevelant curriculum as either a "most important" or "very important" factor contributing to dropping out. Eleven principals perceived "irrelevant curriculum" as an important factor.

Because thousands of students who enter high school not only read well below the national level but also have failed the minimum competency test, this response is difficult to interpret. Students who fail the minimum competency test are not prepared for the high school curriculum and to that extent, at least, it is irrelevant for them. To be fair, it must be said that in responding to this question, principals may have correctly assumed that "readiness" for the curriculum is much different from "relevance" of the curriculum.

Following in order of frequency mentioned after "course failure," "truancy," and "class cuts," were "pregnancy" and "peer pressure." With notable exceptions like the *Aspira Chicago Hispanic Dropout Study* (Aspira Inc. of Illinois and Kyle, 1984), few studies have carefully assessed the impact of such factors as "pregnancy" and "peer pressure" on student dropout rates. Yet the principals regard both as major deterrents to student retention. Access to aggregated Chicago-area hospital data on births to teenage girls may help to test the validity of the principals' perception of the teenage pregnancy problem.

Student Truancy

TYPE	MOST	VERY	IMPORTANT	SOMEWHAT	LEAST
Selective Academic	0	33.3	0	33.3	33.3
Selective Vocational	0	33.3	33.3	33.3	0
Non-Selective Vocational	40.0	26.7	26.7	6.7	0
Non-Selective Segregated	29.4	38.2	26.5	5.9	0
Non-Typical	22.2	0	22.2	22.2	33.3

Figure 4-2.

Similarly, more in-depth interviews and qualitative assessments of the school climate may prove helpful in determining the nature and extent of "peer pressure" to leave school. This kind of information is essential if counseling potential dropouts is to be effective.

Although recent news accounts and Kyle's 1985 study give the impression that fear of gangs operating in the schools and neighborhoods contribute extensively to students' dropping out, only 11 principals cited "fear of gangs in the *school*" as an "important," "very important," or "most important," factor contributing to dropping out. A greater number, 24 principals, cited "gangs in the *neighborhood*" as "important," "very important," "most important." It should be noted that only two principals cited "fear of gangs in the *neighborhood:*": as a "most important factor."

Of the ten possible contributors to dropping out, the three which, according to the principals contribute least to dropping out are, in descending order, "irrelevant curriculum," "language problems" and

Student Class Cuts

TYPE	MOST	VERY	IMPORTANT	SOMEWHAT	LEAST
Selective Academic	0	33.3	66.7	0	0
Selective Vocational	33.3	33.3	0	33.3	0
Non-Selective Vocational	20.0	40.0	33.3	6.7	0
Non-Selective Segregated	35.3	29.4	23.5	11.8	0
Non-Typical	0	11.1	22.2	0	66.7

Figure 4-3.

Pregnancy

TYPE	MOST	VERY	IMPORTANT	SOMEWHAT	LEAST
Selective Academic	0	0	66.7	0	33.3
Selective Vocational	0	0	50.0	0	50.0
Non-Selective Vocational	0	6.7	20.0	46.7	26.7
Non-Selective Segregated	11.4	25.7	37.1	14.3	11.4
Non-Typical	22.2	11.1	0	11.1	2.1

Figure 4-4.

"teacher absenteeism." We have already commented briefly on the curriculum and dropping out.

While difficulty with language may not contribute directly to dropping out, it is hard to reconcile this principal perception with the fact that Hispanic students are dropping out in proportionately larger numbers than whites, blacks or Asians. Neither does it square with School

Peer Pressure

TYPE	MOST	VERY	IMPORTANT	SOMEWHAT	LEAST
Selective Academic	0	0	0	33.3	66.7
Selective Vocational	0	33.3	33.3	0	33.3
Non-Selective Vocational	0	13.3	40.0	46.7	0
Non-Selective Segregated	14.3	28.6	11.4	31.4	14.3
Non-Typical	0	22.2	11.1	11.1	55.6

Figure 4-5.

Fear of Gangs in the Schools

TYPE	MOST	VERY	IMPORTANT	SOMEWHAT	LEAST
Selective Academic	0	0	0	0	100.0
Selective Vocational	0	0	0	33.3	66.7
Non-Selective Vocational	0	0	13.3	46.7	40.0
Non-Selective Segregated	5.9	5.9	23.5	26.5	38.2
Non-Typical	0	0	0	33.3	66.7

Figure 4-6.

Board's data showing that Hispanics are more likely to have better attendance in their bilingual classes when compared with their non-bilingual classes. We need more research like the 1984 Steinburg, Blinde and Chan study of dropping out among language minority student groups.

Fear of Gangs in the Neighborhood

TYPE	MOST	VERY	IMPORTANT	SOMEWHAT	LEAST
Selective Academic	0	0	0	33.3	66.7
Selective Vocational	0	0	33.3	0	66.7
Non-Selective Vocational	0	6.7	20.0	46.7	26.7
Non-Selective Segregated	11.4	20.0	20.0	28.6	20.0
Non-Typical	11.1	0	11.1	33.3	44.4

Figure 4-7.

Irrelevant Curriculum

TYPE	MOST	VERY	IMPORTANT	SOMEWHAT	LEAST
Selective Academic	0	0	0	33.3	66.7
Selective Vocational	0	0	33.3	33.3	33.3
Non-Selective Vocational	0	7.7	15.4	46.2	30.8
Non-Selective Segregated	2.9	2.9	20.0	31.4	42.9
Non-Typical	0	0	11.1	33.3	55.6

Figure 4-8.

In addition to the factors that contribute to dropping out, we were also interested in knowing which events occurring within the community at large contribute to students not attending school. Among the choices principals considered were: "bad weather," "gang activity," "locally high unemployment rates," "family upheavals like divorce and death," and "teacher strikes." Again, principals were asked to designate other events

Student Language Problems

TYPE	MOST	VERY	IMPORTANT	SOMEWHAT	LEAST
Selective Academic	0	0	0	0	100.0
Selective Vocational	0	0	0	33.3	66.7
Non-Selective Vocational	0	0	13.3	46.7	40.0
Non-Selective Segregated	0	8.6	8.6	20.0	62.9
Non-Typical	0	0	0	22.2	77.8

Figure 4-9.

Teacher Absences

TYPE	MOST	VERY	IMPORTANT	SOMEWHAT	LEAST
Selective Academic	0	0	33.3	33.3	33.3
Selective Vocational	0	0	0	0	100.0
Non-Selective Vocational	0	0	0	20.0	80.0
Non-Selective Segregated	0	0	14.3	17.1	68.6
Non-Typical	0	11.1	0	11.1	77.8

Figure 4-10.

within the community and not listed in the survey which also contribute to students not attending school. Forty-three principals identified "family upheaval" as a "serious" or "very serious" contributor to dropping out. Twenty-four cite "locally high unemployment rates" as a contributor. In descending order of frequency mentioned, "bad weather," "gang activity" and "teacher strikes" were identified as contributing to student absenteeism.

Among the other contributing phenomena cited were: "peer influence," "return to homeland," "baby-sitting," "lack of parental support," and "drug abuse."

Because absenteeism often precedes dropping out, we decided to test the principals' perception of the scope of the absentee problem. Fifty-three of the 64 respondents consider absenteeism as a "moderately serious," "serious" or "very serious" problem in their schools. Fifty-seven believe class cuts are a "moderately serious," "serious" or "very serious" problem.

WHEN ARE STUDENTS TRUANT?

Principals identified five critical months associated with truancy. In descending order of frequency mentioned, June (24), May (16), December (15), January (14) and September (14) are the months when students are most likely to be truant.

In an effort to identify the capability of schools to address the problem of truancy, we asked the principals to indicate the average weekly caseload of the truant officers assigned to their schools. Not all principals responded to this question. Also two schools indicated that in a given week they may have an average of two or three thousand students absent. Eliminating these two schools and seventeen nonrespondents, the average for the forty-six responding schools was about 70 students per week. A number of principals indicated that their truant officers are available to their schools only two afternoons or two mornings per week.

WHEN DO STUDENTS DROP OUT?

According to the principals, the five months in order of frequency mentioned when students are most likely to drop out are: June (21), January (17), September (14), May (12) and February (10).

ACCURACY OF REVISED ATTENDANCE
AND LEAVE CODE SYSTEMS

Confusion about how to classify dropouts leads to bogus reports of an 8 percent dropout rate. Most principals regard their recently revised attendance and leave code system as either accurate (39) or very accurate (20).

While the principals believe that the reporting system is generally correct, they did make suggestions to improve the system especially at the local level. Their recommendations focused on such matters as computerization of the entire attendance and class cut accounting within the school and between the school and the central office.

Other suggestions centered on in-service education of all teachers to ensure that the new attendance system would be used efficiently and effectively.

A number of principals surfaced the need to hire full or part time clerks in the office to help with attendance.

PARENTS, THE SCHOOLS AND DROPPING OUT

The vast majority of principals, 62, believe parents can help in the schools' efforts to prevent truancy and dropping out. The principals suggested activities that parents can undertake at home with their children and activities that would involve parents directly with the school. At-home activities included: helping students with homework, providing a time and place to do homework, monitoring their children's departure time from school whenever possible, and avoiding keeping students at home to baby-sit, guard the house, or shop. At-school activities embrace a variety of volunteer work such as supervising in the library or cafeteria, and, more importantly, working with networks of parents in an effort to decrease class cuts, truancy and dropping out.

BUSINESS, THE SCHOOL AND DROPPING OUT

In addition to providing such programs as adopt-a-school, career counseling, and part-time work, principals believe business leaders can provide other powerful incentives for students to remain in school. Specifically, principals believe business can provide tutors, job mentors and successful role models to schools. They can also donate rewards for attendance, provide schools with state-of-the-art, high-tech equipment, and even intervene directly with students who have been identified by the schools as especially prone to dropping out.

ADEQUACY AND AVAILABILITY OF BOOKS AND MATERIALS

Teachers and students require books and materials to accomplish the goals and objectives of the curriculum. In response to the question concerning the adequacy of books and materials, most principals (40) who responded to this question believe that they have sufficient materials to support their academic programs. Nine principals, however, all of whom are located in integrated general (3) and segregated, general high schools (6) do not believe their books and supplies are adequate.

Adequacy is one dimension of the curricular materials problem; availability is another. Thus, principals were asked to respond to a question concerning the availability of books for each semester. Again, most principals (45) believe their schools receive books in a timely fashion. Twelve principals, eleven of whom are located in integrated general (3) schools or segregated general (8) schools do not believe that their books are available on time. It should be mentioned that no attempt was made to verify when principals actually ordered their textbooks. The recently revised ordering system appears to be effective.

PRINCIPAL TURNOVER

It is well established that principal turnover has a destabilizing effect on schools. We attempted to identify the type of school that experiences high rates of principal change. Principals were asked: "Including you, how many principals have there been at your school within the last 15 years?" It is interesting to note that there is relative stability among principals appointed to selective academic and selective vocational schools. That is, within the last 15 years, principals in selective schools have had a tenure of at least five years. Quite another pattern unfolds in integrated and segregated general high schools. Thirty-nine schools reported having more than one principal within the last 15 years. Among the segregated general high schools, six had three principals, seven had four principals and two had five principals, all within the last 15 years.

SUMMER SCHOOL/EVENING CLASSES
AND THE CHILD AT-RISK

Principals were queried concerning the value of summer school and evening classes to the child at risk of dropping out of school. Fifty-nine of the 60 principals who responded to this question believe summer school is helpful. Fifty-two of 58 respondents agree that evening classes may help prevent dropping out.

When asked whether or not they would be willing to have summer school and evening classes at their own school buildings, 56 of 59 principals said they would welcome summer school at their sites. For a variety of reasons including quality control, only 38 of 57 principals indicated that they would welcome evening classes at their schools.

CONCLUSION

Research on the dropout is not a new phenomenon. For many years, but particularly during the sixties, numerous studies attempted to fathom the depths of this complex problem. Like other studies, ours demonstrate that many factors must be considered to assess the nature and extent of the dropout problem. We agree with Rumberger (1987) that what is needed now is a comprehensive, causal model of the dropout process. Rumberger has suggested what elements need to be considered to develop such a model or series of models and his suggestions provide an appropriate conclusion to this chapter.

Future research on the dropout should attempt to uncover the processes that underlie and lead to the dropout problem.

The next generation of research should explore the interrelationships among the various factors associated with dropping out.

Researchers must also attempt to measure the long-term, cumulative effects of the various factors contributing to dropping out.

Future research should recognize that there are different types of dropouts, no "typical" dropout. Thus a comprehensive model should account for white middleclass dropouts as well as inner-city black dropouts.

REFERENCES

Kyle, C.L., Lane, J.J. and Sween, J.A., Triana (1986). A., *We Have A Choice: Students At Risk of Leaving Chicago Public Schools.* Chicago. Chicago Area Studies Center and Center for Research on Hispanics. DePaul University.

Steinberg, L., Blinde, L.P. and Chan, K.S. (1984). *Dropping Out Among Language Minority Youth.* Review of Educational Research 54(1), 113–132.

Rumberger, R. W. (1987) *High School Dropouts: A Review of Issues and Evidence.* Review of Educational Research. 57(2) 101–121.

Chapter 5

ENGAGEMENT, NOT REMEDIATION OR HIGHER STANDARDS

GARY G. WEHLAGE

A year-long study of fourteen schools and programs for at-risk students by the National Center on Effective Secondary Schools produced several important conclusions about their effectiveness. The explanation for their effectiveness with potential dropouts can be summarized by saying, they succeed in establishing social bonds between the student and the school. According to this theory, social bonding of individuals to an institution occurs when the following elements become operable: attachment, commitment, involvement and belief (Hirschi, 1969). This chapter will address the component of "involvement" which we have chosen to expand and rename "engagement" because this term captures more of the spirit of what occurs in successful schools. Engagement refers to the investment of student attention and effort in the activities and work of schooling. While each of the other elements of social bonding—attachment, commitment, belief—are closely intertwined with engagement, for analytic purposes we have extracted it from the broader theory and treat engagement as a separate and distinct element.

Our research on students and programs demonstrates that there is great diversity among the group labeled "at-risk." For example, students differ on race and ethnicity and gender, whether they are substance abusers or not, where they fall on the socioeconomic scale, the extent to which they are behavior problems in school, whether they are in trouble with the law, and for females, whether they are pregnant and/or mothering. In addition, we discovered that at-risk students displayed a broad range of academic achievement and potential; some of them very competent in the essential skills required by schools. Having noted this diversity, it is important to emphasize that most students at-risk of dropping out also have some common characteristics such as truancy, course failure, and credit deficiency toward graduation. These characteristics suggest that a high degree of disengagement from school is common among them. The literature on dropouts has given much attention to describing those student characteristics that correlate with dropping out. While this focus on students is important, it is an incomplete view of the problem. Failure for most students is better seen as a process of mutual rejection by the student and the school. This mutual rejection develops from an interaction of a number of conditions, some of which are characteristics of the students, but others are institutional characteristics. Disengagement from school should be seen as a interactive process rather than as some fundamental mental inability or social flaw in the backgrounds of students.

This chapter will offer insights into how school characteristics interact with students to produce engagement and disengagement. In doing this we will expose a number of the assumptions that control our views of school, curriculum, teaching and learning. The following section offers two scenarios of programs studied by our research project that were successful in engaging at-risk students. These will be followed by an analysis of the impediments preventing schools from successfully engaging a broad range of students as well as those who are clearly at-risk of dropping out.

READING, WRITING AND REPORTING

The Media Academy is a school-within-a-school at Fremont High School in Oakland, California. The students are black, Hispanic or recent immigrants from Asia. The Media Academy is nonselective, seeking volunteers among entering tenth graders who are interested in the electronic and print media. The academic achievement of the volunteers varies widely. Some score below the tenth percentile on standardized tests of reading and mathematics while others score above the eightieth percentile. In many respects Media Academy students are typical of the students at Fremont, an inner-city high school with a poor reputation for academic success.

Conversations with Media Academy students indicate that most of them have a number of personal, family and academic obstacles to overcome. For some, English is their second language. Almost all are poor, many from single-parent homes. Before entering the Media Academy, most of the students found school neither completely discouraging, on the one hand, nor did they find it motivating or satisfying, on the other. Most Media Academy students struggle reluctantly with their academic courses. They have been only modestly successful in a school system that has been accused of being discouraged with itself and projecting low expectations for most of its students.

The Media Academy contains a broad middle group of urban students that have some of the characteristics of those who drop out. Because they are poor and minority, some with little push from their homes, expectations and aspirations for themselves are often low both in terms of education and future work. For some who seem to be motivated to acquire education beyond high school, they exhibit a naivete about what one must do academically in high school to get into a college. While they may be less at-risk of dropping out than the most traumatized students we saw in other schools, school is only marginally attractive, and unexpected events in a student's life can easily tip the balance of interest away from school to the streets, early pregnancy or a low-paying job.

The Media Academy is designed as a three year "major" built around journalism, English and social studies. These courses are planned to supplement one another and are the core of the Academy curriculum. In addition, the "lead teacher" has assembled an advisory panel of media professionals who have raised a modest amount of additional money to support the program. Much more important is that they make their businesses and themselves available to the Academy. Students visit the local newspaper, television and radio stations where they can interact with a broad range of people working in the media industry. Experts in advertising, cartooning and reporting come to the Academy to demonstrate their skills.

In addition to publishing an award-winning school newspaper, the Media Academy publishes a Spanish-English paper for a local ethnic community. Students are given opportunities to produce public service commercials for television and radio; for example, how do you say "no" to drugs. The following vignette describes one event that suggests the power of the Media Academy to engage students.

. . . The setting is not a school classroom. No one would mistake this room for a classroom because the atmosphere reeks with money, high technology and success. This is a conference room in a large modern office complex housing a variety of international businesses. There are plush chairs, heavy wooden furniture, thick carpets and fine drapery. The room is equipped with a large television screen and on it appears the face of John Drury, a television anchorman and personality from the San Francisco Bay area. Instead of the usual group of middle aged businessmen in three-piece suits, the conference room is filled with fourteen and fifteen year old high school sophomores. These are fifty Media Academy students who have been brought to the Harbor Bay Teleport, the focal point of which is a satellite communication system used by international businesses to communicate worldwide. In this case, the satellite is allowing students to converse with Mr. Drury across the bay from Oakland to San Francisco. The use of this facility was made possible by the cooperation of Harbor Bay Teleport Corporation, one of the many community sponsors who have joined forces to promote the development of the special program, the Media Academy.

The purpose of this adventure into the world of high technology is to create an opportunity for the students and a media professional, Mr. Drury, to discuss the media profession. The format is to have five or six students, seated at a table with microphones, asking him questions. This format allows him to describe and comment on the media business based on his professional experience of many years. After a few minutes of questioning by one group of students, another group moves to the table for its turn, and so on. They have been encouraged by their teacher to frame both initial and follow-up questions about the media field. While each student is to have prepared several questions in advance as part of a class assignment, only those who have volunteered need come to the table to ask their questions of Mr. Drury.

The questions asked the anchorman range from the personal to the professional and from the concrete to the abstract. One student asks about the high school he attended. To the students' surprise he graduated from their high school, Fremont, nearly forty years ago. Another student pursues the work of being an anchorman: Where does he get the stories he reports each day? Miguel asks, "What are some good jobs in television other than being an anchor?" Chanel, a black student, asks about the opportunities for minorities in media.

One of the students who has volunteered to ask questions is Maria, a recent immigrant from Mexico. Her journalism teacher, Mr. O'Donoghue, comments before the session that her volunteering surprises him because she has been extremely shy in classes during the first semester. In addition to this being her first year in an American school, her command of English is obviously a handicap. The journalism, English and history classes have been particularly difficult for her. In preparation for this day, Mr. O'Donoghue, has helped her put some ideas and questions in standard English. When her turn comes at the table, she asks the initial question in carefully measured words, trying to pronounce each correctly. "Does one have to pass any kind of examination to become a television reporter?" When Mr. Drury completes his answer, Maria asserts her prerogative and asks a follow-up question: "Is a college degree in journalism required for one to be a television reporter?" At the end of her turn, as Maria moves away from the table, Mr. O'Donoghue catches her eye and signals a well-done sign.

Later, near the conclusion of the forty-five minute session, after all volunteers have been able to ask their questions, the teacher invites any student with an additional question to the table. Maria, who is seated at the very back of the room, winds her way between chairs and students toward the table. Several students are there ahead of her and begin to question Mr. Drury. Maria edges between them to get close to a microphone. Time is almost up, but she finds the appropriate moment and asks her question before the end of the session. It is a good question, one about the responsibility of the media for encouraging crisis events involving the safety of human lives. "Does television make more people do things like take hostages because they know television will be there?" For Maria, having the confidence to ask these questions was important, signifying a step down the road toward success and achievement in school.

Later, in commenting on this scene, Mr. O'Donoghue says, "What a breakthrough; what a confidence-builder for her! She can be a real success story! If she works on her English—and she is working hard now—she can be a winner. This program can do a lot for her."

LEARNING BY DOING

The students at Croom Vocational High School, Upper Marlboro, Maryland, are of a different sort than those at the Media Academy. While this school also draws students from a large urban area, with a majority being black, they come from much more impoverished homes and generally have a much more limited set of life experiences than those at the Media Academy. Student scores on standardized academic tests cluster in the bottom quartile. Academic failure has been frequent and they are discouraged students when they choose Croom. It is unlikely many of them could graduate from their home high school given that they are over sixteen, often credit deficient and generally unhappy with their school experiences, having run afoul of various rules. In response to these conditions, Croom offers a two-year program. It is a combination of vocational and academic course work leading to a high school diploma and/or vocational certification in one of seven areas, such as auto mechanics, grounds keeping and office work.

Practical work in the vocational areas is facilitated by both specially equipped shops and the very environment in which the school is located. Croom has a large campus, about 28 acres, with numerous buildings that provide opportunities for applying the knowledge and skills learned in the shops. Food service students prepare the noon meal each day for all Croom students and staff; classrooms are painted, doors repaired and new window screens are built; groundskeeping students maintain the lawn, flowers and shrubs; the auto shop has a constant supply of vehicles from the staff and local residents. The results of the work these students do in the various shops is directly observable by them, their peers and the adults at the school.

The Croom campus has been created out of a former Nike missile base, one of a number that formerly surrounded Washington D.C. The atmosphere is quite different from that found in most high schools. The carefully maintained lawn, shrubs and flowers remind one more of a college campus than a high school. Unlike the modern concrete school structures that compress large numbers of students into a single building for the entire day, 125 Croom students are scattered throughout a dozen buildings. No clanging bells mark the time for passing. There are no hall monitors or hall passes. There is no graffiti on the walls of any of the buildings. The well kept grounds are free of litter. A first-time visitor to the school is routinely cautioned by the student guide that everyone walks on the concrete walkways to avoid wearing paths across the lawn.

The setting for the following glimpse of Croom students and teachers is the auto shop. Scattered around the grounds is an array of vehicles. Some of them look like they are literally junk while others seem to be in various stages of being dismantled, repaired, or restored. Visible a few hundred yards away are the horticulture, groundskeeping and building trades shops.

The auto shop teachers, like those in the other vocational areas, seem adept at teaching the students what they need to know when they need to know it. For example, the newest or least competent students are assigned the simplest tasks, while more accomplished students take on more difficult assignments. One morning while observing the auto shop, I saw one student performing an oil change on a car, while a second student changed the fuel filter on a Volkswagen diesel. Still a third student was replacing a worn-out clutch on a pickup truck. Another was replacing the disc brakes on a Ford EXP, and another was dismantling an eight cylinder engine pulled from an old Chrysler Imperial which was in the process of being restored by the school.

During all this activity the shop teacher and his aide made carefully timed moves from student to student to monitor each procedure. Rather than seeing these adults as teachers, they were more like tutors, coaches and master craftsmen guiding their apprentices. As each step of an operation was performed, one-to-one instruction was provided, including reminders to be thinking ahead about the next step.

The strategy of tutoring and coaching often emphasized a type of problem solving. For example, the teacher might challenge the student to consider what could be the cause of a problem: "What do you think you're going to find when you pull that (brake) drum?" Also woven into the tutoring and coaching were requests to speculate about the unanticipated. For example, ordinarily disc brake calipers on a newer car move freely. But on an older car "they may become rusted and bind. Then what will you do?" Students are challenged to think ahead to the next several steps in their work. While changing the oil on a vehicle, a student was scolded for standing and watching the oil run from the engine. The teacher took the moment to instruct the young man about certain realities on the job; in a real garage the mechanic would use that time to grease the car and gather the filter and oil needed to complete the work.

The Media Academy and Croom provide particularly good examples of the diversity of students falling under the at-risk label. They also provide good examples of the engagement that can occur when students are challenged with an appropriate set of experiences in a different environment. The Media Academy and Croom demonstrate a variation of curriculum that is "experiential learning." It involves carefully designed and closely supervised experiences related to work in the adult world. The curriculum in each case is matched to the students' abilities and interests. Each provides opportunities to produce concrete products that have value to both students and adults. The adults with whom they come in contact treat these young people with respect. There is a tutorial and mentor relationship between adults and students. The experiences provide the students opportunities to make the transition to adulthood. The curriculum provides a rich set of experiences that is likely to stimulate their aspirations and interests. In the case of the Media Academy where a number of students have the potential for going to college, the curriculum does not impose a ceiling on their opportunities. In both programs the level of engagement in the curriculum was high by any standards.

THE PROBLEM OF ENGAGEMENT IN CONTEMPORARY SCHOOLS

The spate of studies on American schools in recent years confirms that the problem of low engagement in school work is a general phenomenon and not restricted to those labeled "at-risk." Various observational studies have confirmed what Cusick (1973) noted years ago—students are frequently mere "spectators" in the educational process. They stand on the sidelines watching and waiting. Consequently, the mental effort expended on school is minimal. Weeks go by in which no more than a few hours of concentrated effort by students can be observed. This lack of engagement is due to absences, the interruption of nonacademic activities, lost class time from inefficient teaching and boredom from an uninspired curriculum. There is evidence that the average teenager spends more time watching television each week than actively pursuing school work. While at-risk students make their lack of engagement obvious, it is generally agreed by observers to be a pernicious problem among a majority of high school students. Both Goodlad (1984) and Sizer (1984) indicate that students display a high degree of passivity in the classroom. Sizer observed from his study that American high school students are "all too often docile, compliant, and without initiative." These characteristics suggest a fundamental disengagement from the tasks that result in learning and achievement.

The lack of student engagement and consequent achievement is clearly a pernicious problem in American education. The profession needs to give serious thought to its root causes before school reforms are undertaken. "Raising standards" in an effort to coerce students into greater effort may have the desired effect on some portion, but what about those who are already doubtful about the value of academic effort? Based on the research reported here and numerous studies of schools' three significant impediments that lie behind a lack of student engagement are described. They are: (1) school is not structured to be extrinsically motivating because achievement is not tied to any obvious reward. (2) The learning process used in schools is too narrow, ignoring the way people learn in settings other than school and contributing to the view that school is not part of the "real world." (3) Educators are so obsessed with the "coverage" of subject matter that school knowledge is superficial and prevents students from gaining a sense of competence from achieving. Any equation for contemporary school reform must address these three impediments affecting both those who now "get by" and graduate as well as those who drop out.

Achievement and Reward Disjuncture

First, from a student's viewpoint there is little motivation to do well in school because, for the great majority of students, school achievement is not extrinsically rewarding. For the noncollege bound there is no relationship between achievement and subsequent employment after high school. Bishop (1987) argues that connecting school achievement to employment is an important lever for increasing the engagement of students. He sees the low engagement by most students resulting from the fact that the labor market fails to reward effort and achievement in high school. Employment upon leaving high school has little or nothing to do with how well one did in courses. The only thing that counts is having a diploma.

For those going on to most colleges, it is enough to "get by" with modest grades and test scores for admission to state universities. For those interested in attending a prestigious college, there is a need to compete and excel, but this is only a small fraction of the high school population. However, this competition is a zero-sum game that rewards only a very few and discourages many who might achieve much more. The result of these conditions is the creation of a peer culture that actively discourages effort at academic achievement. Most classrooms are infused with an implicit assumption shared by the students that no one will try too hard and thereby raise the level of expectations and performance for others. Disengagement from academics is "cool" in the peer culture. This phenomenon has been carried to an extreme among some black youth who denigrate success in academic work as a form of "acting white" (Fordham and Ogbu, 1986).

For those youth not planning to attend a college but rather seek employment upon graduation, their perception is that one does not need to do well in school. This is probably accurate. There is apparently no connection between school performance and their chances of gaining employment. Success in getting a good job is not dependent on how hard one studied in high school. Most employers do not make use of transcripts, but rather seek evidence of a diploma and good character. The "good job" that most students want is tied more directly to local labor market conditions, national economic trends and the network of connections that an individual has when pursuing employment.

In addition, the wage one receives upon obtaining employment is not affected by school performance. Bishop cites data indicating that high school grades and test scores have no effect on the wage rate a recent graduate earns. Generally, employers peg wages to the level of the job, not the past performance or ability as measured by tests. Eventually, employees with higher ability and productivity due to educational achievement are likely to be rewarded down the road by their employers, but the vagaries of promised benefits some years later have little motivating effect on a high school adolescent. Thus the lack of an extrinsically rewarding relationship between achievement and employment discourages engagement by most students.

Bishop suggests that employers and schools cooperate in an effort to tie school achievement and test performance more closely to hiring practices. He claims that if employers scrutinized a graduate's academic records, it could pay off in the hiring of more productive employees and create an incentive system that would drive student engagement. We see this as both impractical and a bit naive.

We would prefer to see educators take Bishop's general point about lack of extrinsic rewards and act in two ways. First, schools could develop more interesting vocational related curricula that connect adolescents to employment. Second, attention could be given to developing new methods of evaluating students' competencies in a variety of areas. Such evaluation needs to find and emphasize a greater variety of strengths students can display. Croom Vocational, for example, provides incentives by linking its graduates to work available in the private sector. Certification and evaluation of students' vocational skills is more complex than giving grades and test scores. The result is that Croom graduates are considered good potential employees and are relatively easy to place. The Media Academy students can obtain summer jobs in the field if their school work is satisfactory. They have a view of the relation between school and work that is probably much more sophisticated than most students.

Connecting school and work would be an important motivational factor for many youth. However, providing extrinsic motivation for achievement is, in our judgement, only part of the solution. This strategy assumes that young people can always see where their self-interest lies and be motivated to act on it. Appealing to people's self-interest is probably a better strategy than coercing them to work harder by raising academic and graduation standards. But even together, coercion and self-interest are not enough on which to build a school reform movement. There are other substantive reforms in schooling that must occur also. These reforms have their roots in a more comprehensive and adequate conception of learning, and a restructured curriculum that is much less fragmented and superficial. These reforms are likely to produce greater intrinsic motivation and sustain students when school becomes difficult and requires substantial effort of them.

The Narrow Conception of School Learning

Reforms that will bring about greater student engagement must be based in part on different assumptions about how learning can occur and what competencies can be developed and rewarded. One way of examining the assumptions behind school learning is to compare it with learning that occurs outside of school. Lauren Resnick (1987) by contrasting learning in and out of school, highlights how school learning is narrowly conceived in comparison to the demands for learning and use of knowledge in non-school contexts. This narrowness gives school learning an air of unreality. It also means that only some skills and knowledge are rewarded among the range that are needed to be successful outside of school. She points to two characteristics of school learning that make it narrow.

First, the learning process is highly individualistic in school and it ignores the socially-shared learning process that occurs and is required in many settings outside of school. In school, individuals are to acquire a specified body of knowledge and skills, and the acquisition of these is relatively independent of other individuals. Each person works alone in the acquisition process. There is little interdependence in school learning. In fact, we have made a fetish out of the need to individualize learning. There is little sense of group effort to achieve or to solve a common problem. In contrast, learning outside the school is almost always embedded in some interdependent process in which group learning and sharing of information is often an indispensible characteristic.

Modern organizations are examples of the practice of group learning, utilizing teams of people who are interdependent. Some of the most important innovations in manufacturing productivity have developed around cooperative work-groups. Health care is a good example of the emphasis on group sharing of knowledge. Gone is the general practitioner in solitary practice. When a patient enters a clinic to be examined and treated for some malady, there is by necessity a cooperative effort in which knowledge is generated and shared by all those serving the patient. In addition to doctors, there are nurses, technicians, pharmacists and clerical people who must work together to diagnose and prescribe for the patient. There is remarkably little of a group or cooperative orientation to learning in schools. Only recently has a conception of "cooperative learning" emerged from research that demonstrates effectiveness in promoting learning among a range of students (Newmann and Thompson, 1987). This approach to learning is not widely employed, however, in American schools.

Second, school learning is narrow as a consequence of the way achievement is construed. Achievement is most commonly defined as the acquisition of knowledge that can be recalled by students. Typically, teachers ask students to organize their thoughts on carefully circumscribed subject matter in order to respond correctly to subsequent questions. Achievement is answering teacher questions. These questions require students to respond verbally to teacher cues, marking the correct answer from those supplied on a test, or writing statements that demonstrate that the knowledge has been mastered. Given the perceived unreality and incredibility of much subject matter, teacher questions become strange, obscure, and make teachers appear eccentric. From a student perspective teacher questions seem contrived and unrelated to much that occurs outside the institution itself. This competence of correctly answering teacher questions is so restricted that it seems unimportant to the present or future of many students.

Taken together, the individualistic approach to learning and the requirement of responding to teacher questions, make it easy for many students to become disengaged from the process. It is not clear to the student that the knowledge that one accrues from this process is important in any way. The contextual purpose for acquiring such knowledge is isolated within the school. School learning appears to be for teachers. For students, the emphasis is on learning the abstract symbols of school knowledge — algebraic equations, Latin names of phyla in biology, names dates and terms from history—in the absence of real people, problems or activities. Learning in school is learning the rules for using the symbols out of any recognizable context. Moreover, it is apparent to students that the version of "applying" this knowledge that is required by school, taking tests, is something rarely required in practical settings. On the other hand, the context for acquiring out of school knowledge is its practical usefulness whether the field is medicine, law, automobile production or carpentry. Knowledge out of school has purpose. It has social value to the individual and some larger group. The "test" for out of school learning is successful application in a practical setting.

To the extent that learning in school can become a socially-shared process in which students work together in a cooperative framework, then greater student engagement can be expected. To the extent the knowledge students are asked to learn can be perceived as having some social purpose, then greater engagement will likely result. This does not mean that every lesson must be obviously "relevant" to students. Educators can certainly ask students to suspend judgment about the "relevance" of knowledge, but the *persistent* separation of school from the world outside is maintained with considerable costs. Disengagement of the many is almost certainly one obvious cost.

Coverage and a Superficial, Trivialized Curriculum

The curriculum is dominated by an obsession with coverage of vast amounts of information in many different subjects. Coverage is characterized by racing through topic after topic in order to "expose" students to the key concepts and facts of a school subject. The coverage process fragments knowledge and produces only superficial understanding that inhibits students' gaining a sense of competence from learning.

Critics have bemoaned the cheapening of the curriculum through a proliferation of courses and the creation of a "shopping mall" mentality of having students choose courses based on whatever strikes their fancy (Powell, Farrar and Cohen, 1985). While not disputing this claim, we believe that a more serious problem is the obsession with coverage that characterizes even the traditional "solid" academic courses in most high schools. The problem seems to be that there is no end of good things to which students should be exposed. As more and more knowledge is developed, teachers feel obligated to cover this knowledge—to expose students to all the topics, ideas and facts that are included in a typical course.

The obsession with coverage is a frustrating, losing battle for both teacher and student. Consider the enormity of the task implied by covering "United States History: Reconstruction to the Present." Not only does the course cover a large span of time, which obviously gets longer each year, but there are historians hard at work generating more and more knowledge about a myriad of topics. And new knowledge does not necessarily replace the old; newly discovered facts and interpretations must be compared with old views of what happened. Not only is more knowledge being generated about Grant, Teddy and Franklin Roosevelt and John F. Kennedy, but whole new topics are being constantly generated. Increasing interest and demand for a view of history that reflects the roles of women and minorities, for example, has created new bodies of knowledge that must be given their due. Traditional fields of specialization, like foreign policy and labor history, have been subdivided to create additional topics that beckon for attention by the textbook writer, teacher and student. The disciplines of history, the social sciences, literature and the humanities are probably more seriously affected by this proliferation of knowledge than others. Certainly the sciences, too, have their problem with an expanding body of knowledge that teachers feel obligated to cover. The reality is that students and teachers can never be successful if they continue their efforts at coverage.

Newmann (1987) sees coverage as a destructive "addiction" suffered by educators. This addiction destroys the curriculum by making it superficial. As teachers and students race through topic after topic, only the most surface level of understanding can be expected. Teachers feel obligated to cover all of the topics of the book or official curriculum, and yet they know that much has been left out, not understood or even misunderstood. Newmann argues that the addiction to coverage reveals an illusion that people can master all that might be important to know. This illusion produces a tremendous waste of time in schools since most of what is learned passes out of the student's head shortly after the obligatory test. But more insidious than wasting time is the "mindlessness" that coverage encourages.

"Classrooms become places where material must be learned, even though it may seem nonsensical to students (because there is no time to explain), where students are denied the opportunities to explore related topics they may be curious about (because their interests may wander too far from the official topics to be covered), where teachers' talents for teaching subtle nuances and complexities are squelched. As a result many students stop asking questions soon after early elementary grades; they passively allow teachers and texts to pour material into their heads to be stored for future reproduction. . . . " (Newmann, 1987).

Newmann outlines the only feasible alternative to coverage, and that is a curriculum designed to treat selected topics in depth. His conception of depth is borrowed from Sizer (1984) who uses the phrase "less is more" when discussing curriculum. The meaning of this phrase must be clear. Less refers to less mindless coverage and less acquisition of superficial knowledge. More refers to greater mastery of fewer topics. More also refers to greater complexity of understanding and more thoughtfulness about those topics investigated. More does not refer to more reliance on a skills oriented curriculum; but it does imply greater competency in those skills that are acquired while studying topics in depth.

Whether the attention is on special interventions with at-risk students or the general student population, the problem of engagement is a central issue. The three impediments stand in the way of student engagement producing underachievement for some and contributing to the decision to drop out among others. Schools cannot hope to make major inroads on the dropout problem as long as these impediments exist, whether in conventional schools or even in alternatives intended as dropout prevention.

IMPLICATIONS FOR SCHOOL REFORM

One practical implication of this analysis for school reforms is to authorize alternatives and special interventions with at-risk students to expand their conceptions of learning and curriculum. Encourage educators in development of curricula that have a connection with the world of work and promise some pay-off in employment if students demonstrate their competence. Tap those skills and interests that many students have but are not now rewarded by the narrow conception of learning embedded in school. Eliminate the superficial coverage of vast amounts of material with in-depth experiences that provide an opportunity for students to gain a sense of competency.

At-risk students are already seriously disengaged. It seems highly unlikely that either a policy of remediation or one of imposing higher academic standards will have the desired effect of increasing engagement or achievement. Both of these strategies suggest only more of the same fare that those dropping out already find unacceptable. While there are many alternatives in existence, their effectiveness is often curtailed by the tendency for school districts and state regulation to impose the same standards and requirements on alternatives as on conventional schools. This prevents them from having the legitimacy and authority to develop the kinds of interventions that would most likely engage at-risk students. Why force alternatives to look like conventional schools when conventional schools are part of the problem creating dropouts? Authorizing expanded conceptions of learning and curriculum can encourage the kinds of school reform that would lead to greater engagement by a broad range of students. Just as the dropout problem is the observed tip of a much broader disengagement from school, interventions with at-risk students can show the possibilities of a general reform of schooling for the great majority of students.

By extending learning beyond the restricted school conception now employed, and providing a closer link with the world of action outside the school, a more compelling environment can be created for students. For many young people who are now disengaged and unrewarded by the narrow curriculum, an increased range of opportunities for competence is important. The curriculum should be based on depth, not coverage of formal course titles. School could provide more avenues to develop and display competence that is not now rewarded in school, but is valued in the world outside.

One way of attacking the impediments to engagement is through an experiential curriculum and mode of learning. It can provide for both individualistic and group learning. Experiential learning builds upon an interaction between the knowledge and skills of the classroom and the experience of applying them in problem solving settings. This kind of curriculum is precisely what was found in the Media Academy with students learning the skills and knowledge of the media in class, but also experiencing their application in the contexts of real world radio, television, newspapers and advertising. They also applied their skills and knowledge to the production of their own newspapers for the school and local community. Moreover, this application occurred in a group setting in which students cooperated and shared with one another in the production of newspapers and commercials.

In a less sophisticated form, Croom Vocational High School also utilizes an experiential curriculum. Coming from a poor urban background, these students lacked experiences in areas such as painting, lawn and garden care and auto repair. The vocational shops provide a base of applied knowledge and problem solving that prepare students for the transition into the world of employment opportunities that they would otherwise not have.

Finally, these programs were good places for teachers. Morale and satisfaction were high among teachers. They along with their students were engaged.

Endnotes

1. This paper was prepared at the National Center on Effective Secondary Schools, School of Education, University of Wisconsin-Madison which is supported in part by a grant from the Office of Educational Research and Improvement (Grant No. G00869007). Any opinions, findings, and conclusions or recommendations expressed in this publication are those of the author and do not necessarily reflect the views of this agency or the U.S. Department of Education.

2. I wish to thank my colleagues at the National Center on Effective Secondary Schools, University of Wisconsin-Madison, for their help in clarifying my thinking about "academic engagement" and for their assistance in collecting the data in this chapter that describe several schools and programs for at-risk students.

REFERENCES

Bishop, J. (1987) *Why high school students learn so little and what can be done about it.* Cornell University: Center for Advanced Human Resource Studies.

Cusick, P. (1973) *Inside High School: The students' world.* New York: Holt, Rinehart, & Winston.

Goodlad, J. (1984) *A place called school.* New York: McGraw-Hill.

Hirschi, T. (1969) *Causes of delinquency.* Berkeley: University of California Press.

Newmann, F. (1987) *Can depth replace coverage in the high school curriculum?* National Center on Effective Secondary Schools, University of Wisconsin, Madison.

Newmann, F. and Thompson, J. (1987) *Effects of cooperative learning on achievement in secondary schools: A summary of research.* National Center on Effective Secondary Schools, University of Wisconsin, Madison.

Powell, A., Farrar, E. and Cohen, D. (1985) *The shopping mall high school.* Boston: Houghton Mifflin.

Resnick, L. (1988) Learning in school and out. *Educational Researcher,* 16 (9).

Sizer, T. (1984) *Horace's Compromise.* Boston: Houghton Mifflin.

Chapter 6

FROM GRADE TO GRADE?
PROMOTION POLICIES AND AT-RISK YOUTH

FLOYD M. HAMMACK

When should pupils move from one grade to another; when should they be retained? The complex questions which lie behind this seemingly simple educational problem are the subject of this chapter. For those students who are not doing well in school, who are "at-risk," being promoted or held back by school authorities may be a critical decision. For teachers and school administrators who must make the decision to promote or hold back students, not only is the progress of individual students at stake, but so too are the performance figures for the school. In our current time of educational accountability and assessment, high retention rates and test scores are scrutinized by the public and by state educational authorities. Finally, for boards of education and central district and state education authorities, the development of policy regarding promotion can signal to the public at large the degree to which reform is being taken seriously and tax revenues effectively spent.

Although some students may be held back because of small physical size or emotional immaturity, the primary reason is inadequate mastery of knowledge and skills deemed appropriate for pupils of each age (Jackson, 1975; Smith and Shepard, 1987). Among the variety of remedies educators have for addressing a student's learning problems, holding back is probably the most significant, yet it is a practice about which we know relatively little. What we do know throws into question the usefulness of the practice for raising student achievement levels. At the same time, states and school systems are increasingly turning to stricter standards for promotion and for graduation.

This chapter takes the view that most of the problems at-risk children have in school are not the product of school policies but rather of factors outside of the school and over which the school has little direct control. Nevertheless, school policies do have consequences for students, and many are highly negative for at-risk students. Moreover, school personnel and educational policy-makers are often not aware of such unintended negative consequences.

The analysis which follows is guided by the requirements of any policy analysis: Why do current policies exist? What are the goals the policy choice seeks to maximize? What are the alternatives, and what does the research evidence have to say about alternatives to achieve the goal?

In order to understand the origins of promotion policies, this essay will selectively review the history of the organization of schools and the curriculum. This brief historical review provides the necessary background for understanding why promotion policies have become a controversial issue. The next part of the chapter reviews what we know about current practices of promotion and retention in grade. Next, the chapter brings together the writings of the recent educational reform reports on promotion policies. These reports, and the broader concern over educational achievement which they represent, have raised promotion to its current status as a significant educational issue. Next, the chapter explores these current recommendations in the light of the historical review presented earlier. The educational assessment and minimum competency testing movement are the vehicles most frequently recommended and used to assure compliance with current reform standards. Yet, these movements are not without problems, and their goals and practices need to be assessed. Two school systems which have implemented strict promotion policies are discussed. Next, the available evidence for holding back and for promotion are examined. Alternatives to current and recommended practices are reviewed at the end of the chapter.

To anticipate the chapter's conclusion, there is no consistent evidence that holding back students improves their mastery of material not previously mastered over the learning gained among promoted students with equal educational problems. In addition, holding back does little to aid them getting back on the normal age/grade progression. The conclusion developed here includes questioning of the rigidity of the school's timetable for educational progress and a discussion of noneducational, or at least indirectly educational, rationales for holding back students not meeting a specified standard. These indirect justifications for strict promotion policies—stressing as they do organizational alignment, consistency and toughness—may be more important than the improvement of the educational performance of failing students.

HISTORY

Elementary school students, when asked what grade they are in, can easily answer. Their grade is central to their school experience, and incorporates their age and school identity. But, as Tyack (1974:44) makes clear, it was not always so.

> In 1883, Henry Barnard ... maintained that a classroom containing students of widely varying ages and attainment was not only inefficient but also inhumane. ... From Horace Mann in Massachusettes to Calvin Stowe in Ohio to John Pierce in Michigan, leading common school crusaders urged communities to replace the heterogeneous grouping of students with a systematic plan of graduation ...

Tyack (1973:45–46) goes on to relate how, in the interests of efficiency and, one presumes, humanity, William Harvey Wells, in 1864, developed curricula in accordance to grades so that when teachers were assigned to a grade they had available a single set of learning materials for all of the students in the class. This sets the stage for how schools were organized, especially in urban areas. A school class became homogeneous with respect to age, scholastic expectations and curricula. Whereas, earlier, teachers had engaged in what Labaree calls "individual craft instruction" —because of the individual attention required by the diverse age and achievement levels of undifferentiated classrooms—whole group instruction (or "large-scale batch production") became the dominant methodology (Labaree, 1984). The press of large numbers of students needing schooling resulted in the "One Best System" of education detailed by Tyack (1974). In short, schools became highly organized and a single, "rational" organizational form emerged across the country.

By the turn of the century, however, reformers were becoming alarmed by the number of pupils who did not finish their elementary or their secondary education. Especially in urban areas, the student population was increasing and changing rapidly during the last years of the nineteenth century and the first decades of the twentieth century (Trow, 1961). School attendance was more likely to be required by law, and students were far more likely to be either immigrants themselves or the children of immigrants. Where earlier movement from grade to grade had been based on the models of learning typified by Well's strict curriculum, the rate of failure began to increase as students became more heterogeneous. As Labaree (1984:71) found in Philadelphia, promotion standards were increasingly relaxed. The reasons for this change, argues Labaree, include a new notion of the purposes of schooling. Education was becoming a right for all students, not just those able to pass its rigorous promotion expectations. Consequently, those expectations became more diverse, and included vocational and other nonacademic subjects as well. Secondly, as it is today, repetition of grades was expensive and inherently inefficient. Leonard Ayers, an early critic of nonpromotion, repeatedly referred to the costs of keeping students back; in effect, he argued, a nonpromoted student costs twice as much (for each grade repeated) to educate as one who is promoted (Ayers, 1908; Labaree, 1984). Finally, schools, especially secondary schools, instituted tracking and differentiated curricula within grades to handle the variety of levels of student achievement at each grade.

Hence, as the one best system came to be organized, and the number of its students expanded, the expectations for scholastic performance became less strict. "Social" promotion, based primarily on age, became common, and where tests were used, they most likely determined track placement or eligibility for special schools. This pattern, although criticized at many points in our educational history, has remained with us until quite recently. In contrast, European systems never developed a social promotion system (Clark, 1985). Their secondary schools remained tied to the colleges and universities for which they prepared entrants. Our secondary schools undertook to educate all students, not just those selected for college preparation (Trow, 1961), and thus we were faced with the problem still with us today: how to educate most children through early adulthood.

CURRENT PRACTICE

Contemporary elementary and secondary schools are generally organized along grades in which students spend an academic year studying a specified curriculum. There is a clear, linear progression to schooling: students enter in kindergarten, progress to the first grade, pass through succeeding grades and move on to middle or junior high or high schools in an orderly and yearly sequence of promotions. This "timetable" for the educational career is rigid with little opportunity for "stopping out" or diversion, without significant consequence (Roth, 1963). To get off the main sequence implies a significant deviation from what everyone is expected to accomplish. "Skipping" a grade, although deviant, does not carry the stigma being held back does. In fact, being held back is one of the worst fears of childhood (Goleman, 1988). Moreover, those who are held back cannot legally opt out of school as compulsory school attendance for those under 16 does not allow such flexibility. Most schools have only one sequence, and a student not promoted must be "held back a year" to repeat the curriculum of the previous year. Generally, decisions about holding back are made by local educational authorities following local school, district or state policies. Parents may be consulted; students hardly ever.

Although most school systems have provisions for "special education," which has its own sequencing rules, there is only one set of grades and curricula which is designed for all other students. Ability or achievement grouping among or within classes may well take place, but schools limit the instructional variety offered students. For most students, this lack of variety does not pose a serious problem; they have little difficulty mastering the basic expectations inherent in the school organization just described. However, Smith and Shepard (1987:130), using census data on school enrollments by age, estimate that between 15 and 19 percent of all students are retained in a grade at some point during their elementary or secondary education. No other national evidence for nonpromotion (or retention rates) could be found.[1]

The criteria for retention may vary widely, but, again, no systematic national research exists on their variety. We do know, however, that a number of states are using minimum competency tests as indicators of student progress, and have tied grade promotion to passage of these tests. According to recent state surveys, eight states tied passing such tests to grade promotion (Digest: 105). In most cases, however, the state mandates allow for local districts to devise more flexible policies, and do not use test scores alone in the promotion decision.[2] Failing students are often put into "transitional" classes, or promoted "provisionally" or "with deficiencies."

In 1981 New York City introduced a "promotion gates" testing program, using the California Achievement Test of reading. It set its standard at 3.7 for fourth graders (one year below the national norm) and at 6.2 for seventh graders (one and one-half years below the national norm). No other criteria were allowed; teachers' recommendations, parental or student objections nor developmental factors were used, only test scores. At the first testing, about 17 percent of the fourth graders failed, and 26 percent of the seventh graders did not meet the standard (Labaree, 1984:76). Special classes were set up for the "gates" students during the following summer, and the students were tested again. Those who failed a second time were put into special "gates" classes for the next school year, when they took the examination again. Some students were enrolled in gates classes for two years before being promoted.

More recently, New York has begun to use the Degrees of Reading Power test and pass rates have increased—according to school officials due to improved instruction and perhaps to the differences in the test. About 10–15 percent of students at both grades now do not pass. Those students who do not pass after one year in a gates class are now promoted to a transitional class. A longitudinal evaluation of the retained students against a comparable control group, carried out in 1986, concludes that "The promotion gates policy has had a small, short-term effect on student achievement which is not sustained three years after program participation. The short-term effects are achieved at the expense of an increase in the proportion of students who subsequently drop out of school" (Office of Educational Assessment, 1986:2). Achievement gains of the retained students were no better than for those who were promoted. The report goes to recommend that " . . . such low-achieving, at-risk students not be held over unless there is a clear plan of follow-up services throughout their school career . . . " (1986:2).

Madaus and Greaney (1985) report on the strict promotion testing system used in Ireland from 1943 to 1968. The percentage promoted out of the primary system on the basis of the examination hovered around 85 percent. What is more valuable in their work, however, is the review of the consequences produced by the examination. They provide evidence that once the examination was seen as a real hurdle, teachers began to teach to the test. While that result is easily anticipated, the impact on retention rates at earlier grades is not. Schools were more likely to hold students back *before* they took the examination in anticipation of their failure (Madaus and Greaney, 1985:287) than had been the case before the test was made mandatory. This delaying of weaker students allowed these students to reach legal school-leaving age without having to take the examinations. This strategy had the effect of increasing the promotion rate, while raising the dropout rate, a relation which is clearly possible during the current reform period.

Jackson (1975) estimated that during the 1971–1972 school year, about one million students were held back. Hence, pulling all these sources together, our best national estimates are that about 15 to 19 percent of all students are held back at least one year during their elementary or secondary school career, and that this figure is probably higher, above 22 percent, for urban systems. But these figures are highly depended on state and local policies and these policies shift, and they are not equivalent in their use of terms.

Beyond these few statistics and reports, however, there is little available research to inform us of the extent of nonpromotion or of the criteria schools use to implement this policy. There is some evidence that retention rates have been declining (Selden, 1982), but no studies following elementary cohorts of students through the educational system and estimating patterns of nonpromotion have been undertaken. Thus, whether rates of "social" promotion have increased or stayed where they have been for many years is not known. Without such knowledge, moreover, we cannot estimate the degree to which the practice has contributed to lower average test scores, or other problems of the educational system.

Yet, school systems continue to focus on promotion policies. The state of Georgia has recently announced that it will "... require all school districts to consider kindergartners' scores on a standardized test in deciding whether to promote them to the 1st grade" (Gold, 1988:1). The state superintendent of schools asserted that the purpose of the test was not to set up a gate, but to aid in the identification of areas of need students have and to begin the process of remediation (Gold, 1988:15). Of course, the testing of students for promotion, whether the scores become the sole criteria for promotion or not, necessarily constitutes a gate.

Clearly, social promotion policies (even of kindergartners), while once championed by Ayers and other educational reformers as the means to educational, social and economic efficiency, have come to be identified by more recent reform reports as a primary source of the decline of scholastic performance among our elementary and secondary school students. The exploration of this ironic turn of events is the next area of discussion.

THE EDUCATIONAL REFORM COMMISSIONS

The current period of educational reform was initiated by the 1983 publication of the President's Commission on Educational Excellence, whose report, *A Nation at Risk*, forcefully linked the failure of our educational system to our national economic decline. Among its many recommendations for change to strengthen our nation's education, the Commission stated that "standardized tests of achievement . . . should be administered at major transition points from one level of schooling to another . . . The purpose of these tests would be to: (a) certify the student's credentials; (b) identify the need for remedial intervention; and (c) identify the opportunity for advanced or accelerated work" (1983:27–28). In addition, the report recommended that "placement and grouping of students, as well as promotion and graduation policies, should be guided by the academic progress of students and their instructional needs, rather than by rigid adherence to age" (1983:29–30). The language of the last recommendation is particularly interesting. School systems should not adhere to "rigid" standards of age, but rather to (flexible?) standards of academic progress.

But the President's Commission was not alone in recommending the move from social or age-related promotion to a system based on test scores. The Education Commission of the States' Task Force on Education for Economic Growth released another of the 1983 reports, *Action for Excellence: A Comprehensive Plan to Improve Our Nation's Schools*. It recommended, among other things, that " . . . programs be established to monitor student progress through periodic testing of general achievement and specific skills. . . . We recommend, moreover, that the practice of 'social,' or chronological, promotion be abolished; promotion from grade to grade should be based on mastery, not age" (1983:39).

A final example is the National Science Board Commission on Precollegiate Education in Mathematics, Science and Technology, whose report *Educating Americans for the 21st Century*, also recommended testing and standards. "Every State should establish rigorous standards for high school graduation, and local school districts should provide rigorous standards for grade promotion. We should curtail the process of social promotion" (1983:x). These three reports are not the only ones to recommend strict standards of grade promotion, but they are among the most widely read and influential. They provide a virtual consensus among reformers on the issue of grade promotion: schools should establish clear performance standards and strictly hold students to them before allowing movement from one grade to another. Age should not be a factor, nor should "social" considerations, like peer relations, be taken into account. Strict promotion standards are seen as a way to stop the decline in students' performance, and tests are a way to bring a high degree of accountability into the educational system.

While evidence on the effects of strict promotion policies will be reviewed in somewhat more detail below, it is worth noting here that in none of the three reports quoted here, nor others not quoted, is any evidence offered for the ability of strict promotion standards to improve student performance. In fact, the best research evidence, to the degree that it can be summarized, suggests the opposite: holding back students who do not meet the performance expectations does not improve the likelihood of their mastering future educational expectations. The best reviews of this research literature (Jackson, 1975; Selden, 1982; Holmes and Matthews, 1984; Smith and Shepard, 1987) conclude that retention does virtually nothing in comparison to social (or age-based) promotion in improving student achievement.

Moreover, there is now good evidence that for those students who get off the main sequence, who are "held back" and do not catch up, the chances of eventually dropping out before high school graduation are very good (Hammack, 1986). Examining dropout reports from a number of major urban areas makes clear the very high dropout rates for overage high school students. Something contributes to students being overage, of course, and often it is earlier poor academic performance which resulted in their being held back. The available remedies, special education, nonpromotion and remedial instruction do not appear to work well in improving learning and keeping at-risk students in school (Olson, 1985).

However, the issue has not become one of simply instituting stricter promotion standards; today, the issue is minimum competency and states' willingness to test and to key educational progress to test perform-ance. A full discussion of this policy is beyond the scope of this chapter;[3] but its implications for the education of at-risk youth are critical and will be examined.

MINIMUM COMPETENCY TESTING

As noted earlier, eight states now tie grade promotion directly to test performance, and 25 require students to pass such a test to graduate from high school. But the movement does not stop at the elementary and secondary level. The state of Florida now requires all public college freshmen to pass a state developed and administered competency test in order to move on to sophomore status.

The minimum competency testing movement predates the current education reform recommendations. It has its origins in efforts to clearly (re)establish minimum expectations of schooling and to link those expectations to school performance. Making schools more accountable for the educational performance of their students requires both a test of achievement and a standard against which to measure the average scores of students in individual schools. These efforts to increase school accountability stem from a widespread rejection of the conclusion that schools have little independent effect on student performance, once ability and family background are accounted for. That conclusion was overstated (Coleman, 1966; Jencks, 1972), but stimulated what has come to be called the effective schools movement (Austin, 1979).

The idea of this effort is that truly effective schools did exist, and once identified and studied, the factors associated with their success could be spread to other, less effective, schools (Edmonds, 1979; Klitgaard and Hall, 1974). Among the factors identified as characteristic of effective schools are clear and strongly held standards or expectations for student achievement.[4] The literature produced by this movement has therefore stressed the need for clear and enforced educational standards in addition to other factors, such as leadership and school climate as important.

But such standards and the associated tests assume that there is a consensus about what third graders, for example, need to know and be able to do. As Daniel Resnick (1980:24) notes, "Testing for minimum acceptable competence as opposed to scaled norm-referenced performance assumes that competency can be defined in agreed upon ways, successfully taught, and appropriately measured. These conditions do not yet describe the present environment." Nevertheless, as has been noted earlier, the use of such tests continues.

Writing (1985:12) with Lauren Resnick, Resnick relates testing with assignment to curriculum track. They begin by noting that the United States is virtually alone among advanced industrial societies in granting diplomas on the basis of school attendance rather than on test performance. The tests we do give—*except* for minimum competency tests—are not designed to be taught to nor studied for, and, as a consequence, cannot help shape the curriculum nor serve as incentives for student effort. Only minimum competency tests can serve these monitoring and assessment purposes, providing that consensus can be achieved about their content and use. These authors note that curriculum tracks (and class homogeneous ability groups) allow for a diversity of educational goals and thus standards which have helped create the declines in national test scores. The Resnicks are strongly in favor of raising standards of instruction and performance for all students in middle schools and of using tests both to assess skill acquisition and to monitor student and school progress.

Although students in the United States are tested more than those in any other country, the state-wide use of tests for promotion and graduation is relatively new. The testing of students for monitoring the educational system has been carried out on samples of students for many years, but the new testing programs include *all* students and are for the purpose of certifying performance, not monitoring schooling (though they may be used for that reason as well). In addition, there are clear sanctions and rewards associated with test performance: promotion and graduation (Airasian, 1987).

However, as noted above, the best evidence available discourages a strong positive assessment of strict promotion standards as a means of improving educational performance. In fact, Smith and Shepard (1987) go so far as to assert:

> Let us not mince words; we see little justification for retentions or for programs that add a year to a pupil's career in school. The evidence is quite clear and nearly unequivocal that the achievement and adjustment of retained children are no better—and in most instances are worse—than those of comparable children who are promoted. *Retention is one part of the current reform packages that does not work.* Moreover, retention and policies associated with it are costly both to taxpayers and to the pupils affected (1987:134).

Holmes and Matthews, after reviewing 44 studies qualifying for their meta-analysis, are almost as emphatic: "Those who continue to retain pupils at grade level do so despite cumulative research evidence showing that the potential for negative effects consistently outweighs positive outcomes" (1984:232). Even earlier, Jackson concluded his extensive review of the research then available by stating, "Thus those educators who retain pupils in a grade do so without valid research that such treatment will provide greater benefits to students with academic or adjustment difficulties than will promotion to the next grade" (1975: 627).

WHY DO WE CONTINUE TO RETAIN STUDENTS?

Airasian alerts us to the changing purposes of testing, and to the goals a testing policy seeks to achieve. The national commissions cited earlier all expressed concern that our educational system was in decline; that students were not learning as much as citizenship and employment require, especially as international economic competition grows more intense. Hence, the establishment of standards and holding students and schools to those standards is an attempt to improve educational performance. In the process, as governors, state legislatures and state boards of education have been the primary initiators of the new testing schemes, they have been strengthening their control of education at the expense of local schools and districts. A second goal of stricter promotion policies and the development of minimum competency test programs, then, has been to enhance state control of education (see Dougherty, 1988, for a related argument).

Another goal, though not explicit, is also operating in the effort to tighten promotion standards. As Christopher Hurn (1985: 274–76) has pointed out, the authority of schools over their students has diminished considerably since the 1960s. Court decisions extending student rights, combined with a heightened tendency to question institutional authorities reduced schools' "previously great discretion to punish and discipline students as they saw fit" (1985:276). By the mid-seventies, these forces had produced a clear "reduction of the schools' moral authority to inspire and motivate students to give of their best, and a weakening of the mutual trust and good will upon which that moral authority ultimately depended" (1985:276).

By 1987, this loss of institutional authority resulted in the widespread popularity of Edwin Hirsch's (1987) cultural literacy list. The reception of this book provides strong evidence for Hurn's argument, and the backlash the loss of authority has generated. Hirsch is explicit in his desire to support the political and intellectual atmosphere needed to support the consensus on "what everybody needs to know" that is required for minimum competency testing. The reestablishment of the cultural and moral authority of the schools is, perhaps, an even more important goal of stricter standards than aiding the scholastic improvement of students not progressing as quickly as schools expect.[5]

If our intent is to help at-risk students succeed in school, however, stricter retention policies seem unlikely to be effective. At the same time, we need to avoid a relaxation of the standards which exist by the teachers and administrators who are facing the students who fail those standards (McDill, Natriello and Pallas, 1986). What can help? The last section of this chapter reviews, briefly, directions for effective change.

ALTERNATIVE POLICIES

A clear implication of this analysis is that the timetable of schooling is too tight already for some students. The organizational imperatives of large scale schooling outlined above resulted in what Roth, has called "one of our most highly organized and standardized timetables..." (1962:73). While that timetable may satisfy organizational needs, it is not helpful for at-risk students.

In the early grades, mixed grade classes are possible and can be effectively implemented using cooperative learning strategies developed by Slavin (1987). These methods have been found to be "... more effective than traditional methods in increasing basic achievement outcomes on standardized tests of mathematics, reading, and language" (1987:7). When classrooms are organized around cooperation, instead of competition, the differences students bring to school are more likely to be narrowed as the reward system is geared to everyone's gains, not just that of individual students.

Individualization of the diagnosis of student difficulties, combined with a renewed focus on the delivery of educational resources directly to at-risk students and the monitoring of the educational results may reduce the impact of the rigid timetable. Taking the focus off of the timetable, without neglecting expectations for learning, is the goal. The achievement of this goal can be enhanced by a school climate where there are clear and concise rewards based on effort and on the progress students make. The clear connection between student activity and rewards can help where intrinsic motivation or prior commitment to school is lacking (McDill, Natriello and Pallas, 1986).

What is also very clear is that merely instituting a new promotion policy will be unlikely to improve failing students' performance. The school system's average performance data may rise, but only because its dropout rate has also risen or the number of special education students on separate examination standards has also risen (Office of Educational Assessment, 1986; Hammack, 1986; Wehlage and Rutter, 1986; Viadero, 1988). What is essential is that additional resources be directed not just to the measurement of student progress, but as well to the education of those not keeping up with the main sequence. As New York City discovered, a really strict promotion policy can be very expensive. Whether that money is best spent for gates classes or in some other instructional scheme (like cooperative learning) is an important question for which no single answer is available. But merely assuming that students who are exposed twice to the general curriculum will catch up with their age peers is not supported by available research.

Perhaps it is time for an entitlement program for those students not meeting a standard in the early elementary grades. Such a program would force school districts to devote resources toward the at-risk student. The example of special education programs could be instructive here. The creation of "child study teams" for *every* student falling behind (or better yet, for every student) could be a beginning; such teams might be required to formulate "individual educational plans" for students who are otherwise unable to keep up with the timetable. The implications of these more elaborate instructional designs need exploration, but a more strict promotion policy and a one-year remedial class are not the answer for at-risk youth.

Endnotes

1. Attempts to obtain reliable data regarding the national- or state-wide policy and practice, specifically rates of retardation for nonspecial education elementary students, were not productive. Contacts with United States Department of Education's Office of Educational Research and Improvement, The Education Commission of the States and several city and state education departments and boards of education were made in order to determine whether studies of retention rates by grade level were available. Some city reports, Austin, Los Angeles and Oklahoma City among them, are available, but reflect cross-sectional studies of policies recently put in place.

2. The *requirement* to hold back elementary level students on the basis of test scores alone seems rare. Secondary school graduation is more likely to be controlled by tests.

3. See Resnick, 1980; Jaeger and Tittle, 1980; Haney and Madaus, 1978, for a good introduction the literature on minimum competency testing.

4. Good sources on the search for effective schools are: Brookover, 1979; Rosenholtz, 1985; and Ralph and Fennessey, 1983.

5. See the Fall, 1986 issue of *Teachers College Record* edited by Nyberg and Farber, which was devoted to essays concerning "Authority in Education."

REFERENCES

Airasian, Peter W. 1987. "State Mandated Testing and Educational Reform: Context and Consequences." *American Journal of Education.* 95(May):393–412.

Austin, Gilbert R. 1979. "Exemplary Schools and the Search for Effectiveness." *Educational Leadership* October: 10–14.

Ayers, Leonard. 1908. *Laggards in Our Schools.* New York: Russell Sage Foundation.

Brookover, Wilber. 1979. *School Social Systems and Student Achievement: Schools Can Make a Difference.* New York: Praeger.

Coleman, James. et. al. 1966. *Equality in Educational Opportunity.* Washington, D.C.: Government Printing Office.

Dougherty, Kevin. 1988. "Educators as Politicians: Toward a Fuller Understanding of their Role." Unpublished manuscript, Department of Sociology, Manhattan College.

Edmonds, Ronald. 1979. "Effective Schools for the Urban Poor." *Educational Leadership* 38: 15–24.

Gold, Deborah L. 1988. "Georgia To Test Kindergartners For Promotion." *Education Week,* VII, 23 (March, 2): 1, 15.

Goleman, Daniel. 1988. "What Do Children Fear Most? Their Answers are Surprising." *The New York Times.* March 17, B9.

Hammack, Floyd M. 1986. "Large School Systems' Dropout Reports: An Analysis of Definitions, Procedures, and Findings." Pp. 20–37 in Gary Natriello (Ed.), *School Dropouts: Patterns and Policies.* New York City: Teachers College Press.

Haney, Walter and George F. Madaus. 1978. "Making Sense of the Competency Testing Movement." *Harvard Educational Review* 48: 462–84.

Hirsch, E. D. Jr. 1987. *Cultural Literacy: What Every American Needs to Know.* Boston: Houghton Mifflin.

Holmes, C. Thomas and Kenneth M. Matthews. 1984. "The Effects of Nonpromotion on Elementary and Junior High Pupils: A Meta-Analysis." *Review of Educational Research* 54 (Summer): 225–236.

Hurn, Christopher J. 1985. *The Limits and Possibilities of Schooling: An Introduction to the Sociology of Education.* Second Edition. Boston: Allyn and Bacon.

Jackson, Gregg B. 1975. "The Research Evidence on the Effects of Grade Retention." *Review of Educational Research* 45:613–635.

Jaeger, Richard M. and Carol Kehr Tittle (eds). 1980. *Minimum Competency Achievement Testing: Motives, Models, Measures and Consequences.* San Francisco: McCutchan.

Jencks, Christopher, et.al. 1972. *Inequality.* New York: Basic Books.

Klitgaard, Robert E. and George Hall. 1973. *A Statistical Search for Unusually Effective Schools.* Santa Monica: The Rand Corporation.

Labaree, David F. 1984. "Setting the Standard: Alternative Policies for Student Promotion." *Harvard Educational Review* 54 (February):67–87.

Madaus, George F. and Vincent Greaney. 1985. "The Irish Experience in Competency Testing: Implications for American Education." *American Journal of Education* 93 (February):268–294.

National Commission on Excellence in Education. 1983. *A Nation At Risk: The Imperative for Educational Reform.* Washington, D.C.: Government Printing Office.

Nyberg, Davis and Paul Farber, (eds.). 1986. "Authority in Education." *Teachers College Record* 88 (Fall): whole issue.

Office of Educational Assessment. 1986. "Evaluation Update on the Effects of the Promotional Policy Program." New York: New York City Board of Education.

Olson, Lynn. 1985. " 'Excellence' Tactics Single Out Weakest, But Offer Little Aid: The Remediation Issue." *Education Week* 4, 38 (June 12): 1, 20–22.

Ralph, John H. and James Fennessey. 1983. "Science or Reform: Some Questions About the Effective Schools Model." *Phi Delta Kappan* June: 689–694.

Resnick, Daniel P. 1980. "Minimum Competency Testing Historically Considered." Pp. 3–29 in David C. Berliner (ed.), *Review of Research in Education,* #8. Washington, D.C.: American Educational Research Association.

Resnick, Daniel P. and Lauren B. Resnick. 1985. "Standards, Curriculum, and Performance: A Historical and Comparative Perspective." *Educational Researcher,* April, 5–20.

Task Force on Education for Economic Growth. 1983. *Action for Excellence: A Comprehensive Plan To Improve Our Nation's Schools.* Denver: Education Commission of the States.

The National Science Board Commission on Precollegiate Education in Mathematics, Science and Technology. 1983. *Educating Americans for the 21st Century.* Washington, D.C.: National Science Foundation.

Rosenholtz, Susan J. 1985. "Effective Schools: Interpreting the Evidence." *American Journal of Education* 93:352–88.

Roth, Julius. *Timetables: Structuring the passage of time in hospital and other careers.* Indianapolis, Bobbs-Merrill, 1963.

Selden, Steven. 1982. "Promotion Policy." Pp. 1467–1474 in Harold E. Mitzel, III, *Encyclopedia of Educational Research.* New York: Free Press.

Smith, Mary Lee and Lorrie A. Shepard. 1987. "What Doesn't Work: Explaining Policies of Retention in the Early Grades" *Phi Delta Kappan,* October: 129–134.

Viadero, Debra. 1988. "Study Documents Jump in Special Education Enrollments." *Education Week* 7, 23 (March, 2):17.

Wehlage, Gary G. and Robert A. Rutter. 1986. "Dropping Out: How Much do Schools Contribute to the Problem?" Pp 70–88 in Gary Natriello (ed.), *School Dropouts: Patterns and Policies.* New York: Teachers College Press.

Chapter 7

LEGAL PROTECTIONS FOR AT RISK CHILDREN

JULIE UNDERWOOD

INTRODUCTION

American society places a high value on education. Education is seen as the best way to improve oneself in our society, a way to climb the social and economic ladder to success. The American legal system, however, has not incorporated this value into law, in that the right to an education has not been found to be a federal constitutional right (*San Antonio School Dist. v. Rodriguez,* 411 U.S. 1 (1973)). However, the right to access to the American public school system has been guaranteed on an equal basis regardless of race, sex or handicapping condition. Although access to education has been opened considerably over the last thirty years, female, handicapped, minority and lower socioeconomic status children run the highest risk of school failure. Many experts attribute this to a lack of commitment to provide services and make these students successful, on the part of the public school system. The education a child receives once within the system may not be equal in quality to that received by others, nor meet his or her needs. Over the last thirty years the courts and the U.S. Congress have interpreted and implemented legislation to ensure equal treatment of students by outlawing discrimination on the basis of race, sex and handicap. The impact these pieces of legislation and judicial interpretations have had on the public schools is the focus of this chapter. In addition, the legislative and judicial treatment of other circumstances which may place children at risk for school failure, such as child abuse, and recent state legislative enactments for at-risk children will be reviewed.

Children at-risk are generally defined as those who are not likely to complete high school successfully. Currently there are legal protections for those children to either help them deal with their problems, protect them from discrimination or enhance their chances of success. What will be reviewed are federal statutes or standards in each area; specific state legislation in each area will not be reviewed.

HANDICAPPED

The federal law, Education for All Handicapped Children Act of 1975 (20 U.S.C.A. 1401), assures that all handicapped children have access to a free appropriate public education and related services designed to meet their unique needs. It defines handicapped children as:

> mentally retarded, hard of hearing, deaf, orthopedically impaired, other health impaired, speech-impaired, visually handicapped, seriously emotionally disturbed, or children with specific learning disabilities who, by reason thereof, require special education and related services (20 U.S.C.A. 1401 a-1).

The Act assures that all handicapped children have access to a free appropriate public education. The appropriate educational program must be tailored to each handicapped child's educational needs. An individualized educational plan (IEP) is designed for each child and reevaluation of the plan must be conducted at least annually. The IEP must include the following information: the child's present level of performance; a statement of goals; a statement of what particular kind of special education and related services are to be provided; a statement about the degree of mainstreaming that will be provided; and a plan for evaluation.

The key to compliance with the Education for All Handicapped Children Act is to determine what constitutes an appropriate education for each child. The United States Supreme Court has interpreted the statute to require that services for the handicapped student be individualized through the individualized education plan and be sufficient to permit the child to benefit from the instruction provided (*Hendrick Hudson District Board of Education v. Rowley*, 458 U.S. 176, 102 S.Ct. 3034 (1982)).

The Education for All Handicapped Children Act defines an appropriate education as providing for special education and "related services." Related services are defined as

> transportation, and such developmental, corrective, and other supportive services (including speech pathology and audiology, psychological

services, physical and occupational therapy, recreation, and medical and counseling services, except that such medical services shall be for diagnostic and evaluation purposes only) (20 U.S.C.A. 1401 (17)).

The Supreme Court has interpreted this mandate as requiring a school district to provide those services necessary for the child to receive educational benefits from his/her educational program. Schools, however, are not required to provide ongoing medical services which are required by state law to be performed by a physician (*Irving Ind. School District v. Tatro*, 104 S.Ct. 3371 (1984)). Nor are they required to perform highly technical and involved nursing services which go beyond the scope of school nursing functions (506 E.H.L.R. 103 (SEA IL 1984)).

Another requirement of the Education for All Handicapped Act is that children must be educated in the least restrictive environment appropriate to their needs. Children also must be mainstreamed or placed in physical proximity to their nonhandicapped peers whenever appropriate (20 U.S.C.A. 1412(5)(B)). This requires the team developing the individualized educational plan to select from all possible appropriate placements, the one which is least restrictive for that individual child (45 CFR 121a.552 Comment.). A determination of restrictiveness should include considerations of the child's educational, emotional, social and physical needs. It should place a child in a position which makes him or her able to lead a life most closely approximating one of a "normal" child. The requirement to mainstream children when appropriate is not a mandate to place all handicapped children full time in regular classrooms, but only to place them in contact with nonhandicapped peers when appropriate. At times the mandate to place a child in the least restrictive environment will take precedence over the statutory preference for mainstreamed placements.

The statute contains a complex system of procedural safeguards for the children and parents served. These safeguards include (1) access by parents to relevant school records, (2) a parental right to be involved in the initial placement decision and any subsequent changes in placement, (3) opportunity for a fair and impartial hearing, including the right to be represented by an attorney or advocate, (4) opportunity to appeal the hearing officer's decision through a court, (5) a right of the child to remain in the current placement during the pendency of the hearing proceedings, and (6) attorneys' fees to a prevailing party.

The other major provision protecting the handicapped is Section 504 of the Rehabilitation Act of 1973 (29 U.S.C.A. 794). Section 504 prohibits discrimination against handicapped persons in any federally assisted program or activity. This means that institutions may not:

(1) deny or limit services to handicapped people or establish different eligibility requirements for them,

(2) provide handicapped people with services which are not as effective as those provided to others,

(3) provide services in a way which limits handicapped persons' participation, or

(4) provide separate or different services to handicapped persons, except when necessary to make the services as effective as those provided to others.

Although the Education for All Handicapped Children Act is of primary importance to K–12 schools, Section 504 is also important because it is broader in scope. Section 504 deals with all handicapped people, not just students, and in some instances provides students nonacademic rights which they may not have under the Education for All Handicapped Children Act.

One of the most noticeable effects of Section 504 is the structural changes in buildings which allow for physical accessibility. Physical access is an area which is frequently misunderstood. Although each program must be readily accessible to handicapped persons, not every part of every facility need be accessible. The key is in allowing opportunity for participation in the class or program. Every room need not be accessible but every program must be. This can be achieved by moving programs to accessible places, as well as by making structural changes to the facility.

Under Section 504 a school cannot deny a handicapped student a chance to participate in a program if he/she is otherwise qualified. In addition, the school is required to make minor modifications to accommodate the handicapping condition. If reasonable accommodations cannot be made which would allow the person to function efficiently and safely in a program, it is not discriminatory to deny participation (*Southeastern Community College v. Davis*, 442 U.S. 397 (1979)).

In a case where a severely physically handicapped high school student wanted to attend a school sponsored trip to Spain, the court held that the school was not required to allow her to go. The student's stature (3 1/2 feet) and severe congenital limb deficiencies made it difficult for her to walk on uneven surfaces and for long periods of time. After examining the activities that were contemplated for the trip, the court found that the girl would not be capable of keeping up with the group. Thus, she was not qualified to participate and exclusion did not violate Section 504 (*Wolf v. South Colonie Central School Dist.*, 534 F. Supp. 758 (N.D.N.Y. 1982)).

In cases dealing with handicapped students' involvement in athletics, the courts have required the schools to allow the students to participate if they are "otherwise qualified" to play the sport. If they try out for the team and are able to compete effectively, they have demonstrated their qualification to participate. Thus, the courts have ruled in favor of a student with one eye who was barred from all contact sports (*Kampmeier v. Nyquist*, 553 F.2d 296 (2d Cir. 1977)); a student with one kidney who was barred from the wrestling team (*Poole v. South Plainfield Board of Education*, 490 F.Supp. 948 (D.N.J. 1980)); a student with one eye who was barred from the football team (*Wright v. Columbia University*, 520 F. Supp. 789 (E.D.Pa. 1981)); and a student with one kidney who was barred from the football team (*Grube v. Bethlehem Area School District*, 550 F. Supp. (E.D. Pa. 1982)).

The final area of special consideration for handicapped students is the area of student discipline. This area involves both the Education for All Handicapped Children Act and Section 504. In dealing with discipline of handicapped students the first question one must ask is whether the behavior involved is a manifestation of the child's handicap. Stated in another way, one must first determine if there is a nexus between the behavior in question and the disability. Students cannot be disciplined for a behavior which is a manifestation of their disability. To do so would merely be disciplining the handicap, or imposing penalties on a student because he/she is handicapped. This would violate Section 504's prohibition on discrimination on the basis of handicap (*S-1 v. Turlington*, 635 F.2d 342 (5th Cir. 1981); (*Prince William v. Malone*, 762 F.2d 1210 (4th Cir. 1985)).

Making a determination of whether a behavior is related to a student's handicap is difficult, and must be decided by taking the whole child into consideration, not the label, or the identified handicapping condition. The determination should be made by a "knowledgeable group of people" (*S-1 v. Turlington*, 635 F.2d 342 (5th Cir. 1981)). Logically this seems to imply members of the IEP team or others who have worked with the child and his/her handicap. If there is a nexus between the behavior and the handicap, then the behavior should be worked on through an individualized behavior program developed as a part of the IEP rather than the disciplinary consequences used for the general student population.

If the behavior is not related to the handicap, regular procedure may be followed with some modifications. If a student is to be removed from the current educational placement for a period greater than ten days, the change in placement must follow EHA procedures rather than regular disciplinary procedures for the school (*S-1 v. Turlington*, 635 F.2d 342 (5th Cir. 1981); *Honig v. Doe*, 56 U.S.L.W. 4091 (1988)). If a student is to be removed or expelled from the school, some appropriate educational program must be provided to the student to satisfy his/her rights to an education under the Education for All Handicapped Children Act. In addition, if there is a conflict between the school and the parents regarding these decisions, the Act requires that the student remain in his/her current educational placement until a resolution is reached. This is true even if the student is disruptive or even potentially dangerous. The Court suggests that if this situation occurs schools can seek relief in the courts (*Honig v. Doe*, 56 U.S.L.W. 4091 (1988)).

MINORITY AND DISADVANTAGED YOUTH

Racial Discrimination

Almost thirty-five years after the United States Supreme Court issued its landmark decision which outlawed apartheid practices in the American public schools (*Brown v. Bd. of Education* 347 U.S. 483 (1954)), racial discrimination still remains as a serious problem in our public schools. Even in the 1980s over 60 percent of the black students in America attend predominantly black schools. In addition, minority students are more often suspended from schools and tracked into low ability groups, and have been found more likely not to finish school with a high school diploma.

De jure segregation, apartheid, is a prohibited practice constitutionally and under state statutes. However, schools remain racially unbalanced due to other factors, such as housing patterns and attendance area boundaries. Courts have mandated remedies for this de facto segregation by mandating inter and intra district busing and redistricting. The courts do not require statistical balance in the public schools, but imbalances must be justified by nondiscriminatory bases.

The constitutional demand to desegregate schools does not mean that
every school in every community must always reflect the racial composition of the school system as a whole. . . . It should be clear that the
existence of some small number of one-race schools . . . is not in and of
itself a mark of a system which still practices segregation by law.
But . . . the burden upon school authorities will be to satisfy the court
that their racial composition is not the result of present or past discriminatory action on their part (*Swann v. Charlotte-Mecklenburg Board of
Education,* 402 U.S. at 24-26).

Judicial and Office of Civil Rights orders requiring pairing of schools,
redrawing of attendance districts, assignment of students across district
lines, and busing students to nonneighborhood schools have all been
upheld as remedial measures to remedy racial segregation. School district policies allowing for open enrollment within the district alone have
been found not to be a sufficient remedy for segregation. The issue of
whether a district is in fact segregated and which remedy is sufficient is
heavily dependent on the facts of the individual case.

Nationally, at the high school level, black students are suspended
three times as often as whites. Minority students comprise 25 percent of
the school population and yet they comprise 40 percent of all students
suspended or expelled. It is often alleged that this is caused, not by
minority students presenting an actual disruption more often than white
students, but by racism in the public schools.

Although discipline policies are now written in a race neutral manner,
they are too often applied discriminatorily. Policies generally contain
vague terms and leave the teachers and administrators with a good deal
of discretion in their application. Unfortunately, this can lead to discriminatory applications and interpretations. A reported example of this
is a school rule banning weapons which was interpreted to include hair
picks. Any student possessing a hair pick could be disciplined under this
interpretation. The discriminatory impact of such an interpretation
is obvious.

Such discriminatory application of disciplinary rules would be grounds
for judicial relief. However, since the rules are racially neutral on their
face, to be successful, the plaintiff would have to present evidence of
discriminatory motives. Actual proof of animus is extremely rare. The
courts have held that absent a legitimate educational reason if the practice would forseeably result in discrimination, discriminatory intent can
be inferred.

Although the state has the authority to set reasonable promotion and graduation requirements, these cannot be racially discriminatory. Different testing criteria cannot be used for minority and non-minority students (*Harkless v. Sweeney Independent School District,* 554 F.2d 1353 (5th Cir. 1977)). A common issue is when facially neutral tests and requirements are discriminatory because they have a disparate negative impact on minority groups. For example, black students are three times as likely to be identified as educably mentally retarded; they are only half as likely to be identified as gifted. In addition, they are more likely not to receive a high school diploma when standardized testing is used as a criterion.

The legality of using student testing techniques which have a disproportion adverse impact on minority students is not settled. Use of the same IQ test was upheld in one case (*Parents in Action in Special Education v. Hannon,* 506 F.Supp. 831 (N.D. Ill. 1980)) and nullified in another (*Larry P. v. Riles,* 495 F. Supp. 926 (N.D. Cal. 1979), aff'd in part 793 F.2d 969 (9th Cir. 1984). In both cases the test was being used for placement of students into special education classes, and was resulting in a disproportionate number of black students being identified as educably mentally retarded. As in the above discriminatory discipline policies noted above, the court will look to see if discrimination was a forseeable result of the practice and if the practice is justifiable for educational reasons.

The issue of the discriminatory results of minimum competency testing also continues to be a subject of litigation. The best known of these cases is *Debra P. v. Turlington,* 474 F. Supp. 244 (M.D. Fla. 1979), aff'd, 644 F.2d 397 (5th Cir. 1981). Here the use of a minimum competency test as a criterion for graduation was challenged on the grounds that it was not a reflection of the material actually taught in the curriculum and because black students were unfairly treated due to the vestiges of previous de jure segregation in the state. To justify the test the Court of Appeals required the district to show that the skills on the test were included in the official curriculum and that the majority of the teachers recognized them as being something they should teach. Not to require that the information be taught would violate notions of fundamental fairness as well as support the testing of a student's culture and noneducational experiences rather than a measure of skills acquired through formal education. In response to the more blatant discrimination charge, the court suspended the use of the test until the students who had been in attendance at segregated schools had passed through the system. This was necessary since the white students had an unfair advantage over the black students by attending different schools in the lower grades.

Language

Generally grievances raised by minority students, other than segregation, involve linguistic barriers. State or school board rules can require that the basic language of instruction in all schools be English. The state, however, cannot instruct in the English language exclusively, by denying interpretation and bilingual instruction to students who cannot use the English language. The principal sources of federal legislation which cover linguistic barriers to educational opportunities are found in Title VI of the Civil Rights Act of 1964 (42 U.S.C.A. 2000a et seq.), the Equal Educational Opportunities Act of 1974 (20 U.S.C.A. 1701 et seq.), and the Bilingual Education Act of 1978 (20 U.S.C.A. 3221 et seq.).

The most noted case in the area is the United States Supreme Court case *Lau v. Nichols* (414 U.S. 563, 94 S.Ct. 786 (1974)). There non-English speaking Chinese students maintained that failure to provide methods for bridging the language gap violated the Civil Rights Act of 1964. The 1964 Act bans discrimination "on the grounds of race, color, or national origin" in "any program or activity receiving federal financial assistance." The Department of Health, Education and Welfare has issued guidelines which state:

> Where inability to speak and understand the English language excludes national origin — minority groups children from effective participation in the educational program offered by a school district, the district must take affirmative steps to rectify the language deficiency (35 C.F.R. 11595).

The Supreme Court held in favor of the children, and in so doing observed that there can be no equality of treatment where the students do not understand English. The Court concluded that:

> Basic English skills are at the very core of what these public schools teach. Imposition of a requirement that, before a child can effectively participate in the educational program, he must already have acquired those basic skills is to make a mockery of public education. We know that those who do not understand English are certain to find their classroom experiences wholly incomprehensible and in no way meaningful (*Lau v. Nichols* 414 U.S. 563 at 566).

The Court did not define the relief required for the children but instead noted that the lower judge had the discretion to fashion appropriate relief by way of an injunction.

The Equal Education Opportunities Act's (EEOA) provision relating to linguistic minorities states

> No state shall deny equal educational opportunity to an individual on account of his or her race, color, sex, or national origin, by . . .
>
> (f) the failure by an educational agency to take appropriate action to overcome language barriers that impede equal participation by its students in its instructional program (20 U.S.C.A. 1703(f)).

This statute is broader than Title VI of the Civil Rights Act because it applies to all public educational agencies and programs, applies to any individual, and applies regardless of evidence of intentional discrimination. Most importantly it has been held that the EEOA imposes an affirmative duty on schools "to take appropriate action to overcome language barriers" (*Morales v. Shannon*, 516 F.2d 411, 415 (5th Cir. 1975), cert. den'd., 423 U.S. 1034 (1975)).

To be successful in an EEOA case the students must be able to identify their language barriers and show how their language barrier impedes their participation in the instructional program. Plaintiffs must next show how the defendants have failed to take appropriate steps to rectify the problem and finally identify the connection between the defendant's failure and the students' learning problems (See *Martin Luther King, School Children v. Michigan Board of Education*, 451 F. Supp. 1324, 1330 (E.D. Mich. 1978)). The courts have given the educational experts a great deal of discretion in determining what remedies would be appropriate in each particular case. The EEOA does not necessarily require any particular form of program or even formal bilingual or bicultural education (See e.g., *Guadalupe Organization, Inc. v. Tempe Elementary School*, 587 F.2d 1022 (9th Cir. 1978)).

Although this statute is most commonly used to redress the grievances of nonEnglish speaking minorities, it has been used by children who spoke "black English." In one case, eleven black children were experiencing educational difficulties due to their use of "black English." The court found that they were being denied equal opportunities under the EEOA by the school's failure to train teachers in that vernacular and help the students bridge the gap from their language to standard American English (*Martin Luther King, School Children v. Michigan Board of Education*, 451 F. Supp. 1324 (E.D. Mich. 1978)).

The most specific statute in the area is the Bilingual Education Act (BEA). It, in part, states:

[T]here are large and growing numbers of children of limited English proficiency . . . the Congress declares it to be the policy of the United States, in order to establish equal educational opportunity for all children (A) to encourage the establishment and operation, where appropriate, of educational programs using bilingual educational practices, techniques and methods, (B) to encourage the establishment of special alternative instructional programs for students of limited English proficiency in school districts where the establishment of bilingual educational programs is not practical . . . , and (C) for that purpose to provide financial assistance to local educational agencies and, . . . to State educational agencies . . . The programs assisted . . . are designed to meet the educational needs of individuals of limited English proficiency with particular attention to children having the greatest need for such programs (20 U.S.C.A. 3222).

Fiscal incentives are intended to induce school districts with high concentrations of linguistic minorities to undertake bilingual and bicultural programs. Like the EEOA, the BEA does not impose any particular philosophy of bilingual education. The statute and implementing regulations use the concepts of "limited English proficiency" meaning children with sufficient difficulty in understanding, speaking, reading or writing the English language to deny them the opportunity to learn successfully in English (20 U.S.C.A. 3223 (1)); "transitional bilingual education" meaning "structured English language instruction, and to the extent necessary to allow a child to achieve competence in the English language, instruction in the child's native language" (20 U.S.C.A. 2332 (4)(A)); "developmental bilingual education" meaning "a full-time program of instruction . . . in structured English-language instruction and instruction in a second language (20 U.S.C.A. 3223 (5)(A)); and "special alternative instructional programs" meaning "programs of instruction [that] have specially designed curricula and are appropriate for the particular linguistic and instructional needs of the children enrolled" (20 U.S.C.A. 3223 (6)). The BEA stresses appreciation of students' cultural heritage in all courses to the extent the same are necessary to allow a child to progress through the educational system (34 C.F.R. 500.4).

Economically Disadvantaged

Originally, federal money was made available to state and local schools through Title I of the ESEA, which is now called Chapter I. The money is to be used to supplement the special educational needs of economically disadvantaged children. Services comparable to those provided in the public schools are to be provided to children who attend private and parochial schools in areas with high concentrations of low-income families.

Since 1965, most of the nation's public school districts and many private schools have used Chapter I programs to help millions of economically disadvantaged children. Students who receive Chapter I services are at high risk for academic failure. Half of these students score below the fifteenth percentile on national achievement tests. Many have moved and changed schools frequently. Fifty percent of the Chapter I students qualify economically for free or reduced lunch programs; slightly more than one-third are minorities. Eligible students receive supplementary small group instruction in reading, writing and communication skills. According to repeated national studies, children who participate in Chapter I programs do better in school than similar children who do not participate in Chapter I programs. And some children, like the children of migrant workers or children in states where there are no kindergartens, attend school in Chapter I programs, when they otherwise might not attend school at all.

Most Chapter I money is used to provide extra help in reading and math for elementary school children whose test scores show that they are not working at or near the level of other children their age. These educational programs are possible because Chapter I funds pay the salaries of teachers and classroom aides to work with economically disadvantaged children in small groups in their own classrooms or in special workrooms, and because Chapter I funds purchase extra materials and equipment, designed to help children who are having trouble learning to read and do math. In addition, Chapter I funds are used to train Chapter I and regular teachers so they are better prepared to help children in need of special educational assistance. Finally, Chapter I funds are used for programs to train and encourage parents to become more involved with their children's education.

In *Bell v. New Jersey and Pennsylvania* (102 S.Ct. 2187 (1983)), the United States Supreme Court held that the federal government may recover from the states funds which had been misused. In the wake of that opinion, there have been a number of cases involving the Secretary of Education's decisions seeking repayment of misused Chapter I funds. Some of these cases are reviewed here to illustrate appropriate and inappropriate uses of Chapter I funds (e.g., *Bennett v. Kentucky Department of Education*, 105 S.Ct. 1544 (1985); *Bennett v. New Jersey*, 105 S.Ct. 1555 (1985)).

In 1985 the United States Supreme Court decided a case in which the state of Kentucky was alleged to have used federal funds to supplant state expenditure for educating disadvantaged children rather than supplementing the state's expenditures as required by Title I of the Elementary and Secondary Act of 1965 (*Bennett v. Kentucky Department of Education*, 105 S.Ct. 1544 (1985)). The Court held that the programs did violate the requirements of Title I. Even though the state's interpretation of the statute was reasonable, the Secretary's interpretation prevailed.

The Fourth Circuit Court of Appeals reviewed the Secretary of Education's order for the refund of funds allegedly misspent under Title I during 1977–79 totalling $317,435. (*Virginia Dept. of Educ. v. Secretary of Educ.*, 806 F.2d 78 (4th Cir. 1986)). The amount included funds spent on a secondary summer school program, a Saturday program, and funds for a home school worker. The Secretary concluded that the programs funded constituted general aid to the schools because they were not targeted to the special educational needs of the Title I eligible students and therefore were not appropriate expenditures under Title I. The Home School Program was designed to reduce absenteeism in the schools which contained Title I children. The employee, after receiving the absentee list for the day, would contact the Title I families on the list, by phone or a visit, inquiring about the absence, after which the same procedure was followed for the non-Title I children. It was found that equivalent services were provided to both groups of children. The summer school program was for the remedial reading, math, and basic skills instruction to Title I children. However, it included summer theater and music programs which were open to all students. It was found that the primary purpose of this was not to provide remedial instruction to Title I students, but to provide continuing music education in the summer. Finally, the Saturday program was not limited to Title I children and offered extracurricular activities such as photography, drill team, needlepoint, reading for pleasure, and other leisure classes. The school's attempt at defending this program under the theory of confidence and self-esteem building and developing a rapport with students was not adopted by the Secretary, and it was determined that these were beyond the scope of the stated Title I purposes.

The Eleventh Circuit Court of Appeals also upheld the Secretary of Education's determination that the state must refund funds for misuse of Title I funds (*Florida Department of Educ. v. Bennett*, 769 F.2d 1501 (11th Cir. 1985)). The United States Department of Education had determined that the state of Florida had not provided "comparable" service to non-Title I schools. This requirement was intended to insure that federal funds were used to provide compensatory programs over and above those normally provided in the schools. The state conceded that the comparability requirement had not been met, but that its slight variance from the requirement (the statute allows for a 5% variance in spending) should not necessitate a full refund of the federal funds for all of the schools involved. The Secretary of Education disagreed with the school, and the court upheld the Secretary's decision, reasoning that it was beyond the scope of review for the court to substitute its view of a more equitable remedy for the decision of the Secretary.

The Ninth Circuit Court of Appeals held in a similar manner and required the state of Hawaii to refund $2,109,618. (*Department of Educ. State of Hawaii v. Bell*, 770 F.2d 1409 (9th Cir. 1985)). In addition to the comparability of services question raised in the Eleventh Circuit case, the state attacked the statute's no-supplant requirement as unreasonable (20 U.S.C.A. 241a, b(3), e). The court again deferred to the Secretary of Education's interpretation of the statutory requirements and upheld its decision.

Homeless

A federal statute effecting the education of homeless children was passed by Congress in June, 1987 and signed into law in July, 1987 (P.L. 100-77). The McKinney Homeless Assistance Act is a package of several programs dealing with homeless people. The Act has as its stated educational intent that homeless children have access to a free, appropriate public education on an equal basis with nonhomeless children. The statute is intended to discourage states from using state residency laws to bar homeless children from attending public schools. The stated policy of the sections regarding education is

> (1) each State educational agency shall assure that each child of a homeless individual and each homeless youth have access to a free, appropriate public education which would be provided to the children of a resident of a State and is consistent with the State school attendance laws; and
> (2) in any State that has a residency requirement as a component of its compulsory school attendance laws, the State will review and undertake steps to revise such laws to assure that the children of homeless individuals and homeless youth are afforded a free and appropriate public education. (Section 721). The McKinney Act provides federal funds to

states which develop a state plan to provide education to the homeless. The state plans must be designed so that local educational agencies will comply with the federal Act's provision for access. School districts in participating states must enroll homeless children in either the district in which the child was originally enrolled or in the district in which the child is actually living, whichever is determined to be in the child's best interest (Section 722(e)(3)). The placement of the child must be made without regard to whether the child is living with the parents (Section 722(e)(4)). School districts must provide other educational services in a nondiscriminatory manner to homeless children such as special education, compensatory education and transportation (Section 722(e)(5)).

Successful implementation of this Act will require the participation of all states. The deadline for state applications was April 30, 1988. As of February 1, 1988 only eleven states had completed applications (Arkansas, California, Kansas, Kentucky, Massachusetts, New Jersey, Ohio, Pennsylvania, Tennessee, Washington, and West Virginia).

SEX DISCRIMINATION

The courts have been called upon to address various forms of sex discrimination in the public school system. The most common areas of litigation include differential treatment in athletics and academic programming, and classifications of students due to pregnancy or marital status. Only the issues of differential treatment in academic programming and classifications due to pregnancy and marital status will be reviewed here.

Equal Treatment

Sex discrimination can be challenged either on the basis of the constitutional theory of equal protection or under the federal statute, Title IX of the Education Amendment of 1972. In order for the courts to uphold a state's classification of people on the basis of sex, the state must have an important interest and the classification must be substantially related to that interest (*Craig v. Boren*, 429 U.S. 190, 197 (1976)).

Under the constitutional theory of equal protection the courts have struck down sex-based criteria for admission to educational programs. For example, in two cases courts struck differential admissions standards even though they were designed to ensure equal enrollment in a college preparatory program (*Bray v. Lee*, 337 F. Supp. 934 (D. Mass. 1972);

Berkelman v. San Francisco Unified School Dist., 501 F.2d 1264 (9th Cir. 1974)). However, a court has upheld the maintenance of sex-segregated high schools in which the enrollment was voluntary and the programs were found to be essentially equal in quality (*Vorchheimer v. School District of Philadelphia,* 532 F. 2d 880 (3rd Cir. 1976), aff'd by an equally divided court, 430 U.S. 703 (1977)). Courts have consistently struck policies which have provided unequal educational opportunities for females and males. For example, the exclusion of females from traditionally male courses in the industrial arts have been found to be unconstitutional (E.g., *Seward v. Della,* No. 134173 (Cal. Super. Ct. 1973)).

Title IX of the Education Amendments of 1972, states that

> No person in the United States shall, on the basis of sex, be excluded from participation in, be denied the benefits of, or be subjected to discrimination under any education program or activity receiving federal financial assistance 20 US.C. 1681 (a).

The implementing regulations of this statute specifically prohibit sex discrimination in admissions, counseling, courses, financial aids and scholarships, and extra curricular activities. A student may not be precluded from any right, privilege, advantage or opportunity because of sex. Under Title IX a school which receives federal financial assistance may not require or refuse participation in any course by any of its students on the basis of sex. This includes courses in physical education, industrial, business, vocational, technical, home economics, etc. Some segregation may occur within the course, such as separating sexes when playing contact sports, or separating vocal groups for vocal range. In addition, whenever a school finds that a course has a disparate distribution of enrollment on the basis of sex, it must take action to determine that sex bias on the part of the school is not responsible for the result (Section 86.360). Sex segregated honoraries and extracurricular clubs would also be illegal under Title IX (E.g., *Iron Arrow Honor Society v. Heckler,* 702 F.2d 549 (5th Cir. 1983) vacated as moot, 464 U.S. 67 (1983)).

Litigation under Title IX was effectively suspended for a time due to a case which ruled that the statute was limited to programs directly receiving federal financial assistance (*Grove City College v. Bell,* 465 U.S. 202 (1982)). However, that court ruling was negated by the Congressional passage of the Civil Rights Restoration Act of 1987. This took effect in March, 1988. As a result all school programs will be required to be in compliance with Title IX's regulations regarding sex neutrality if the school district receives federal financial assistance. A resurgence in compliance monitoring and litigation will be the likely result.

Pregnancy and Marriage

Until the early 1970s schools generally tried to rid themselves of the problems presented by student marriages and pregnancies by simply suspending or expelling the students involved. This absolved pregnant girls from the obligations of compulsory attendance and allowed them to stay at home, hidden from their peers. Usually this meant the end of the student's education. Gradually during the 1970s schools began to rescind their rules regarding marriage and enact rules which allowed girls a choice of attending a separate school, having home instruction during pregnancy or attending separate classes for pregnant students.

The legal issue involved is whether a student can be excluded due to pregnancy or parenthood. The weight of recent authority is that pregnancy or marriage is not a valid reason to exclude a student from an education. Related issues are whether the pregnant student can be required to leave the regular school program and participate in a special school program, or take only homebound instruction, and whether a student can be excluded from extracurricular activities due to pregnancy or parenthood. Although some conflict on these issues exists, it is generally held that they too are prohibited practices. These practices can be challenged under the due process clause of state or federal constitutions, the equal protection clause of state or federal constitutions, or as a violation of Title IX of the Education Amendments of 1972. The implementing regulations for Title IX specifically state that

> A recipient shall not discriminate against any student, or exclude student from its education program or activity, including any class or extracurricular activity, on the basis of such student's pregnancy or recovery therefrom, unless the student requests voluntarily to participate in a separate portion of the program or activity of the recipient (34 C.F.R. 106.40 (b)(1)).

Previously a potential difficulty for a plaintiff in a Title IX suit is that the statute was limited to programs that receive federal financial assistance (*Grove City College v. Bell*, 465 U.S. 202 (1982)). As a result, if a pregnant student were excluded from a program or activity that did not receive federal assistance, Title IX would not prevent exclusion or discrimination. However, that court ruling was negated by the Congressional passage of the Civil Rights Restoration Act of 1987 in January

1988. Thus, in the future litigants will be able to directly challenge sex discrimination under Title IX. Previously most litigants have challenged discrimination on the basis of pregnancy under constitutional theories.

Generally to justify classifying people, the courts require that the state have a rational basis for the classification. The state must have an important interest and the classification must be substantially related to that interest if the classification is based on sex or if the student has been denied an education. Finally, if the classification infringes on an individual's fundamental rights, the state must have a compelling reason and the classification must be necessary to further that reason.

The prevailing opinion is that a student may not be denied an education solely due to pregnancy, marriage or parental status. In *O'Neill v. Dent* (364 F. Supp 565 (E.D.N.Y. 1973)) a regulation excluding a married student from a military school was invalidated. In *Shull v. Columbus Mun. Separate School District* (338 F. Supp 1376 (N.D. Miss. 1972)) the court held that a student could not be excluded from school solely because she was an unwed mother. Similarly another court upheld the right of an unwed mother to attend full-time regular classes if such attendance was not dangerous to her physical or mental health and if there was no other reason for her exclusion (*Ordway v. Hargraves* 323 F. Supp. 1155 (D. Mass. 1971)). Clearly the prevailing authority requires a school district to prove that the presence of a pregnant student will substantially disrupt the school, and will not uphold a general policy excluding all pregnant students from school.

In one case, however, the court upheld the school's decision to require an unwed mother to attend night school, tuition-free, rather than regular classes. The court found that the student's fundamental right of procreation was not violated because night classes were made available to the student. The court upheld the policy under the rationality test finding that since these students were "more precocious," their presence in regular classes may be disturbing. Thus, the policy was rationally related to the school's interest in maintaining discipline in the school (*Houston v. Prosser*, 361 F. Supp. 295 (N.D. Ga. 1973)).

The cases in the area of exclusion from extracurricular activities is just as consistent. The courts have held that a school may not exclude a student from participation in extracurricular activities solely due to marriage or pregnancy (*Indian High School Athletic Ass'n v. Raike*, 329 N.E.2d 66 (Ind. Ct. App. 1975); (*Bell v. Lone Oak Indep. School Dist.*, 507

S.W.2d 636 (Tex. Civ. App. 1974); *Hollon v. Mathis Indep. School Dist.*, 358 F. Supp 1269 (S.D. Tex. 1972); *Moran v. School District 7, Yellowstone County*, 350 F.Supp. 1180 (D. Mont. 1972); *Davis v. Meek*, 344 F. Supp. 298 (N.D. Ohio 1972); *Holt v. Shleton*, 341 F. Supp 821 (M.D. Tenn. 1972); *Romans v. Crenshaw*, 354 F. Supp. 868 (S.D. Tex 1972)). In one case, the court found that exclusion of a married student from extracurricular activities violated the fundamental right to marry and struck the policy on equal protection grounds (*Beeson v. Kiowa County School Dist.*, 567 P.2d 801 (Colo. Ct. App. 1977)).

CHILD ABUSE AND NEGLECT

Reports of child abuse, and especially sexual abuse, have increased significantly over the past few years. The rise is due, in part, to national media attention, school programs which raise students' awareness about their "right to be safe" and the clarification and expansion of reporting requirements. Children under five are most often the victims of maltreatment, accounting for almost 40 percent of all abuse/neglect reports. Although sexual abuse is reported most frequently for older children, 25 percent of sexual abuse reports concern children under five. Physical abuse, neglect and emotional abuse occur most frequently within families, with 80 percent of the reports citing parents as the abusers. Thirty percent of sexual abuse is by parents, with other family members accounting for 16 percent. No one yet knows how many cases remain unreported. Abuse has long-term serious consequences for its victims. Abused children are more likely than other children to be developmentally delayed and emotionally disturbed. As adults they have a high probability of becoming abusive parents, psychiatric parents and criminals.

In 1974 the federal Child Abuse Prevention and Treatment Act was enacted (42 U.S.C.A. 5101 et seq.). This statute provides a model legislative response to the problem of child abuse and neglect. Since then all fifty states and the District of Columbia have enacted similar child abuse protection statutes. These generally contain provisions mandating the reporting of suspected child abuse by those who work with children, encouraging reporting by others, providing good faith immunity to both groups of reporters, and providing penalties for the failure of mandatory reporters to report.

An integral part of all of the child protection statutes is the mandated reporting of suspected child abuse or neglect by certain professionals.

Mandatory reporters are basically those people who have access to children during the course of their professional duties. All states and the District of Columbia require teachers and other school officials who deal directly with children, to report child abuse. Although educators do not have the medical expertise to make an actual diagnosis of abuse or neglect they can generally surmise the cause of unexplained or unusual injuries. They see children on a day-to-day basis and are more likely to recognize inconcurrencies in a child's appearance or behavior (Rowe, 1981). In 1985, 15 percent of reports of all possible child abuse or neglect cases came from school personnel.

In addition to the mandatory reporters, most state protection statutes permit the reporting of child abuse by anyone who knows or has reasonable cause to suspect that a child is being abused or neglected. It is from this group of permissive reporters that most child abuse reports are made totalling 46 percent in 1985.

Abuse is generally seen as an intentional act and is sometimes referred to as an act of commission. Implicit in most definitions of abuse is that the injury is deliberately inflicted. Abuse includes bodily violation (e.g., beating, burning, cutting, exposure), sexual molestation and mental injury (e.g., sleep deprivation, beration and sensory overload or deprivation) (Schwartz, Arthur & Hirsch, 1982).

Neglect, on the other hand, is generally the failure to provide for the child and is sometimes referred to as an act of omission. Neglect is a failure to provide for a child's physical or emotional needs. Neglect is a parent or a guardian's failure to meet the basic needs of the child when they are otherwise able to do so. It includes the failure to: (1) meet nutritional needs; (2) meet needs of physical shelter from the elements and physical harm from the environment; (3) protect the child from dangers in the environment within the control of the parent; (4) meet health needs, including specific medical care; (5) meet emotional needs; (6) meet intellectual needs; or (7) meet needs of moral guidance and supervision (Besharov, 1978; Schwartz, Arthur, & Hirsch, 1982).

The states are relatively consistent in the degree of certainty an educator must have before he/she is required to report a situation of possible child abuse. The "statutory message is virtually the same—individuals are required to report when they should believe or suspect that a child has been abused [or neglected]" (Wayne Law Review, 1981, 189).

One of the common features of all of the state child protection statutes is the immunity from civil or criminal liability granted to those reporters who act in good faith. The federal statute also contains a provision for immunity for good faith reporters (42 U.S.C.A. 5103 (b)(2)(A)). This provision was intended to combat the fear of liability by protecting reporters from possible legal repercussions for reporting and thereby encourage the processing of reports. The statutes protect from legal attack all acts required or permitted by the statutes, including reporting as well as evidence gathering, such as taking photographs or interviewing the child. Even with the protection of immunity granted by the statutes, many educators are hesitant to report suspected child abuse and neglect. Thus, there are several ways to compel compliance with the statutes.

To carry out the legislative mandates of child abuse reporting, most statutes carry penalties for the failure to report. Although some states provide for both civil and criminal penalties most states provide for only criminal sanctions, and a minority provide for only civil penalties. In addition, a school district may pursue the matter through disciplinary proceedings of its own. A district can discipline an employee for failure to follow its own policies regarding the reporting of suspected child abuse just as it can discipline for failure to follow any district regulation. A civil suit may be filed on behalf of the child for damages caused by the failure to report. A type of civil liability can be imposed on a mandatory reporter who failed to report suspected child abuse of neglect through a simple negligence action. There it is claimed that the mandatory reporter's failure to report was a cause of the child's subsequent injuries. Finally, there is the possibility of criminal sanctions for the failure of a mandatory reporter to report suspected child abuse or neglect. Most states have criminal sanctions available for an educator's failure to report suspected child abuse. Seven state statutes provide for the imposition of fines for failure to report, eighteen states provide for fines or imprisonment, twenty-two states provide for the prescribed penalties for misdemeanors (typically up to $1,000 fine and less than one year in jail.)

Educators are mandatory reporters in all of the child protection statutes. This means generally that a teacher or other school official who works directly with students on a regular basis must report any suspected child abuse or neglect that they see in their professional capacity to the social service agency. To define exactly a suspicion of child abuse or neglect is difficult; however, it appears that a teacher should report a suspicion of mistreatment, whether done by an act of commission or omission. Although this may cause abuse and neglect to be overreported the statutes protect reporters who act in good faith from any civil or criminal liability, even if their report turns out to be erroneous. This immunity is designed to encourage hesitant reporters to report. Also provided to encourage reporting are various consequences for a mandatory reporter's failure to report suspected child abuse or neglect. There are three types of consequences for failure of a mandatory reporter to report suspected child abuse.

1. An educator can be disciplined by the school system for failure to report suspected abuse or neglect contrary to school policy.

2. An educator can be sued civilly in a negligence action for damages which were caused by a negligent failure to report suspected abuse or neglect.

3. Most statutes delineate criminal sanctions for failure to report.

RECENT STATE LEGISLATIVE ACTION

In April of 1983, the National Commission on Excellence in Education released "A Nation At Risk," a report highly critical of public education. This was only one of the first of such treatises to be released in the mid-1980s. In response, many state legislatures enacted programs to address the issues raised. Most of legislative reform dealt with the status of teaching as a profession, and the curriculum in the public schools. In the area which affects students directly, curricular reform, many state legislatures from 1983–86 made broad changes. Legislatures responded to the criticism of poor student performance by raising academic standards, mandating increased curricular requirements, mandating student testing for promotion and graduation, and lengthening the school day or year.

One of the possible results of these increased academic requirements is increased failure or dropout rates of at-risk students. The report recommendations and legislative responses may increase the conflicts between the demands for schools and other demands placed on students. Increased minimum requirements for achievement alone may lead to more student failure without apparent remedy. Students with these problems will have to be dealt with if increased standards are to do anything positive for them. Without additional attention it is likely that the only result will be the negative one of increasing school failure. Fortunately, many states have realized this possibility and have enacted special programs for "at-risk" students.

Legislative attention in this area generally falls into five categories: substance abuse, alternative education, school attendance, teenage parent and early identification. Thirteen states enacted legislation in the area of substance abuse. These generally mandated instruction in the areas of drug and alcohol abuse. Louisiana enacted a program of chemical testing for alcohol for likely student users. Utah mandated the reporting of drug and alcohol use by students. In the area of alternative education or instruction, eleven states enacted programs. Not all states developed the common notion of alternative education for the nontraditional student. For example, Illinois' program includes grants for remedial summer school. Kentucky and Texas include remedial instruction within the school. A related type of legislation is programs dealing with the prevention of dropouts and truancy. Nine states enacted this type of legislation. Four states enacted legislation dealing with the problems of the teenage parent. Arizona, California, and Florida all enacted programs for assessment as early as kindergarten. Connecticut enacted a program of testing with a battery of psychometric, academic and motor skills tests for identification of high-risk students. Maryland, Rhode Island and Wisconsin enacted legislation on suicide prevention for school-age children.

SUMMARY

The Education for All Handicapped Children Act assures that all handicapped children have access to a free appropriate public education and related services designed to meet their unique needs. The appropriate educational program must be tailored to each handicapped child's educational needs through the formulation of an individualized educational program. Within the IEP the child must receive the level of educational and related services necessary for him or her to receive educational benefits. In addition, the program must be provided in the least restrictive environment. The child and parent's rights under this statute are protected through a complex set of procedural safeguards and opportunities to challenge the educational system through due process procedures.

Section 504 of the Rehabilitation Act also serves to protect the rights of the handicapped. It prohibits discrimination against handicapped persons in any program receiving federal financial assistance. This means that schools may not deny the benefits of programs to handicapped persons who are otherwise qualified to receive them. In some situations schools will have to make reasonable accommodations for the handicapped person in order to allow them to participate in programs or activities.

Both constitutional and federal statutory provisions prohibit discrimination on the basis of race. Racially segregated or apartheid schools have been found to be unconstitutional, but we still are faced with schools in which one race substantially predominates. The courts and the Office of Civil Rights have devised a number of remedies for this problem. Whether a school district will actually be ordered to undertake a proactive integration plan is heavily dependent on the facts of the specific case.

Although we do not often see blatently racially discriminatory policies in schools, racial discrimination is evident in the schools in the form of practices which have the effect of being racially discriminatory, or racially discriminatory enforcement of school practices. Since these are not racially biased on their face, some evidence of discriminatory motive must be shown in order to be successful in a court action. The courts have held that absent a legitimate educational reason for the practice when it would forseeably result in discrimination, discriminatory intent can be inferred.

Generally, grievances raised by minority students, other than segregation, often involve linguistic barriers to educational success. State or school board rules can require that the basic language of instruction be English. The state, however, cannot instruct in the English language exclusively, by denying interpretation and bilingual instruction to students who cannot use the English language. Federal statutes have been held to impose an affirmative duty on schools to take action to overcome language barriers for these children. The courts, however, have given the educational experts a great deal of discretion in determining what approach to take. The statutes do not necessarily require any particular form of program, philosophy of bilingual education or even formal bilingual education.

Federal funds are available through Chapter I of the Elementary and Secondary Education Act to supplement the special educational needs of economically disadvantaged children. Most Chapter I money is used to provide extra help in reading and math for elementary school children whose test scores show that they are not working at or near the level of other children their age. The courts have recently enforced Department of Education's actions for a refund of these funds where it has been shown that they were not used for the specific services needed for at-risk children.

The McKinney Homeless Assistance Act was passed into law in 1987. It contains provisions requiring that homeless children have access to a free, appropriate public education on an equal basis with nonhomeless children. The statute is intended to prevent states from using state residency laws to bar homeless children from attending public schools.

The courts have been called upon to address various forms of sex discrimination in the public school system. The most common areas of litigation include differential treatment in academic programming and athletics and classification of students due to pregnancy or marital status. Differential treatment on the basis of sex has been struck under the federal constitution and statutes. Schools cannot use separate admissions requirements, nor can admissions to programs be limited to only one sex. In addition, whenever a school finds that a course has a disparate distribution of enrollment on the basis of sex, it must take action to determine that sex bias on the part of the school was not responsible for the result. The weight of judicial authority is that pregnancy or parental status is not a valid reason to exclude a child from the educational system. Related issues are whether a pregnant student can be required to leave the regular school program and participate in a special school program, or take only homebound instruction, and whether a student can be excluded from extracurricular activities due to pregnancy or parenthood. Although some conflict on these issues exists, it is generally held that they, too, are prohibited practices.

Child abuse reporting statutes in all states require educators to report suspected child abuse and neglect. To define exactly a suspicion of child abuse or neglect is difficult; however, it appears that a teacher should report a suspicion of mistreatment, whether done by an act of commission or omission. An educator's failure to report suspected child abuse and neglect can result in sanctions such as disciplinary actions, negligence actions and criminal sanctions.

Many state legislatures have recently addressed the needs and problems of at-risk children. Legislative attention in this area generally includes programs to address substance abuse, provide alternative education, improve school performance, provide services for teenage parents and identify at-risk children at the earliest possible opportunity.

The foregoing are all examples of legal authority to improve the status of children at-risk, and increase their chances for educational success.

However, although many of these provisions have been in place for a number of years they do not guarantee that the public educational system has the commitment necessary to serve these children and prevent the tragic loss of their potential through school failure. Even though they have these protections, their success continues to be in jeopardy especially in light of recent moves to increase academic requirements and standards. The only avenue for success appears to be in institutionalizing the spirit of the legal protections these children have in the educational system. Until this occurs constant vigilence is necessary to protect them through the letter of the law.

APPENDIX

State Legislation

Alaska	Alaska Stat. 14.30.360 (1984)
Arizona	Ariz. Rev. Stat. Ann. 15-715 (1985), 15-712, 15-796 (1986)
Arkansas	Ark. Stat. Ann. 80.1921 (1985); 1985 Ark. Acts 1047
California	1985 Cal. Legis. Serv. 456, 1145, 1216, 1530; 1986 Cal. Legis. Serv. 871
Colorado	Colo. Rev. Stat. 22-1-110, 22-52-101 et. seq. (1985), 22-2-114.1 (1986)
Connecticut	Conn. Gen. Stat. Ann. 10-202a, 10-202c (West 1986)
Florida	Fla. Stat. Ann. 232.301 (West 1984), 230.2316, 232.302 (1986)
Illinois	Ill. Ann. Stat. ch. 122, 2-3.41, 2-3.61, 2-3.66 (Smith-Hurd 1984)
Indiana	Ind. Code Ann. 20-10.1-4-9 (Burns 1985)
Kentucky	Ky. Rev. Stat. Ann. 158.148 (Bobbs-Merrill 1985), 158.750 (Bobbs-Merrill 1986)
Louisiana	La. Rev. Stat. Ann. 17-1993 (West 1984); 1985 La. Acts 828
Maine	Me. Rev. Stat. Ann. tit. 20-A, 4729 (1983), 5151 (1985)
Maryland	Md. Educ. Code Ann. 7-4A-01 (1986)
Massachusetts	Mass. Ann. Laws ch. 188, 52 (Law. Co-op. 1985)
Michigan	Mich. Comp. Laws Ann. 388.1641, 388.1648, 388.1693 (West 1986)
Minnesota	Minn. Stat. Ann. 124.246, 126.66 (1984)
Mississippi	Miss. Code Ann. 37-21-7 (1986)
Nebraska	Neb. Rev. Stat. 79-4, 140.05 (1986)
New Mexico	N.M. Stat. Ann. 22-2-8.6 (1986)
North Carolina	1985 N.C. Adv. Legis. Serv. SB 1, IV, 31
North Dakota	N.D. Cent. Code 15-21.1-01-04, 15-38.13-1 (1985)
Pennsylvania	Pa. Stat. Ann. tit. 24 15-1547 (Purdon 1986)
Rhode Island	R.I. Gen. Laws 16-22-12 (1985), 16-22-14 (1986)
Tennessee	Tenn. Code Ann. 49-6-1007 (1985), 49-6-3402 (1986)
Texas	Tex. Educ. Code Ann. 11.205, 16.052(d), 16.153 (Vernon 1984)
Utah	Utah Code Ann. 53-14-4-1, 53-22(b)-2 (1986)
Vermont	Vt. Stat. Ann. tit. 16, 909 (1983)
Virginia	Va. Code 22.1-253.6 (1986)
Washington	Wash. Rev. Code Ann. 28A.97.010 (1983), 28A.03.380, 28A.58.802 (1984)
Wisconsin	Wis. Stat. Ann. 115-36, 115.365, 115.367, 115.91, 118.153 (1985)

REFERENCES

American Association for Protecting Children, Inc. (1987). *Highlights of Official Child Neglect and Abuse Reporting.*

Board of Inquiry Project. (1985). *Barriers to Excellence: Our Children At Risk.* Boston: National Coalition of Advocates for Students.

Besharov, D. J., and Baden, M. (1978). *The abused and neglected child: Multi-Disciplinary Court Practice* 11–12. New York: Practicing Law Institute.

Center for Law and Education, Inc. (1987, September) *Newsnotes.* Vol. 38, p. 3. Cambridge, MA: Center for Law and Education, Inc.

Civil Liability for Teachers' Negligent Failure to Report Suspected Child Abuse. (1981). 28 *Wayne Law Review* 183, 189.

Martin, H. P. (1986). Abused children—what happens eventually. In K. Oates (Ed.) *Child Abuse,* pp. 154–169. N.J.: Citadel Press.

National Commission on Excellence in Education. (1983). *A Nation at Risk: The Imperative for Educational Reform.* Washington, DC: U.S. Government Printing Office.

Rowe (1981). Beyond reporting—How teachers can help victims of child abuse. *Today's Education.*

Schwartz, A., and Hirsch, H. (1982). Child abuse and neglect: A survey of the law. *Medical Trial Technique Quarterly, 28,* 247.

28 *Wayne Law Review,* 183, 189. (1981). Civil liability for teachers' negligent failure to report suspected child abuse.

TABLE OF CASES

Hollon v. Mathis Indep. School Dist., 358 F. Supp 1269 (S.D. Tex. 1973).

Holt v. Shelton, 341 F. Supp 821 (M.D. Tenn. 1972).

Honig v. Doe, 108 S.Ct. 592, 56 U.S.L.W. 4091 (1988).

Houston v. Prosser, 361 F. Supp. 295 (N.D. Ga. 1973).

Indian High School Athletic Ass'n v. Raike, (164 Ind. App. 169) 329 N.E.2d 66 (1975).

Irving Ind. School District v. Tatro, 468 U.S. 883, 104 S.Ct. 3371 (1984).

Kampmeier v. Nyquist, 553 F.2d 296 (2d Cir. 1977).

Larry P. v. Riles, 495 F. Supp. 926 (N.D. Cal 1979), aff'd in part 793 F.2d 969 (9th Cir. 1984).

Lau v. Nichols, 414 U.S. 563, 94 S.Ct. 786 (1974).

Martin Luther King Junior Elementary School Children v. Michigan Board of Education, 451 F. Supp. 1324, 1330 (E.D. Mich. 1978).

Morales v. Shannon, 516 F.2d 411, 415 (5th Cir. 1975), cert. den'd. 423 U.S. 1034, 96 S.Ct. 566 (1975).

Moran v. School District 7, Yellowstone County, 350 F. Supp. 1180 (D. Mont. 1972).

O'Neill v. Dent, 364 F. Supp. 565 (E.D.N.Y. 1973).

Ordway v. Hargraves, 323 F. Supp. 1155 (D. Mass. 1971).

Parents in Action in Special Education v. Hannon, 506 F.Supp. 831 (N.D.Al. 1980).

Poole v. South Plainfield Board of Education, 490 F. Supp. 948 (D.N.J. 1980).

Prince William v. Malone, 762 F.2d 1210 (4th Cir. 1985).

Romans v. Crenshaw, 354 F. Supp. 868 (S.D. Tex 1971).

Seward v. Della, No. 134 173 (Cal. Super. Ct. 1973).

Shull v. Columbus Mun. Separate School District, 338 F. Supp 1376 (N.D. Miss. 1972).

Southeastern Community College v. Davis, 442 U.S. 397 (1979), 99 S.Ct. 2361.

S-1 v. Turlington, 635 F.2d 342 (5th Cir. 1981).

Swann v. Charlotte-Mecklenburg Board of Education, 402 U.S. 1, 91 S.Ct. 1267 (1971).

Virginia Dept. of Educ. v. Secretary of Educ., 806 F.2d 78 (4th Cir. 1986).

Wolf v. South Colonie Central School District, 534 F. Supp. 758 (N.D.N.Y. 1982); aff'd by Wolf v. South Colonie Central School District, 714 F.2d 119 (2nd Cir. Oct. 20, 1982).

Wright v. Columbia University, 520 F. Supp. 789 (E.D. Pa. 1981).

Chapter 8

STUDENT CHARACTERISTICS
AND THE PERSISTENCE/DROPOUT
BEHAVIOR OF HISPANIC STUDENTS

ANGELA PEREZ MILLER

INTRODUCTION

The research literature surrounding the topic of dropouts has travelled through a series of issues: accurately assessing the numbers and defining the dropouts, gathering school or systemwide baseline data, examining student characteristics, surveying self-reported reasons for dropping out and finally examining the schools themselves and their school characteristics and educational environments that contribute to placing students at risk (in danger of ending their formal education by dropping out) or to the dropout behavior of students. This recent focalization on the school environment itself appears to be worthy of extensive research and investigation. Through the act of dropping out, students reject the social relationships and definitions of knowledge that schools promote (Fine and Rosenberg, 1983) and thus make the notion of a dropout a contextual one (Tobin and Ventresca, 1987). Despite the progression of research on dropouts and at-risk students to an examination of the problem within an institutional or societal context, analyses of at risk/dropout students invariably highlight those students' individual differences or inadequacies.

Fine and Rosenberg (1983) propose that dropouts as a group challenge the belief that educational systems are the "great equalizers" that provide the path to equal opportunity and economic success. Their study countered the belief that high school dropouts are "academically and motivationally helpless and economically doomed" (p. 270). By searching for individual student deficits we continue to preserve and protect the educational and economical systems from criticism and their identification as contributors to the act of dropping out.

Our concern with the large numbers of at-risk students and high Hispanic dropout rates must be examined within the context of the education reform issues that are sweeping the country. Recent research indicates that these are potentially competing issues. Researchers suggest that school reforms directed at challenging content, time spent in school and achievement standards may have both positive and negative effects on the retention of students until graduation. Nationally, the rate of retention until graduation has declined since 1980 from 76 percent to 73 percent, and Hodginkinson (1985) anticipates that state reform programs will cause a further decline. Raising standards may challenge students to work harder, and working harder may lead to greater achievement. However, unless additional support is provided to students, the reforms may produce one of two negative results: "an improvement in aggregate measures of student performance chiefly attributable to the increasing selectivity of American schools (i.e., an increase in the dropout rate), or a relaxation of the standards as they are implemented by educators who must confront first-hand the negative consequences of such reforms" (McDill, Natriello and Pallas, 1985, p. 29). Fine (1986) maintains that such "reforms" merely divert attention from the unjust social and economic conditions surrounding minority, urban adolescents. She asks pointedly, "What would happen, in our present-day economy, to these young men and women if they all graduate? Would their employment and/or poverty prospects improve individually as well as collectively?" (p. 407).

In Chicago, as in many large U.S. cities (where minority students are numerically in the majority), educational reform task forces, which include numerous representatives of business and industry, decry the quality of education that is provided to our youngsters amid declarations that our graduates are unemployable. Chicago's minority student population is 23.4 percent Hispanic, 60.1 percent black, and 2.8 percent Asian (Chicago Public Schools, 1988). The irony is that some of these same concerned businessmen have little difficulty transplanting their factories across the U.S. border into Mexico and creating "maquiladoras" (assembly plants) where the pay for Mexican labor is $12 to $15 per week. "This is capitalism with its ugliest face," asserted the director of the AFL–CIO region that includes California. "Firms create unemployment and wreck lives on the American side, and exploit the desperation of Mexicans on the other" (Warren, 1988, p. 19). A number of Chicago metropolitan area firms have "maquiladoras" in Mexico.

The research continues to support the need to concern ourselves with the at-risk population among our Hispanic students: First of all because of the growing numbers of language minority students, particularly those that are Hispanic; second, because of the large numbers of at-risk Hispanic students that are present in large urban school systems; and, last, because of the assumptions, perceptions, conceptions or misconceptions regarding Hispanic students who are associated with being at risk. This particularly includes those misconceptions regarding students who belong to a language minority (LM) and/or are limited-English-proficient (LEP).

The Hispanic population is the fastest-growing minority population in the United States (Usdan, 1984). The Census Bureau reports that as of March, 1987 the Hispanic population was 18.8 million with a growth rate that continues to be five times as fast as the rest of the population ("Hispanic Population," 1987). Consequently, the Hispanic population is estimated to range from 25 to 30 million by the year 2000, or 11 percent of the total population (Hispanic Policy Development Project (HPDP), 1984).

The Hispanics are also a young population. Almost one-third of the Hispanic population is under the age of fifteen years compared to one-fifth of the general population. Puerto Ricans and Mexican Americans constitute the youngest Hispanic groups, with a median age of twenty-two (Ford Foundation, 1984). The average black is 25 years old and the average white is 31 years old (Hodgkinson, 1985).

Dropout has become almost synonymous with Hispanic students. Nationally, the Hispanic dropout rates reported for our urban high schools are alarmingly high; New York, 80 percent and Los Angeles, 50 percent (HDPD, 1984). Statistics for the Chicago Public Schools for the class of 1985 show that Hispanics have higher dropout rates (48.2%) than whites (42.3%), blacks (46%) or Asians (17.5%) (Chicago Public Schools, 1987).

This young and growing Hispanic population and the disproportionate numbers of dropouts demands that we focus our attention on issues of educational attainment.

STUDENT AND SCHOOL CHARACTERISTICS
RELATED TO DROPPING OUT

The reasons youth drop out of high school are varied; however, they are often interrelated and generally fall into three major categories: those related to school experiences, those related to the family condition and those related to economic factors (Ekstrom et al., 1986; Fine, 1986; McDill et al., 1985; Rumberger, 1983; United States General Accounting Office (USGAO), 1986).

A summary of Hispanic studies, local and national, indicates that three major causes for dropping out of school for Hispanic students (not ranked) are academic failure (HPDP, 1984; Steinberg, Blinde and Chan, 1984; Michigan State Board of Education (MSBE), 1986; Miller, 1985), family related economic reasons (HPDP, 1984; Lucas, 1971; Miller, 1985; Rumberger, 1983; Steinberg et al., 1984) and individual personal problems (Lucas, 1971; Miller, 1985; Rumberger, 1983). Background characteristics that are strongly associated with dropping out are SES (MSBE, 1986; Steinberg et al., 1984; USGAO, 1986) and race/ethnicity (Designs for Change, 1985; Hess and Lauber, 1985; Rumberger, 1983; Steinberg et al., 1984; USGAO, 1986).

Four major Chicago studies (Designs for Change, 1985; Hess and Lauber, 1985; Kyle et al., 1986; Hess et al., 1986) have contributed descriptive information on student and school characteristics related to high dropout rates. Chicago public high schools that experience high dropout rates have students who enter high school overaged (15 years old by December first of the year they enter high school), are functioning below average in reading, have failed minimum competency tests and thereby experience academic failure. The school characteristics associated with high dropout rates are those high schools that are non-selective and segregated (Designs for Change, 1985), lack strong administrative leadership (Hess et al., 1986), lack order and discipline (Hess et al., 1986), have a high failure rate (Kyle et al., 1986; Hess et al., 1986) and are dominated by passive instruction with minimal student and teacher interaction in the classroom (Hess et al., 1986).

The Hess and Greer (1987) study, *Bending the Twig*, supports the need to direct our dropout prevention efforts toward the elementary school level. This study found that elementary schools that had high numbers of dropouts graduated large percentages of students who were reading below grade level and were overage. Schools with higher levels of low-income students had higher dropout rates, and minority schools had a higher proportion of low income students. The retention of students after third grade significantly raised the dropout rate. In fact, retention did not reduce but did increase the dropout rate.

In this Chicago study of elementary school graduates from the class of 1978 that would eventually become the high school class of 1982, the researchers generalize their findings in describing the characteristics of typical dropouts in Chicago schools as those students "who are poor readers, overage, poor and Hispanic" (Hess and Greer, 1987, p. 13).

Tobin and Ventresca (1987) and Ogbu and Matute-Bianchi (1986) perceive societal, political and educational responses to minority students' school failure as too narrow, in that historically we have continued to repeat the same ineffective responses and initiatives. The research on at-risk students and dropout is generally descriptive and merely tells us how minority students fail but do not explain why some minority students persist and achieve in school in spite of language and cultural differences. Ogbu and Matute-Bianchi (1986) propose that a broader conceptual framework needs to be developed that links the relationships between educational institutions and individuals to sociocultural and historical forces. This broader conceptual framework would not only describe but also explain the reasons for the process of minority student school failure which places them at risk.

There is the need, at this point, to inject the notion of persistence, as opposed to dropping out, as a characteristic that exists among our Hispanic students. Persistence is the ability to remain in high school until completion/graduation (Miller, 1987). Persistence is not researched as a characteristic that exists among our Hispanic students. Descriptive studies such as those cited above (Chicago studies) provide valuable baseline data and information on dropouts for the school system and for individual schools. However, by dealing with the problem at an aggregate level, negative characteristics are generalized to the total student population, usually based on racial/ethnic membership, without considering the individual attributes of students that are of a more positive nature. These positive attributes are the ones that need to be examined in order to promote persistence among Hispanic students.

Dropout studies generally do not differentiate between the differing Hispanic subgroups and aggregate all Spanish-speaking, language minority students under the umbrella term "Hispanic." Research on Hispanic persisters and dropouts is needed that considers the differing cultures, language dominance, second language proficiency and educational experiences of Hispanic subgroups.

LANGUAGE AND CULTURE

In addition to the above explanations as to why Hispanic students do not do well in school, social scientists have focused on the role of language and cultural differences in relationship to minority school failure (Ogbu and Matute-Bianchi, 1986). Research studies on Hispanic students tend to emerge from an ethnocentric perspective. This perspective supports the position that positive goal and value orientations and educational aspirations are those orientations and aspirations which are most similar to those of the Anglo-American culture. Too often, the posture taken by researchers on language and culture is one represented by a group of studies on Mexican Americans that Ramirez and Castaneda (1974) label the "damaging culture" hypothesis. The damaging culture hypothesis maintains that the culture and values of Mexican Americans are the ultimate cause of their low economic status and low academic achievement, thereby stressing the notion that Mexican Americans who are less affiliated with their ancestral culture will score higher on achievement than a more affiliated group.

The damaging culture view is countered by Buriel's (1984) "cultural integration" hypothesis that contends that integration with one's ancestral culture is conducive to success in American society. Cultural integration is determined by Spanish language usage and generational status. Preservation of the Spanish language over two or more generations reflects a deliberate need to maintain a connection to the ancestral culture. Language and generational status has been widely used as a means to measure acculturation by researchers (Buriel, 1984). Retaining an integration with traditional Mexican culture is a characteristic that may be significantly and positively related to educational achievement. Buriel (1984) found that being fluent in Spanish and coming from a Spanish-speaking home was positively associated with better grades in school.

Research studies (Buriel and Vasquez, 1982; Kagan and Zahn, 1975; Willig et al., 1983) have supported the notion that first- and second-generation or low acculturated, language minority students perform better academically than subsequent, moderately acculturated generations of the same group. It is important to emphasize that acculturation is not one-dimensional but multidimensional and bidirectional and that it encompasses not only the degree of assimilation but also types of assimilation. Some ethnic groups or individuals totally embrace a high degree of acculturation, some resist acculturation while others are more eclectic and integrate cultures (Mendoza and Martinez, 1981).

Ogbu and Matute-Bianchi's (1986) work identifies three different kinds of minority groups: autonomous, immigrant and subordinate or caste-like minorities. Most of our Mexican students fall into the immigrant minority group, whose children have the potential to perform well in school. As a group, the immigrant minorities are positive, moved here voluntarily and have high expectations which influence their children's behavior and academic performance in school (Chiswick, 1982; Ogbu and Matute-Bianchi, 1986). This is in contrast to the school experiences of the caste-like minorities, minorities who become incorporated into a society involuntarily and permanently through slavery, conquest or colonization, which represent persistent and disproportionate school failure. Autonomous minorities are minorities in a numerical sense. They do not experience persistent disproportionate school failure and have a "cultural frame of reference" (p. 87) which enhances their situation and generates success (Ogbu and Matute-Bianchi, 1986).

In 1984, a survey was completed anonymously by 1,180 students at the predominantly Mexican (91%), Benito Juarez High School in Chicago. Of the 1,180 respondents, 132 were students in the bilingual program. The results of the survey serve to reinforce two of the major recurring causes of dropping out previously cited: economic problems (having to work to help the family) and academic failure. Among the general population of students, the first and second reasons reported by the students, that of economics and academic failure, were selected as potential reasons for dropping out (19 percent and 15 percent, respectively). However, when the responses of the bilingual program students (LEP, immigrant minority group) are separated from the total group, the economic reason is chosen by 51 percent of these students, whereas only half (26%) chose course failure as the probable reason for dropping out (Miller, 1985).

In this instance, the survey results of students in the bilingual program indicate that these students are less likely to drop out due to academic failure, thus supporting the notion that an integration with traditional Mexican culture (Buriel, 1984) and immigrant minority group status (Ogbu and Matute-Bianchi, 1986) is positively related to educational achievement.

In a review of the literature, Buriel (1984) found Mexican immigrants to be achievement-oriented and to have more years of schooling prior to immigrating than the national average of schooling for the general Mexican population. Immigrants are a highly self-selected group who have more ability and work motivation than their fellow counterparts who remain at home (Chiswick, 1982; Ogbu and Matute-Bianchi, 1986) and of course a willingness to make a change. Basically, the incentive to immigrate is an economic one. The high selection of having to work to help the family as a probable reason for not completing high school by Juarez students represents a strong sensitivity to or feelings of responsibility to assist the family economically.

Because of the geographic proximity of Mexico and the United States, we have a continuous source of first-generation Mexican immigrants and the sociocultural conditions for reinforcement of traditional Mexican culture.

HISPANIC STUDENT CHARACTERISTICS AND DROPPING OUT

Although the recent trend in dropout research is that of examining school characteristics that may contribute to dropping out, the focus continues on student characteristics associated with dropping out. For this reason the discussion that follows will be directed to those student characteristics that are most frequently associated with dropping out for Hispanic students in Chicago Public Schools; that of low SES, race/ethnicity, poor reading ability, and being overage.

Socioeconomic Status

A background characteristic often associated with a Hispanic dropout is socioeconomic status (Arias, 1986; Michigan State Board of Education, 1986; Steinberg et al., 1984; USGAO, 1986). A Chicago study (Hess and Greer, 1987) found that elementary schools that have high dropout rates have higher numbers of low income students. Generally, researchers are staying away from this issue as well as that of racial/ethnic background, because they argue that schools can do nothing about a student's background characteristics that contribute to dropping out (Wehlage and

Rutter, 1986; Fine, 1984). In addition, if you focus on background characteristics you can justify not being able to do anything about improving the condition of at-risk/dropout students.

However, there have been studies (Hernandez, 1973; Kagan and Zahn, 1975; Steinberg et al., 1984) that deemphasize the importance of SES in contributing to the dropping out of school. Kagan and Zahn (1975) in their study of Mexican American children ruled out SES as a factor in explaining their poorer school performance. They concluded that a plausible explanation for the school achievement gap to be "a function of an interaction between the Mexican American child's experiences and values and the school's teaching material and teaching styles" (p. 648). In a review of the literature, Steinberg et al. (1984) found SES to be a strong predictor of dropping out; however, when SES was held constant, Hispanic youngsters dropped out at a rate higher than youngsters of other racial/ethnic backgrounds.

In a study of white, black and Hispanic elementary children in the Chicago metropolitan area, black and Hispanic children who are in the process of moving up the SES scale or in the process of acculturation, experience what Willig and her associates (Willig et al., 1983) call "debilitating motivational variables that include low self-concept of academic ability, and high anxiety in relation to school performance" (p. 407).

Thus, being at risk based on low SES is not consistently found in the research literature as being strongly related to dropping out among Hispanic students.

Race and Ethnicity

A student's race/ethnicity is another background characteristic found to be strongly associated with dropping out (Arias, 1986; Designs for Change, 1985; Hess and Lauber, 1985; Rumberger, 1983; Steinberg et al., 1984; USGAO, 1986). For the purpose of this discussion this issue will be examined as a language and culture factor. Language must be included when discussing race/ethnicity and or defining the group identity of Hispanics. Language is the medium used by members of a group to transmit information and behavior; therefore, it is the vehicle for transmitting the culture within an ethnic group (Jankowski, 1986).

As previously stated, the findings of Buriel (1984) and others indicate that being fluent in Spanish and coming from a Spanish-speaking home is positively associated with better grades in English and math. This would indicate that bilingualism is not a handicap but an asset when it comes to learning. In addition, there are studies that indicate that students who retain an integration with traditional Mexican culture are more likely to experience success in school; as acculturation increased, achievement decreased, especially among those students who were in the process of shifting from one sociocultural group to another.

A recent study in a California high school examined the differences in school performance among Japanese and Mexican descent students (Matute-Bianchi, 1986). Although the researcher used only one category of Japanese students, there were five categories indicated for the Mexican descent students: recent Mexican immigrant, Mexican-oriented, Mexican American, Chicano and Cholo.

The first two category of students, recent Mexican immigrant and Mexican-oriented, are more closely related to the previously mentioned type of student who retains an integration with traditional Mexican culture. The cultural discontinuities that develop from cultural differences,such as being LEP, unfamiliarity with the school culture or curriculum, apparently does not threaten their identity as Mexicans. They and the more socially integrated Mexican Americans are identified as the successful students.

The Chicanos and Cholos, on the other hand, are alienated from school and appear to resist certain aspects of the school culture, especially the behavior required to succeed in school academically. They identify this behavior with the more Americanized students of Mexican descent which they call "Wannabees." "Wannabees" are those students who want to be white or want to be Anglo (Matute-Bianchi, 1986). The researcher identifies the dilemma experienced by the Chicano student as choosing between doing well in school and being Chicano. They perceive participation in the culture of the dominant group, that is, the school culture, as denying one's identity as a Chicano. Therefore, school rules and regulations are to be resisted, challenged and opposed, which leads to alienation from the academic system of the school and of course being "at risk."

The Willig et al. (1983) study included Anglo, black and Hispanic students in grades four to eight who were studied in order to examine success and failure in school. This study differentiated among the groups of Hispanic children that represented three degrees of acculturation to Anglo-American culture. The low acculturated group was comprised of children who came from families where both parents and the child were born in Mexico; the moderately acculturated group was represented by children from families where some or any of the previously mentioned family members were born in the United States; and the highly acculturated group where both parents and the child were born in the United States. The researchers assessed achievement attributions, test anxiety, defensiveness, school performance and select background characteristics. Hispanic children demonstrated higher test anxiety than black and white children and a tendency to attribute failure to lack of ability but not to task difficulty. They found that the moderately acculturated children, those in the process of shifting from one sociocultural group to another, reflect the highest at-risk factors: debilitating attributions, and higher defensiveness and anxiety scores.

These two studies (Matute-Bianchi, 1986; Willig et al., 1983) illustrate the effects of different levels of acculturation as a factor in influencing the ability of Hispanic students to integrate into the academic and social systems of a school.

Too often, educators as well as parents assume that abandonment of traditional ethnic culture and assimilation into the dominant Anglo culture will enhance academic, economic and social success (Mendoza, 1984). However, the work of the above researchers suggests that a culturally integrated individual is more likely to succeed.

Academic Achievement

Chicago high schools that experience high dropout rates have students who are functioning below their grade level in reading (Designs for Change, 1985; Hess and Lauber, 1985). The Hess and Lauber (1985) study found that predominantly Hispanic schools had 71 percent of their entering freshman reading at below average levels compared to the predominantly black schools (53%); and the predominantly white schools which had 73 percent of their students reading at an average level or above.

In addition to the above concern of underachieving Hispanic students, there appears to be a need to more clearly define a limited-English-proficient student and not just within the confines of a bilingual program. As educators we must recognize the difficulties that language minority or limited-English-proficient (LM/LEP) students must confront in their effort to succeed academically in a general program of instruction in English. Students exiting bilingual programs may have reached an acceptable level of conversational English proficiency but may not necessarily have mastered the academic English vocabulary peculiar to a specific subject area such as social studies or science (Miller, 1984). Cummins (1984) has found evidence that children develop oral proficiency in two years but may take five to seven years to acquire the language skills needed to function successfully in an all English instructional program.

It is not possible to discuss the education of LM/LEP children and their academic achievement without considering the issue of language. Among the language conflicts that have been identified by researchers are language interference, when a student tries to function in one language and substitutes elements of another language (Hernandez, 1973); and the transference of information in one language to situations involving the use of a second language versus the notion that bilinguals have their linguistic knowledge organized into two separate memories (Scarborough, Gerar and Cortese, 1984). These concepts in turn lead to the notion of a bilingual dual coding system or the independence versus the interdependence of bilingual memory. One study supporting the dual coding model maintains that the "bilinguals' two verbal systems and a common imagery system are all partially interconnected but capable of functioning independently" (Paivio and Lambert, 1981, p. 538).

Additionally, various studies support the reinforcement of native language as being positively related to English language learning (Cummins, 1984). A study of 5,000 secondary bilingual education students in New York City found that mathematics achievement was positively related to parent's occupation, student attendance and native language achievement. The researchers concluded that the native language ability of bilingual students has a strong relationship to how well these high school students will perform academically. In this same study they found that the most important predictor of English language achievement is achievement in the native language followed by language use and years in the United States (Torres and Villegas, 1985). There have been various studies (Anderson and Johnson, 1971; Kagan and Zahn, 1975; Willig et al., 1983) that argue against the use of reading ability in English as the sole reliable predictor for the academic ability of Hispanic, LM/LEP students. These studies indicate that mathematical competence is a better indicator of academic ability. Anderson and Johnson (1971) found that although Mexican American high school students on the whole receive lower grades in English than their Anglo classmates, "there appears to be no difference in mathematical competence between Mexican American students and other students" (p. 297). In addition, there appeared to be no difference in mathematics grades among Mexican American children from four generations.

Kagan and Zahn (1975) in examining the achievement gap between Anglo and Mexican American elementary school children found the achievement gap is greater in reading than in math. The researchers discounted bilingualism as a factor in explaining the reading achievement gap, as most of the Mexican American subjects were third-generation Mexican Americans who spoke only English, even in their homes. They proposed the notion that "mathematics is relatively culture free compared to reading which may contain culturally nonrelevant content" (Kagan and Zahn, 1975, p. 648).

These studies, however, should not encourage us to discount the role of language in the teaching of mathematics. Using native language to teach mathematical concepts and its usage in solving word problems in mathematics remain necessary. Even LEP students who are skilled in mathematics may continue to need native language support services, even as they advance and perform at mathematics levels above the norms of their peers.

Educational Assessment

A discussion regarding the achievement levels of Hispanic students requires a discussion regarding educational assessment. As a result of recent school reform initiatives, there is increasing attention given to test results as indicators of individual student achievement and/or a school's effectiveness. This focus magnifies the conflicts between the educational goals of quality and equality of educational opportunity. Decisions made on the basis of test results have not only educational consequences for minority and non-minority students but will also eventually influence the social and economic distribution of resources (Airasian, 1987). School system policies and procedures regarding educational assessment are relevant and determining factors that affect Hispanic achievement test results.

Since educational assessment is primarily language-dependent, it is difficult to ignore certain factors that have important implications for the assessment of LM/LEP students: that of limited exposure to specific second language (L2) learning experiences and how knowldge in one's first language (L1) does not automatically transfer to situations involving the use or acquisition of a second language (Miller, 1984). It is evident that assessment of intelligence or achievement of LEP or bilingual students is most valid when done in the student's first language (Oakland and Matuszek, 1977).

Although our schools are required to assess a student's English language proficiency and/or reading ability, few collect data on native language proficiency which research has shown to be a significant predictor of English language achievement (Hakuta and Gould, 1987). An assessment of a student's native language strengths has more potential in promoting persistence than just an English language assessment of an LEP that indicates only language weaknesses.

Some educators would propose that language dominance be determined in order to assist in a decision as to which language is to be used in testing and that the language used in testing should be the dominant language. While assessment of a student's language dominancy is necessary for administering tests to determine the level of ability in both languages, it is also important to consider the student's ability to function in each of the languages he/she speaks. Since code-switching is a characteristic of Mexican American speakers (Matluck and Mace, 1973), then an assessment in both L1 and L2 would produce a more accurate assessment of a student's academic ability. Paivio and Lambert (1981) maintain that bilinguals have a dual coding system, which suggests that cognitive thinking during a test being performed in L1 is then translated into L2 the language of the test. The ultimate goal of test administration should be to use the test language or languages that will maximize and more accurately reflect the language minority student's ability level. Therefore, educational assessment of bilingual students should be executed in both languages in order to maximize the student's opportunity to be assessed accurately.

DeAvila and Havassy (1974) in their article on the testing of minority students state that:

> Tests that require answers of fact assume that all children taking the test will have had about the same exposure to the facts being tested. Any number of examples involving vocabulary bear out the spuriousness of this assumption. It is impossible to determine whether minority chil-

dren miss a test item because they have never been exposed to a word or because they lack the capacity to understand the word. Problems of this type are found in virtually any test of mental ability which uses a score on a vocabulary subtest to infer ultimate capability. (p. 73)

Therefore, the relationship of language and assessment has monumental implications for the policies and practices of public school systems that have within their population LM/LEP students. The assumption can be made that the subtests related to language, reading comprehension, and written expression in English will reflect an accurate achievement level in the English language for the LM/LEP student. However, a student who has perhaps spent several years of study in a non-English-speaking country, and possibly one to three more years in a bilingual program in the United States, is not going to be properly assessed in the content areas, the subtests of mathematics, social studies, and science, by a standardized test given only in English (Miller, 1984). Consequently, students who are taught the content areas in their native language may not demonstrate the actual level of achievement when they are assessed only in English.

Given that educational and intellectual assessment is primarily language-dependent and that the LM/LEP student's ability to function in English will be determined by that student's exposure to specific second language learning experiences and will be further, if not hampered certainly not helped by the fact that first language skills are not automatically transferred for use in a second language, then it follows that the only fair, accurate and appropriate assessment of a language minority student, in a general, bilingual or special program, is to administer achievement tests in the content areas in the student's first language and second language and separate language assessment instruments for English and the student's native language.

Overage

Few studies exist that indicate overage is a factor strongly related to Hispanic students who are at risk. However, there are studies that have found overage to be strongly associated with the dropout behavior of the general student population (Schulz et al., 1986; Hess and Greer, 1987; Gampert and Opperman, 1987). The Hess and Greer (1987) study found that the pattern of overage among Hispanic students followed systemwide patterns. However, in their study, being overage was weakly related to

Hispanic dropouts. In an earlier study, Hess and Lauber (1985) theorized that language transition problems reduced the effects of peer sanctions against overaged Hispanic students. In their 1985 high school study they found that schools that were over 50 percent Hispanic had the highest proportion of overage entering freshman students in the system (35%). However, the Hispanic dropout rates for overage students are similar to that of white students but less than that of black students.

In the Chicago study (Hess and Greer, 1987) of the elementary school years and dropout rates, the researchers found that retention of students after the third grade significantly raised the dropout rate. When a fourteen year old, low achieving student is retained for one year and enters high school at age 15 years with an improved reading level (at least one stanine), that student's dropout potential is higher than that of a similar 14 year old who was not retained (Chicago Public Schools, 1987).

Similar findings emerged from a longitudinal study (Gampert and Opperman, 1987) of the "Gates" promotional policy in New York City. Fourth and seventh graders not meeting promotional criteria (one year or more below grade level in fourth grade and one-and-a-half years or more below grade level in seventh grade) were retained for one year and received intensive remedial instruction in reading and mathematics. The remedial support provided an immediate and temporary effect in the students by increasing reading achievement. However, in the long term, the students returned to previous levels of reading achievement and became more at risk for dropping out (Gampert and Opperman, 1987).

SUMMARY

Based on the above discussion, we can conclude the following regarding student characteristics and how they contribute to the persistence/dropout behavior of Hispanic high school students.

Research does not indicate that SES is consistently found to have a strong relationship to the dropping out of Hispanic students. When studies have controlled for the effects of SES, Hispanic students were found to drop out at rates higher than other minority students. This implies that other factors related to the process of dropping out are more significantly related to dropping out than SES.

Generational status, degree of acculturation and the use of native language have a strong relationship to experiencing success in school. First and second generations perform better than subsequent generations.

Low acculturation and high acculturation are more positively related to school performance than those students who are moderately acculturated. Retaining an integration with traditional Mexican culture is generally positively related to educational achievement. Spanish language fluency and coming from a Spanish-speaking home is positively associated with better grades in school.

Math achievement appears to be a better predictor of academic ability as well as native language achievement for language minority/limited-English-proficient students. However, given that educational and intellectual assessment is primarily language-dependent, a more accurate and appropriate assessment of Hispanic, LM/LEP students would be to use language assessment instruments for English and Spanish and administer tests in the content areas in both Spanish and English.

Although being overage when entering high school does not appear to be strongly associated with the dropping out for Hispanic students, it must be considered as potentially detrimental if being overage is a result of retention in the elementary years. Several studies have demonstrated the negative effects of retention on the persistence behavior of all students, regardless of race/ethnicity, gender or SES.

CONCLUSIONS

In order to promote persistence among our Hispanic youngsters, teachers and administrators should consider the following strategies: (a) promote the native language and culture of the student and specifically encourage the continued formal learning of the native language as well as English; (b) give careful consideration to the use of math scores as a more reliable predictor of academic ability; (c) institute the use of a more thorough and fair educational assessment process for LM/LEP students that takes into consideration the students' linguistic and cultural background; and (d) although being overage is weakly associated with dropping out among Hispanic students, it is a condition to be avoided, especially if it is a result of retention, as all studies indicate that retention has negative effects on the persistence behavior of all students.

Research studies indicate that we can no longer focus our concern and dropout prevention efforts at the school level or upon the individual student. When we consider our "at-risk" student population we are referring to a large proportion of our Hispanic student population. Prevention and intervention for our at-risk youth has become a concern for the total educational system as well as the social and economic systems surrounding it.

When we consider the dropout prevention programs in operation, although greatly needed, they are serving only a small number of our at-risk population. Therefore, we need to examine the organization, structure, curriculum, assessment practices and the educational environment to determine how to prevent the dropping out of so many Hispanic students so that we can effectively engage them in our schools. We must create a school culture that produces persisters. This effort must include the sociocultural, economical and political forces that affect the persistence/dropout behavior of Hispanic students.

REFERENCES

Airasian, P. W. (1987). State mandated testing and educational reform: Context and consequences. *American Journal of Education, 95,* 393–412.

Anderson, J. G. and Johnson, W. H. (1971). Stability and change among three generations of Mexican-Americans: Factors affecting achievement. *American Educational Research Journal, 8,* 285–309.

Arias, M. B. (1986). The context of education for Hispanic students: An overview. *American Journal of Education, 95,* 26–57.

Buriel, R. (1984). Traditional culture integration and adjustment. In J. L. Martinez, Jr. and R. H. Mendoza (Eds.), *Chicano psychology,* (pp. 95–130). New York: Academic Press, Inc.

Buriel, R. and Vasquez, R. (1982). Stereotypes of Mexican descent persons. *Journal of Cross-Cultural Psychology, 13,* 59–70.

Chicago Public Schools. (1987). *Dropouts: A descriptive review of the class of 1985 and trend analysis of 1982–85 classes.* Chicago, Illinois: Author.

Chicago Public Schools. (1988). *Racial/Ethnic survey — students: As of October 30, 1987.* Chicago: Author.

Chiswick, B. R. (1982). The economic progress of immigrants: Some apparently universal patterns. In B. R. Chiswick (Ed.), *The gateway: U.S. immigration issues and policies* (pp. 119–158). Washington, D.C.: American Enterprise Institute for Public Policy Research.

Cummins, J. (1984). *Bilingualism and special education: Issues in assessment and pedagogy.* England: Multilingual Matters, Ltd.

De Avila, E. and Havassy, B. (1974). The testing of minority children—a neo-Piagetian approach. *Today's Education, 63,* 72–75.

Designs for Change. (1985). *The bottom line: Chicago's failing schools and how to help them.* Chicago: Author.

Ekstrom, R. B., Goertz, M. E., Pollack, J. M., and Rock, D. A. (1986). Who drops out of high school and why? Findings from a national study. *Teachers College Record, 87,* 356–373.

Fine, M. (1986). Why urban adolescents drop into and out of public high school. *Teachers College Record, 87,* 393–409.

Fine, M. and Rosenberg, P. (1983). Dropping out of high school: The ideology of school and work. *Journal of Education, 165,* 257–272.

Gampert, R. D. and Opperman, P. (1987). *Longitudinal study of the effects of promotional policy in the New York Public Schools.* Paper presented at the annual meeting of the American Educational Research Association, Washington, D.C.

Hakuta, K. and Gould, L. J. (1987). Synthesis of research on bilingual education. *Educational Leadership, 44,* 38–45.

Hernandez, N. G. (1973). Variables affecting achievement of middle school Mexican-American students. *Review of Educational Research, 43,* 1–33.

Hess, G.A., Jr. and Greer, J.L. (1987). Bending the twig: The elementary years and dropout rates in the Chicago Public Schools. Chicago: Chicago Panel on Public School Policy and Finance.

Hess, G.A., Jr. and Lauber, D. (1985). *Dropouts from the Chicago Public Schools.* Chicago: Chicago on Public School Finance.

Hess, G.A., Jr., Wells, E., Prindle, C., Liffman, P., and Kaplan, B. (1986). *"Where's room 185?" How schools can reduce their dropout problem.* Chicago: Chicago Panel on Public School Policy and Finance.

Hispanic Policy Development Project, Inc. (1984). *Make something happen: Hispanics and urban school reform.* New York: National Commission on Secondary Education for Hispanics, Vols. I & II.

Hispanic population up in U.S. (1987, September). *Chicago Tribune,* p. 3.

Hodgkinson, H. L. (1985). *All one system: Demographics of education, kindergarten through graduate school.* ISBN 0-937846-93-7. Washington, D.C.: Institute for Educational Leadership, Inc.

Jankowski, M.S. (1986). *City bound: Urban life and political attitudes among Chicano youth.* Albuquerque, New Mexico: University of New Mexico Press.

Kagan, S. and Zahn, F.L. (1975). Field dependence and the school achievement gap between Anglo-American and Mexican-American children. *Journal of Educational Psychology, 67,* 643–650.

Kyle, C. L., Lane, J., Sween, J. A. and Triana, A. (1986). *We have a choice—students at risk of leaving Chicago public schools.* Chicago: DePaul University, Chicago Area Studies Center and Center for Research on Hispanics.

Lucas, I. (1971). *Puerto Rican dropouts in Chicago: Numbers and motivations.* Council on Urban Education, Project No. O–E-108.

Matluck, J. H. and Mace, G. J. (1973). Language characteristics of Mexican-American children: Implications for assessment. *Journal of School Psychology, 2,* 365–386.

Matute-Bianchi, M. E. (1986). Ethnic identities and patterns of school success and failure among Mexican-descent and Japanese-American students in a California high school: An ethnographic analysis. *American Journal of Education, 95,* 233–255.

McDill, E. L., Natriello, G., and Pallas, A. M. (1985). *Raising standards and retaining students: The impact of reform recommendations on potential dropouts.* (Report No. 358).

Mendoza, R. H. and Martinez, J. L. (1981). In A. Baron, Jr. (Ed.), *Explorations in Chicano psychology*, (pp. 71–82). New York: Praeger Publishers.

Michigan State Board of Education. (1986). *Hispanic school dropouts and Hispanic student performance on the MEAP tests*. Michigan: Author.

Miller A. (1984). *Issues related to the assessment of minority language students*. Unpublished manuscript.

Miller, A. (1985). *Benito Juarez High School and dropout*. Unpublished manuscript.

Miller A. (1987). *An analysis of the persistence/dropout behavior of Hispanic students in a Chicago public high school*. In progress.

Oakland, T. and Matuszek, P. (1977). Using tests in nondiscriminatory assessment. In T. Oakland (Ed.), *Psychological and educational assessment of minority children*, (pp. 52–69). New York: Brunner & Mazel.

Ogbu, J. U. and Matute-Bianchi, M. E. (1986). Understanding sociocultural factors: Knowledge, identity, and school adjustment. In *Beyond language: Social and cultural factors in schooling language minority students* (pp. 73–142). Los Angeles, California: Evaluation, Dissemination and Assessment Center, California State University.

Paivio, A. and Lambert, W. (1981). Dual coding and bilingual memory. *Journal of Verbal Learning and Verbal Behavior, 20,* 532–539.

Ramirez, M. and Castaneda, A. (1974). *Cultural democracy, bicognitive development and education*. New York: Academic Press.

Rumberger, R. (1983). Dropping out of high school: The influence of race, sex, and family background. *American Educational Research Journal, 20,* 199–200.

Scarborough, D. L., Gerard, L. and Cortese, C. (1984). Independence of lexical access in bilingual work recognition. *Journal of Verbal Learning and Verbal Behavior, 23,* 84–99.

Schulz, E. M., Toles, R., Rice, W. K., Jr., Brauer, I. and Harvey, J. (1986). *The association of dropout rates with student attributes*. Paper presented at the annual meeting of the American Educational Research Association, San Francisco, California.

Steinberg, L., Blinde, P. O. and Chan, K. S. (1984). Dropping out among language minority youth. *Review of Educational Research, 54,* 113–132.

Tobin, W. A. and Ventresca, M. (1987). *Early school leavers: Historical perspectives and some new questions*. Paper presented at the annual meeting of the American Educational Research Association, Washington, D.C.

Torres, J. S. and Villegas, J. J. (1985). *Relationships among student characteristics, achievement, and school context in E.S.E.A. Title VII high school programs*. Paper presented at the annual meeting of the American Educational Research Asociation, Washington, D.C.

United States General Accounting Office. (1986). *School dropouts: The extent and nature of the problem*. (USGAO publication No.HRD86-106BR). Washington, D.C.: U.S. Government Printing Office.

Usdan, M. D. (1984). New trends in urban demography. *Education and Urban Society, 16,* 399–414.

Warren, J. (1988, January 24). U.S. plants in Mexico foster boom, worry. *Chicago Tribune*, p. 19.

Wehlage, G. G. and Rutter, R. A. (1986). Dropping out: How much do schools contribute to the problem? *Teachers College Record, 86*, 374–392.

Willig, A. C., Harnisch, D. L., Hill, K. T., and Maehr, M. L. (1983). Sociocultural and educational correlates of success-failure attributions and evaluation anxiety in the school setting for black, Hispanic, and Anglo children. *American Educational Research Journal, 20*, 385–410.

Chapter 9

EFFECTIVE TEACHING AND SCHOOLING FOR BLACK CHILDREN

EDITH R. SIMS

During the past ten years, much has been written about effective schools, their characteristics and teaching behaviors which enhance student achievement. As a result, this country has been deluged with recommendations, reform programs and education summits designed to improve education and to insure that all children have equal access to opportunities to prepare for productive citizenship. The foray of educational initiatives has resulted in many positive changes taking place in school districts throughout the nation. Some districts have responded by developing local objectives which identify learning outcomes expected for students in their state as well as in their district. Racially-isolated schools in some urban districts have benefited from an infusion of desegregation monies from the federal government.

Unfortunately, too few initiatives have been developed to specifically address the needs of black students who attend secondary schools. While these students are inherently no different from their counterparts in affluent areas or other parts of this country, their circumstances are dramatically different.

The high percentage of unemployed males and females sixteen years of age or older, the reduction in entitlement programs for the elderly, and an increase in the number of single parent families headed by females, often force many inner city students to reside in overcrowded or low-income housing for the poor. Because of their socioeconomic condition, black students, through no choice of their own, are often deprived of materials in the home which enhance intellectual development. Consequently, they enter secondary school with a poor self-concept, low self-esteem and a lack of confidence in facing new or challenging situations, anxiety and undue stress. These factors often lead to unsatisfactory performance in school.

Invariably, students who enter high school, burdened with problems related to the socioeconomic status of their families, have difficulty making the social adjustment required to be successful. Seeking to be accepted by their peers, they often become attached to social groups which are more likely to exhibit atypical or disruptive behavior.

The population at risk includes overage black children who graduate from elementary school at age fifteen regardless of their level of achievement. When overage low-achieving students leave elementary school without having demonstrated a mastery of basic competencies and skills, they are more likely to leave high school before acquiring the cognitive and affective skills to become a competent, productive citizen in a pluralistic society. Predictably, this population has experienced, or will experience, problems related to truancy, attendance and poor achievement. Many educators know from experience and research that these behaviors are evident as early as sixth or seventh grade, yet few accept the challenge to create innovative and alternative programs designed to meet their needs.

Are there predictors of children at risk? While there is no sole predictor, black children at risk are usually slow learners, poor, overage, low achievers, have poor attendance records, low self-esteem, a poor self concept and disruptive behavior. After or during the first year of high school, some will experience some difficulty with the law, use or abuse drugs, become involved in some form of gang-related activity, become a teenage unmarried parent and drop out of school.

This chapter will identify and review policies, strategies, and programs at George Henry Corliss High School proven to be effective in increasing student achievement and improving the quality of education made available to students as they prepare for productive citizenship.

George Henry Corliss High School is an inner-city school located on the far south side of Chicago in the Pullman community. The diversity of its population may be seen in the variety of occupations held, ranging from professional to semiskilled and unskilled workers, as well as unemployed and welfare recipients. The community, however, has seen an economic development decline in recent years. According to the 1980 census, the medium family income was $21,000. Salient facts and pertinent information about the school may be seen in Figure 9-1.

	GRADE 9	GRADE 12
MEDIAN READING PERCENTILE:	27	25
MEDIAN MATH PERCENTILE:	25	30

LOW INCOME FAMILIES	45.5%
RACIAL COMPOSITION	100% BLACK
STABILITY	97.1%
LIMITED ENGLISH	0
STUDENT ATTENDANCE	88.2%
FREE/REDUCED LUNCHES	588
MEMBERSHIP	1900
NUMBER OF TEACHERS	116

Figure 9-1. Salient Facts About Corliss High School (Fall 1986).

The purpose of schools is to provide quality programs and educational opportunities to ensure that all students who attend them will become intellectually, socially and economically productive. Researchers and educators agree that schools which effectively serve inner-city students, have definite characteristics: (Edmonds 1978; Edmonds 1982; Brookover et al. 1982)

- a school climate conducive to teaching and learning
- a clearly defined mission or vision
- strong but nonthreatening leadership
- high but reasonable expectations for success
- valid methods of assessment
- some parent involvement

The undergirding philosophy of Corliss High School is that all children can learn regardless of their race, family background or socioeconomic conditions. The mission of the school is to prepare students for citizenship and to graduate them with the academic, social and employable skills which will enable them to become productive responsible members of society. Moreover, the principal and administrative team organize and manage the school to reflect that mission and philosophy. The students are expected to demonstrate minimum mastery at all levels, attend classes regularly and promptly, be prepared for work, and to conduct themselves with respect and dignity at all times. Most of the teachers are well prepared and routinely exhibit effective teaching behaviors in their classrooms. The teachers use a variety of teaching strategies and instructional materials to cover curriculum content and to meet the diverse needs of their students. Student progress is monitored and assessed; praise and corrective feedback are often given; there is a built-in incentive awards program to recognize students for achievement, good attendance and good citizenship. The teachers are also recognized for good attendance and achievement.

The process of school improvement requires time, hard work and commitment from all factions involved in the education process; parents, community, educational and career service staffs, and students. Determined to ensure that all students have an opportunity to be successful, the principal utilizes the strengths of all factions involved to develop strategies to increase the likelihood that students will succeed.

In December, 1984, the school formed a school improvement committee to develop a school plan to eliminate those factors from the school environment which impeded teaching and learning and to replace them with collective actions for improvement. The committee, composed of representatives from the administrative, professional and career service staffs, the local school advisory council, and teachers, through the use of the Faculty Survey (Fig. 9-2), identified eight factors which negatively affected school improvement and student achievement.

1. Too little time to teach because of too much paperwork
2. Low teacher morale
3. Lack of administrative support
4. Disrespectful attitude of students
5. Teachers not involved in decisions which affect them
6. Failure of administration to seek ideas from teachers before establishing policies
7. Excessive class "cutting" and tardiness
8. Student apathy and high failure rate

Through collaborative efforts, a policy of closed campus was agreed upon and instituted. There was an immediate increase in the amount of time available for teaching, a decrease in the number of gang-related incidents, and more time for individual student counseling and parent conferences. Under the closed-campus program, students arrive at school in the morning, and remain in the school building for all lunch periods as well as for all other school-related activities until the end of their school day.

Expressed Concerns/Factors	Serious Concern	Moderate Concern	Marginal Concern	Little Concern
I. Excessive paperwork encroaching on teaching time.				
A. Daily division records				
B. Phone logs.				
C. Program office forms/reports.				
D. Cut slip processing.				
E. Teacher absence forms.				
F. Class interruptions to sign various forms.				
G.				
H.				
II. Low teacher morale.				
A. Administration related causes.				
1. Lack of administrative support.				
a. Apathetic administrators.				
b. Particular philosophical approach.				
c. Personality conflict between teacher & administrator.				
d. Heavy work load of administrator.				
e. Personality conflict among administrators.				
2. Inconsistent administrative procedures.				
a. Record keeping.				
b. Paperwork.				
c. Class cutting.				
d. Student discipline.				
3. Excessive leniency in disciplining students.				
4. Ineffective disciplinary procedures.				
5. Professional status of teachers not always respected.				
6. Teachers not consulted before policy changes are enacted.				
7. Some teachers subjected to more disciplinary action than others.				
8. No assistant principal available in an emergency.				
9. Some teachers appear to have extra privileges.				
10. Uniform Discipline Code ineffective in dealing with chronic behavioral problems.				
11. Excessive, unnecessary program changes.				
12.				
13.				

Expressed Concerns/Factors	Serious Concern	Moderate Concern	Marginal Concern	Little Concern
B. Teacher related causes.				
1. Unwillingness of some teachers to come to the aid of others needing assistance.				
2. Failure to consistently comply with existing rules/policies.				
3. Failure to treat all colleagues in a professional manner.				
4. Failure to carry out duty assignments consistently.				
5. Apathetic attitude toward anything beyond one's own classes.				
6.				
7.				
C. Student related causes.				
1. Disrespectful attitude toward teachers.				
2. Apathetic about learning.				
3. Excessive tardiness to school and to classes.				
4. Excessive class cutting.				
5. Failure to abide by school rules and regulations.				
6. Excessive hall activity during class periods and division.				
7. Lack of parental involvement.				
8.				
9.				

Additional Comments:

Figure 9-2. Faculty Survey Used to Develop School Improvement Plan.

Before teaching and learning can occur, a healthful and safe learning environment, with minimal distractions and incidents of disruptive behavior, is essential. Encouraged by the positive outcomes of the closed-campus policy, a Code of Conduct, unlike the school district's uniformed discipline code, specifically states and uniquely defines the infractions and corresponding penalties for those which frequently occurred at the school. For example, in the district's uniformed discipline code, there is a broad heading, "Failing to Abide by Rules and Regulations." Infractions under this heading carry a maximum suspension of one to five days out-of-school. The Corliss Code of Conduct delineates infractions and specifically states that "leaving trays on the lunchroom table" and "in building without an identification card" carry one to five days out-of-school suspension.

Those infractions which occurred most frequently at the school are listed in Figure 9-3. The school district's uniformed discipline code addressed the more serious offenses listed below.

Arrest and Ten (10) Days Suspension—Out of School

1. Use and/or possession of narcotics
2. Gang-related activities
3. Concealing dangerous weapons
4. Verbal and/or physical assault on staff members
5. Robbery
6. Theft

Expulsion from school is also considered for violations in this section.

Positive outcomes from the implementation of the two initiatives, closed campus policy and the Corliss Code of Conduct, were a marked improvement in the behavior of students, a reduction in the incidents of vandalism, a reduction in "paperwork" associated with in and out-of-school suspensions, an improvement in the general appearance of the building, and an increase in the amount of time for teaching.

Incentives and Rewards

An effective long-term strategy for school improvement requires two components: sanctions and rewards. When sanctions are imposed, it is essential to simultaneously put in place an incentive plan to reward students for academic achievement, attendance, good citizenship and excellence in behavior. Incentives and rewards should be based upon

A. **Ten (10) Days Suspension—Out of School**

　　1. Food Fights (direct involvement)
　　2. Drinking Alcoholic Beverages
　　3. Exploding firecrackers in building
　　4. False activation of fire alarm
　　5. Defacing or damage to school property

B. **Five (5) Days Suspension—Out of School**

　　1. Fighting
　　2. Leaving school without permission
　　3. Smoking cigarettes in building
　　4. Forging or falsifying school forms

C. **Three (3) Days Suspension—Out of School**

　　1. Loitering in gymnasium
　　2. Refusing to obey a directive by a staff member

D. **Two (2) Days Suspension—Out of School**

　　1. Use of Profanity in building
　　2. Being in corridors without a pass during class periods
　　3. Eating in unassigned lunchroom

E. **Two (2) Days Suspension—In House**

　　1. Leaving trays on lunchroom tables
　　2. Eating outside the lunchroom in classroom, gym, corridor, etc.
　　3. Refusing to show I.D. Card
　　4. In building without I.D. card
　　5. Misconduct in class, library, or assembly hall.

F. **One (1) Day Suspension—In House**

　　1. Being improperly dressed
　　2. Leaving classroom without permission
　　3. Cheating in class or copying the work of another student
　　4. Caught in the act of class cutting
　　5. Excessive tardies to class
　　6. Wearing hats in building
　　7. Wearing picks or combs in hair (applicable to young men only)
　　8. Bringing radios in building
　　9. Wearing sunglasses in building
　　10. Wearing earrings in school (applicable to young men only)
　　11. Wearing plastic bags, hair nets or shower caps on head when in the building.

Figure 9-3. Penalties for Violation of Corliss Code of Conduct.

objective, explicit criteria, and standards which allow all students an opportunity to work for them. A variety of incentives may be used to motivate students to achieve success. Students who maintain a perfect attendance record for each month (no tardies, no cuts and no absences) are eligible to participate in a Monthly Attendance Lotto for cash awards of $50, $25, and $15 for first, second, and third prizes respectively. While cash prizes may not be appropriate for younger children, they appeal to inner-city high school students for several reasons: daily carfare, increased personal needs, school fees, extra money for sports events and nonessential material possessions. Students regularly and publicly receive awards for attendance, citizenship and achievement. Incentive Awards for each category are listed in Figure 9-4.

Rewards which cultivate character, bolster self-esteem and instill school pride are essential in any long-term improvement plan. Students who have no discipline referrals each month, exemplary service to the school, or outstanding contributions to special clubs, events, or activities are eligible for good citizenship awards. Rewards in this category, highly visible and long-lasting, include plaques, certificates, ribbons, key chains and school pins.

Built in rewards for achievement (grade for class performance and success on standardized tests) are enhanced when students are frequently and publicly recognized for their accomplishments. Academic achievement awards are presented to students who distinguish themselves by qualifying for the Regular Honor Roll when they earn on a 4.0 scale, a grade point average of 3.0 and 3.5 or above, respectively. Academic awards, presented at the end of each marking periods, include trophies, free tickets to all school activities, and achievement buttons. See Figure 9-4 for the Incentive Awards for attendance, citizenship and scholarship.

SCHOOL AND COMMUNITY PROGRAMS

Because of strict budgetary constraints and cutbacks in funds available for basic skills and literacy programs for secondary schools in areas with a high rate of poverty, school administrators are compelled to develop their own programs or look for existing ones in the community to provide needed services to students. Programs which enhance the cognitive and affective development of black inner-city students, briefly described in this section, are highly recommended.

$$$$$$$$$$$$$$$$$$$$$$$$$$$$$$$$$$$$ *ATTENDANCE LOTTO* $$$$$$$$$$$$$$$$$$$$$$$$$$$$$$$$$$$$$$

1st Prize $50.00	2nd Prize $25.00	3rd Prize $15.00

Lotto tickets will be issued monthly to students who—

1. Have not cut any class or division during the month
2. Have not been tardy to their first period class (second period if that is their starting time)
3. Perfect Attendance in division for the month

•••••••••••••••••••••••••••••••••••• *GOOD CITIZENSHIP* ••

Plaques, School Letter, Pins, Key Chains, Certificates

—One free ticket to a school activity of his/her choice (basketball, football game, school dance, etc.)

—Certificates to obtain free tickets to a Chicago White Sox's Baseball Game

Students who exhibit the following traits will be nominated by their division teacher each month for good citizenship awards:
1) Dependability,
2) Courtesy,
3) Service to School,
4) Participation in clubs and/or activities.
To be eligible, a student must have no discipline referrals.

•• *ACADEMIC* ••

PRINCIPAL'S HONOR ROLL	GPA	3.5 or above
HONOR ROLL	GPA	3.0 or above

—Trophy at end of each marking period
—Free tickets to all school activities
—Certificate to obtain free tickets to a Chicago White Sox's Baseball Game
—One free theatre ticket
—End of year pizza party
—Achievement button

Students who have a cumulative grade point average of 4.0 or better for four years will be presented a plaque at graduation.

Figure 9-4. Incentive Awards for Attendance, Citizenship and Achievement.

Youth Motivation

A youth motivation program under the auspices of the Merit Employment Division of the Chicago Commerce and Industry is available to all Chicago public high schools that have a significant number of minority students. Two major objectives of the program are (1) to motivate young people to stay in school and acquire skills which will prepare them for the future and (2) to provide an opportunity for face-to-face relationships with success models in various fields of work.

Chicago Youth Centers

Chicago Youth Centers offer several programs designed to enhance the social needs of inner-city students. Two of them, *Reaching Into Successful Employment,* (RISE), and *Fresh Start,* are beneficial to secondary students. The *RISE* program helps nonproductive students improve their attendance, build self-esteem, and acquire coping skills to deal with problems related to their home and environment. The *Fresh Start* program is designed to enhance the affective skills of overage, low-achieving freshmen students by assisting them with goal setting, decision making, and problem solving.

Peer Tutoring

Peer-tutoring programs are beneficial to both the tutors and students being tutored. Students who excel academically in vocational classes and students who have a composite of 20 or above on the American College Tests (ACT) are eligible to become a tutor in vocational and academic areas respectively. The tutors are paid minimum wages from funds generated through local fund-raising endeavors.

Career and Skill Development

The Career and Skill Development program answers the needs for vocational development. The idea of learning new skills, related to business, such as resume writing, job application procedures and interviewing techniques are fully covered in the Career and Skill Development program with all participating students.

By giving the student various approaches and alternatives in regard to careers and colleges, the center supplies background experience for the students' effective career search.

Child Development

The Child Development program is unique to the public schools by having an onsight preschool room that sees seventy-five (75) three (3) and four (4) year old children each week. The high school child development students act as tutors giving the preschool individualized instruction. The child development program is in its ninth (9th) year, growing and improving each year. It is a program where everyone is a winner.

T.V. Studio

Fortunately, the school is equipped with a modern, bi-level T.V. studio that is unrivaled by any high school in Chicago today. The studio facilities include a professional "state of the art" T.V. lighting system, special effects switching system, dural format, portable television system. This system can facilitate live programming to the entire school through a closed circuit interlink. This switcher can also provide special effects for the three phase editing system and the film slide and tape chain through which students can integrate 16 millimeter film and slides into live or prerecorded productions. After two years of television production, Corliss' students can demonstrate the knowledge and skills that can lead to a successful television center.

VOCATIONAL EDUCATION PROGRAMS

According to a recent study by the Hiring Policy Goals Committee, a school reform committee set up by the late Mayor of Chicago, Harold Washington, 32 percent of the 16,000 graduates in the class of 1985 were unemployed and 31 percent were employed in "dead-end jobs." Such alarming statistics validate the need for work-study programs for at-risk students. Vocational education programs at Corliss High School offer students an opportunity to enroll in any one of the three available work-study programs to earn credit toward graduation and job-related experience. Having an opportunity to experience the world of work while still in school motivates students to remain in school and obtain marketable skills which lead to employability in solid stable jobs and positions of upward mobility.

Distributive Education (D.E.)

Distributive Education is a cooperative work program offered to eleventh and twelfth graders who wish to prepare for a career in Marketing or Merchandising. The student works in an approved training station, such as a retail store or service business organization, in a marketing or merchandising occupation and follows a training plan designed to relate classroom work to the employment activity. Preference is given to students who have taken Salesmanship or other business subjects prior to or during enrollment in the program.

Cooperative Work Training (C.W.T.)

The Cooperative Work Training program, an early intervention program, differs from the other cooperative programs in the type of student for which it is designed. These potential dropout students are 16 years of age or older, low achievers and/or slow learners, and are placed at training stations to develop a specific skill. Work experiences need not provide training and job rotation as do the more sophisticated programs, such as Office Occupations (O.O.), Distributive Education (D.E.), Industrial Related Occupations (I.C.E.), or Home Economics Related Occupations (H.E.R.O.).

Home Economics Related Occupations (H.E.R.O.)

Home Economics Related Occupations program offers on-the-job training in areas which involve the knowledge and skills of some phase of home economics such as food service, clothing services, child care services, and home furnishings services. Students in this program attend a related class in which instruction is given by the coordinator to reinforce skill development in their area of employment, in addition to career counseling, consumer education, labor laws, safety and personal characteristics necessary to achieve job success. This program is open to all eleventh and twelfth grade students who have completed one or more courses in home economics.

STAFF DEVELOPMENT AND STUDENT ACHIEVEMENT

Most educators will agree that (1) there is a need to increase student achievement in inner-city schools and (2) student achievement may be accelerated through improved instruction. How to improve instruction and accelerate student achievement becomes a question and a challenge. Obviously, staff development is essential to the improvement process, yet little time is allocated for it by some school districts. Currently, two full days (one for opening school and one for closing school), and three half-days are allocated for staff development during the school year. To obtain additional time, eight 40-minute class periods are reduced by four minutes. Operating on a Friday Faculty Meeting Schedule, the educational staff participated in biweekly, thirty-two minute sessions to review research about effective teaching behaviors, classroom management and successful strategies for teaching inner-city secondary students.

Staff development is crucial to the improvement of instruction, but because of the scarcity of time available for it, those factors which have an impact on student achievement (Squires, Huitt, and Segars, 1983) are discussed and assessed in inservice sessions.

School Climate: The school environment is safe, orderly, clean and conducive to teaching and learning; students take care of school property.

Organization for Effectiveness: Counselors and administrators are placed to support teachers by freeing them from major distractions and giving them more time to plan and teach; attendance procedures are clearly understood by students and teachers.

Curriculum Content: Curriculum committees develop units, unit tests and final examinations for the core areas of English, mathematics, science and social studies; curriculum content is aligned with the skills and knowledge required on the Tests of Achievement and Proficiency (TAP).

Curriculum Coverage: A supervisory process of classroom observations and a weekly review of lesson plans is instituted to help in monitoring the amount of material covered during a semester; students master academic assignments.

Student Involvement: Assistant principals are involved in monitoring student behavior and detaining students in a tardy center to minimize distractions, class tardiness and problems related to classroom management; students spend the majority of class time actually working on content and learning activities.

Expectations For Success: Teachers spend most of the class period in organized learning activities; students are praised and rewarded for demonstrated achievement instead of mediocre or poor performance; homework is required, collected and graded; teachers expect students to succeed.

Effective Teaching Behaviors: Effective teaching behaviors, based on well-documented research, are thoroughly and frequently presented by the principal; the principal supervises and evaluates teachers and rewards them for good work.

When Corliss opened its doors to the first freshmen class in 1974, its motto was "In Pursuit of Excellence." Since that time, that motto has been posted throughout the building as a visual reminder to students that excellence in education is a never-ending process. The curriculum, comprehensive in scope, is designed to challenge students as they acquire marketable skills for employment and for success in postsecondary education. Therefore, programs and courses which help students acquire the basic skills which will prepare them to function in a pluralistic society take precedence over all other activities. Priority is given to the teaching of comprehension and using sources of information in all disciplines. A great deal of instructional time and emphasis are placed on the everyday skills of generalization, inference, map and chart reading, determining direction and distance and interpreting data.

Black, inner-city, secondary students also need praise, encouragement and a built-in ratio of success for their efforts and performance. To be effective, teachers must not only possess an excellent grasp of their subject matter, but must also be creative, innovative and able to use a variety of instructional materials and methods of instruction. Generally, methods of instruction which allow the whole class to be involved are more effective than small group instruction or seat work where students work independently. Effective secondary teachers report that standing, moving about the classroom and interacting with students encourage positive behavior as well as increase student involvement and participation in class activities. Teachers who routinely vary their methods of instruction while modifying and augmenting the curriculum to ensure that the majority of the students in their classes attain a minimum level of mastery before they are awarded a grade of satisfactory or better for their achievement and performance, have been highly successful in the teaching of at-risk students.

A comprehensive secondary curriculum for at-risk students must be all inclusive: a college preparatory curriculum for the college-bound, gifted programs for the talented and gifted, and vocational programs for regular, educable mentally handicapped and learning disabled. This curriculum design motivates students to stay in school and learn skills for employability and productivity.

SPECIAL PROGRAMS

In keeping with its philosophy that all children, regardless of their race or socioeconomic conditions, can learn and its mission to graduate students who are intellectually and socially prepared for citizenship, a variety of programs are made available to students. *The Principal's Scholars Program (PSP),* a cooperative project at the University of Illinois at Urbana-Champaign and Ada S. McKinley Educational Agency (ASM) is open to students who pursue a college preparatory curriculum, and are interested in gaining entrance into colleges and universities. *The Students, Teachers, Educators and Parents (STEP)* is a cooperative educational program designed by DePaul University for minority secondary students. It is a four-year program which assists students in further enhancing the academic and personal skills essential to their success in college. The program is open to all freshmen who have average grades and are committed to excellence. Parents and students are involved in monthly meetings with university staff to discuss progress, achievement and the concerns of the school and participants.

A federally-funded *Options for knowledge, Integrated Humanities Program for Talented and Gifted Students* enables gifted and talented students to concentrate on areas of interest in the humanities, develop leadership skills, prepare for college entrance examinations and receive in-depth study in science and mathematics with special emphasis on Health Science Career Exploration.

Black children enjoy and appreciate learning about their heritage and the contributions blacks have made and are making to society. School programs which teach teachers how to incorporate black culture into their disciplines are useful and highly successful. *Teaching About Africa (TAA)*, a social studies program implemented in twenty-two Chicago public high schools, allows teachers to share strategies for building positive images of Africa and to teach the curriculum from a global perspective while highlighting the heritage and contributions of different races and nationalities.

Although these programs are still in their infant stage, teachers and parents are overwhelmed with the motivation and enthusiasm of their students. In time, there will be a significant increase in achievement and performance.

PARTNERSHIPS

The business community is now finding it more difficult to find high school graduates prepared to enter the job market. As a consequence, more businesses are eager to accept their moral and social responsibility with enlightened interest. They welcome an opportunity to participate in Adopt-A–School programs throughout the country.

Since schools need more than monetary support, businesses are encouraged to form a school/business partnership to support the school in many and varied endeavors. Some of the more common services provided and desired (Adams, 1987,10) are as follows:

- academic incentives to students
- technical assistance to special programs and projects
- jobs for graduates
- hands-on experience for teachers
- access to modern equipment and technology
- human resources in academic disciplines
- teacher recognition projects

Corliss High School has two adopters; WBBM–TV and St. Paul Federal Bank. While the focus of the WBBM–TV adoption is on television talent and technicians, it is not confined to the television department. A court artist demonstrated sketching in the art laboratory; a television reporter lectured English classes on how to research news stories; a television technical director showed students how to edit video tape. In the television classes, **WBBM–TV** artists have helped students build sets, producers have given lectures on news production techniques and writers have talked to classes about news writing.

St. Paul Federal Bank for Savings adopted Corliss and Pullman Elementary School. As an outgrowth of its Thrift Education Program, St. Paul provided the resources and equipment for the production of professional quality video tapes to teach elementary school students the basics of spending and saving money and high school students about preparing for careers. Education took place at many levels. The Pullman elementary students prepared to "teach" other students about money and banking, while the Corliss television students were given the opportunity to work under real world working conditions. They were introduced to the production process on a step-by-step, hands-on basis, by professionals who expected an excellent product and within specified deadlines.

The script was written and developed by students at Corliss. Through the generosity of St. Paul Federal, the tapes will be made available to other elementary schools in the Chicago metropolitan area. As an adoptive parent, St. Paul Federal Bank is committed to employing graduates of Corliss and also helping them to become productive members of society.

PARENT INVOLVEMENT

The acceleration of achievement may be greatly enhanced through parent involvement. Research findings indicate that a strong partnership between the school, the parents and the community increase the effectiveness of the educational program (Dulaney, 1987). Students whose parents take an active role in their children's education generally perform better than those whose parents are not involved in the education process.

Lengthy teachers' strikes, declining achievement scores and unemployable graduates have refocused attention on parents and their impact on education. Parents, quickly becoming aware of state and local legislation which mandate their involvement in local school improvement councils, are now rallying behind supporters of education reform. Educators throughout the country now recognize parents as partners in the education process. Parents, willing to become involved, are happy to provide teachers with information about their children which will enhance the teacher's effectiveness. Many teachers, however, are reluctant to encourage parents to become involved for various reasons.

- Parents may be tempted to share confidential information
- Parent involvement activities require too much planning and supervision
- Parents may have ulterior motives or hidden agendas
- Parents may have difficulty keeping school commitments

Successful parent-involvement programs are carefully planned to maximize the training and skills of parents. Parents should be allowed flexibility in schedules, given various options for becoming involved, made aware of building standards and procedures, and provided with information and techniques for helping students achieve and perform.

Parents of students at Corliss High School are expected and encouraged to exercise their rights and responsibilities to become involved in the education of their children. A variety of avenues, including parent letters, school newsletters and Parent-Teacher Association (PTA) meetings are used to recruit parents as well as keep them informed about the school's programs, procedures and activities. Parent volunteers, appreciated and respected, are used for corridor supervision, fund-raising, and to assist classroom teachers and the attendance office staff. Generally, when parents are involved, they are more positive about the school and are more willing and prepared to garner support for educational programs and initiatives. The Parent-Teacher Association and Local School Improvement Council, both supportive of parent involvement, diligently work to disseminate information about the school, its goals and objectives, school budget and reform issues in education.

AN ALTERNATIVE PROGRAM

Despite the alarming statistics concerning the high dropout rate of at-risk students nationwide, few alternative programs are available to high school dropouts eighteen years of age and older. The General Educational Development (GED) Collegiate Scholarship Program for Chicago Public School Dropouts Residing in Chicago Housing Authority (CHA) Communities is an exemplary program available to high school dropouts who reside in the CHA communities.

The program is specifically designed to meet the academic, social and economic needs of high school dropouts. It offers hope and a second chance to eligible persons who reside in these communities. The objective of the program is to recruit eligible candidates and prepare them for success when taking the GED Examination. Successful candidates are given an opportunity to enroll in a college or university of their choice.

Realizing the need for support in the cognitive and affective domains, the skills and knowledge required to pass the GED Examination are taught in three-hour classes five days per week. Five areas, reading, writing, mathematics, social studies and science, are taught and assessed regularly. When a candidate scores a composite of 200 or more on the GED Practice Examination, he/she is encouraged to take the official GED Examination which requires at least 225 points to be successful.

Candidates who are successful and enter higher education are supported by guidance and counseling programs. Preparation for the college-work world is done by discussing career planning, self-concept, image building and success. Guest speakers and individual monitors are presented regularly.

The program, in its first year, has had a dramatic impact. Nine participants are enrolled in Chicago State University. Successful candidates still become leaders in the CHA communities and develop other initiatives to help dropouts acquire the basic skills and competencies to become productive citizens.

REFERENCES

Adams, Don, "New Data on Partnerships," *Pro Education*, April 1987, 10, 12.

Brookover, Wilbur, Laurence Beamer, Helen Efthim, Douglas Hathaway, Laurence Lezotte, Stephen Miller, Joseph Passalacqua and Louis Tornatzky, *Creating Effective Schools: An Inservice Program for Enhancing School Learning Climate and Achievement.* Learning Publications, Inc. Holmes Beach, Florida, 1982.

Chicago Education Summit Hiring Policy Goals Committee, Chicago, 1986.

Davis, Samuel C., "GED Collegiate Scholarship Program," unpublished, 1987.

Dulaney, Kathy H., "A Comprehensive Approach for Parent and Community Involvement, "*Illinois School Journal* vol. 67, no. 1, (Spring 1987), 42–48.

Edmonds, Ronald R., "Effective Schools for the Urban Poor," *Educational Leadership*, Oct. 1978:15–23.

Edmonds, Ronald R., "Program of School Improvement: An Overview," *Educational Leadership*, Dec. 1982:4–10.

Lunenburg, Frederick C., "Another Face of School Climate," *Illinois School Journal* vol. 67, no.1, (Spring 1987) 3–10.

Reed, Sally and Craig Sautter, "Programs for Teens at Risk," *Instructor* vol. 1 (Fall 1987), 28–29.

Slezak, James, *Odyssey to Excellence.* Merritt, San Francisco, California 1984.

Squires, David A., William G. Huitt, and John K. Segars, *Effective Schools and Classrooms — A Research Based Perspective.* ASCD, Alexandria, Virginia, 1983.

Chapter 10

IS BEHAVIOR TOWARD STUDENTS
BASED ON EXPECTATIONS??

KATHRYN C. WIGGINS

Have you ever seen sadness reflected in the eyes of a child who wants to learn, but doesn't know how? Have you ever heard angered frustration voiced by a high school student who is tired of failing? Have you ever felt despair in a quest to meet the needs of all students? A great body of research in education today and reports from national commissions suggest that the nation and our children are "at risk" because teachers do not teach well and students are not learning. Other studies indicate that it is possible for schools and teachers to make a difference, but there is no clear model for effectiveness in any situation (Berliner, 1979; Brookover & Lezotte, 1977, Brophy and Good, 1986; Hutchins, 1987).

What is apparent from these investigations is that learning in the classroom is influenced by student and teacher attributes and expectations, the teacher's content expertise and process behaviors, the school's climate and administrative policies, and the support of parents and society in general. Each of these factors is empowered with relative degrees of input in the overall design and selection of the specific ingredients that form the completed learning environment or its participants. Society's interest in education is often swayed by political maneuvers. Finances or location usually influence parents in the selection of a school. Reliance is placed on school professionals, burdened with resource constraints and guided by legal principles, to orchestrate a child's educational program. Teachers and students are assigned to each other, and for better or worse, they spend a year or more performing what is expected. This limited interaction among the partakers of our educational system causes a fragmented approach to goal setting, procedural implementation and system evaluation. Ultimately, the quality of the school experience for children is jeopardized.

The information presented in this chapter will focus on a discussion of teacher expectations and how they seem to influence differential behavior toward students. It would be simplistic to suggest that children's performances can be improved merely by having teachers reflect high expectations, but research suggests a correlation exists. Expectancy theories will be defined briefly, with particular attention drawn to how they are communicated within the classroom. Results from specific studies will be summarized and the information that is gleaned will lead to this chapter's concluding generalizations.

EXPECTANCY

Research on expectancy theories has its origins in the field of psychology (Tolman, 1932; Gibson, 1941; Mac Corquodale and Meehl, 1954). Complex definitions of the construct "expectancy" refer to a type of judgement being made that leads one to arrive at assumptions about consequences and thus, behave accordingly. Recently, theorists interested in interpersonal perception, especially related to teaching and learning, have investigated how perceptions are formulated and if they affect educational outcomes.

A general classification of expectancy effects is offered by Babad (1982). "Golem" effects are undesirable negative effects indicating that expectations result in retarded achievement. "Galatea" effects are desirable effects which result from high expectation that positively influence achievement. According to Brophy (1985), "most expectation effects observed in the classrooms are Golem effects rather than Galatea and are produced by teachers who are overreactive (Brophy & Good, 1974), high biased (Babad, 1982), or high differentiating (Brattesoni et al., 1981)" (p. 316).

Further investigation into expectation effects identifies two types commonly found in the classroom. The first is defined by Mertin (1957) as the "self-fulfilling prophecy" where "a false definition of the situation evokes a new behavior which makes the originally false conception come true" (p. 423). Mertin's original example included a description of a bank that was rumored to be on the verge of bankruptcy. Before long, people acted on that rumor and withdrew their money. Eventually, so much money was withdrawn that bankruptcy was inevitable. The implication derived from this scenario illustrates that outcome is dependent on actualized behavior. Using the bank example, if no one withdrew money, the bank would not have perished. Teachers' impressions of students can lead them to develop particular expectations, some of which can be false. If their subsequent teaching behaviors maintain these expectations and induce specific student behaviors, then the self-fulfilling prophecy will occur.

"Sustaining expectation effects" is the second major phenomenon found in the classroom. According to Cooper and Good (1983), sustaining expectation effects "occur when teachers respond on the basis of their existing expectations for students rather than to changes in student performance" (p. 6). In contrast to the self-fulfilling prophecy effect which begins with inaccurate expectations, the sustaining expectation effect begins with true expectations. The teacher's familiarity with the student's past performance or identified ability "label" influences the teacher to expect only the current or past level of performance. Hence, the student's learning activities are limited to a particular curriculum or set of teaching behaviors (Rist, 1970).

Some encouraging information was arrived at from studies of in-service teachers and sustaining expectation effects (Brophy and Good, 1974). Findings suggest that teachers show a willingness to alter their expectation levels if faced with consistent student performance that differs from the past performance and/or is contrary to assumptions. Not only were these teachers' expectations flexible, but they tended to be accurate if based on valid data (i.e., school records, performance on academic activities).

COMMUNICATING EXPECTATIONS

In an attempt to clarify the developmental steps that are involved in communicating teacher expectations, Brophy and Good (1974) created a four-step model of the process:

1. Teachers develop expectations which predict student behavior.
2. Teachers behave differently to each student based on the expectation.
3. Through the teacher's behaviors, the student is informed about the behavior that is expected from him/her and this impacts on his/her self-concept and motivation.

4. If the teacher behavior persists and the student reacts accordingly, the final student behavior will correspond to the initial expectation.

Whatever the expectation, a good deal of the mediation involves nonverbal communication processes (Dusek, 1985). Additionally, there appear to be differences in the receptive clarity of these nonverbal communication channels, as well as an individual's sensitivity to them (Conn, Edwards, et al, 1968). Research in these areas is not abundant, but it suggests that many students may be unaware of nonverbal signals from teachers, either by choice or inability to perceive them (Given, 1974). Students who have low esteem and confidence, students who are troubled or distracted, students with sensory input systems that are lacking, students who integrate information incorrectly, will miss the silent language of instruction and feedback that could alter their behavior.

BEHAVIOR-EVALUATION-EXPECTATION LINKAGE

A preponderant amount of research has focused on the connection between teacher expectations of students and resulting student behaviors, as well as teacher behaviors and resulting student expectations of self. The linkages that exist between teachers and students and their expectations and behaviors are illustrated in Figure 10-1. Each component in the model affects the formation of the others. Teachers are in a position to observe student behaviors. If these behaviors follow a somewhat consistent pattern (i.e., doing or not doing assignments, giving or not giving effort, succeeding or not succeeding on tests), teachers formulate an evaluation (judgement) which tends to influence their expectations about future student performance and their own teaching abilities. Teacher behaviors in the classroom communicate messages to students which suggest expectations. Students receive this information, assess it as best they can, and formulate their own expectations which are revealed through their responding behaviors. The linkage cycle is dynamic and very much dependent upon the amount and quality of interaction that takes place between teachers and students.

What types of behaviors lead to an evaluation of performance? Morrison and McIntyre (1969) clustered teacher reactions into three areas of student behaviors: pupil achievement, general classroom behavior and attitudes toward the teacher, and peer relationships. Nash (1973) determined that it was a combination of achievement and personal attributes

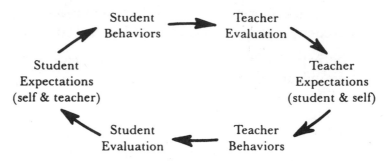

Figure 10-1. Behavior-Evaluation-Expectation Linkage.

that formed the basis for teacher perceptions of students. His study revealed that teachers tended to rate higher those students who were achievers. Those students who did not achieve were seen as being duller than they really were. Other studies show that teachers gain information about students through such questionable indices as physical appearance (Bruan, 1976), race and social class (Weinstein and Middlestadt, 1979) and gender (Bank, Biddle and Good, 1980). Whether consciously or subconsciously, teachers choose from a variety of factors in order to develop a profile of a student.

Expectation effects are not present in all classes and often depend on the characteristics of the participants involved. In describing teachers, Brophy and Good (1974) suggest three categories. "Proactive" teachers are clear about what it is they are to teach and believe in their own teaching capabilities. These teachers are most likely to have positive effects on students and high expectations for all (p. 314). Then there are "overreactive" teachers who set rigid expectations for all students. The low achievers would be expected to do poorly, and often very little is done to help them go beyond, since they are behaving normally for their expectation level. Finally, we have the majority of teachers who are "reactive" in their behavior. Expectation levels fluctuate, depending upon new information.

Of the types of teachers described, it is apparent that the most effective would be one who combines both proactive and reactive characteristics. Not only are they confident about instructional content and teaching ability, but they also respond to the needs of students and actively attempt to address them.

In a study of physical education student teachers, Babad, Inbar, and Rosenthal (1982) attempted to determine levels of teacher bias after student teachers were given background information about the children's social status. The data indicated that highly biased teachers reflected much larger expectation differences between high and low expectation students. The no bias teachers seemed to make accurate predictions of their students' performance levels and did not exaggerate these differences. Similar findings were reported in a study done by Brattesani, et al. (1981).

How teachers define their role may have an influence on the things they stress in the classroom and consequently their expectations (Good and Brophy, 1978, 1980). Some teachers will emphasize content (observed more in secondary school), while others will stress socialization (observed more in elementary school). In the content-oriented classroom, it is usually the high achievers that have more opportunity to interact with the teacher and receive more praise and feedback than the low achievers who may avoid participation due to a lack of ability. In the socialization-oriented classroom, interaction with all students is frequent and the pace of the curriculum tends to be slower. The low achiever may actually do better in this situation, but the achievement of the class as a whole may be low simply because they were not exposed to a sufficient amount of content in lieu of time spent on socialization (Brophy, 1979; Fisher, 1980).

Students gauge their own evaluation of the teacher's expectations and determine if they can meet them successfully. Those students who are keenly sensitive or highly dependent will be more influenced by the teacher behaviors (Zuckerman, 1978). This may be especially true for younger children. Those students who are less sensitive to the subtle communication cues of the teacher are more at risk of missing important directives. Also, the shy, quiet student who avoids interactive participation is more likely to be perceived incorrectly by the teacher and, therefore, more likely to have false expectations. The student who eagerly participates often will have more opportunity to be perceived correctly (Brophy and Good, 1974).

Students who disrupt classroom activities or threaten a teacher's control will receive more feedback about behavior and less about content. This could lead to their receiving less academic encouragement. "In general, where students and teachers are mutually hostile, the potential for positive self-fulfilling prophecy (Galatea) effects seems minimal, but the probability of negative (Golem) effects is high" (Dusek, 1985).

STUDIES

Now that we have reviewed some of the participant characteristics in the linkage process, a selected sample of investigations and their results should offer further insight. From the myriad of data, we see relationships being established between teacher expectations and student learning. Although these studies are not free from methodological or analytical weaknesses, they do suggest some interesting trends. Rosenthal (1985) summarizes the four ways that teachers seem to treat students differently and suggests that these areas are the ones most in need of attention. Through nonverbal and verbal cues, teachers create a "warmer socioemotional climate" and give more "differentiated feedback" to those students who earn special approval (Rosenthal, 1985, p. 54). Additionally, more actual teaching takes place and the subject matter that is presented to the "special" students is often more challenging. It appears that the "approved" students receive many more opportunities for responding to questions, and are given more time to think through their answers. All of these differentiated behaviors can send devastating messages to those students who are not included in the "select" group.

Factors associated with specific situations and/or types of environment can contribute to differentiated behaviors between teachers and students (Brophy & Evertson, 1978). Examples of such factors include grade level, size of group, and pace of lesson. As one looks at grade level characteristics, it is apparant that the environment and curricular emphasis are different between primary grades and middle or upper grades. Very often, teachers in the primary grades create opportunities for learning to occur in small groups and focus content as well as socialization and personal development. This type of situation can allow a more personal contact between teacher and student, since the teacher usually attempts to individualize the material and the pace to meet the needs of the small group.

While the early grades use small group activities more often, the upper grades tend to do things in a whole class format with an emphasis on content rather than socialization (Brophy & Good, 1974). In this type of situation, there generally is a quantitative reduction of interaction between teacher and students. Keeping the pace of a whole group activity can cause a teacher to avoid calling on low-expectancy students who may slow things down and lead to student frustration (Weinstein, 1976). Thus, high-expectancy students will be given more opportunity to respond to teacher questions.

One of the first educational applications of the concept of self-fulfilling prophecy was done by Rosenthal and Jacobson (1968) in an experimental study of expectancy effects on elementary children. Teachers were told that the scores achieved by a random sample of students revealed that they would make surprising gains in "intellectual competence" during the coming months. At the conclusion of the year, results revealed that these children not only made significant gains, but were perceived by their teachers as being happier, more curious and interesting.

This study has received much dispute and was replicated several times. Jose and Cody (1971) found no significant differences in learning between groups. Dusek and O'Connell (1973) concluded that "the child's academic potential determined the teacher's expectation rather than the reverse" (p. 375). Also, they reported that neither the false test scores nor the biased statements suggested to the teachers seemed to affect the children's achievement scores. Despite the issues related to the original Rosenthal study, indications from it and other investigations suggest that teacher expectations can and do affect students, although these expectation effects do not always occur, and differ in degree and type (Brophy and Good, 1974; Braun, 1976; Good, 1980).

Hall and Merkel (1985) raise questions about the consequences of parents and teachers having expectations that are too high. Based on Rotter's (1954) social learning theory, problems will arise when the value of a reinforcer is very high (i.e., good grades), but the expectancy for receiving the reinforcer is very low. The student who is asked to give a performance that is beyond his/her capabilities will use such survival strategies as cheating, taking short cuts, or merely avoiding any participation. A study done by Covington and Omelich (1979) indicated that even if teachers reward effort, students who try, but do not succeed at a task, will be hesitant to try again.

Suggestions from several studies indicate that there are differing amounts of praise and criticism given to high versus low achievers (Rejeski, Darracott, and Hutslar, 1979; Taylor, 1979). Although it was not a universal finding, some data indicated that low-expectancy groups receive less praise and more criticism than higher groups (Cooper and Baron, 1977). Other studies showed no significant differences (Alpert, 1974), and some data revealed that the low reading groups were given more direct control, positive reinforcement and error correction than the other reading groups (Haskins, Walden and Ramey, 1983).

In an attempt to assess the accuracy of teacher perceptions and come to some understanding of teacher-student interactions, Brophy and Evertson conducted a longitudinal "student attributes" study (1981). Twenty-seven teachers and their students in four different grade levels were included over approximately two years. The factors that were analyzed included teachers' expectations, teachers' free response descriptions, coding of classroom behaviors and teacher-student interactions. Some of the results indicated the following:

A. Teacher halo effect seemed to be present. Students perceived favorably on achievement and/or conduct were perceived more favorably on other attributes. It was noted that teacher attributes were more closely associated with perceptions than with personal qualities.

B. The teacher ranking, the adjective descriptions and the classroom observation data revealed that girls were more successfully adjusted to the role of student than boys and were thus perceived more favorably by the teachers.

C. When comparing calm versus restless, and mature versus immature students, teacher ratings indicating success at school correlated highly with calm and mature attributes, and teachers, generally, had negative reactions to restless and immature students.

D. Focusing on work habits, those students identified as "careful" were given high ratings in school success. Interestingly, those students viewed as careless were not viewed as negatively as those who were restless.

E. Teacher perceptions were found to be related to such variables as creativity, persistence, student attractiveness, noticeable students, student cooperation and attachment to the teacher.

All of these variables, in differing degrees, showed some affect on the quality and quantity of teacher-student interaction. One implication from this study is that those students who are able to conform to the teacher's expectations of the role of the student will have an easier time succeeding in that classroom. Those students who are unable to adjust or fulfill their role will present frustrations and problems to the teacher. This may produce negative responses from the teacher which could alter the opportunities for success made available to the student.

Teachers who are faced with children who do not fulfill role expectations can react in a variety of ways. Giving up on a student is an unacceptable response. After repeated attempts to find a solution, failure can lead a teacher to simply ignore the problem student or rationalize the blame away to someone else or factors beyond his/her control (Weiner, 1979). This situation finds students and teachers ultimately "rejecting" each other and responding negatively throughout the year in an attempt to tolerate what is happening in the learning environment (Brophy, 1981). If a teacher wished to eliminate the dilemma and improve the situation, remediation must be pursued which employs alternative approaches to instruction and motivation, getting assistance and increasing effort and time commitment.

CONCLUSION

The extent of the influence that teacher expectations has on students is not clear, but we do know these effects exist. Although the most recent investigations suggest that these effects are less intense than originally indicated, student attitudes seem to be the most affected by the expectation phenomena. Good teaching does not come easily to anyone, and difficulties are to be expected when dealing with masses of students. Increased understanding of expectation effects and how they can be used in a positive manner will help teachers nurture the potential in each student. The following list suggests some teacher behaviors that might minimize the presence of negative effects:

1. It is not appropriate to maintain equal expectations for all students. Some degree of individualization is necessary if each student's unique characteristics are considered.
2. It is not appropriate to compare high achievers to low achievers. Separate norms should be established.
3. A high degree of interaction between teacher and student should be maintained.
4. Assessing students frequently will allow a teacher to interact more often with the student and set incremental challenges that are current with the student's abilities.
5. Give task specific feedback in combination with praise. Specific

feedback promotes skill improvement, while praise promotes in-creased effort through positive attitudes.

6. Concentrate on HOW to teach content and structure the lesson to include a variety of teaching techniques that will address different learning styles.

7. Identify teaching strengths and weaknesses and implement changes that will lead to more effectiveness.

The sensitive, reflective teacher who has invested the time in getting to know the students as individuals rather than stereotypes or group members will have an advantage in overcoming the problems associated with determining and communicating realistic expectations. One thing is apparent! Teachers have the power to employ good instructional techniques that can help to buffer or even eliminate negative expectation effects.

REFERENCES

Albert, J. (1974). Teacher behavior across ability groups. A consideration of the mediation of Pygmalian effects. *Journal of Educational Psychology*, 66, 348–353.

Adams, G. (1978). Racial membership and physical attractiveness effects on pre-school teachers' expectation. *Child Study Journal*, 8, 29–41.

Babad, E. Y., Inbar, J., & Rosenthal, R. (1982). Pygmalian, Galatea, and the Golem: Investigations of biased and unbiased teachers. *Journal of Educational Psychology*, 74, 459–474.

Bank, B., Biddle, B., & Good, T. (1980). Sex roles, classroom instruction, and reading achievement. *Journal of Educational Psychology*, 72, 119–132.

Berliner, D. (1979). Tempus educare. In D. Peterson & H. Wallberg (Eds.), Research in reading: Concepts, findings and implications. Berkeley, CA: McCutchan.

Blair, T. (1988). Emerging patterns of teaching: From methods to field experiences. Columbus, Ohio: Merrill.

Brattesani, K., Weinstein, R., Middlestadt, S., & Marshall, H. (1981). Using student perceptions of teacher behavior to predict student outcomes. Paper presented at the annual meeting of American Educational Psychology Association, Los Angeles, April.

Braun, C. (1976). Teacher expectation: Sociopsychological dynamics. *Review of Educational Research*, 46, 185–213.

Brookover, W., & Lezotte, L. (1977). Changes in school characteristics coincident with changes in student achievement. Occasional Paper No. 17. East Lansing, MI: Michigan State University, College of Urban Development. (ERIC NO. ED 181 005)

Brophy, J. (1979). Teacher behavior and its effects. *Journal of Educational Psychology,* 71, 733–750.

Brophy, J. (1985). Teacher-student interaction. In Dusek, J. (Ed). Teacher expectancies. Hillsdale, New Jersey: Lawrence Erlbaum Associates, p. 303–328.

Brophy, J. & Evertson, C. (1981). Student characteristics and teaching. New York: Longman.

Brophy, J. & Evertson, C. (1978). Context variables in teaching. *Educational Psychologist,* 12, 310–316.

Brophy, J., & Good, T. (1974). Teacher-student relationships: Causes and consequences. New York: Halt Pinchart & Winston.

Brophy, J., & Good, T. (1986). Teacher behavior and student achievement. In M.C. Wittrock (Ed.). *Handbook of research on teaching* (pp. 328–378) (3rd ed.). New York: Macmillan.

Conn, L., Edwards, C., Rosenthal, R., & Crowne, D. (1968). Perceptions of emotion and response of teachers' expectancy by elementary school children. *Psychological Reports,* 22, 27–34.

Cooper, H., & Baron, R. (1977). Academic expectations and attributed responsibility as predictors of professional teacher's reinforcement behavior. *Journal of Educational Psychology,* 69, 409–418.

Cooper, H., & Good, T. (1983). Pygmalian grows up: studies in the expectation communication process. New York: Longman.

Covington, M., & Omelich, C. (1979). Effort: the double-edge sword in school achievement. *Journal of Educational Psychology,* 71, 169–182.

Dusek, J. (1985). Teacher expectations. Hillsdale, New Jersey: Lawrence Erlbaum Associates.

Dusek, J., & O'Connel, E. (1973). Teacher expectancy on the achievement test performance of elementary school children. *Journal of Educational Psychology,* 65, 371–377.

Fisher, C., Gerliner, D., Filby, N., Marliave, R., Cahen, L., & Dishaw, M. (1980). Teaching behaviors, academic learning time, and student achievement: An overview. In C. Denham & A. Lieberman (Eds.). Time to learn. Washington, D.C.: National Institute of Education.

Gibson, J. (1941). A critical review of set in contemporary experimental psychology. *Psychological Bulletin,* 38, 781–817.

Given, B. (1974). Teacher expectancy and pupil performance: The relationship to verbal and non-verbal communication by teachers of learning disabled children. *Dissertation Abstracts International,* 35, 1529A.

Good, T. (1980). Classroom expectations: Teacher-pupil interactions. In J. McMillan (Ed.). The Social psychology of school learning. New York: Academic Press.

Good, T., & Brophy, J. (1978). Looking in classrooms (2nd ed.). New York: Harper & Row.

Good, T., & Brophy, J. (1980). Educational psychology: A realistic approach (2nd ed.). New York: Holt, Rinehart, & Winston.

Hall, V., & Merkel, S. (1985). Teacher expectancy effects and educational psychology. In J. Dusek (Ed.) Teacher Expectations. Hillsdale, New Jersey: Lawrence Erlbaum Associates.

Haskins, R., Walden, T., & Ramey, C. (1983). Teacher and student behavior in high and low ability groups. *Journal of Educational Psychology,* 75, 865–876.

Hutchins, T. (Ed.). (1987). Effective classroom instruction. Bloomington, IN: Phi Delta Kappa Center on Evaluation Development, Research.

Jose, J., & Cody, J. (1971). Teacher-pupil interaction as it relates to attempted changes in teacher expectancy of academic ability and achievement. *American Educational Research Journal,* 8, 39–49.

Merton, R. (1948). The self-fulfilling prophecy. *Antioch Review,* 8, 193–210.

Merton, R. (1957). Social theory and social structure. New York: Free Press.

Mac Corquodale, K., & Meehl, P. (1954). Edward C. Tolman. In W. Estes, S. Koch, K. Mac Corquodale, P. Meehl, C. Mueller, W. Schoenfield, & W. Verplanck (Eds.) Modern learning theory. New York: Appleton-Century-Crofts.

McDonald, F. I. (1976). Beginning teacher evaluation study. Phase III, Summary. Princeton, New Jersey: Educational Testing Service.

Morrison, A., & McIntyre, D. (1969). Teachers and teaching. Baltimore: Penguin Books.

Nash, R. (1973). Classrooms observed: The teacher's perception and the pupil's performance. Boston: Routledge and Kegan Paul.

Rejeski, W., Darracott, C., & Hutslar, S. (1979). Pygmalian in youth sport: A field study. *Journal of Sports Psychology,* 1, 311–319.

Rist, R. (1970). Student social class and teacher expectations: The self-fulfilling prophecy in ghetto education. *Harvard Educational Review,* 40, 411–451.

Rosenthal, R. (1985). From unconscious experimenter bias to teacher expectancy effects. In Dusek, J. (Ed.) Teacher expectancies. Hillsdale, New Jersey: Lawrence Erlbaum Associates, p. 37–65.

Rosenthal, R. (1983). Teaching functions in instructional programs. *The Elementary School Journal,* 83, 335–352.

Rosenthal, R. (1974). On the social psychology of the self-fulfilling prophecy: Further evidence for pygmalian effects and their mediating mechanisms. New York: MSS Modular Publications.

Rosenthal, R., & Jacovson, L. (1966). Teachers' expectancies: determinants of pupils' I.Q. gains. *Psychological Reports,* 19, 115–118.

Rosenthal, R., & Jacobson, L. (1968). Pygmalian in the classroom. New York: Holt, Rinehart & Winston.

Rotter, J. (1954). Social learning and clinical psychology. Englewood Cliffs, New Jersey: Prentice-Hall.

Taylor, M. (1979). Race, sex, and the expression of self-fulfilling prophecies in a laboratory teaching situation. *Journal of Personality and Social Psychology,* 37, 897–912.

Tolman, E.C. (1932). Purposive behavior in animals and men. New York: Appleton-Century-Crofts.

Weiner, B. (1979). A theory of motivation for some classroom experiences. *Journal of Educational Psychology,* 71, 3–25.

Weinstein, R. & Middlestadt, S. (1979). Student perceptions of teacher interactions with male high and low achievers. *Journal of Educational Psychology,* 71, 421–431.

Weinstein, R. (1976). Reading group membership in first grade: teacher behaviors and pupil experience over time. *Journal of Educational Psychology,* 68, 103–116.

Zuckerman, M., DeFrank, R., Hall, J., & Rosenthal, R. (1978). Accuracy of nonverbal communication as determinant of interpersonal expectancy effects. *Environmental Psychology and Nonverbal Behavior,* 2, 206–214.

Chapter 11

TEACHER-STUDENT INTERACTION

Eileen McGuire

Attention is often directed toward the inability of students to cope with urban schooling and failure. Implied is the notion that school disorders and failures exist primarily because students in recent years have developed a disdain for authority and lack of respect for adult school leaders.

However, a contrasting point of view suggests that students are not totally responsible for the disorder and chaos that exist in some public schools. The following review is presented to illustrate that factors other than student behavior may exist within schools which contribute to school disruptions and lack of success.

The teacher is clearly recognized as the central figure in the classroom; the teacher is both the authority figure and the instructional leader in the classroom; the teacher is responsible for establishing a climate that is conducive to learning, one that is responsive to the needs of the individual learner, and a climate that encourages and facilitates the total development of pupils. All of this should be orchestrated in an environment that is relatively free from elements that can detract from the learning process. The role of the urban classroom teacher in an inner city setting becomes more complex in that often he or she must establish such a classroom environment in spite of a conglomeration of negative factors associated with low socioeconomic conditions of urban communities.

The preexisting attitude regarding integration that teachers bring to school can have significant impact on the climate that is ultimately established within the classroom. Such attitudes, if viewed negatively by pupils, may impede the accomplishment of specific learning tasks, activities, and goals. Green (1975) indicates that children from low socioeconomic or urban communities are often confronted in the classroom

174

by teachers who view them as intellectually deprived and unlikely to succeed. These initial attitudes could well determine the kinds of activities that are undertaken in the classroom and further hamper the development of positive student-teacher relations.

Teacher opinion of students and expectations for them may in fact affect subsequent student behaviors and achievement outcomes. Purkey and Smith (1983) theorized that student achievement is strongly affected by the school social system, which varies from school to school and even within similar subsamples with socioeconomic status and racial composition controlled. In the analysis of two pairs of public elementary schools (matched in terms of racial composition, mean socioeconomic status, and urban location—each pair had one high- and one low-achieving school), Purkey and Smith found substantive differences in: (1) time spent on instruction, (2) commitment to (and assumed responsibility for) student achievement, (3) expectations for student achievement, (4) ability grouping procedures, and (5) use of appropriate reinforcement practices. In sum, an effective school was described as one "characterized by high evaluations of students, high expectations, high norms of achievement, with appropriate patterns of reinforcement and instruction," in which students "acquire a sense of control over their environment and overcome the feelings of futility which characterize the students in many schools" (p. 435).

The problem associated with teaching in urban schools is further exacerbated when other factors such as middle class values and attitudes are considered. Much criticism has been directed toward the inability of middle class teachers to relate in a positive manner to minority students. It has been found that teachers with positive attitudes toward integration had fewer discipline problems and required fewer discipline measures in their classrooms than teachers with negative attitudes (Peretti, 1975).

In a report edited by Johnson (1973) for the Far West Laboratory for Educational Research and Development, Dorothy Clement cites (pp. 224–35) studies which indicate that institutional adjustment, or conformity to school rules and values, is an important factor in the formulation of teacher judgments. These studies show that the attitudes teachers hold toward their individual students can influence the ways that they treat the students. Feshbach (1969) provided some information about the kinds of student attributes that attract or repel teachers. Results showed that teachers most generally preferred rigid, conforming and orderly students. The next most popular group were dependent, passive and acquiescent students, followed by flexible, nonconforming and untidy students.

Of all instructional grouping practices in the elementary grades, intraclassroom reading grouping is the most likely to be important in establishing a socioeconomic and achievement link. In the elementary schools, the reading group to which a child is assigned is primarily a matter of a single teacher's judgment. Because achievement tests correlate positively with socioeconomic status, some degree of socioeconomic segregation in classrooms would occur were test scores to be the sole criterion in grouping decisions. However, tests are seldom the only criterion. Instead, some schools frequently encourage teachers to use their own judgment and to consider criteria other than tests (Rist, 1970). These additional criteria might be more closely correlated with SES than reading ability. Rist implies this in stating that dress and cleanliness were among grouping criteria in the class he studied.

Rist's work is an ethnographic study of a single class of children over a three-year period; Rist describes how home background differences among kindergarten pupils can be transformed into achievement differences among third graders. He suggests that teachers initially divide pupils into instructional groups on the bases of social, class-related criteria and then give more instructional time to higher groups.

Characteristically, low groups are less engaged with the lesson than high groups. In low groups children tend to distract one another, are low in social maturity and children are perceived as troublemakers and those who don't pay attention. Teachers tolerate more interruptions and discipline students more, thus giving less instruction.

Soon real differences in achievement emerge, affecting children's capacity to learn new material and influencing subsequent teachers' judgments and expectations. Hence, Rist argues, lower class students emerge from their elementary schooling less academically able than their classmates. This suggests the potential importance of grouping practices in the elementary school for understanding the consequences of high school tracking.

Goodlad (1984) in his book, *A Place Called School*, found that ability grouping and tracking appear not to produce the expected gains in students' achievement. Students of average and especially low achievement tend to do less well when placed in middle or low than in mixed groups.

Goodlad says studies have shown there to be lower self-esteem, more school misconduct, higher drop-out rates and higher delinquency among students in lower tracks.

Finally, he says minority students and those from the lowest socioeconomic groups have been found in disproportionate numbers in classes at the lowest track levels, and children from upper socioeconomic levels have been found to be consistently overrepresented in higher tracks. And the courts have ruled, in a number of cases brought to them, that classification of students on criteria that result in disproportionate racial groupings is discriminatory and therefore unconstitutional.

Tracking researchers have tended not to examine the teaching practices associated with tracking; they have concentrated almost exclusively on effects of the practice.

Brophy and Good (1979) reporting on a study conducted by Leacok noted differences in teachers' behavior in middle class white schools; student inattention was taken as an indication of teacher need to arouse student interest, but the same behavior in a lower class black school was rationalized as boredom due to limited student attention span.

Faulk (1972) cites the teachers' lack of understanding of the students as a primary causal factor in most problems which occur in desegregated schools. He sees teacher attitudes as being most critical, and attributes teacher lack of contact with blacks as a cause of problems and misunderstandings between teachers and black students.

Kron and Faber (1973) discuss a reaction which may be common among in experienced teachers or teachers who have been transferred to schools of a different "sub culture" than the one with which they are familiar. This reaction, which is termed "culture shock," is manifested by a number of symptoms, including depression, self-doubt, hostility, fatigue and anger. Kron and Faber suggest that culture shock is common among teachers who have been transferred. The fact that individual teachers experience differing degrees of the malady suggests that some have more tolerance for unfamiliar situations, and for a number of reasons, can adjust with less difficulty.

A similar teacher reaction can be seen in desegregated classrooms. A white teacher from Indianapolis reported having feelings of "resentment" and "inadequacy" when her classroom was integrated. Reports of teachers crying in their principal's offices are not uncommon (Orfield, 1976).

The sense of inadequacy felt by the teacher is further documented by Orfield (1976). He reports that often teachers face a "professional crisis" with the realization that they are not effective with children from backgrounds with which they are unfamiliar. He says that when these good teachers are confronted with large numbers of students who do not respond in the school's typical way, they must either blame the newcomers or recognize and acknowledge a very serious professional inadequacy.

Lack of teacher acceptance of individual differences is evident in the existence of a status hierarchy among teachers which dictates that a teacher's status is determined by the type of student, grade or subject which he or she teaches (Uredevor, 1967). Therefore, students of lower academic levels may indeed be resented by their teachers, and this condition could be a source of conflict within the student-teacher relationship. Orfield (1976) discusses a case study of three California schools which found that older teachers from schools that had been considered "high status" schools prior to desegregation seemed to have the greatest degree of difficulty in adjusting to desegregation. They expressed hostility over their perception that their school had been invaded by strange children with no respect for their ideas of what a classroom should be like.

One apprehension which many teachers have relative to classroom discipline is that of losing control of the students (Niemeyer, 1965). The point at which the students are considered to be "out of control" is defined by the teacher, and the student who goes beyond the arbitrarily determined point of control may be considered a "discipline problem."

A study conducted by Stebbins (1970) sought to obtain information on teacher definitions of disorderly conduct. Stebbins found that, for teachers included in the study, reaction to disruption was based not only on consideration of the behavior, but upon some identification of the students involved in terms of the level of their past academic performance and deportment. Because the teacher's evaluation of and reaction to various behaviors is dependent, in part, upon the classroom activity, the teacher's academic success expectations of the student, and the teacher's behavioral expectations of the student, the same type of behavior may be evaluated differently and receive different responses.

Students somehow sense how their teachers view them. Students respond well when they are liked and respected by the teachers. Racist views or middle class contempt for lower socioeconomic groups almost absolutely obstruct communication and destroy the chances for effective teaching (Brophy and Good, 1979).

A reasonable conclusion of this research is that the quality of teaching makes a considerable difference in students learning and behavior. Teachers influence students in a number of ways that curriculum alone cannot.

An investigation of classroom practices at an urban public school was conducted to determine the impact of teacher behavior. The majority of classroom time at this school was allotted for academic activity. In general, however, it did not appear that this time was used economically. The teachers here did not spend a great amount of time engaged in academic interaction with their students. The following description of a morning's observation in a classroom generally reflects the kind of instruction and amount of time spent on instruction. Class began at 9:00. Students entered the room and took out a sheet of paper and began copying an assignment from the board without the teacher telling them to do so. The teacher was busy working at the desk for twenty-five minutes as the students worked. At 9:20 she began giving directions for a class assignment. While the students were working on the assignment, the teacher worked at the desk. A reading group was called to the back of the room at 9:45. They were assigned a story to read to themselves; they read quietly for fifteen minutes. The class went to the library at 10:00. The class returned to the room at 10:35 following a lavatory break. They resumed working on their board assignment. At 10:40 another group was called to the back of the room. The teacher interacted with them verbally. They were given an assignment in their workbooks. They returned to their seats at 10:50 and another group was called back. This group responded to various questions asked by the teacher and read sentences aloud.

For the most part, the morning appears to have been well planned by the teacher. The students were engaged all morning in academic activity; however, there was relatively little teacher-student interaction. The teacher answered questions that were raised by individual students, but most of the teacher's time was spent at the desk and as long as the students were quiet there was little interaction between the teacher and the students, whether they had finished their assignments or not.

One teacher's classroom regressed to virtually no time spent on instruction—total chaos. All of his time was spent on trying to maintain order.

A similar format was observed in different classrooms, with the primary difference in teacher-student interaction being determined by how noisy the students were. It appeared that, while the teachers here attempted to keep their students busy, not a great deal of time was spent on group or individual instruction. In three of the classrooms, it was noticed that where attempts at keeping students busy failed, the teacher spent a large amount of time attempting to maintain discipline. The time spent attempting to maintain discipline varied considerably among teachers.

My observations suggest that some of the teachers at this school tend to write off large numbers of their students. Conversations with teachers generally indicated that they did not feel that the majority of their students were capable of high achievement. One teacher pointed out that this attitude should be obvious by the manner in which the teachers utilized the several remedial programs that were established in the school. In the teacher's own words, the remedial programs were nothing more than "dumping grounds" for teachers who did not want to be bothered with certain students, particularly if they presented behavioral problems in the classroom. It was obvious that large numbers of students were required to attend the remedial math and reading programs.

For the most part, the teachers indicated that such large numbers of students were required to receive remedial instruction because of their poor academic skills. They attributed these "poor" skills to the background and family environments of their students. One teacher pointed out that there was relatively little that she, as a teacher, could do to overcome the negative effects on achievement that were caused by social class and family environment. Several other teachers with whom I talked agreed that the lower achievement their students maintained was due primarily to their family backgrounds and that there was relatively little that they could do to overcome the effects of these conditions on achievement.

Confusing reinforcement messages were not evident in all classrooms observed. Appropriate reinforcement patterns were consistently observed in one classroom. The curriculum materials were placed around the room with easy accessibility for students' use and enjoyment; upon completion of the whole group instructional task, the students read extensively from books, magazines and newspapers. They wrote summaries from various supplemental science and social studies books. They also were able to listen to prerecorded readings with headsets. The classroom was stimulating and disciplined. The teacher made very clear the purpose of every activity. The students understood how to do each task. The students knew what they were supposed to do when they finished a task. In this classroom more of the precious time available for learning was spent on activities of academic value.

The teacher placed a high priority on subject matter learning. The whole group instructional format was used most of the time to keep the pace of instruction moving. Information about the topic was always being given to everybody.

The following description of a morning's observation of reading generally reflects the instruction and amount of time spent on instruction. Class began at 9:00. Students entered the room, and took out homework assignments and turned them in as their name was called by the teacher. They took out a sheet of paper and began working on a quiz covering the homework. At 9:15 the teacher collected the quiz. At 9:20 she began the reading lesson with the whole group. The students were given information about the story they were going to read. She asked the students what they thought and wrote their responses on the board. She assigned three pages to be read silently. The students appeared eager to participate. They checked the responses on the board and found two of them to be correct. The whole group's attention was then directed to another set of other questions on a chart. They discussed the questions and possible solutions and then were instructed to read and find out if their predictions were correct. The students again appeared to do so eagerly. They were instructed to write the information on their papers and were instructed how to complete the assignments. They were also told what they were to do when they finished the task. The students moved to other tasks without disruption. Positive reinforcement was given for work well done.

The grouping practices were fluid and students were grouped according to need for extra instruction on a given task. The teacher was free to give additional instruction to those who needed it the most.

When asked what kind of progress she expected her students to make at the end of the year she indicated they would do very well. She believed that the students learn more because they know more—the more they know the more they learn. She made sure everybody knew what they needed to know to learn.

The teacher assumed all of the responsibility for the class and the instruction, but it appeared the students were taking the responsibility for the learning. Much of the time was spent on instruction and very little was discipline.

There was very little discussion with the teacher about ability level or economic status as it really did not appear to matter much in this classroom.

Conversations with teachers, as well as observations of their classroom behavior, suggested that the expectations the teachers held for their students' immediate and future academic performance were low. Teachers were generally reluctant to accept responsibility for the low achievement that their students maintained. They were quick to point out that the vast majority of their students came from poor families and, very frequently, from problem homes. They presented this as the primary cause of the low achievement of their students. This excuse was given almost without exception by the teachers.

When asked what percentage of their students were capable of mastering the materials presented in class, the answers varied from one-third to 60 percent. When one teacher indicated that perhaps 50 percent were capable of mastering the curriculum material presented, we asked about the other 50 percent. The teacher replied that they would be lost academically. Another teacher pointed out that most of her students could master the material if they would do their homework, but the problem was that the students would not do what they were told.

In general, the teachers demonstrated that they did not set clear and concrete achievement goals for their students. When asked about achievement goals, they generally replied that they tried to help each student as much as they could.

My observations of the teachers, their behaviors and their attitudes in low achieving classrooms suggested that commitment to high achievement was very low. The teachers indicated that they did not expect much from their students academically and reflected this in their classroom behavior.

Perhaps the most salient example of lack of commitment to higher achievement in one room was expressed by the teacher who could not control his classroom. The teacher was asked to attend meetings after school to discuss methods of improving instruction and improve overall effectiveness in his classroom. He refused to attend unless he was paid. When the district superintendent ordered him to attend he expressed the opinion that there was nothing that could be said or done to increase achievement in his classroom. He did not set high standards for academic performance witnessed by the assignments written on the board—100 addition, subtraction, multiplication and division facts daily. He said they can't do math until they know the facts. This teacher did not spend any time in the classroom interacting with his students academically—the only interaction was commands to obey which the children basically ignored. In general, the other teachers did not spend a great deal of time in the classroom interacting with their students. They did not demonstrate much resourcefulness in the classroom, and they did not feel that the majority of their students were capable of high achievement. These factors, and others led me to conclude that commitment to higher achievement in these rooms was low.

In contrasting the observed differences in the factors that appear to have been related to academic climate, this study could be misconstrued as suggesting that higher achieving rooms were perfect examples of how it should be—and lower rooms how classrooms should not be. This is not the case. Perhaps the most important finding is that the teachers in the higher achieving rooms demonstrate attitudes and behaviors that were conducive to higher achievement, and the lower achieving classrooms did not.

The presentation and discussion of those factors that appear to have been related to the achievement levels maintained in the classrooms observed is not intended to suggest that simply incorporating one of these factors will cause an increase in achievement. These factors appear to have been highly interrelated and shared one common factor—teachers who believed that their students could achieve and took responsibility for that achievement. Higher achievement became a reality; the students produced.

BIBLIOGRAPHY

Brophy, J., Classroom organization and management. *Elementary School Journal,* 1983, 265–285.

Brophy, J. and Good, T., *Teacher-student relationships: Causes and consequences.* New York: Holt, Rinehart, and Winston, 1979.

Faulk, H., Desegregation in McKeesport. *Integrated Education,* 1972, 10, 35–48.

Feshbach, N., Student teacher preferences for students varying in personality characteristics. *Journal of Educational Psychology,* 1969, 60, 126–132.

Goodlad, J., *A Place Called School.* New York: McGraw Hill, 1984.

Green, R., Investing in youth: an approach to discipline in urban schools. *Journal of Educational Research,* 1975, 59, 36–39.

Johnson, J., Low income children and their teachers. *Far West Laboratory for Education Research and Development.* November, 1973.

Kron, K. and Faber, C., How does the teacher cope with culture shock? *Clearing House,* 1973, 47, 506–509.

Niemeyer, J., *The Inner City Teacher.* New York: Charles E. Merrill, 1966.

Orfield, G., How to make desegregation work. *Law and Contemporary Problems,* 1975, 39, 314–340.

Peretti, F. and Swenson, K., Teachers' attitudes and interacial discipline problems. *Illinois School Journal,* 1975, 55, 49–55.

Purkey, S. and Smith, M., Effective schools. *The Elementary School Journal,* 1983, 427–437.

Rist, R., Student social class and teacher expectations: the self-fulfilling prophecy in ghetto education. *Harvard Educational Review,* 1970, 40, 411–451.

Stebbins, R., The meaning of disorderly behavior, *Sociology of Education,* 1970, 44, 217–236.

Uredevor, L., The effects of desegregation upon school discipline. *Journal of Secondary Education,* 1967, 42, 91–97.

Chapter 12

THE VIDEO CHILD—AT RISK
AND LEARNING THEORY

SISTER FRANCES RYAN

INTRODUCTION

A few decades ago, Marshall McLuhan (1967) caught well the scene of the 1990s when he said, "The medium is the message." Video America is a reality. Carolyn Marvin, an associate professor of communications at Annenberg School, cautions that after the invention of the telephone in 1876, people were worried about "telephone addicts" and that myths conveying "horror stories" were not helpful. Rather, in video America there is a need to develop new roles and rules to integrate and use new medium forms (Collins, 1988).

This chapter looks at how the video child-at-risk is affected in one's learning style within the video environment and the need in education to arrive at better forms of adaptation to the question: What are some roles and rules for the child's learning style in a video environment?

STATEMENT OF THE PROBLEM

Mr. Joseph is an investment counselor for Shearson-Lehman-Hutton. He spends ten hours a day consulting the green screen of his Quatrain, the blue monitor of his IBM XT and the green display of his Bond Brain. While Mr. Joseph is on his way home, he rents a movie. Before slipping it into his Panasonic videocassette recorder, he might play a Nintendo video game with his six-year-old son, Ricky. Mr. Joseph's tennis game has improved considerably since he began using his Sony® video camera to monitor his serve.

For Mr. Joseph's son, Ricky, the video environment becomes the medium. As more screens are at play, school, home and his parents' work, Ricky lives at a time where he experiences a turning point in the medium of his learning environment. "The first generation of children grew up being entertained by video, but the second generation is being taught by video" (Collins, 1988, p. 13).

David Kearns (1988), chairman of the Xerox Corporation, commenting on the growing relationships between business and schools, points out that, educationally, there are some major concerns. "Well over one-fourth of today's school children are black or Hispanic and about one-third of them never make it to graduation day. They're being failed by a system that's not responsive to their needs" (p. 567). It is "sobering to note that America's public schools graduate 700,000 functionally illiterate children every year and that 700,000 more drop out" (p. 566).

Mr. Kearns' concern is that these students are the core of the labor pool in the 1990s.

Is there a relationship between the intensified video environment and the learning deficiencies resulting in illiteracy and school dropout situations? Is there a lack of adaptation to newer forms of learning and a need for restructuring learning environments?

REVIEW OF FIELD STUDIES ON VIDEO CHILDREN

Chart I

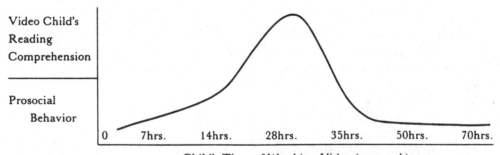

Child's Time of Watching Video (per week)

Studies (Morgan and Gross, 1982; Rice, 1988) suggest that educational programs such as "Sesame Street" and formats such as "Mr. Rogers' Neighborhood," correlated with video watching within 14–28 hours a week, can enhance the learning experience for the video child. Rice (1986) shows how reading comprehension and language development is increased with his studies on preschool-kindergarten children. Morgan and Gross (1982) use the term "cultivation" being enhanced with the child in reading comprehension watching a time-specific amount of video. Pearl, Bauthelet and Lazar (1982) observed that children evidence better prosocial learning (for example, cooperativeness and sharing) under specific conditions of watching video (Singer and Singer, 1983).

However, over the 35–40-hour intervals of watching video, reading comprehension scores decline (Morgan and Gross, 1982). Several studies have also shown a high correlation between violent television shows and subsequent aggression that occurs in the video child-at-risk (Eron, 1982; Milansky et al., 1982). The studies at Yale University show that excessive video watching by children influences a lessening of language usage, poor imagination, less waiting ability and motoric restlessness, less communication in the family and social groups and poor school adjustment (Singer and Singer, 1983).

Excess video program watching by children, particularly commercials, influence the way they learn in cognitive development. The University of Kansas studies (Wright and Huston, 1983) show it promotes more passive learning rather than active learning by the child. It fosters low-level cognitive processing and takes away time and energy from more creative or intellectually stimulating activities (Postman, 1979; Winn, 1977). Salomon (1981) has demonstrated that video does not challenge the child to as strong an amount of invested mental effort (AIME) as in reading comprehension.

Is there, then, a possibility that the video child-at-risk is unable to adapt to our present learning styles demanded in education? Educators point to a growing characteristic in the classroom, the bored child. Teachers verbalize the need to be "entertainers" in the classroom, and "teacher burnout" continues in increasing numbers. Conversely, Elkind (1984) in *The Hurried Child* suggests at the other part of the spectrum the rigid, overachieving child showing high stress characteristics. This overachieving video child-at-risk is unable to structure his/her own time but is highly dependent on outside structure with little room for flexibility. These children are not able to fill their free time and have an intolerance for daily activities that are not chock full of sight and sound (Kiebey, 1988).

THE PROPHECY OF MARSHALL MCLUHAN

While McLuhan (1963) is known for his concept of the "global village," McLuhan also presented his theory of communication and culture that suggest the "print society" is going out and the "visual arts society" is growing in numbers.

From prehistoric times to 1451, the "Tribal Village" era characterized communication by face-to-face contact. Media were nonexistent. In face-to-face contact, all the senses were used and people were more group-oriented. Nonlinear thinking with nonrational, nonsequential qualities conveyed communication of information. The trades were concerned with home-manufactured articles, and generally, in occupations, people were crafts-people.

In 1451, the Guttenberg Bible was printed and ushered in the "print-oriented society." There was contact with other lives through reading and the printed media. Because of print, there was an emphasis on vision and the use of one sense, either visual or auditory in nature. Information was rational and sequential in nature. People were more inner-directed and self-oriented in their life-styles. The industrial era produced assembly lines and automation.

In the late twentieth century, the "neotribal society" emerged through the invention of electronic media and personal contact through technology (The Global Village). Because technology uses a multisensual approach, visual, auditory, and in intensified affective situations, kinesthetic forms, the person is highly engaged in the medium. The rapidity of images gives rational-nonrational content promoting nonlinear thinking and a tolerance for nonsequential information. In the visual arts-neotribal society, people are interactive and dependent on computer automation. McLuhan predicts that although we seem to be in a stage of passivity towards automation, the neotribal society will eventually have people as "inventors" who will be able to manipulate and master active forms of engagement and interaction through technology.

The contrast of the print society with the use of one sense in learning styles, as, for example, visual sense in reading or auditory sense in the lecture style, compared to the multisensual approach in technology, seems to have a major implication for why the video child learns differently today. There are major shifts in cognitive structures between the conditioning of media watching for over ten hours a week in preschool years to the print society dominated orientation of the average school in its expected learning styles.

Many children in lower SES families who have excessive viewing habits are at risk for school situations. In its worse form, we have children who are technological isolates. Even children in higher SES families are unable to adapt to current learning styles and often are labelled "learning disabled" children. Singer and Singer (1983) looked at the correlation of SES, reading comprehension and television variables and concluded that excessive television viewing lessens reading comprehension. Much more research is needed in this area.

THE LEARNING THEORY SHIFT

David Perkins (1986) of Harvard University cites three central concerns in learning theory regarding (a) *acquisition,* (b) *internalization* and (c) *transfer.* Acquisition calls for attention, recognition and rehearsal. Looking at an average television show, one can discern certain characteristics. The average attention span to a commercial time is about seven to eight minutes. Then one to two minutes are spent in shifts of thirty-second commercials with rapid pace, constant intercutting, interruptions and shifts in sound level (Singer and Singer, 1983). Using a multisensual modality approach, the video child acquires information for about eight minutes before the abrupt shift in sequencing material begins with commercials. The acquisition time in the classroom for the video child-at-risk remains the same in the time-conditioning process; however, the teacher does not "shift" for commercials and the video child-at-risk is unable to adapt to this new learning pattern.

Internalization processes are also influenced by the use of rational-nonrational material in media. Problem solving already worked out in the media format promotes a passive rather than interactive approach in the use of mental effort (Salomon, 1981). The video child-at-risk becomes dependent on technology as a way to learn and think, with passivity being a predominant characteristic of the child's learning patterns. Higher sequencing of thought and reflective, abstract powers are not challenged. The emergence of "critical thinking skills" (Marzono and Arredondo, 1986; Swartz, 1986) as a growing trend in curriculum shows an innovative answer to a growing need in students.

Transfer and elaboration problems are often met with difficulty because of poor imagination skills and lack of communication seen with the video child-at-risk. Guided imagery exercises have grown in use to promote the use of imagination.

The video child-at-risk shows two chief learning profiles: (1) *the bored, disinterested learner* and (2) *the overachieving rigid learner.*

THE BORED, DISINTERESTED LEARNER

Sheila Ribordy, professor of clinical psychology at DePaul University, has developed the following profile of the bored, disinterested learning style of the video child-at-risk:

This child has short attention span, often with normal to superior intelligence. There is an underachievement pattern compared to the child's potential.

Preoccupied, in a dreamworld, the child is restless and easily distractible. In learning style, she or he has difficulty with problem-solving situations, is disorganized and does not use reflective skills with abstract concepts. The child is characterized by being present-oriented with poor delay of gratification and is impulsive in making decisions. Thus, she or he does not plan ahead, requires limits and won't take responsibility for self. The video child-at-risk is often bored and disinterested unless there is an intense situation requiring use of all the senses and there is a rapidity of images. Their characteristics range from being socially immature and isolated with poor imagination and creativity. Self-initiating projects and responsibility for self are difficult.

THE OVERACHIEVING, RIGID LEARNER

Ribordy (1988) describes the overachieving, rigid learner style from the video child-at-risk as being anxious, intense, obsessive in thought patterns, compulsive in behavior with many rituals in his or her daily routine. The overachiever is rigid and organized but very dependent on the routine in school being predictable, and loves structure. This child has a low tolerance for ambiguity, with poor abstraction skills. Trial-and-error problem-solving skills are preferred. Socially, the overachieving learner is uncomfortable and has a poor sense of humor. This child has unrealistically high expectations of self and seems to be under constant pressure. She or he has an excessive need for reassurance and is worried about future events. Consequently, the overachiever has somatic complaints such as stomachaches, headaches, frequent colds, even colitis or ulcers. Tasks that require imagination and creativity can be difficult for this learner.

APPROACHES WORKING WITH
THE VIDEO CHILD–AT–RISK

The purpose of strategies is to assist the child to become a master of technology, not a passive, conditioned victim of excessive video-watching patterns. Future technology promises more interactive opportunity for children, such as video discs and programs giving a sequence of choices and allowing the child to follow those choices to their consequences. Even with these innovations, the child needs to learn to achieve a balance in one's life-style in the use of video technology.

APPROACHES WITH THE PARENTS

With the use of parent conferences and PTA meetings, dialogue about the hours the child views video can be discussed. Jason (1985) has used behavioral modification and taken reinforcers to reduce the hours of video viewing with the child and the use of alternative entertainment activities such as sports, music and hobbies.

The use of specific questions and concrete examples help the parents. Parents seem motivated when they have a rationale to follow in relating to the video child-at-risk. First, it is helpful to discuss the parents' habits at video-watching activities. Is the television, computer, VCR, frequently used in the home? Regarding the child, how many hours of TV, computer and video games does your child experience in the day? What time does the child go to bed with or without TV? Such questions can pinpoint the issues.

The Illinois Parents-Teachers Association (1983) has initiated a statewide project called "Television: Meeting the Challenge: The Illinois PTA Project on TV Viewing Skills." This program helps parents select programs carefully and assists the child to understand by parental reflections the difference between real life and make-believe, television programming and the printed word, and commercials and the subliminal, hidden message. In this program, children are taught by their parents the difference in style between drama, news, public affairs and comedies. A sense of "critiquing the message" helps the child to be more interactive with media. Finally, curtailing the hours and knowing when to turn television off gives the child more alternatives in how she or he learns about the world.

Parents can be very helpful in assisting the video child-at-risk to become more tolerant of quiet times; the child enjoys quietness, starting with short fifteen- to thirty-minute periods. Monitoring homework in a quiet place, rewarded by alternative entertainment activities afterwards, teaches the child about inner choices that can be rewarding and balances the child's time activities. The use of games can be used to lengthen attention span and to help focus the child on an activity. Games with the parents also promote interactions and communication versus passive television-viewing patterns. Family communication patterns change as well as the patterns of the excessive video-watching child-at-risk. In lower socioeconomic status families, economical and diverse activities need to be suggested for the families. Home visits can be helpful regarding observation of family space, media habits, and alternative resources.

APPROACHES WITH THE CHILD

For the educator, the excessive video child-at-risk presents a challenge. The video child-at-risk needs time to build new habits and patterns of choices in his/her life-style. The thirty to thirty-five hours at school and homework obligations offer a rich opportunity to use new types of multisensory experiences.

The child requires interaction with the learning task to promote active learning styles. By the use of participant modeling in the relationship between the educator and volunteers in the classroom with the video child-at-risk, she or he learns new learning styles.

The use of a brief overview and "reinforcers markers" in the classroom to provide predictability enforces the active learning style and allows the video child-at-risk to be an active participant in the change process.

Accurate assessment and diagnosis is needed before an effective plan can be mapped out for the child. The method of P.O.A. can be helpful in assessment: P—Problem/Personal Issue; O—Outcome; A—Approach. In Figure 12-1, the learning functions of acquisition, internalization and transfer are illustrated to pinpoint strengths and difficulties the video child-at-risk may have in her or his learning style. Labeling the problem or social/personal issues in interactions, the educator then looks at O—Outcome. What outcome does the educator desire of the child after

ACQUISITION	INTERNALIZATION	TRANSFER
Take in data according to favorite representational system	Memorization — Recall long term/short term	Apply
(Teacher: Help with cross-representational acquisition)	Classify	Elaborate
Comprehension of data	Categorize	Dramatize
Visual System	Distinguish	Paint
Auditory System	Differentiate	Summarize
Kinesthetic System	Compare	Rewrite
Multisensual System	Evaluate	Paraphrase
	Identify	Restate
	Label	Match
	Plan	Give Examples
	Hypothesize	Locate
	Critique	Transform/Combine
	Infer	Speculate
	Modify	Value
	Invent	Synthesize
	Reversibility of Thought	
	Conservation	
	Abstraction	
	Analyze	

Figure 12-1.

the desired change in learning style? Finally, the A—approach is a specific way for the educator to promote the desired outcome in the video child-at-risk.

In Figure 12-2, various strategies are suggested in learning activities including the use of video technologies. The main purpose is not an avoidance of technology but rather the child's mastery of technology including interaction and active reflection on media. Another goal is the use of technology in combination with other alternative multisensory experiences in life.

In working with the bored student, the educator finds ways to challenge the child. Gradually lengthening the attention span and stimulating the bored student through multisensory tasks, the teacher brings the child from a conditioned response that is known to other ways of learning responses. The educator can encourage the child's decision-making powers and sense of control by giving the student choices and responsibilities regarding activities and assignments. The bored student usually is academically delayed in certain academic tasks and needs to have the larger tasks broken into separate steps. Reflective abilities can be enhanced by question and journal essays.

VISUAL STRATEGIES	AUDITORY STRATEGIES	KINESTHETIC STRATEGIES	MULTISENSUAL STRATEGIES
Charts/Graphs	Tapes	Math/Manipulatives	Nature Walks
Pictures	Records	Role Playing— historical and literary characters	Field Trips
Handouts	Lecture	Cutting	Abacus
Colored Chalk	Story Telling	Pasting	Puppetry
Chalkboard/ Board work	Music	Science Experiments	"Structured Play"
Maps	Old Radio Shows	Taking care of plants, rocks, animals, gardens	Teaching another student at chalkboard
Bulletin Boards	Spelling Bees		
VCR Cassettes	Concerts	Gym-Sports Activities	Group Projects
Flashcards	Guest Speakers	Writing on board	Television
Flannel boards	Group Participation	"Simon says . . . "	Word/Math games
Overheads	Hearing words on flashcards	Art Projects	Sand blocks/ letters
Film Strips/		Puzzles	
Comic Strips/ Cartoons	Foreign Language tape lab-centers	Aerobic Exercises	Show-n-Tell
		Relaxation Exercises	Scrabble
Television/Movies	Reading to class	Food/Cooking Projects	Science Use of Experiments
video camera	Student repetition of teacher directions	Cleaning-up Activities	
Computer/Printouts		Choreographic/Dance Activities to music	Pantomime
Video games			"Motor-Programs"
Newspapers	Speeches	Pottery-Making	Group Projects
Photographs	Socratic method (use of dialog)	Plays/Skits	Teaching flannel Board project
Letter-Writing		Finger Painting	
Journals	Mini-Surveys	Sculpture	
Create your own dictionaries			

Figure 12-2.

With the overachieving child, the teacher attempts to minimize anxiety by relaxation activities and well-timed reassurances. Through the educator's relationship, the overachieving student can be encouraged to slow down, to have fun in learning and even to survive mistakes. The child needs to develop realistic expectations. By giving clear directions, the educator minimizes ambiguity and then gradually gets the overachieving child to provide his/her own structure. Because the overachieving student is focused on academic success, the child needs to be bolstered and reinforced in social interactions and skills. The outcome of these interactions would be to reinforce independence and self-initiation.

The use of the P.O.A. method is illustrated in working with Chris, a sixth grader, who seems bored in the classroom.

One of Chris's problems seems to be in the area of acquisition because of a short attention span; Chris's strengths appear to be in kinesthetic activities and active learning activities. The outcome is to lengthen

Chris's attention span from six to seven minutes to about ten minutes. In collaboration with Chris's parents, the approach is to engage Chris in certain games that encourage longer attention span such as checkers or scrabble for linguistic use. The games also help Chris with his kinesthetic modality of learning and his gifted way of expanding his attention span. In the classroom, Chris takes particular interest in the science projects. By assignment to watering and growing potato plants and keeping a record, Chris learns to concentrate on a project that interests him and fits easily to his learning style. Chris becomes more involved through this plan, and his attention span lengthens to ten-minute activities with little difficulty.

APPROACHES WITH THE EDUCATOR

Two areas seem primarily affected by media conditioning of students. The first area is that students learn through multisensory experiences and need to be encouraged to use one sense for certain activities by the use of visual or auditory or kinesthetic strategies in the classroom. The second area relates to timing in the relationship between the educator and the students. The video child is conditioned to about a six- to eight-minute attention span, even less with younger children. Educators in their curriculum planning will need special emphasis not only on content areas but use of diverse process activities that involve children in active learning styles. Processing with certain time intervals appropriate to the age of the child, certain activities (Fig. 12-2) can incorporate a variety of experiences that helps the video child adjust to the classroom.

Diversified curriculum planning calls for creativity and focus on other styles of learning than used by the educator. For example, if the educator is usually visually dominated in her or his teaching style, use of auditory, kinesthetic or multisensory styles needs some concentration. Teaching process and timing as well as content planning in curriculum development can assist the educator in working with the media student.

SUMMARY

In summary, the relationship of the video child-at-risk and changes in how the child learns is discussed. Studies defining excessive video watching are used to show two learning styles that have emerged, namely, the bored student and the overachieving, rigid student. McLuhan's studies (1963) showing the neotribal period relying on the image society and slowly leaving the print society points to shifts in learning acquisitions. Lower SES children seem particularly vulnerable to being video children-at-risk. Lastly, strategies and approaches are discussed for the parents, children and educators in assisting the video child to become a master of technology rather than a victim of it.

REFERENCES

Bradford, J. (1979). *Human Cognition.* Belmont, CA: Wadsworth.

Collins, Glen (1988). "From a Vast Wasteland to A Brave New World" *New York Times.* March 20. 13.

Dacey, J. (1982). *Adolescents Today.* Glenview, IL: 145, Scott Foresman.

Elkind, David (1984). *The Hurried Child.* Reading; Addison-Wesley.

Eron, L.D. (1982) Parent-child interaction, television violence and aggression of children. *American Psychologist,* 37, 197–211.

Jason, L.A. (1985). Using a token-actuated timer to reduce television viewing. *Journal of Applied Behavior Analysis.* 18, 269–272.

Jason, L.A. and Rooney-Rebeck, P. (1984). Reducing excessive television viewing. *Child and Family Behavior Therapy.* 6, 61–69.

Kearns, David T. (1988). An Education Recovery Plan for America *Phi Delta Kappa.* April. 565:570.

Kirbey, R. (1988). Television Used as escape by frequent viewers Guidepost: American Association for Counseling and Development. Feb. 25, 16. *Journal of Communications* 36, No. 3.

McLuhan, Marshall (1967) *The Medium is the Message.* New York: Bantam.

Marzaro, R. and Arredondo, D. (1986). Restructuring Schools through the Teaching of Thinking Skills. *Educational Leadership.* May, 20–26.

Milausby, J.R., Kessler, R., Stipp, H., and Rubens, W.S. (1982). Television and aggression: Results of a panel study. In D. Pearl, L. Bouthilet and J. Lazar (Eds). *Television and Behavior: Ten Years of Scientific Progress and Implications for the Eighties.* (Vol. 2) Washington D.C., U.S. Government Printing Office.)

Morgan, M. and Gross, L. (1982). Television and educational achievement and aspiration. In D. Pearl, L. Bouthilet and J. Lazer (Eds.). *Television and Behavior; Ten Years of Scientific Progress and Implications for the Eighties.* (Vol. 1) Washington D.C.: U.S. Government Printing Office).

Pearl, D., Bouthilet, L. and Lazar, (Eds). (1982) *Television and Behavior: Ten Years of Scientific Progress and Implications for the Eighties.* (Vol. 1 and 2). Washington D.C.: U.S. Government Printing Office.

Perkins, D. (1986). Thinking frames. *Educational Leadership.* May 4–10.

Postman, N. (1979). *Teaching as a Conserving Activity.* New York: Delacourt.

Ribordy, S. and S. Frances Ryan (1988). Media and Learning Theory Workshop. DePaul University.

Rice, M. (1986). Television can have a positive influence on children's language development, *Phi Delta Kappa.* February, 472.

Salomon, G. (1981). *Children and the Worlds of Television.* San Francisco: Jossey-Bass.

Singer, J. and Singer, D. (1983). Psychologists look at television (Yale University). Cognitive, developmental, personality and social policy implications. *American Psychologist.* July, 826–834.

Swartz, R. (1986). Restructuring Curriculum for Critical Thinking. *Educational Leadership.* May 43–44.

Winn, M. (1977). *The Plug-In Drug.* New York: Viking.

Wright, J. and Huston, A. (1983). A matter of form: potentials of television for young viewers. *American Psychologist.* July, 835–843.

Chapter 13

AT RISK: A PEDOGENIC ILLNESS?

Gerald Wm. Foster And Sandra Pellens-Meinhard

INTRODUCTION

Out of the twenty-two states in which the SAT is the predominate college entrance exam, Oregon ranked second in 1987 (Oregon, 1988). Yet one out of every four Oregon high school students drops out. In a system as successful as Oregon's, it should be possible to reduce the number of students who drop out. They are currently proposing two solutions: (1) identifying at an early age "at-risk" youth (those with problems that lead to dropping out); and (2) helping them overcome the problems which contribute to their leaving school (Oregon, 1987).

Not that we as educators haven't been trying to act on these two solutions for a long time. In the first case we have already created every conceivable group to accommodate students with problems: learning disabilities, emotionally disturbed, physically handicapped, gifted, average ability and now a special category for *Children at Risk*. But labels, labels! Children are placed in categories like these in an attempt to help them become successful learners. In other cases, children are given labels related to socioeconomic status, racial and/or cultural background in an attempt to improve their educational status. But the question is does the labelling really help?

People are identified by labels; designer labels for clothes, career labels for work, I.Q. for intelligence, academic grades for class work, etc. But labeling children may take away their unique and individual identities, giving them a false understanding of themselves. Marilyn Ferguson claimed that "Labelling (remedial, gifted, minimally brain dysfunctional, etc.) contributes to self-fulfilling prophecy" (1980, 290). The focus is no longer on individuals but on groups and their characteristics. Thus, whatever the process or criteria for placing children into categories, labeling only sets them apart from other children.

It is important to keep in mind that in our effort to help students become successful learners, the categories or labels may have become overemphasized and the individual learner, neglected. It is also important to keep in mind that the defined categories such as learning disabilities, behavioral and emotional disorders, gifted, and remedial are based upon perceived characteristics of learners. In other words, characteristics such as achievement, I.Q., and class grades which are not inherent characteristics of children but are reflections of acceptable societal standards and norms are used to group students. Normalcy for intelligence and behavior are defined, therefore, according to a range of criteria that characterizes a "best fit" for our educational system and not for the individual student.

A better alternative might be to describe students in terms of their class performances vs. their ability to develop understanding. Student responses to teachers at different *levels* of understanding will, of course, be different, producing a normal variety instead of an abnormal homogeneity.

A NEW APPROACH TO GROUPING STUDENTS

If we match differences in students' learning with differences in teachers' instructions, we may be able to begin to explain the cause for some "at-risk" situations. We can describe students in terms of these two dimensions and their reaction to different instructional techniques. First, using a traditional attribute of student growth—student performance measures or generally what is referred to as achievement—we find students' success described by hard work, high recall test scores, frequent participation, homework completion, careful and neat work, and so forth. Its index is most often grades.

Now consider the other attribute describing students—understanding. Because some students understand more deeply than others, many topics require capabilities students simply don't have. For these students much of the work is produced mechanically and algorithmically, without any understanding of "why." All of us can probably think back on our own school experiences and recall topics in which we were successful according to the teacher's terms, but failures in developing any understanding. We know the feeling of fear (or at least uneasiness) at being asked just the right question that would expose our nonunderstanding since evaluation of understanding generally displays the student's methods and organization of content and not a memorized answer.

Instruction which focuses on conceptual understanding attempts to dissociate the student's understanding from imitative and memory behavior by relying on using what the student can initiate rather than reproduce. Evaluation takes forms which help students see the depth of their own understanding so they can focus on their internal capabilities rather than external instruction. Other sources used to determine understanding include independent work, initiation of participation, projects, group work, reasoning in a topic, and so forth. The measurement index most often used is a developmental scale of comprehension.

If we place the two attributes of successful achievement and understanding together in a logical multiplication, we will produce a table which describes various categories of today's students. With a focus on performance, there are two types of students: (1) those who achieve and who are rewarded with high grades and (2) those who are failures because of their lack of success or interest in meeting daily work assignments and performance requirements on tests. As for student capability to understand, we also have two types: (1) those who successfully understand (comprehend the content logic of what is being taught) and (2) those who do not. We then have four possible types of students due to the interaction of achievement (performance success) and understanding (comprehension success).

If these four types really exist then we should be able to describe students in each cell. We find in the first cell of Figure 13-1 (reading left to right, top to bottom), the understanders who do their work and achieve high grades and rewards. They are the students to whom we usually refer to when we say that some students learn in spite of poor teaching.

Cell two describes students who understand reasonably well but have a history of not being rewarded by the normal educational system. They make up a sizable portion of the students we label "at risk" and who actually do drop out.

The third cell describes students who achieve but do not really understand. These students work hard and by and large are rewarded for their superficial understanding by good grades. But even in awarding them good grades, their teachers often feel a concern that they don't really comprehend; they just "play the game" well.

Finally, in the last cell we find the students who have weak understand-

ACHIEVEMENT

	High	Low
High	Hard worker, successful on comprehension and performance (cell 1)	Turned off, failure based or boredom (cell 2)
UNDERSTANDING **Low**	Hard worker, success based on memorized algorithmic performance (cell 3)	Special Education, failure based, or lack of comprehension and performance (cell 4)

Figure 13-1. Achievement Versus Understanding in Students.

ing and achieve poorly. They are the dropouts and special education students whose development is not aided by the current system and who have ceased to care about school.

ROLE OF THE AFFECTIVE IN LEARNING

In addition, all children can be at risk because of impositions put upon them by society, economics, cultural, physical and educational conditions of the environment. Once we begin to see the impact adults have on the emotional as well as the intellectual development of children, especially in the school setting, we can begin to see why each student has a chance of being put at risk.

As much as learning seems under the control of adults, it is the development of the affective in the child that is the most tightly controlled by adults. And a teacher is one of those adults. In school, motivation (or lack thereof) is often cited as a major factor in getting students to learn. Yet we act as if that motivation to learn or resist learning isn't found in the affective component of knowing. We praise behavior that helps a child get the right answer rather than encouraging creativity. Following procedures and time schedules are more important than the individual needs of children. Alice Miller wrote, "It is among the commonplace of education that we often first cut off the living root and then try to replace its natural functions by artificial means. Thus we suppress the child's curiosity. For example, there are questions one should not ask, and then when he lacks a natural interest in learning he is offered special coaching for his scholastic difficulties" (1981, 75).

Piaget (1981) believed there is a "constant and dialectic interaction between affectivity and intelligence" (p. 25). In other words, a child's motivation to learn and develop intellectually depends upon the desire to understand his/her environment. His hypothesis states that "affectivity can cause acceleration and retardation in the development of intelligence, that it can disturb intellectual functioning and modify its content" (p. 43). Thus, it is possible that children who are labeled as emotionally disturbed, learning disabled, or behaviorly disturbed acquire these behaviors because their affective development has been blocked by societal, familial, and/or school interventions.

Marilyn Ferguson stated, "Worse yet, not only is the mind broken, but too often, so is the spirit. Allopathic teaching produces the equivalent of iatrogenic, or 'doctor-caused,' illness . . . teacher-caused learning disabilities. We might call these pedogenic illnesses. The child who may have come to school intact, with budding courage to risk and explore, finds stress enough to permanently diminish that adventure" (p. 283). We as teachers can prevent pedogenic illnesses (Ferguson, 1980) by helping students see themselves for what they know and understand about their own feelings as well as about the world around them. In other words, we act as mirrors so that they can reflect upon new thoughts and ideas that will continually reshape their own feelings and understandings. If students are not allowed to explore (at the very least in an educational setting) their own feelings and thoughts, they can become children at risk.

Teachers who do not have an understanding of their role in relation to the child as a learner put students at risk. In spite of the vast array of teaching methods, there is little awareness of the factor or factors that separate teachers who know how to develop understanding in children through appropriate cognitive and affective methods from those who do not.

ROLE OF AFFECTIVE TEACHING

A key question in teacher development has to do with how teachers think about teaching. How is it that some teachers distort inquiry methods to didactic ones while some create dialectical (student structured) teaching situations out of cookbook approaches? Is it a simple matter of the quantity of experiences which would lead to a "more is going to produce better" response; or, is it a matter of a shift in the quality of thinking which would lead to an "understanding makes the difference" response?

Educators need to realize that for the majority of teachers, adopting a student-structured approach (understanding makes the difference) may be very difficult not because it simply requires more work in the classroom, but because it requires a qualitatively different conceptualization of teaching. What teachers think about teaching affects how they teach. Otherwise, how can they teach a student-structured classroom the same way they teach a textbook-structured program? Teaching appears to have a developmental factor which would explain the differences in how and what is being taught. If that is so, the crucial question then becomes what would the development look like and how could we analyze teaching for its presence?

Shavelson and Stern (1981) have done extensive review of the literature to assess what research says about teachers' pedagogical thoughts, judgements, decisions and behavior. Research on interactive teaching reveals that teachers have mental scripts that routinize teaching behaviors.

> In sum, teachers' main concern during interactive teaching is to maintain the flow of activity. To interrupt this flow to reflect on an alternative and consider the possibility of changing a routine drastically increases the information processing demands on the teacher and increases the probability of classroom management problems (p. 484).

Thus without some conceptualization of what interactive teaching is and why an active student-structured program based on promoting students' thinking is more beneficial than the traditional textbook approach, teachers are likely to use prior mental scripts that are incompatible with student-structured teaching. In spite of the extensive review of Shavelson and Stearn, there is little evidence to suggest that teachers have the know how or understanding to take risks required to use alternative behaviors compatible with different learning modes.

A more recent study by Prawat (1985) revealed that elementary teachers place an inordinately high priority on affective concerns. For example, forty teachers in the sample were asked the following question, "Of the various things you do as a teacher which do you consider to be the most important?" Their responses related to having positive interactions with students, feeling good about *one's* self (not about the students' self), and students doing neat work.

Beyond emphasizing the affective domain, the most common cognitive response was simple basic skill acquisition. "Twice as many teachers responded to the questions in a predominately affective as opposed to cognitive fashion" (p. 592). Is it no wonder then, that promoting understanding and conceptual comprehension in student-structured classrooms may make no sense and, in fact, may seem reprehensible to classroom teachers?

SCHEMES OF TEACHING

Using this study and Shavelson and Stearn's review, a pattern begins to emerge. One might surmise that the majority of teachers (both elementary and secondary) have an unconscious basic schema of teaching rather than a conceptual or conscious understanding of teaching. This contention is supported by the following evidence:

(1) Laboratory and classroom studies indicate that when students are grouped or treated like a whole class, teachers make pedagogical decisions, especially planning decisions, on the basis of the group or whole class and not on the active needs of the individual student (Shavelson and Stern, 1981, p. 475).

(2) The average common script used by teachers during interactive teaching is one of structuring, soliciting, responding, and reacting, where teachers ask questions and students respond (Shavelson and Stern, 1981, p. 484).

(3) The majority of responses falling into the cognitive category referred to promoting basic skills acquisition and the learning of specific objectives. (Prawat, 1985, p. 592).

From this summary, it would appear that teaching is a static, routinized activity bounded by feeling, beliefs and perceptions about what students need to know. Indeed, the key here seems to be the unconscious logic or belief system which constitutes "what the student needs to know." Student-structured teaching requires a qualitatively different view of learning and the role of the teacher in the classroom. Thus a search must be made for evidence of qualitative shifts in teacher thinking compatible to interactive teaching and the means necessary to help teachers make those shifts.

Lampert (1984) described a project that attempted to train teachers to recognize intuitive knowledge in children as opposed to formal knowledge taught in schools. Through anecdotal incidents she discovered that knowledge is conveyed to students in ways which is both socially useful and meaningful to the teacher herself... What is most striking about the thinking of the M.I.T. project teachers is that although they analyzed their work into a set of forced choices, they did not seem to have to make such choices in their practice... They did not have an analytic language for reflecting on their practice to counter the contradictory themes that developed in their thinking about intuitive and formal knowledge (p. 13).

This study is more revealing about teacher thinking than Prawat's study because Lampert recognized the relationships in the teacher's thought patterns and behaviors. She admitted that the project did not go far enough in examining "their ways of thinking about teaching." Taking teacher stories as evidence for their thinking about *why* they do *what* they do means developing new ideas about both how to analyze what teaching is and how to measure it.

We believe Piaget's findings can provide insight into how teachers develop understanding about teaching. Before we apply his theory to teaching, it might be useful to review the development of knowledge.

THE DEVELOPMENT OF COMPREHENSION

Piaget identified four different levels of knowledge formation. The first level is the sensorimotor stage (0–3 years) in which a child develops coordination of physical actions; the second, identified as the preoperational stage (3–5 years), is the stage at which a child begins to interpret his/her world through symbolism and language development. The third stage, concrete operational (age 5–12), finds the child beginning to internalize his/her actions upon concrete objects into the formation of mental structures. The final level (formal operational stage of 12 +), is characterized by the development of mental structures abstracted from other mental structures.

Concept development can be typified by these different stages. In the preoperational stage, knowledge is dependent on the raw perceptions of the individual. Knowledge is based upon how an object or an idea is viewed unrelated to the logic which interrelates empirical experiences. In other words a tree "grows in size" as the person approaches it from a far distance. Knowledge changes as events change. Thoughts and ideas are regulated by external influences.

The next stage in the development of a concept is relating actions to logic. Reality is structured through acting upon objects and abstracting logical relationships. This is the beginning of true concept formation. Using the same example, the person knows that logic dictates a tree height stays constant even though perception says it changes. A person's thoughts have an internal regulation because of the development of mental structures.

In the final stages of concept development, the concept may be enriched by its abstraction from general mental structures rather than abstractions from specific concrete experiences. Thus, concepts can be derived from other concepts and various possibilities for a solution can be related. Using the same example of the tree, knowing that any object's size does not depend upon distance from an object can be related to thoughts that are no longer tied to specific experience or examples.

THE DEVELOPMENT OF TEACHING

Teaching is a concept. More particularly, teaching and how it relates to individual disciplines is also a concept. Understanding the logic on which successful teaching is based is no different than understanding the logic on which the understanding of spatial relationships (geometry) is based. In addition, people can be at different levels of understanding a concept whether that concept is geometry or teaching. Thus it is possible that teachers will be at different levels of conceptualizing teaching even though they may have had the same methods training and are using the same curriculum material. Not only do teachers have to conceptualize different aspect of the curriculum, but they also must conceptualize their role in the classroom, how children learn, and how evaluation of learning must proceed. Meinhard (1986, a & b) has used Piaget's theory of intellectual development to conceptualize teaching development in hierarchial stages. Based on how teachers understand knowledge, he described the act of delivering that knowledge (teaching) by the same logical relationships that typify Piaget's model.

By using Piaget's equilibration model of activity to reconstitute teachers' increasingly precise and integrated conceptions of knowledge, Meinhard related the structural components as the teachers construct them, and begins their coordination and incorporation into an increasingly comprehensive conception of knowledge. The components whose contributions a teacher must account for are the (1) subject (student), (2) object (content) and (3) development of understanding.

A NEW APPROACH TO GROUPING TEACHERS

Initially it is apparently an awareness of the observables that forms the most primitive attempts at instruction (preoperational stage), followed by a conceptualization of the logic of the coordinations between the subject and object (concrete operational stage), which finally culminates in the constructive mechanisms of equilibration which account for the development of the subject/object relationship (formal operational stage). A synopsis of Meinhard's stages follows:

Stage 1: Static Notions and Procedural Teaching

Teachers' ideas of knowledge begin with the primacy of observables as the source of knowledge for students. Conceptions of assimilation are extremely vague and undifferentiated at this stage. The diffuse phenomenalistic and impressionistic notions of behavior and knowledge make it appear that there is no subject and no active assimilation mechanism. Without awareness of transformations in knowledge, learning appears as data that is moved from the object to the student, stored, and then used to produce behavior. Hence there is a characteristic one-way relationship [Object→Subject] between the student and the environment in teachers' explanations at this level. The tabula rasa notion causes the subject to disappear making knowledge and behavior disconnected and independent.

Teaching at Stage 1 is procedural because of its fundamental emphasis on knowledge as knowing how to do something or the corresponding emphasis on the transmission of facts and names. With only functional structures constituting their understanding, teaching is only factual knowledge needed to act in the world and using algorithms to get answers. These teachers look to a source of authority to know what to teach and so remain content with arbitrary "scope and sequence" assertions of textbooks. Since the passive learner is necessary for the reception phase of learning, classroom management of behavior focuses on controlling and eliminating activity. There is no understanding of development in the learner. Practice is used to reinforce what was taught or transmitted. With no ability to see logical relationships in activity, assessment is based in observable compliance to procedure. Learning is simply a change in outward behavior no matter how trite.

Stage 2: Dialectial Understanding and Conceptual Teaching

Operational thought, in contrast to preoperational thinking in Stage 1, is typified by its shift to rational systems. When reasoning of the teacher develops from the one-way functional structure of Stage 1 to close itself by grouping together reversible transformations, it forms a stable structure useful to the teacher in coordinating teaching behaviors with student learning. For the teacher, the subject and object now become true reciprocals in an equilibrium relationship with mutual effects on each other (Subject → Object). No longer does the student arise secondarily as an outcome of experience, but the capabilities of the student determine the nature of the selection and interpretation of the educational stimulus.

Student attention is no longer a passive reception but the outward contact of an internal set of coordinations. When teachers become aware of these patterns to behavior, they will become aware of thoughtful reasoning and reflection in their students. A relativism emerges that not only explains why the same words can have different meanings to different students, but also explains the shift in teaching to a cooperative teacher/student partnership in the exploration of subject matter. Instead of telling students what to think, the conceptual teacher realizes that only by creating situations in which students display their ignorance on the larger conceptual organizing schemes of subject matter, can they set about planning a curriculum that will assist and support the individual student in making sense out of the "facts" of the subject matter, lowering the "at-risk" climate of the classroom. Likewise, evaluation at Stage 2 focuses on student understanding rather than on a behavioral compliance or simple answer production.

Stage 3: Developmental Understanding and Explanatory Teaching

Stage 3 teachers' understanding of the presence of an assimilatory structure enriches their ability to structurally specify the coordinations of students' cognitive activity with a qualitatively new explanatory structure— that of development. With the ability to specify the development of various logic comes the realization that they can be ordered. Following this comes teachers' notions of the internal change mechanisms, a conception of growth and development which is not only a seriation of stages, but which also encompasses a conception of inclusion of predecessor to successor stages:

(SUBJECT——OBJECT) < (Subject——Object) < (subject——object).

Since learning is now assimilation at work, stage 3 teachers enrich the previous conceptualization of methods of learning and understanding to a conceptualization of the development of those methods which make human learning possible in the first place.

At Stage 3, teachers focus on the assimilations of students as the tool of development—the notion of learning to learn. It is these teachers who are most likely to spark life-long learning attitudes and problem-solving procedures in their students. Attention is on qualitative changes in students' thinking rather than on what was learned. Teaching emphasizes student initiative and reflective thought as fundamental methods of inquiry. By developing the learner's ability for independent investigation, teaching emphasis on inquiry also produces the independent learner. With the disappearance of overt teaching, the oversight, encouragement, and questioning of Stage 3 teachers include a concern for staying out of the way of the learner. Evaluation not only takes into account the presence of a logical system but also the maturing of that system over the educational experience (See Fig. 13-2).

Is there evidence for these levels of teaching development? One way to find out is to collect data on what teachers think about teaching. Piaget used interviews and anecdotal data to interpret mental development of children on specific concepts. Through similar techniques, teachers should be capable of producing interviews which would reveal the stage of their development in teaching. In fact, Lampert (1984) recently supported the importance of gathering anecdotal incidences from teachers to find out what they are thinking.

While there are numerous ways to collect these data, one example would be to find out how a teacher conceptualized teaching by asking the following questions: (1) what is your curricular objective; (2) what teaching method would you use; (3) what would students do; and (4) what will the student be learning? Data could also be collected from pre- and in-service teachers on a series of reflections that record their thoughts on particular issues related to teaching.

Data from situations described above were gathered from teachers who matriculated through pre- and in-service teaching methods courses. Participants were asked to write down any thoughts that occurred during their time spent in class (called reflections). Data were also drawn from a variety of other sources such as methods texts, an Association for Super-

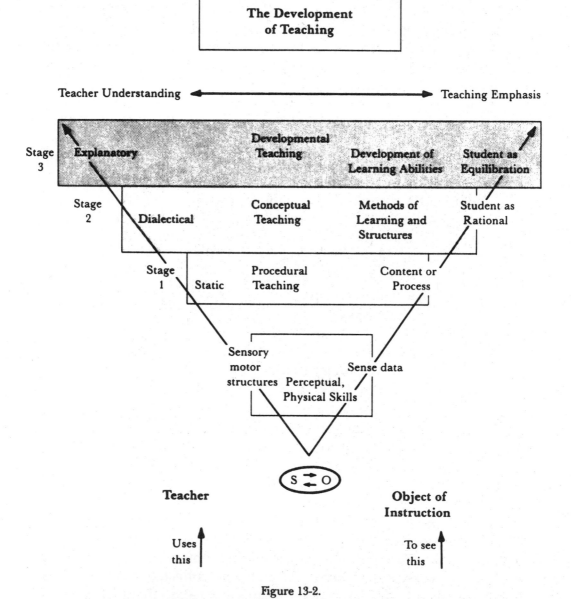

Figure 13-2.

vision and Curriculum Development (ASCD) questionnaire, and journal articles.

The easiest illustrations of the three levels are the following examples of actual teacher comments given during a science in-service program:

Teacher #1: "Tell me what I should tell my students about bubbles."

Teacher #2: "When you think concepts it is easy to design activities compared to thinking facts."

Teacher #3: "When I work with students I try to understand how or what a student is thinking as he/she acts upon the objects in a science activity."

In the first example the teacher has accepted the charge of teaching process science but is focused upon the facts her students need to know about bubbles. In other words, she is thinking of definite outcomes from activities and how she can transmit those outcomes. In example #2 the teacher appears to be aware of the logic necessary to relate concepts to one another rather than simply to teach isolated facts. She is tuned into a total picture of "bubbles" and sees different possibilities for the activities and her students. In the last example, the teacher is no longer concerned about science facts or even concepts but what learning or development is occurring with her students (and concerned, therefore, in the richest sense with the comprehension of facts and concepts).

Given additional examples from classroom teachers and other sources, the pattern of development illustrated above becomes more evident. It may be helpful to keep in mind certain words from Meinhard's model that characterize each stage. In Stage 1 you will find words such as train, facts, tell, cover the content and behavioral objectives. At Stage 2, teachers are more likely to use language that includes comprehend, construct, point-of-view, and affect. The Stage 3 teacher will exhibit language that focuses on learning to learn, development, increasing capabilities, and initiation.

Stage 1

Multiplication facts are necessary! Even if they are taught by drill and rote memory.

All children can be taught and their behavior can be managed. Lower performing children need to be taught at a faster-than-average rate, not at the same or a slower rate; and programs designed to teach them need to be more highly structured, not less.

Stage 2

I think a teacher needs to learn when to give more directions and when to leave it up to the learner.

I am a textbook basher—I became more involved in my course,

probably in exact proportion to my enthusiasm for the materials I had chosen to use. I also became more involved with my students. I established a situation where they needed me more for exposition and where we all had to do interpretive work together. Happily, I found that students enjoyed the more demanding materials that had replaced the textbooks they had used as crutches on the road to learning—But (giving up textbooks) means giving up multiple answer tests for essay exams.

Stage 3

The primary purpose of classroom materials and activities should be to provide opportunities for the students to construct operational structures rather than for mere memorization of facts. Activities should have many different entering points, so that a child can begin an activity at a level consistent with his/her intellectual development. Activities should be open-ended; there should be no preset ending points or outcomes. Students should find and report their own results.

The principal goal of education is to create people who are capable of doing new things, not simply repeating what other generations have done—people who are creative, inventive and discoverers. The second goal of education is to form minds that can be critical, can verify, and not accept everything they are offered.

In comparing the above examples, it becomes obvious that a teacher at Stage 1 also thinks in terms of isolated events. Ideas and events are connected or related in a linear fashion. Solutions and conclusions to problems are simplified to generalized procedures that all students should know regardless of their capabilities. Answers are seen as either black or white and final. As you move through the examples of the different levels to Stage 3, it becomes apparent that teachers at this level think in terms of "everything related to everything." Solutions and conclusions to educational problems are no longer simplified and final but complex and ever changing. The Stage 3 teacher does not feel as though he/she has arrived at the answers to education but takes risks to formulate and try out new ideas. They support students in taking the same risks which reduces their chance of being at risk. Thus, we can say that a Stage 1 teacher is more likely to create an environment that produces at-risk children than a Stage 3 teacher because of the emphasis upon performance and achievement rather than individualized growth and development.

In the introduction, we wrote about two components to the "at-risk" problem. One had to do with identifying at-risk students early enough, and the other had to do with helping them overcome the problems that contribute to their leaving school. Granted, there are many problems that occur outside of the school setting which create pressures for dropping out. But educators themselves, in the way they have arranged their classroom and in the way they teach, may be making a major contribution to the problem.

Julia Thomason (1984) talked about the school as zoo and stated, "School keepers also study living conditions for their charges. Often, however, they attempt to adapt the "animal" to the environment" (p. 3). We need very carefully to begin to examine how our students are surviving (the student matrix) and what it is about our own teaching practices (the stages of teaching) that forces students into unnatural survival modes.

One conclusion that we could make from the information presented here is that when students at all levels of cognitive and social abilities are forced "to adapt" to Stage 1 teaching, we will find students fitting the categories of *all* four cells of the matrix. Thus it is Stage 1 teaching that places students cognitively and socially "at risk." Because these teachers are the ones who teach from a single "transmittal" script and need to "feel good" about it, their classrooms and curricula may show too little regard for the students' needs or behaviors. As a result, these teachers "must spend inordinate amounts of time and energy in unsuccessful efforts to make the "creatures" (students) change. Is it any wonder that so many students fail to flourish or that some do not even survive?" (Thomason, 1984, 3). As we develop instruction to reflect the higher states of teaching, we will expect more and more cells to disappear. When the teacher forsakes memorization and algorithmic learning, the matrix will reflect simply two cells: those who put up defenses to having their non-comprehension revealed (often accompanied with hostile reactions), and those who can enjoy learning because their individual needs are being met.

Finally, when teaching focuses on the development of the individual with regards to a mastery of the epistemology of a discipline, all cells should disappear because all learners will be receiving the help they need at a level which is both appropriate and provocative. The negative aspect of being found to be in error will be removed since learning will be acknowledged to simply be a growth process from somewhere lesser to somewhere greater.

And eliminating the negative aspects of ignorance may be the place for most teachers to start on developing their own teaching. Classrooms need to be a place where teachers *want* to know all the mistakes, dumb questions and ignorance that their students have to offer. Teachers need to realize that it is only by knowing what their students *do not* know that they will really support and promote their cognitive development. Again, students who are encouraged to take risks are less likely to be at risk. Educators should, therefore, think about applying the "180 degree rule" of classroom interaction. When something is not going right, try turning the problem up-side-down; look at it from the student's point of view; ask yourself how would you like to learn if you were the student; and always, always think of yourself as an educator (pulling out what the student knows) as opposed to a teacher (stuffing in what you want them to know). If teachers will shift to supporting their students who display their ignorance instead of punishing them for it, our classrooms will be much healthier places and much less likely to put our students at risk of cognitively or socially opting out.

In many cases, teachers never go beyond the status quo because their ideas and behaviors do not fit the standards set for them. For examples, they are expected to cover certain material by a set date, students are expected to achieve at a certain level, and classrooms are to be quiet and orderly. In an article in the *Chicago Tribune*, Casey Banas (1987) reported in reference to a particular school in Michigan: "A teacher with a good idea often doesn't have a chance since the idea must run a lengthy administrative gauntlet of eight steps, including the principal, curriculum committee, various levels of administrators, and eventually, the school board, for approval. There is plenty of motion in the school system, but few results" (p. 7). If teachers are kept at a plateau by the status quo, then their students' opportunities will be minimal, creating an environment for teacher-caused learning disabilities. Thus, there is a cycle of at-risk teachers producing at-risk students unless they have the opportunity to grow and develop professionally. This may mean, at times, a painful analysis of who we are, how we perform, and to what extent we are part of the real problem. Only then will being part of the solution be our rightful claim as educators.

REFERENCES

Banas, C., "Teachers' Self-Esteem Deemed a Main Issue," *Chicago Tribune*, Section 1, p. 7, Dec. 28, 1987.

Ferguson, M., *The Aquarian Conspiracy: Personal and Social Transformation in the 1980's* 1980, J.P. Archer, Inc., New York.

Kahl, S., and Harms, N. C., "Project Synthesis: Purpose, Organization and Procedures." In *What Research Says to the Science Teacher, Vol. 3,* pp. 5–11. Edited by Norris C. Harms and Robert E. Yager. Washington, D.C.: National Science Teachers Association, 1981.

Lampert, M., "Teaching About Thinking and Thinking About Teaching." *Journal of Curriculum Studies,* 16 (1984): 1–18.

McNair, K., "Capturing Inflight Decisions: Thoughts While Teaching." *Educational Research Quarterly,* 3 (1978–1979): 16–25.

Meinhard, R., "Teacher Development," Unpublished manuscript, 1986.

Meinhard, R. and Pellens, S., "Development in Education: Generating its Implications," *Educational Science Forum,* 2 (July, 1986): 1–5.

Miller, A., *The Drama of the Gifted Child,* 1981, Basic Books, New York.

Oregon Department of Education, Salem, Or. 97310, 1988.

Oregon Issue Backgrounder, Department of Human Resources, Salem, Or. 97310, August, 1987.

Piaget, J., *Intelligence and Affectivity: Their Relationship During Child Development,* 1981, Annual Reviews Monograph, Palo Alto, California.

Prawat, R. S., "Affective Versus Cognitive Goal Orientations in Elementary Teachers." *American Educational Research Journal,* 22 (1985); 587–604.

Shavelson, R. J., and Stern, P., "Research on Teachers' Pedagogical Thoughts, Judgements, Decisions, and Behavior." *Review of Educational Research,* 51 (1981): 455–498.

Thomason, Julia, "Nurturing the Nature of Early Adolescents— Or a Day at the Zoo," *Middle School Journal,* vol. 25, no. 4, Aug. (1984).

Chapter 14

A GENDER AT RISK

Joan M. Lakebrink

The authors of *A Nation at Risk* declare that "All, regardless of race or class or economic status, are entitled to a fair chance and to the tools for developing their individual powers of mind and spirit to the utmost" (1983, p. 4). Perhaps the exclusion of gender in this statement means that the authors assumed that gender was not a limiting factor in education, or that they were satisfied with the situation in which many females find themselves: limited in both educational and life choices. In either scenario, the oversight is unfortunate at best, insidious at worst.

SCHOOL GOALS

Shakeshaft (1986) dispels the myth that the culture of schools is female and therefore schools are good places for girls but not for boys. Schools, in fact, may not be very good for boys or girls, but they certainly are not nurturing for girls. One must stand with her in her shock at Theodore Sizer's statement that, "It is revealing how much less discrimination there is in high schools than in other American institutions. For many young women, the most liberated hours of their week are in schools" (1984, p. 79).

Jane Roland Martin studied the goals of education, from what is taught in classrooms to general purposes, and concluded that schools exist to serve the public lives of men. Schools were created in response to what males need to know in order to become public people; therefore, the very nature of schooling is fashioned in a male (white male) image (1985).

School curricula and modes of instruction are based on male development. "Although females mature earlier, are ready for verbal and math skills at a younger age, and have control of small-motor skills sooner than males, the curriculum has been constructed to mirror the development of males" (Shakeshaft, 1986, p. 500). Girls, consequently, are ahead but must remain patient, most likely become bored or hold back and learn to wait for someone else's instructions even though they may not be meaningful to them.

The proverbial wisdom of educating boys and girls in a co-educational environment also favors male development over girls. In American society boys are encouraged to compete, and generally the ethos of the school is competition. The presence of girls, however, serves as a socializing factor for boys. Girls tend to grow better academically and socially in a single-gender school. They exhibit higher self-esteem, become more involved with academic life and develop a wider range of social and leadership skills. Yet the predominant mode of public schooling is coeducational, which favors males and may be detrimental for females.

INSTRUCTION

The competition ethic built into so much instruction in school tends to reward boys' proclivity to the "I win, you lose" philosophy but becomes problematic for girls. Carol Gilligan (1982) found that competition-based teaching techniques were divisive for girls and threatened the connections between group members. Girls preferred the connection that cooperative learning provided. In fact, cooperative learning approaches have been used successfully "to raise achievement levels of students across lines of gender, race, ethnicity, and ability; to break down racial and ethnic barriers to friendship; and to positively affect self-esteem, attitudes toward school and concern for others" (Harvey, 1986, 511–2).

Cooperative learning approaches, however, need to be established carefully if they are to be effective. Lockheed and Harris (1984) studied the interactions of students engaged in small, mixed-gender instructional groups in elementary classrooms. They found that teachers used small group instruction only about 11 percent of the time, mostly in physical education and reading, rarely in art, language arts and social studies classes. These groups tended to be unstructured mixed-gender groups matched by ability. The results of the study suggest that this arrangement may actually have confirmed sex stereotypes. Boys experienced more leadership experiences that consequently improved the perceptions of themselves as problem solvers.

Girls tended not to have these experiences and therefore became less enthusiastic about work in cooperative groups. Girls in classes with more instructional groups were less likely to want to work in mixed-gender groups than were girls in classes in fewer instructional groups. In other studies, the researchers (Lockheed, Harris and Nemceff, 1983) found that males tended to be perceived as leaders and to be perceived as having better ideas than females in collaborative groups. Webb (1982) found different response patterns in high school mathematics groups. Boys received explanations from both girls and boys within the unstructured mixed-gender groups that were matched by ability. Girls, however, received explanations from other girls because boys did not respond to the girls' questions. Obviously, casual use of small, unstructured, mixed-gender groups for instructional purposes may, in fact, hinder equitable status for male and female students. More observation and diligence is needed in the investigation of the internal dynamics of cooperative groups for learning.

In addition to the structure of schooling, teacher-student interaction frequently inhibits learning for girls. A number of studies have found that boys receive more teacher time and more effective teacher time than do girls. Boys receive more active instruction, listening, praise and punishment. Moreover, this attention is given differentially: boys receive most of their positive feedback for academic behavior and most of their negative feedback for nonacademic behavior. Girls, on the other hand, receive most of their negative behavior for academic work and most of their positive feedback for nonacademic behavior (Council, 1980). Teachers tend to further instruct male students when they have problems or questions, but often do the task for female students. They provide more opportunities for boys to interact—ask questions, answer questions, give opinions and engage in activities.

Myra Sadker and David Sadker (1986) conducted a major study of classroom interaction from 1980 to 1984 with funding from the National Institute of Education. Data were collected from more than 100 fourth, sixth and eighth grade classrooms in four states and the District of Columbia. Rural, urban and suburban class were represented in the sample; classes included were predominantly white, predominantly black and predominantly integrated. Teachers observed were male and female, representing white and minority groups teaching in areas of language arts, social studies and mathematics.

The results were astounding. Male students received more attention from teachers no matter what the grade, subject matter, or whether the teacher was female or male, minority or white. Furthermore, classrooms were generally found to be inequitable with "have" and "have nots" of teacher attention. Different environments existed in the classrooms for different students.

Researchers identified three distinct groups of students in classrooms. About a quarter of the students did not interact with the teacher at all during class. A second groups, the majority of students, typically interacted with the teacher once during class. A third group, fewer than ten percent of the class, were classified as "salient" students, dominating the teacher's time.

Sadker and Sadker further identified the types of teacher interaction available to students. They found three types of precise teacher reactions to students plus a general acceptance of student comments. The most prevalent precise feedback (about one-third of teacher comments) was remediation, helping students correct or improve responses. Praise, giving precise, positive reactions to students' comments or work, constituted about ten percent of teacher reactions. Criticism, explicit statements that an answer is incorrect, accounted for about 5 percent of teacher interaction with students. The fourth category of response was a simple acknowledgement of student comments, such as "okay" or "uh-huh." Over half of teacher comments were observed to fall in this category.

The more precise comments providing remediation, criticism and praise were given significantly more often to male students. More equitable treatment was observed in the distribution of the casual acceptance responses. The authors noted that these responses carry the least impact for learning.

The researchers noted that the majority of classrooms in the study were gender-segregated. Teachers tended to gravitate to the boys' side of the classroom where they spent more time and attention. Teachers also accepted boys' responses more readily than girls'. Boys called out and demanded attention more than girls, but they were usually allowed to give a response when they called out. Girls, on the other hand, were instructed to raise their hands and wait to be recognized. Boys were trained, therefore, to be assertive, while girls were taught to be passive and consequently not integral to classroom discussion.

On the face of such findings, one tends to be skeptical. Certainly, teachers do not intend to discriminate against girls—probably one-half of their students. In order to raise consciousness of teachers as they interact with students, Sadker and Sadker developed training for teachers in which research evidence was presented about bias in teacher/student interaction. Teachers also engaged in microteaching where they practiced equitable teaching skills, received feedback and practiced again. The sessions were videotaped so teachers could see their own interaction patterns. Teachers expressed surprise when they recognized their own biased patterns of interactions. Even teachers who viewed themselves as very aware of the issue of equity saw a need for change.

The results of biased interaction patterns are overwhelming. Proverbial wisdom suggests that girls exceed boys in verbal skills while boys out-perform girls in mathematics. Achievement test scores of high school seniors in 1972 support this assumption. By 1980, however, data from the National Center for Education Statistics indicate that boys are almost even with girls in reading but score higher in vocabulary and mathematics (Rock b, n.d.). A longitudinal study (Rock, a, n.d.) of high school sophomores and seniors found female students had lower achievement test scores than male students in vocabulary, reading, mathematics and science. Only in writing did females score higher.

PROGRAMS AND SERVICES

Test programs are being investigated for gender and racial biases. Rosser (1987) claimed that sex bias in the Scholastic Admissions Tests (SAT) and other college admissions tests are costing young women millions of dollars in merit scholarship aid. Girls score an average sixty-one points lower than boys on the SAT and six units lower on the ACT. These tests are purported to indicate success in first-year college, yet girls earn higher grades than males in high school and in college. Scholarships based on these tests are now awarded to males over females at more than a three to two margin.

Mathematics, science and computer science are special areas of concern for women. Not only are there differential interaction patterns in these classes, but course selection tends to favor boys over girls. In other words, girls tend to take fewer mathematics, science and computer science courses, and they tend to be enrolled in introductory or lower level courses rather than advanced courses. It is puzzling to determine why this is so in light of research on ability. In elementary school, more similarities are found between the sexes than differences and when there are differences, they tend to favor girls. At the junior high school level about half of the few sex differences favor girls. However, in high school and beyond, many sex differences in achievement are noted and favor boys rather than girls (Lockheed et al., 1985).

Alexander and Pollas (1943) found that performance on the SAT–M was highly responsive to the variations in high school mathematics coursetaking, even when prior levels of performance were controlled. Furthermore, variations in course selection can somewhat be explained by differential expectations rather than mathematics performance. Elizabeth Fennema (1982) found that girls feel less confident in their abilities in mathematics than do boys. Furthermore, decreased expectations of female success in mathematics by both sexes precede rather than follow the decline in mathematics achievement by girls.

Czerniak and Chiarelott (1985) found that feelings of anxiety toward science are more prevalent among females than males. Furthermore, these differences in anxiety appear even at the fourth grade level. These findings support Kohlberg's (1966) suggestion that sex-typed behavior is begun in preschool and is continued to be shaped during the elementary school years. These high levels of anxiety correlate with low science achievement scores.

The authors point out that nothing in the literature indicates a biological or genetic reason why females should be less adept at science than males. They therefore conclude that the relationship between science anxiety and lower achievement demonstrates a learned aversion toward science. Interestingly, Steinkemp and Macker (1984) found greatest male superiority in motivational orientation occurred in developed countries, including the United States and in advanced socioeconomic groups.

Steinkemp and Macker (1984) suggest that some differences can be accounted for by science-related, out-of-school activities, usually engaged in by boys rather than by girls. This would explain why boys' motivation toward physical science surpasses that of girls, while girls tend to favor the biological sciences and chemistry. Also, girls function less well with the discovery approach often used in science classes; they prefer more direction and continual feedback on their performance. If educators are to provide effective education for all students, including females, they will need to have invitational, nonthreatening science experiences among preschool and early elementary students as well as in junior and high school. Teachers also need to become aware of their own science anxiety and examine their teaching of science to determine if anxiety is modeled for students. Positive role models and more stress on "feminine" interests such as health, food, children and safety could be helpful in making science more attractive to females. Counselors and teachers need to make conscious efforts to socialize students toward science in equitable ways if gender-related orientation is to dissipate.

The assumption of gender differences and interests in mathematics, science and computer science leads to denial of equal access to development. Educators would do well to analyze teaching practices in these courses. Urging male students to try harder while praising female students for any effort is differential treatment. Explaining proper procedures in problem solving for male students and doing problems for female students is differential treatment. When mathematics has been viewed as an area of study for all students, girls have been found to be better problem solvers than in settings where mathematics is presumed to be a boys' domain (Lockheed et al., 1985, 11).

Schools can make a difference for girls in mathematics, science and computer science through counseling as well. Enrollment figures can be examined to determine patterns of proportional representation of girls in courses generally and also advanced classes. If enrollments tend to be differentially low, the school needs to assert that mathematics and science are for everyone. Some students may need specific encouragement. Students may need to perceive specific connections between these areas of study and careers. Teaching techniques need to be used so girls receive experiences in manipulating objects, using spatial skills and other hands-on activities which will help them succeed in mathematics and science. Interaction of high quality needs to be enhanced so girls are encouraged in problem solving and performance.

Educational services beyond classrooms need to be examined to determine if girls are receiving the special attention they may need. Currently girls represent about 33 percent of the elementary and secondary students identified as needing special education services. The areas of greatest difference in rate are those particularly influenced by subjective judgments, the categories of learning disabled and emotionally disturbed. Referrals of boys because of academic or behavior problems occur more often than girls. This lack of referral for girls cannot be taken to mean they have fewer problems. What does occur is that girls are referred later when they are farther behind academically and their problems are more severe (Mercer, 1973).

CURRICULAR MATERIALS

Curricular materials likewise tend to ignore female students. Bias in books, films and other materials tend to be biased through invisibility of female characters, blatant or subtle stereotyping and male-exclusive language. Few stories in reading or literature portray women as major characters; examples of professions tend to portray males rather than females in high-profile, high-paying and highly technical positions. History, likewise, tends to be a study of men; if women have a place, they tend to relegated to a supplemental women's history course. The message is that males are important and females are somehow "other." Language used in curricular materials and by many educators tend to be male-exclusive. Studies indicate that the generic "he" tends to be understood as male only rather than all people. Children, when asked to draw a caveman, drew pictures of a man; when they were asked to draw cave people they included women and children (Sadker and Sadker, 1982, 71). Girls tend to view themselves as less important as they see themselves ignored. The author recalls an incident in a graduate course in which a male student asserted that authors of a textbook were sexist because they used "she" rather than "he." Upon closer examination, the class discovered that the use of "he" and "she" tended to be rather equitably dispersed in the text. As Shakeshaft (1986, 501) suggested, "If the issue of language were truly irrelevant, there would be little resistance to changing it."

PARENTHOOD

A particularly difficult problem in education arises for women who become parents before the age of eighteen. This group of women continues to be the most discriminated against in educational and employment opportunities (Howe and Edelman, 1985). This is an immense problem particularly because adolescents in the United States have among the highest pregnancy rates of any developed nation in the world (Planned Parenthood, 1984). According to NCES (1983) statistics based on self-reporting, over 23 percent of the females who drop out of high school do so because of pregnancy. Many experts testify that the percentages are closer to 50 or 60 percent.

There is some discussion on whether pregnancy creates problems in education or is one consequence of educational problems. A counselor perceives teenage pregnancy as the beginning of "a life pattern of lost educational opportunities, unstable family life, poor employability, and welfare dependency" (Board of Inquiry, 1985, 22). Rhoda Schulzinger, Staff Director of Full Access and Rights to Educational Coalition in New York, concluded from studies that young persons who are poor achievers in school and who have low educational aspirations are more likely to become sexually active. " . . . If an adolescent girl feels that she is not going to be a high achiever and that there are no jobs or opportunities for her, she may decide that having a child at age 16 may not really disrupt her life" (Board of Inquiry, 1985, 22).

Pregnancy does disrupt teenagers' lives. Educational problems are magnified because of few support services even in the schools for pregnant teenagers, let alone in regular high schools. Home tutoring generally is unavailable and special schools for pregnant girls do not follow total curricula of general high schools. Once the baby is born, the young mother has difficulty with added responsibilities of parenting. Daycare is scarce for teenagers, especially for those who are poor. Many students who do return to school do not meet attendance requirements. Many do not feel part of the student body and drop out because of lack of support. Young mothers are in a special category of need which schools are not regularly set up to address.

After dropping out the teenager is in high risk of a second pregnancy and probable dependence on welfare. She has poor job skills and would probably be unable to take a job in any case because of her babies. Even job programs are not helpful to her, because she lacks basic skills in reading and mathematics.

Schools must develop more comprehensive programs in their particular communities that encourage youth to delay sexual activity and pregnancy and also to provide support for young parents. The first task is to make schools successful for all students if school dropout rates and adolescent pregnancy rates are to be lowered.

Specific programs of sex education are available in most school districts; however, programs vary greatly in terms of age of students, length of time and programmatic content. More successful programs are extensive in terms of parental and community involvement and content of instruction, but also focus on students' understanding themselves and the decisions they make. Such programs attempt to build self-esteem and help young persons comprehend the links between their personal decisions, vocational choice and parenthood.

Information needs to be straightforward, but data from school health programs suggest that access to medical and counseling services is a key element in preventing teen pregnancy. Whether schools operate their own clinics or work cooperatively with nearby clinics, results indicate that students participating in such programs delay sexual activity longer and use contraception more responsibly than do control groups. A Baltimore program reported a 30 percent decline in pregnancy rate in program schools and a 60 percent rise in other schools (Kenney, 1987).

Teens who become parents need programs to help them cope with pregnancy and parenthood plus school. Schools have responded through a variety of models, some school-sponsored, some with health departments, some in special schools and most in regular schools. Such programs include counseling, special education, nutrition, family life and sex education. Medical care is provided by hospitals, clinics and organized community programs. Some programs provide vocational assistance. More than half provide contraception to prevent repeat pregnancies; about one-third provide daycare for infants, and about one-third offer programs for teen fathers (Kenney, 1987).

Schools need to determine what students need in order to complete their education successfully. This may not always coincide with school regulations concerning attendance and probably will demand services not readily offered in many schools. After childbirth the student often struggles with schoolwork and childcare in an environment which she experiences as hostile. Programs need to be broadly based in terms of school services and policies and developed with broad community, parental and student involvement.

Although daycare service is often limited to teen parent support, it may be in the society's best long-term interest to support preschool programs for children of teenage parents. Preschool programs hold the potential for breaking the cycle of poverty. The dramatic possibilities were arrested to by a longitudinal study conducted by the High/Scope Foundation of the Perry Preschool Project in Michigan. An educational consultant from the study claimed, "An economic analysis of our data today has shown that for every $1,000 invested in a year of preschool education, at least $4,000 is returned to society . . . (in) reduced costs for education and legal processing for delinquent behavior, in increased lifetime earnings for participants; still other future returns remain to be calculated" (Howe and Edelman, 1985, 59).

SCHOOL ENVIRONMENT

Schools are assumed to be good places for children to be, yet girls are exposed to abuse at many levels not only in inequitable interaction with teachers in the classroom, but with even more blatant sexist behavior. They may be called sexually derogatory names or propositioned or even raped. Administrators who aggressively eliminate racist or anti-Semitic words and actions ignore or seem to be unaware of sexist insults and put downs. Shakeshaft (1986, 502) recalled "a not uncommon illustration of female marginality" in a Long Island school district in which male teachers attached a nude centerfold over a poster announcing Women's History Week. Female teachers who objected were told they had no sense of humor. The unstated message was that women were sex objects and that a commemoration of women's history was a joke. Had such an occurrence arisen involving race or ethnic origin, administration and fellow teachers would have vehemently objected.

EMPLOYMENT

This environment works against women moving into administrative positions and other positions other than teaching. It is difficult to understand why in 1928 women accounted for more than half of the country's elementary school principals and today, even though women make up more than 80 percent of the teaching force, they account for fewer than a quarter of the principals in those schools. The same adverse statistics appear in sports and physical education. In spite of Title IX of the Educational Amendments of 1972 which specifically prohibits sex discrimination, most of the NCAA Division I women's and men's teams were coached by males in 1984, yet in the early 1970s most women's intercollegiate teams were coached by females.

These data must be examined. Are women incompetent? Schools with women administrators have been shown to have higher student achievement, fewer discipline problems, higher teacher and student morale (Sadker, 1985). Shakeshaft (1986b) cited hundreds of studies documenting direct discrimination against women ranging from negative attitudes to harmful behavior. Women are not promoted because of discrimination.

"Only the Marines are looking for a *few good men;* school district personnel are notorious for looking for lots of white men and *a few good women
and minorities*" (Shakeshaft, 1986a, 502).

Lest this appear to be bitter rhetoric, it would be well to examine what
is lost by not providing educational environments in which female
students and professionals may develop and achieve. Hostile environments inhibit half the student body and the majority of the professional
staff from doing their best. Creating a more positive climate for them
would not only enhance their chances for success (no mean achievement)
but probably would benefit students, teachers and administrators generally.

Coffin and Ekstrom (1979) have found differences in the ways men and
women administrators approach the job and in the climate they create.
Women build relationships. They spend more time with people, communicate more, care about individual differences in students and teachers.
They motivate better. As a result, their staffs are more productive, have
higher morale and rate women higher. Students are more involved in
school activities and enjoy higher morale. Parents also are more favorably disposed toward the schools and districts run by women and are also
more involved in school life.

Women teachers and administrators are more instrumental in learning than men. Not only do they emphasize achievement, but they orchestrate programs and evaluate student progress. They know their teachers
and students, and support them in their work. They create climates that
are more orderly, safer and quieter. They make things work together so
that academic achievement is higher in schools where they are principals.

Women develop a participative leadership that includes teachers,
students and parents. They listen more and provide a great deal of
support. The outcome is a school staff who are aware of and committed
to the goals of learning and they share professionally. Achievement
of learning is emphasized. The climate is "more cooperative than
competitive, ... more experiential than abstract, ... takes a broad view of
the curriculum and has always addressed the whole child'" (Greenberg,
1985).

The characteristics of these schools are similar to the characteristics
observed in effective schools. This explodes the myth that excellence
and equity are at odds with one another. Inequitable education cannot be
called excellent. Furthermore, energy focused on making education
more effective for all students promotes both goals. Equitable education
promotes excellent education.

REFERENCES

Karl L. Alexander and Aaron M. Pallas, "Reply to Benbow and Stanley," *American Educational Research Journal,* Winter 1983, Vol. 20, No. 4, 475–477.

Board of Inquiry, *Barriers to Excellence: Our Children at Risk* (Boston: The National Coalition of Advocates for Students, 1985).

G. C. Coffin and Ruth B. Ekstrom, "Roadblocks to Women's Careers in Educational Administration," in M. C. Berry, ed., *Women in Educational Administration,* (Washington, D.C.: National Association for Women Deans, Administrators, and Counselors, 1979) pp. 53–63.

Council of Chief State School Officers, *Faculty the Future,* Report (Washington, D.C.: Council of Chief State School Officers, 1980).

Charlene Czerniak and Leigh Chiarelott, "Science Anxiety Among Elementary School Students: Equity Issues, *Journal of Educational Equity and Leadership,* Vol. 5, No. 4, Winter 1985, 291–308.

Elizabeth Fennema and Mary Kochler, "The Affective Variable: Confidence in Learning Mathematics." Paper presented at the annual meeting of the American Educational Research Association, New York City, 1982.

Carol Gilligan, *In a Different Voice,* (Cambridge, Mass.: Harvard University Press, 1982).

Selma Greenberg, "So You Want to Talk Theory?" Paper presented at the annual meeting of the American Educational Research Association, special interest group, Research on Women in Education, Boston, 1985.

Glen Harvey, "Finding Reality Among the Myths: Why What You Thought About Sex Equity in Education Isn't So," *Phi Delta Kappan,* March 1986, 509–512.

"High School Drop-Outs," *NCES Bulletins,* November, 1983.

Harold Howe II and Marian Wright Edelman, *Excellence: Our Children at Risk,* (Boston: The National Coalition of Advocates for Students, 1985.

Asta M. Kenney, "Teen Pregnancy: An Issue for Schools," *Phi Delta Kappan,* June 1987.

L. Kholberg, "A Cognitive-Developmental Analysis of Children's Sex-role Concepts and Attitudes," in E. E. Maccoby (ed.), *The Development of Sex Differences,* Stanford, CA: Stanford University Press, 1966).

Marlaine E. Lockheed and Abigail M. Harris, "Cross-Sex Collaborative Learning in Elementary Classrooms," *American Educational Research Journal,* Vol. 21, No. 1 Summer 1984, 275–294.

M. E. Lockheed, A. M. Harris, and W. P. Nemceff, "Sex and Social Influence: Does Sex Function as a Status Characteristic in Mixed-Sex Groups of Children?" *Journal of Educational Psychology* 75, 877–888.

Marlaine Lockheed, Margaret Thorpe, Jeanne Brooks-Gunn, Patricia Casserly, and Ann McAloon, *Understanding Sex/Ethnic Related Differences in Mathematics, Science, and Computer Science for Students in Grades Four to Eight* (Princeton, N.J.: Educational Testing Service, May, 1985).

Jane Roland Martin, *Reclaiming a Conversation: The Ideal of Educated Women,* (New Haven, Conn.: Yale University Press, 1985).

National Commission on Excellence in Education, *A Nation at Risk*, (Washington, D.C.: U.S. Government Printing Office, 1983).

Planned Parenthood of Seattle-Kings County, "Teen Pregnancy Fact Sheet Number One." Paper, March, 1984.

Donald A. Rock et al., *Factors Affecting Test Score Decline 1972-1980*, (Report under review by the National Center for Education Statistics, n.d.).

Phyllis Rosser, *Sex Bias in College Admissions Tests: Why Women Lose Out* (Cambridge: Fair Test, Second Edition, 1987).

Myra Sadker, "Women in Educational Administration: Report Card 4," the NETWORK, Mid-Atlantic Center for Sex Equity, Washington, D.C., 1985.

Myra Sadker and David Sadker, *Sex Equity Handbook for Schools* (New York: Longman, 1982).

Myra Sadker and David Sadker, "Sexism in the Classroom: From Grade School to Graduate School," *Phi Delta Kappan*, March 1986, 512–515.

Charol Shakeshaft, "A Gender at Risk," *Phi Delta Kappan*, March 1986, 499–503.

Charol Shakeshaft, *Women in Educational Administration*, (Beverly Hills, Calif.: Sege, 1986).

Theodore R. Sizer, *Horace's Compromise*, (Boston: Houghton-Mifflin, 1984).

Marjorie W. Steinkemp and Martin L. Macker, "Gender Differences in Motivational Orientations Toward Achievement in School Science: A Quantitative Synthesis," *American Educational Research Journal*, Spring 1984, Vol. 21, No. 1, pp. 39–59.

Chapter 15

LOSING FAITH: RETHINKING THE LD LABEL

JULIA JAMES

As a child in school in the fifties I had trouble distinguishing vowel sounds and my manuscript wouldn't have won a prize. Hidden animals in pictures eluded me and I was a long time automatizing my times tables. Looking back now on my early schooling, as an educator well versed in the intents and excesses of education, I feel quite lucky. My teachers and family helped me learn in my own way, offering lots of encouragement, paying attention to my abilities and differences rather than focusing on what surely could have been viewed as my deficits. They didn't place me at risk by labeling me mildly learning disabled. I can only imagine the kind of self-doubt such a label would have generated over me and how different my life might have been if the messages I received hadn't been enabling.

In time I went on to become valedictorian of my high school class and earned degrees in graduate schools. Still as an adult, I have trouble discerning left from right, can't always remember numbers and I'd rather speak than write. So whereas I perceive myself as an accomplished learner, I recognize that like most of us I have a learning style made up of strengths and weaknesses. The same is true of students in schools where our perception and acceptance of their "learning differences" can either enable or disable them as learners.

It's 1988. We've come a long way in the field of special education. We've improved and enhanced the lives of many individuals. We've learned specialized techniques to teach people with special needs. However, in learning about complexity, it seems we've forgotten to pay attention to some very simple lessons we've long known about the learning process. In large measure we've allowed advances in the technical sphere to obscure the basic and essential human dimension of learning. Out of a desire to help and in the name of science we have dutifully aligned ourselves and our special education systems with the so-called advances in identification, categorization and remediation. We have thereby given heed to a cooler more clinical and pseudoscientific approach that stresses easily quantifiable data on the child over the more subjective judgement of experienced educators. This situation might indeed be tolerable if our instruments of measure and our specialized teaching techniques were doing the job, but today they are increasingly viewed as being of doubtful validity.

Educators, like those in the field of psychology, at times long to model their discipline after the natural sciences. It's the appeal of objectivity, order and justifiability. It's the feeling of surety and security that comes from, "Our data show . . . " over "I think that . . . ". In our litigious society the draw of prescribed, rote formulas for the identification and justification of a child's placement into special programs has the added allure of shifting away a certain onus of responsibility. The overall effect of this objectification is to zero in on the deficits of the younger learner. We reduce the child to measurable increments, and lose our focus on the whole child. We dissect, but don't put back together, forgetting that the whole is so much greater than its sum of parts. We forget that true education always addresses the whole child and all the components of the child's world. The results of this is a dehumanization of a field that must remain passionately human.

In this present light, it has become too easy, perhaps even fashionable, to label children who need a different approach to learning as learning disabled. This is not to deny that there are children with real learning disabilities who need the attention of specialists. But the ever growing special education population is indicative of overclassification and our failure to serve the best interests of our school-age population. I believe that we place children *at risk* when we so glibly pass out the LD label.

How serious is this situation? Since 1976 the number of individuals labeled LD has increased 119 percent. Of the 42 million children in the public school system in 1984–85, some 1.8 million were classified as "learning disabled" and placed in some type of special education program. About 40 percent of the school-aged special education population is now classified in the nebulous category of being learning disabled. Figures from the Office of Special Education and Rehabilitation Services (U.S. Department of Education, November, 1986) show an increase of 34,000 students identified as LD in a period of one year, and more than a

million in the past decade. Keep in mind that during this same period
the total number of students enrolled in the public schools declined by
10 percent.

Whereas the goal of helping children through the creation of more
and more special programs has certainly been moved forth with the best
of intentions, there now must be close examination of the mounting
evidence indicating the deleterious effects of classifying students as LD
at such an alarming rate. The concern generated by this has brought the
accuracy of the entire identification process under serious question.
Researchers Kenneth Kavale and Steven Forness at the University of
California, have thoroughly studied the Wechsler Intelligence Scales
(WISC, WISC–R, and WPPSI), long a backbone of the diagnostic for-
mula used in LD placement, and have concluded:

> The differential diagnosis of LD with the WISC, although intuitively
> appealing, appears unwarranted . . . Regardless of the manner in which
> WISC subtests were grouped and regrouped, no recategorization, profile,
> pattern, or factor cluster emerged as a clinically significant indicator of
> LD. In fact, the average WISC profile for LD does not reveal anything
> extraordinary and appears not unlike that found for the average nor-
> mal child. (Kavale & Forness, 1985, p. 29.)

James Ysseldyke (1987), Institute for Research on Learning Disabilities at the University of Minnesota, reports that by applying one or more
of the definitions now in use for identification, that we would find more
than 80 percent of our entire school-age population qualifying for classification as LD.

Bob Algozzine (1983), contributing editor to *The Journal of Learning
Disabilities,* concludes that no one "has been able to demonstrate . . . that a
specific, distinctly unique group of behaviors differentiate LD children
from many of their classmates. To build an empire on such a foundation
is very dishonest" (p. 9). The same sentiment was echoed by Douglas
Friedrich (1984), Central Michigan University, after his study of 1600
children referred to special education because of suspected learning
disabilities. He and his colleagues analyzed ninety-four formulas that
had been used to diagnose for learning disabilities. He noted, "It seems
such a shame to subject persons to the life-long effects of the label
'learning disabled' when we really don't know what it is" (p. 209).

The nature of the problem is evident in the Education for All Handicapped Children Act of 1975 (Federal Register, 1977), which conjures up
images of severely and profoundly impaired children. In reality, 90

percent of all students served by special education are only "very mildly" handicapped. Indeed, the real basis upon which children are so often miscast into special education roles is found in the research of Shepard, Smith and Vojic (1983) who report that at least half of the learning disabled population could more accurately be described as slow learners, children with second language backgrounds, children who misbehave in class, those who move from one school to another, or as average learners in above-average school districts. While these students may need help in school, it could best be provided through regular education without the LD label.

In part what stands in the way of this is the resilient aftermath of what Harvard psychologist, Howard Gardner (1985), terms the "euphoria of the 1960's and early 1970's, when educational planners felt they could readily ameliorate the world's ills." Since then we have come to the "painful realization that the problems dwarf our understanding, our knowledge, and our ability to act prudently" (p. 392). Still, much of our current special education system was laid down in this era, and tenaciously holds its ground, the massive bulk of its bureaucratic character most difficult to influence, shift or sway.

Another aspect of the problem, arising from this same era, is what Lipsky and Gartner (1987) refer to as the deal cut between general and special education two decades ago. It could be surmised that in the early days of special education, the general education system was left out of the planning as the focus of the times centered on special education. Special educators soon laid claim to a body of knowledge and techniques for working with "special" students. Unfortunately, over time, as Howard Gardner (1985) implies, many of these common techniques, such as sensorimotor training, have been determined to be largely ineffectual. Still, general education was and remains only too happy to hand over these students to a welcoming special education system.

Indeed what happened here historically, repeats itself on a daily basis in classrooms across the country with many regular education teachers absolving themselves of responsibility for their special education students. This can occur when good teachers seek for a child, services they believe they themselves are unable to offer, or when lesser teachers seek to simply be rid of their "problem" students. Either way the effect is much the same with the child launched into a state of limbo.

This is particularly true of LD students who are often mainstreamed and therefore might have their school day split between regular and special education classes. Their special status often casts them into a no man's land in which no one truly accepts responsibility for them. The results are often discouraging and disorienting; a disservice to these students and a particular irony in that the help system being provided now becomes an additional barrier to school success.

It is not out of sinister or cold intent that some teachers invest less effort in these labeled students. It is more a matter of subtle psychological functioning. As education writer Vivian Gussin Paley recently wrote in the New York Times Book Review (1988), if she as a teacher begins viewing a child as learning disabled rather than as having a different learning style, "my relationship with him changes: my vision blurs, the child's words and actions are prejudged."

The power of a label has been well documented. Robert Rosenthal (1968), a professor of psychology at Harvard University, clearly demonstrated the power of positive labeling in the classroom when he established the Pygmalion effect. In this classic experiment, teachers were informed that certain students in their classes had been identified as "late bloomers." Despite the fact that the labels were assigned entirely at random, at year's end the labeled students had made greater progress than any of their classmates. In other words, it was merely the teacher's increased expectations for the student, based on an arbitrarily assigned label, that was then positively communicated to the child, that accounted for the dramatic change in performance.

Such results indicate both the positive power and inherent danger of labeling students. Thomas Armstrong in his book, *In Their Own Way*, writes about the "learned helplessness" that children can develop from negative labeling:

> These children believe that their own efforts to learn will inevitably result in failure. When they succeed, they tend to attribute their triumphs to luck—something outside of themselves. When they fail, they tend to blame themselves and their own lack of ability. After a while they just stop trying. And the label provides them with another reason to fail. (Armstrong, 1987, p. 126)

Thus a deficit label can become a self-fulfilling prophecy. Labeled students may feel and be isolated from peers. The label can bring on increased negative attitudes toward self, learning and school, thereby leading students to doubt themselves and their abilities. Parents and teachers, too, can take part in this cyclical losing of confidence.

The original thrust of Rosenthal's experiment should be repeated here. Children blossom in positive settings. Confidence breeds confidence. Our students learn to believe in themselves through our belief in them. They learn more as we express our confidence and belief in them as learners. Furthermore, this appears to be true regardless of their innate ability level. So when our student or son or daughter seems slow to grasp a concept that other children grasp, when a developmental stage is slow in being reached, we must see that there is a price to pay in rushing too quickly to judgment. For us to panic is to invite the child to panic. To the child it's as if an alarm system has gone off, signaling that a flaw has been found. The underlying communication will likely set the child further back than the remediation process will ever set them ahead. And so where we have been quick to help the child with our formal interventions, let us take the more conservative track of being slow to doubt the capacities of the child to grow strong and straight and persevere.

The final message here is that school systems need to learn to provide help to students in flexible settings without singling them out, without labeling them as defective or deficient. We must accept and appreciate the different ways in which a child can learn. We must expand our curriculum to tap into the many strengths, rather than blindly holding onto single methodologies that judge the child inadequate and flawed.

In the next section of the paper we will look to some of the hopeful developments in our understanding of the learning process and how through their implementation fewer children would be placed at risk.

BEGINNING OF A NEW ERA:
STEPS TO ENDING THE DEFICIENT MODEL

Assessment For Intervention — Reading Styles

All too frequently students are assessed simply in order to diagnose, label and assign them to special education programs. This type of assessment is problematic and dead-ended. What is needed instead is assessment for intervention on the learner's behalf. The aftermath of such testing would not be to explain why the child with his given deficits does not fit into an all too narrowly defined general education delivery system. The purpose would be to provide insights to the particular strengths of individual learners and to help generate instructional strategies geared to the learning styles of these children. This type of assessment precludes the fact that the school system is committed to the creation of a number of alternative programs within the regular educational structure and to the reeducation of classroom teachers. Under such circumstances, students with mild learning disabilities or with other learning problems often would not require the direct services of special education.

An example of the need for the type of special intervention is the student who is identified as LD due to special needs in the area of reading. Indeed approximately 75 percent of LD students reveal reading problems as their primary learning difficulty and approximately 87 percent of LD students receive remedial instruction in reading.

Marie Carbo (1986, 1987) of St. John's University is a pioneer in reading styles research. Recent research on reading styles points to the fact that the instructional methods used in most schools—phonics, whole word, drill and worksheets—are not the best methods for teaching all young children to read. Instructional intervention must be put into practice.

Most poor readers are predominately global, tactile and kinesthetic learners. In U.S. classrooms that reading style is least accommodated. But using Carbo's Reading Styles Inventory would help regular classroom teachers accommodate teaching methods to meet the needs of students rather than trying to alter the individual to fit the narrow structures of the prevalent reading methodology. Rather than spending approximately five hundred dollars per child to put them through the trauma of traditional assessment for special education placement, why not put those dollars toward assessing reading programs and retraining classroom teachers. Sadly, instead, we place students at risk by labeling them LD and providing a segregated program which frequently uses the same methods to remediate them that failed them in the classroom.

Carbo makes the following recommendations for teachers which are based on research findings on learning and reading styles:

1. Identify and match students' reading style strengths, especially their perceptual and their global/analytic abilities.
2. Share information with students about their reading styles.
3. Eliminate phonics from reading achievement tests (phonics is a method, not a goal).
4. Use high-interest, well-written reading materials.
5. Always begin reading lessons with global strategies. (1987, pp. 200–201)

It is important to bear in mind that the technology and methodology needed to make this shift to assessing children for the purpose of helping rather than classifying them have already been developed. It is a question of whether we are willing to reframe our thinking, retrain ourselves and change attitudes. It is a problem in education that too often we, as classroom teachers and administrators, strangely cling to the teaching strategies we witnessed as children sitting in class. The link is not always even conscious, which, of course, makes it all the more resistive to change, so that even when such methods are clearly outmoded or fly in the face of current research we have trouble moving away from them. The heavy consequence of this must be born in mind and challenge us to assess ourselves and our methods. Millions of children in this critical area of reading needn't be placed at risk, if teachers and administrators would take the risk to change.

Assessment for Intervention— Learning Potential Assessment Device

Reuven Feuerstein (1981), an Israeli psychologist, developed the Learning Potential Assessment Device (LPAD). In so doing Feuerstein sought to directly measure the individual's ability to learn, rather than measuring past learning and inferring ability as is the case with traditional intelligence tests. The LPAD is concerned with how an individual learns and the interpretation focuses on the type of instruction that would prove most effective with the learner.

The LPAD is based on Feuerstein's theory of the Mediated Learning Experience (MLE). In a mediated learning experience, someone intentionally intervenes between the person and the environment. In order to provide meaning, clarity and order to interactions that might otherwise be perceived as merely arbitrary in nature. For example, to say to a child, "Go wash your hands," is a command, that while perhaps effective, conveys little in the way of learning of the world. While, of course, the brevity of such a directive is wholly appropriate, the complete and ongoing neglect of reasons why we do things in our daily life keeps the child from building basic reasoned constructs for one's interactions. Thus the good parent and teacher at appropriate times extends the request to, "Go wash your hands before we eat, so you get all the germs off. They could make you sick!" In this manner and repeated through thousands of such "lessons," the person mediating provides very basic insights that in time develop and enhance the thinking process of the young person.

Feuerstein has developed a systematic program, called Instrumental Enrichment (IE), which, he contends, can teach intelligence by way of focusing on the building of these basic and essential thinking constructs. The IE program is paper and pencil exercises that a teacher administers individually or in groups. Instruction is provided an hour a day, three to five days a week over a period of two to three years. The goal is for the child to inculcate a more elaborate mental networking system that increases effective thinking and the capacity to arrive at multiple solutions to problems.

Feuerstein's theory is radical by its very nature. It doesn't accept the inevitability of a child failing to learn. Instead it claims that oftentimes and to a large degree we can work to redress and reform the very foundation of the mind. Recent infant research has indicated the importance of a stimulating environment to the full development of the infant's mental capacities. Feuerstein concurs that this type of stimulation is essential, but contends that where it has been denied it can later be remediated.

Feuerstein's program is increasingly being used and studied in school districts and universities, as well as in the private sector. The true effectiveness and range of applicability of Instrumental Enrichment is yet to be fully determined, though initial results are promising. Early results indicate that improvement is most clearly seen after two or more years in the program with those individuals whose life has been most deprived of mediated experiences.

Assessment for Intervention—SPES

Lynn Meltzer (1987), The Children's Hospital, Boston and Harvard Medical School, developed the Surveys of Problem-Solving Skills (SPES). SPES, which is the Latin word for hope, builds on Feuerstein's approach to evaluating each child's learning potential and on Howard Gardner's (1985) theory of multiple intelligences.

By fourth grade, school work becomes increasingly dependent on the ability to organize and integrate different types of information as well as on the ability to plan, conceptualize and use flexible approaches in a variety of learning situations. SPES is a two part inventory provides a profile of a student's strengths and weaknesses in areas of problem solving strategies and educational skills. The problem solving portion highlights processes such as flexible thinking, thinking about thinking (metacognition), analyzing and solving problems and the ability to justify and explain solutions. The educational skills section provides insight into the child's specific learning style and characteristic error patterns in reading, writing, spelling and math. The tasks on the SPES focus on the importance of identifying how children solve (or fail to solve) problems, rather than merely assessing the correctness of their final solutions.

The SPES profile yields information on the student's developmental level, by characterizing individual differences (not deficits) and developing formulations which contain implications for teaching and treatment a la Feuerstein's Learning Potential Assessment Device. The goal of SPES is the development of a descriptive profile of the student's learning style which will prove useful in designing programs which nurture academic strengths, while addressing academic weaknesses. The resulting educational plan can be put into action by a teacher in a regular classroom. Again the distinctive feature of SPES is that it's not designed to categorize students, but to improve one's understanding of a student as a learner.

Assessment for Intervention—Prereferral System

A primary reason children are unnecessarily labeled LD and thereby placed at risk in the public school setting is the telescopic focus of our present referral process. The tests we employ for diagnosing, the classroom isolation from which teachers often work, the philosophical nature of the deficit model, all lead to an imbalanced studying of the particular weaknesses of a child. Lost is all sight and sense of the complementing strengths that make up the child as a whole. Missing, too, is an appreciation of what psychiatrist-author, Gerald Coles (1987), calls the "interactive" nature of any child's learning. He emphasizes that the prerequisite for understanding any child's learning problem is to gather a broad informational picture of the child and the reciprocal nature of this interaction with the world. Such a model leads away from easy answers and towards vital and necessary questions, such as: Is the curriculum appropriate to this child's learning style? Are there social, emotional issues at play here? Are home problems becoming school learning problems?

The prereferral system takes a giant step towards righting this imbalance by reuniting the school's special and general education staff and by having them seek a broad multidimensional view of a child's environments and how they impact. The focus is so significantly altered that what is being considered is no longer simply children and their learning problems, but the school as an optimal learning environment, the effectiveness of instruction, and the overall appropriateness of curriculum and teaching methods for that child. In this way the support staff works together to understand the interaction of school and whole child and to prevent inappropriate referrals by increasing the skills and knowledge of team members. This mirrors the recommendation of Wayne Otto (1986), University of Wisconsin, who suggests, "Ask not whether students can learn, ask instead how best to teach them" (p. 575).

Simply stated, the goal of these school-based teams is prevention and intervention rather than diagnosis and placement. Prevention and intervention necessitates that many factors (e.g., curricula appropriateness, teacher attitudes and expectations, the conditions and relationships affecting the student's life, as well as personal, biological and developmental issues) be addressed through a broad and caring perspective.

This type of a system is a break from the past and will require endorsement from the school board and superintendent as well as special guidance from the building principal. Since brainstorming is a key factor for high level functioning in these teams, the members of such a team will need training in group dynamics, problem-solving techniques and communication skills. To be effective, members on this team must share power and engage in collaborative decision making. Members must exhibit the ability to be caring, respectful, empathetic, congruent, and open in the school-based support team. There is a need for the individuals participating in this approach to engage in flexible thinking and to be resilient.

If a support team is to be successful a couple of other issues bet thought. One is the challenge of scheduling quality time within the work day for such interactions. Another challenge is that of providing careful, planned follow-up and feedback. As administrators and educators work together a renewed spirit of confidence and cooperation can emerge for decreasing the numbers of students placed at risk and for delivering a meaningful education to all students.

Other Interventions

There are other well-documented approaches (e.g., cooperative learning, the teaching and developing of study skills, thinking strategies and social skills, peer tutoring, teacher consultation) that can have an impact on student success in school and beyond. Labels have been an "answer." They no longer need to be. The doors, for us and the students whose lives we impact, are not closed. The educational leaders of today, whether they are theorists, curriculum developers, superintendents or teachers in the classroom need to tap into the wide array of thinking and research that is now occurring in the educational arena.

Harvard psychologist, Howard Gardner (1985) does this in his outline of a new theory of human intellectual competencies that is the culmination of research that draws together findings from the fields of neurology, psychology, sociology as well as his study of normal adults and children, gifted individuals, *idiots savants*, brain damaged patients, individuals from diverse cultures, and experts from various other lines of work. From this he posits that intelligence is currently recognized only in very narrow and selective forms and postulates the idea of multiple intelligences, the seven "core" forms of which are: linguistic, logical-mathematical, spatial, musical, interpersonal and intrapersonal. Gardner states that, "Only if we expand and reformulate our view of what counts as human intellect will we be able to devise more appropriate ways of assessing it and more effective ways of educating it" (p. 4).

Gardner examines the educational implications of his theory of multiple intelligences, highlighting its value and utility to educational practitioners and policy makers, when he states:

> Too often practitioners involved in efforts of this sort have embraced flawed theories of intelligence or cognition and have, in the process, supported programs that have accomplished little or even proved counterproductive. To aid such individuals, I have developed a framework that, building on the theory of multiple intelligences, can be applied to any educational situation. If the frame put forth here is adopted, it may at least discourage those interventions that seem doomed to failure and encourage those that have a chance for success (p. 70).

Towards these same ends of fully exploring this phenomenon of intelligence which we daily try to educate and measure, Arthur Costa (1987), California State University, outlines the components that characterize intelligent behavior:

- Persistence persevering and using multiple problem-solving strategies
- Deliberateness: in opposition to impulsiveness
- Listening to others with understanding and empathy

- Flexibility in thinking: recasting the problem and looking at it in a new way
- Metacognition: ability to think about one's own thinking
- Checking for accuracy and precision
- Questioning and problem posing
- Drawing on past knowledge and using it in new situations
- Precision of language and thought
- Using all senses
- Using ingenuity, originality, and insightfulness
- A sense of wonder: inquisitiveness, curiosity, and the enjoyment of problem solving (p. 2)

Schools may well improve to the degree we are able to recognize, appreciate and develop such a comprehensive construct of intelligence—not just in our students but in ourselves as well.

In conclusion, I have summarized the work of scholars, researchers and educators. Their ideas concur with my thinking and experiences over the many years working with students, parents, administrators and teachers. I do believe life in schools can be better and more enriching for all the people who spend their valuable time in these institutions.

Too often in classrooms today, students don't have the opportunity to express their true potential. Perhaps the greatest learning disability rests in our not knowing how to teach many of our children. This paints quite a different picture than the one we've become accustomed to seeing on the educational canvas. It calls upon us to grow, to change our thinking and to open ourselves to developing more positive and flexible attitudes that can impact on the students we teach and the institutions in which we teach. The thrust of this thinking would not be on labeling and segregating, but on helping individuals reach their highest potential. This approach would focus on celebrating differences and the many ways there are to think and learn. Finally, as thinking people, ourselves, we need to work to create environments where intelligences of various types can flourish.

As Maxine Green (1987) said so descriptively, "I think we ought to keep a sense of incompleteness, of something unfinished, because along with that also goes a feeling of possibility" (p. 8). Let's keep the subject of how best to educate our young people ever alive and open with our questions, with our sense that it can always be made better and that with time there will be change. Creativity, imagination, openness and laughter need to be our partners as we strive to move forward and create a world where students are no longer placed at risk.

REFERENCES

Adelman, H. and Taylor, L. (1986). The problem of definition and differentiation and the need for a classification schema. *Journal of Learning Disabilities,* 19, 514–520.

Algozzine, B. and Ysseldyke, J. (1986). The future of the LD field: screening and diagnosis. *Journal of Learning Disabilities,* 9, 394–399.

Armstrong, T, L. (1987). *In their own way* Los Angeles: Jeremy P. Tarcher, Inc.

Bok, J., Cooper, M, Dobroth, K. and Siperstein, N. (1987). Special class placement as labels effects on children's attitudes toward learning handicapped peers. *Exceptional Children,* 54, 151–155.

Bos, S., Weller, A, Vaughn, R. (1984–85). At the crossroads: issues in assessment of the learning disabled. *Diagnostique,* 10, 98–111.

Carbo, M, (1987). Deprogramming reading failure: giving unequal learners an equal chance. *Phi Delta Kappan,* 69, 197–207.

Carbo, M. (1987). Reading styles research 'what works' isn't always phonics. *Phi Delta Kappan,* 68, 431–435.

Carbo, M, Dunn, R, Dunn, K. (1986). *Teaching students to read through their individual reading styles.* Englewood Cliffs, New Jersey: Prentice-Hall.

Chance, P. (1981). The remedial thinker. *Psychology Today,* 63–73.

Coles, G. (1987). *The learning mystique.* New York: Pantheon Books.

Costa, A. (1987–8). *Reaching their highest potential.* Tucson: Zephyr Press.

Dixon, V. and Greenburg, D. (1984–85). Assessment in special education: administrators' perspectives. *Diagnostique,* 10, 161–175.

Feuerstein, R. et al. (1981). Cognitive modifiability in adolescence: cognitive structure and the effects of intervention. *The Journal of Special Education,* 5, 269–287.

Friedrich, D., Fuller, G., and Davis, D. (1980). Learning Disabilities: fact and fiction. *Journal of Learning Disabilities,* 17, 209–212.

Fuchs, D., Fuchs, L., Benowitz, S., and Barringer, K. (1987). Norm-referenced tests: are they valid for use with handicapped students. *Exceptional Children,* 54, 263–271.

Gallagher, J. and Weiner, B. (Eds.) (1986). Alternative futures in special education. Virginia: ERIC Clearinghouse on Handicapped and Gifted Children.

Gardner, H. (1985). *Frames of mind* New York: Basic Books.

Glickman, C. (1987). Unlocking school reform: uncertainty as a condition of professionalism. *Phi Delta Kappa,* 69, 120–122.

Graden, J., Casey, A., and Christenson, S. (1985). Implementing a prereferral intervention system: the model. *Exceptional Children,* 51, 377–384.

Green, M. (1987). From the predictable to the possible: recapturing a vision. Address to CASEC Forum. University of Illinois, Chicago.

Harth, R. (1982). The freuerstein perspective on the modification of cognitive performance. *Focus on Exceptional Children,* 15, 2–11.

Joyce, B., Showers, B., and Bennett-Rolheiser, C. (1987). Staff development and student learning: a synthesis of research on models of teaching. *Educational Leadership,* 45, 11–22.

Kavale, K. and Forness, S. (1985). *The science of learning disabilities.* Boston: College Hill Publications, Little Brown.

Lipsky, D. and Gartner, A. (1987). Capable of achievement and worthy of respect: education for handicapped students as of they were full-fledged human beings. *Exceptional Children,* 54, 69–74.

Martin, W. (1987). Developing public policy concerning "regular" or "special" education for children with learning disabilities. *Learning Disabilities Focus,* 3, 11–16.

Meltzer, J. (1987). *Surveys of problem-solving and educational skills.* Cambridge: Educators Publishing Service.

Otto, W, (1986). Ysseldyke and algozzine—those two guys are friends of mine. *Journal of Reading,* 572–575.

Paley, V. (1988). Helping children to fail. *New York Times Book Review,* January 24.

Resnick, L. (1987). *Education and learning to think.* Washington, D.C. National Academy Press.

Rosenthal, R. Jacobsen, L. (1968). *Pygmallion in the classroom: Teacher expectations and pupils' intellectual development.* New York: Holt, Rinehart and Winston.

Shepard, A. (1987). The new push for excellence: widening the schism between regular and special education. *Exceptional Children,* 53, 327–329.

Shepard, L., Smith M., and Vojir, C. (1983). Characteristics of pupils identified as learning disabled. *The Journal of Special Education,* 6, 73–85.

Torgesen, K. (1986) Learning disabilities theory: Its current state and future prospects. *Journal of Learning Disabilities,* 19, 399–408.

Tucker, J. Stevens, L. and Ysseldyke, J. (1983). Learning disabilities: The experts speak out. *Journal of Learning Disabilities,* 16, 6–14.

Vaughn, S. and Bos, C. (Eds). (1987). Research in learning disabilities. Boston: College Hill Publications, Little, Brown.

Will, M. (1986) Educating children with learning problems: A shared responsibility. *Exceptional Children,* 52, 411–415.

Ysseldyke, J. and Christenson, L. (1987). Evaluating students' instructional environments. *Remedial and Special Educations,* 17–24.

CHAPTER 16

SLOW LEARNERS: GRAY AREA CHILDREN

NANCY S. WILLIAMS

Anne, a third grader, was failing in school. Her teachers described her as lazy, inattentive, and distractible. Reading was her worst subject. She could not remember certain sounds or common sight words. A psychoeducational testing battery revealed below-average scores in auditory processing and achievement areas. Nonverbal and verbal IQ measures revealed similar scores, 70 and 68, respectively.

Bill, a seventh grader, had been passed on from year to year. Although Bill could only read at the second grade level, he remained a pleasant, soft-spoken boy, whom everyone liked. Worried parents had Bill tested at a nearby learning disability clinic. Psychoeducational testing revealed low scores in all achievement areas. Poor reading skills lowered comprehension and spelling scores. Bill recognized only a minimum of sight words and had no word-attack skills. Visual processing areas (visual memory, discrimination, analysis) were stronger than auditory processing abilities. Bill also performed well on copying tasks; he liked to draw and seemed to block out his academic failures when he had chalk or pencil in hand. Verbal and nonverbal tests of intellectual functioning revealed test scores of 75 and 79, respectively.

Both Anne's and Bill's parents were told that their child would benefit from individualized instruction, but she or he was not eligible for special education programs.

What can be done for these gray-area children? This chapter will first examine how such children are placed and terminology differences which make references to slow learners difficult. Then, factors that figure in low cognitive performance as well as recommended curricula and teaching strategies will be discussed. Finally, an actual case study will be used to illustrate how slow learners can be successful when given

245

appropriate individualized instruction based on processing strengths and weaknesses.

PLACEMENT CONCERNS

In order to describe the educational needs of children like Anne and Bill, it is important to understand why they are not considered eligible for special education services when they are failing in the regular classroom. First, the particular group to whom this chapter refers is not mentally retarded.

According to the 1973 definition published by the American Association on Mental Deficiency (AAMD), mental retardation refers to subaverage general intellectual functioning (an IQ score below 70) existing concurrently with deficits in adaptive behavior. This is the same definition included in Public Law 94-142, The Education for All Handicapped Children Act, which mandates a free, appropriate public school education for all handicapped children (Federal Register, 1977).

Prior to 1973, the AAMD definition included students with IQ's ranging from 70–84, often referred to as borderline intellectually subnormal. The more stringent 1973 definition was developed, in part, because of the disproportionate number of children from minority backgrounds who were labeled mentally retarded on the basis of IQ tests standardized on middle-class white children (Luick and Snef, 1979).

The borderline retarded category, or slow learner, represents about 13 percent of the normal population on a theoretical distribution of IQ scores (Luick and Snef, 1979). Unfortunately, while demonstrating IQ's too high for programs for the mentally retarded (MR), these children have IQ's too low for learning disability (LD) programs.

According to PL 94-142, "specific learning disability" means a disorder in one or more of the basic psychological processes involved in understanding or in using language, spoken or written, which may manifest itself in an imperfect ability to listen, think, speak, read, write, spell or to do mathematical calculations. The term includes such conditions as perceptual handicaps, brain injury, minimal brain dysfunction, dyslexia and developmental aphasia. The term does not include children who have learning problems which are primarily the result of visual, hearing, or motor handicaps, of mental retardation, of emotional disturbance, or of environmental, cultural, or economic disadvantage (Federal Register, 1977).

Components of this definition include an intellectual capacity of average or better, a discrepancy between expected and actual achievement, a disorder in processing, and learning problems not primarily the cause of sensory impairments, motor handicaps, mental retardation, emotional disturbance, environmental, cultural or economic disadvantage (Kirk and Gallagher, 1983).

While average intellectual functioning is frequently interpreted differently by the diagnostician conducting the evaluation, it generally refers to a score falling between one standard deviation (usually 15 or 16 points) below and above a mean of 100, e.g. 85–115. Slow learners are located in the gray area between average intellectual functioning (IQ 85 and above) and mental retardation (IQ below 70).

Nevertheless, while slow learners technically are not eligible because of a below average IQ, they are frequently placed in LD programs in order to receive individualized instruction. In fact, misplacement of slow learners in LD programs has been so frequent that the Board of Trustees of the Council of Learning Disabilities (CLD) published a position statement recommending that nonhandicapped low achievers and underachievers be removed immediately from LD services and served within the domain of regular education (CLD Board of Trustees Position Statement, 1986).

WHO ARE SLOW LEARNERS?

Terminology Differences

Educators and researchers have written about *low achievers* (Shinn et al., 1986; Ysseldyke et al., 1982; Warner et al., 1980), *slow learners* (Kaluger and Kolson, 1987; Mink, Meyers and Nihira, 1984; Epps, Ysseldyke, and McGue, 1984; Chalfant, 1985; Luick and Senf, 1979), *slow normals* (Belmont and Belmont, 1980), *nonachievers* (Hodges, 1983), *the educationally handicapped* (Mink et al., 1984), and the *retarded performer* (Feuerstein, 1980). Do these labels refer to the same student? It would appear not. While all of the above labels refer to underachievers, these studies actually represent a heterogeneous group of children exhibiting average to below average cognitive abilities.

Research examining differences between learning disabled and *low achieving* students (Warner et al., 1980; Ysseldyke et al., 1982) and LD students and *slow learners* (Epps, Ysseldyke and Mcgue, 1984) find similar characteristics in cognitive ability and achievement. Low achieving students and slow learners in these studies are defined similarly; both demonstrate a low percentile score on a standardized test, fail in the classroom (Warner et al., 1980; Ysseldyke et al., 1982; Shinn et al., 1986), and, like the LD groups to which they are compared, exhibit cognitive abilities in the average range (Ysseldyke et al., 1982; Warner et al., 1980; Epps et al., 1984).

However, other authors use the term *slow learners* (Webber, 1987; Kaluger and Kolson, 1978; Mink, Meyers and Nihira, 1984) as well as *borderline retarded* (Luick and Senf, 1979) and *retarded performers* (Feuerstein, 1980) to refer to students exhibiting below average cognitive abilities. Still other researchers use the term *slow normal* to refer to children at the lower end of the normal range (Belmont and Belmont, 1980).

In sum, one must be aware that terms like *underachiever, slow learner, low achiever, educationally handicapped and retarded performer* refer to various subgroups of underachieving children exhibiting a wide range of cognitive abilities.

Factors Associated with Low Cognitive Performance

According to Feuerstein (1980), the development of cognitive structures is the result of direct exposure to stimuli and mediated learning experiences (MLE), i.e. experiences provided by a mediating agent, usually the parent or caregiver, who selects, organizes, and interprets stimuli (objects, events, ideas) in the child's environment. Deficiencies responsible for retarded cognitive performance belong to a syndrome of cultural deprivation, defined by the Israeli psychologist as conditions in which the essential products of culture are not transmitted or mediated to the individual.

Environmental factors associated with a lack of MLE include lack of adequate parent-child relationships, pathological conditions of parents, a breakdown in cultural transmission, and poverty. Poverty, according to Feuerstein, is associated with reduced opportunities for stimulation and may limit the resources of parents for providing adequate emotional, nutritional, and physical conditions necessary for the child's growth and development. In other words, adverse environmental conditions may contribute to poor parenting skills which in turn limit a child's cognitive development.

Mink, Meyers and Nihira (1984) examined life-style patterns of educationally mentally retarded and educationally handicapped children, the latter described as students exhibiting IQ's mostly below 85 and defined by the authors as severe underachievers in need of special education.

A cluster analysis revealed three distinctive types of families with children exhibiting IQ's between 70 and 84: Type C (IQ mean 74.6); type D (IQ mean 70.6); and type F, (IQ mean 71.2).

Interestingly, most families with educationally handicapped children evidenced environmental conditions similar to Feuerstein's syndrome of cultural deprivation. For example, two of the three groups (C and D) had problematic family environments with poor parent-child relationships and stressful life events. Group D had a high occurrence of stressful life events, a high percentage of problems between child and siblings, a low socioeconomic level, and little provision for learning at home.

The absence of fathers was also noted in this group, although some families had a number of rotating companions in the household. While Group C had the highest number of father figures present, parent-child relationships were the poorest of all groups. Interestingly, Group F had the lowest number of children at home as well as the lowest occurrence of stressful life events.

Finally, while all groups revealed low self-concepts, self-concept was significantly low in Group F, also characterized by having few sociocultural interests (Mink et al., 1984). While no mention is made of cognitive abilities, Wehlage, Rulter and Turnbaugh (1987) report low socioeconomic backgrounds, large families living in cities, urban or rural areas, as well as students' low self-esteem as common characteristics of students at risk of dropping out of school. Further, Edgerton (1979) states that children born and raised in urban ghettos or impoverished rural environments are fifteen times more likely to be labeled mentally retarded than children of the same age from suburbia (Edgerton, 1979).

However, Feuerstein (1980) warns that while conditions of disadvantage may be associated with a lack of mediated learning experiences, not all socioeconomically disadvantaged subgroups are necessarily culturally deprived. Rather, cultural deprivation refers to intrinsic criteria (cognitive functioning), and is the failure on the part of parents or caregivers to provide their children with effective early interactions with environmental stimuli (through mediated learning experiences).

In sum, common characteristics of families with slow learners include poor parent-child relationships, low self-concept, and disadvantaged living conditions (Mink et al., 1984). These factors may contribute to below average cognitive functioning (Edgerton, 1979), a passive cognitive style due to a lack of mediated learning experiences (Feuerstein, 1980), and underachievement (Wehlage, Rulter and Turnbaugh, 1987).

Finally, some argue that schools may contribute to low cognitive performance because they fail to provide support systems for borderline students who are ineligible for special education (Chalfant, 1985). Edgerton writes that children who are poor and come from culturally different backgrounds may be unprepared in terms of language, culture, and motivation to cope effectively with the academic demands of school (1979).

Conversely, Feuerstein (1980) suggests that it simplifies the problem to suggest that altering the school environment will eliminate the poor performance of children, since deficient cognitive functioning is not culture bound or limited to specific school skills. He further states that "even if the 'three R's' of education have been mastered, a lack of the 'fourth R'—reasoning—may lead to maladaptive behavior" (Feuerstein, 1980).

On the other hand, educators have suggested modifications in the school environment as ways to meet the educational needs of slow learners (Canady and Hutchkiss, 1985; Kilby, 1984; Kaluger and Kolson, 1978; Keith, 1982).

CURRICULAR CONCERNS AND OPTIONS

A critical factor influencing learning is pace. Low ability students or slow learners need more time to learn (Kaluger and Kolson, 1978; Canady and Hutchkiss, 1985; Webber, 1987; McDill, Natriello, and Pallas, 1986). Kaluger and Kolson (1978) write that it is unfair to expect slow learners to achieve on the level of average children or to benefit from the same type of instruction. Webber states that slow learners "take longer to acquire knowledge, to appreciate things, to develop that peculiar capacity for acceptance and school success" (1987).

Further, researchers find that students with low ability don't try as hard in overly fast-paced, high-demand classrooms (McDill, Natriello, and Pallas, 1986) and develop negative attitudes toward school, learning, and themselves when pushed regularly through textbooks without mastering the material (Samuels, 1986).

In order to provide slow learners with more time for learning, educators advocate that blocks of time be devoted to skill and content areas (Karweit, 1984; O'Shea and Valcante, 1986; Canady and Hotchkiss, 1985), transitional programs (Kilby, 1984), extended readiness programs (Kaluger and Kolson, 1978), as well as mastery learning techniques (D'Zamko and Hedges, 1988).

Canady and Hotchkiss (1985) suggest parallel block scheduling which provides long blocks of time for content areas (language arts, reading) and enables teachers to actively monitor classroom work. According to these authors, low achieving students benefit from having equal amounts of time allocated for instruction, more supervised seatwork, and greater amounts of teacher-directed instruction. With this type of organization, low achieving students receive as much instructional time as other students. While this seems to be an obvious need, teachers frequently spend more time with high achievers (Canady and Hotchkiss, 1985) and rarely call on low achieving children (Harris and Sipay, 1985).

In addition to block scheduling, Kilby (1984) reports that transitional programs following kindergarten (i.e., junior first grades) provide successful options for students who may face grade repetition and who do not qualify for special education. In these programs, emphasis is placed on language development as well as the acquisition of academic skills.

Follow-up studies comparing students in the program with peers who were eligible but did not attend were impressive. With regard to grade repetition, an average of 27 percent of children not attending the program repeated, whereas only one-tenth of 1 percent of the students attending repeated. Further, placement in LD programs was significantly less frequent among those attending. Two years following the eligibility for Junior First Grade, only 11 percent of the participants, as compared with 32 percent of eligible age peers, had been placed in LD programs (Kilby, 1984).

Like transitional programs such as a Junior First Grade, Kaluger and Kolson recommend a longer readiness period, allowing more time for slow learners to acquire particular skills. According to these authors, a mental age of six is necessary for a student to learn to read under present reading programs and methods. Entrance into school must be delayed for slow learners, since children with an IQ of 75 have a mental age of only four and a half (Kaluger and Kolson, 1978).

Several concerns are evident with transitional programs like the ones described above. First, children enrolled in transitional classes are a year older than classmates in subsequent years (Kilby, 1984). Evidence indicates that students who drop out of school tend to be overage and poor readers (stanine 3 or lower). In fact, overage students with average reading abilities are more likely to drop out (Hess and Greer, 1986).

On the other hand, Belmont and Belmont (1980) suggest that studies of retained children should be designed to determine differences between those who benefit from retention and those who do not. Similar studies should also be developed for students failing to profit from transitional programs.

A second concern of transitional programs, also noted by Kilby (1984), is the need for careful identification procedures for identifying students who would benefit from such programs. Because young children's performances vary, evaluations must be conducted by well-qualified examiners.

According to D'Zamko and Hedges, mastery learning techniques provide students with longer periods of time to master skills. Using mastery learning, pupils are pretested to establish objectives to be achieved, provided with objectives that are part of a planned curriculum, and, when objectives are mastered, given more complex skills (objectives). This procedure is motivating to slower students, since grades do not depend on how quickly students master an objective but rather on mastery itself. The authors suggest that small group instruction, peer teachers, use of programmed instruction, and microcomputers are instructional arrangements that help develop mastery learning in the classroom (D'Zamko and Hedges, 1988).

Finally, Gartland and Rosenberg (1982) suggest that teachers can use class time more effectively for students who require more learning opportunities in order to master concepts and skills of the curriculum. Although the authors address the following recommendations specifically to teachers of learning disabled students, the suggestions seem equally as applicable for slow learners in the regular classroom.

First, teachers should spend at least 50 percent of class time on interactive classroom activities such as demonstrating content material, providing opportunities for students to respond, giving corrective feedback, and reinforcing appropriate student behavior.

Second, teachers should use 35 percent of class time to actively monitor controlled and independent practice activities such as teacher-directed group seatwork and board activities, and independent seatwork. In order to increase students' on-task rates during traditionally off-task periods, the authors suggest that teachers reinforce correct responses, give clear and succinct instructions, assign novel and motivating seatwork activities and use study cubicles.

Finally, teachers should use less than 15 percent of class time on noninstructional activities, such as getting ready for instruction and classroom management (Gartland and Rosenberg, 1987).

TEACHING STRATEGIES

In addition to curricular modifications and options, educators suggest teaching strategies for students with learning problems which encompass effective learning principles (Samuels, 1986; Carlson and Winter, 1980; Conant, 1961; Fields and Lee, 1987; Harris, 1985), adhere to individual learning styles (Hodges, 1987; Dunn and Dunn, 1987), use cognitive strategies (Deshler and Schumaker, 1986), and mediated learning (Feuerstein, 1980; Messerer et al., 1984).

Like Gartland and Rosenberg's emphasis on demonstration of content material and novel, motivating content, Samuels (1986) writes that teachers need to demonstrate and explain step-by-step procedures in order to help handicapped students master basic skills. Carlson and Winter (1980) believe that students with learning difficulties are more likely to acquire a new behavior if they are given model performances to watch and imitate, and provided with appropriate practice in short periods over time.

The authors caution that teachers must first analyze the task to determine underlying concepts and skills that students must know for task mastery and then find out if children have learned these prerequisite skills (Carlson and Winter, 1980). Similarly, Harris (1985) warns that teachers invite failure when they use materials that are too difficult for the child. Feuerstein states that retarded performers fail in academic areas because they are not familiar with content material (1980). Thus, content must be meaningful and based in part on a student's background knowledge of the subject.

With regard to reading, Fields and Lee (1987) write that slow children make a high percentage of errors because basal workbooks covering comprehension skills are often meaningless.

According to Conant (1961), teachers need to develop meaningful courses in both slums and suburbs for pupils with less than average abilities.

In addition, teachers need to determine how students learn best and match instruction and content to a student's learning style (Webber, 1987; Chalfant, 1985; Dunn and Dunn, 1987; Hodges, 1987). Although all learners have individual learning styles, it is imperative that teachers investigate what modality (auditory, visual, kinesthetic) is strongest for slow learners, since failure is generally the rule in the classroom, not success and mastery of content material.

Rather than placing children inappropriately in special education programs in order to receive individualized instruction, Chalfant recommends diagnostic teaching in the classroom, i.e., learning how a student learns or fails to learn, determining the appropriateness of materials and methods, and evaluating a student's progress under different conditions (Chalfant, 1985).

According to Hodges (1987), learning style tests revealed that delinquent nonachievers in a New York City ghetto exhibited strong tactile and kinesthetic abilities and fair to poor auditory abilities. Visual abilities were somewhat stronger than auditory skills but not as strong as tactual, kinesthetic skills. Using this information, a successful reading program was developed using meaningful, global, tactual-kinesthetic experiences. Hodges reports that while none of the students had passed the New York City proficiency tests prior to the implementation of the reading program, 80 percent passed when emphasis was placed on teaching students in the way they could learn (Hodges, 1987).

Finally, educators emphasize the importance of cognitive strategies (Deshler and Schumaker, 1986), or metacognitive learning (the awareness of one's systematic thinking strategies that are needed for learning) (Lerner, 1985) and mediated learning experiences (Feuerstein, 1980; Messerer et al., 1984) for students demonstrating deficiencies in problem-solving and organizational skills.

Deshler and Schumaker (1986) report that mildly handicapped adolescents improve academic performance when taught cognitive strategies, such as how to identify and store information, analyze and solve novel problems, and organize and write material. According to these authors, teaching content is not as effective as improving metacognitive skills, i.e., having students become aware of how they learn and how to take control over their learning (Deshler and Schumaker, 1986). Although Deshler and Schumaker's research involves learning disabled adolescents, it would seem to apply as well to slow learners who exhibit deficiencies in problem solving and organization.

Feuerstein (1980) suggests redeveloping deficient cognitive structures for the retarded learner by analyzing cognitive behavior, locating and interpreting weaknesses, and then selecting techniques appropriate for the specific needs of a child.

According to Feuerstein, deficient functions may occur (1) at the input phase (impairments concerning quantity and quality of data gathered by children as they begin to solve a problem); (2) at the elaborational phase (factors that hinder children in making efficient use of data, such as the inability to select relevant cues); (3) at the output phase (inadequate communication of outcomes, such as lack of precision and accuracy for communicating a response); and (4) with affective-motivational factors.

His Instrumental Enrichment program (FIE) teaches children how to learn and solve problems through mediated learning experiences, learning experiences in which students are verbally guided by a teacher through problem-solving processes. The content-free material, graded in difficulty and complexity, provides successful learning opportunities for students to improve specific difficulties, such as problems in categorization, without being penalized for having inadequate background knowledge (Feuerstein, 1980).

Using Feuerstein's teaching methods of mediated learning, Messerer et al. (1984) found improved problem-solving strategies in a group of post-high school youth demonstrating deficits in cognitive skills. The following example illustrates the procedures used by a teacher-mediator in helping students verbally think through spatial problems included in the Organization of Dots task, a component of Feuerstein's Instrumental Enrichment program.

First, the teacher-mediator asks a series of key questions designed to elicit a definition of the problem as well as potential strategies for solving it. Students work individually developing and trying strategies while the teacher-mediator moves about the classroom clarifying questions and offering encouragement. In the subsequent discussion, students report which strategies worked best and define a general meta-cognitive principle based upon the learning experiences, generalizing the principle to their own experiences.

Finally, the teacher summarizes the lesson, reviewing what was done, which principles were derived, and what was learned. An important factor in this approach is the teacher-mediator who shapes learning opportunities and brings them to the attention of the learner (Messerer et al., 1984).

While mediated learning utilizes verbal strategies in problem-solving situations, Cherkes-Julkowski, Gertner and Norlander (1986) found verbal labeling (or slow inefficient verbal mediation) negatively associated with the performance of slow learners in various group learning situations.

According to these authors, labeling procedures consumed the processing capacity needed to make relevant connections between stimuli. In this study, stimuli consisted of pairs of pictures designed to elicit certain types of strategies. For example, similarities pictures consisted of two pictures from the same category; sentential pictures could be associated within the context of a sentence; rehearsal pictures were "nonsense" shapes that needed labels and thus could be either rehearsed or associated in some fashion.

In contrast to labeling, the researchers found that adequate performance was associated with group repetition of elaborations and suggests that repetitions may be an important learning strategy for slow learners.

Finally, the authors caution that while they found differences in strategies among slow learners, learning disabled and average learners, they found no single strategy for all kinds of stimuli or for all types of learners (Cherkes-Julkowski et al., 1986).

In summary, effective teaching strategies based on individual learning characteristics, and which emphasize explicit and meaningful instruction, task-analysis techniques, appropriate verbal mediation, and curriculum and program adjustments which allow more time for slow learners to develop concepts and skills, are effective options for the administrator and classroom teacher who have the responsibility of teaching the slow learner.

The following case study of a slow learner seen at the DePaul Center for Reading and Learning illustrates how instruction based on a careful analysis of strengths and weaknesses in processing and achievement improved academic skills and self-confidence. The remediation strategies, which include many of the methods and techniques suggested previously, were developed and reported by Patricia Doyle, a clinician at the Center.

CASE STUDY

Diagnosis

Paul is an eighth grader who has been in a learning disability class for most of his school life. After having repeated first grade, he was placed in a special education class. Approaching high school, a thorough evaluation was desired in order to determine if he was in the appropriate program.

A psychoeducational test battery revealed that Paul scored in the borderline range (70–85 IQ) on all instruments used to assess intellectual functioning. Reading, math, and written language aptitude scores were slightly above verbal ability, reasoning, perceptual speed and memory. Assessments evaluating auditory and visual acuity indicated sensory abilities in the normal range.

Tasks assessing auditory processing abilities (memory and perception) revealed weaknesses. Paul had difficulty especially with auditory short-term memory tasks, which required him to repeat words and sentences and to follow a series of oral directions. Visual short-term memory, while stronger than auditory short-term memory, was below average and in keeping with scores on nonverbal cognitive tasks of reasoning and analytical thinking.

Language tests revealed below average receptive and expressive vocabulary. Word-retrieval problems were noted on tasks requiring verbal responses as well as in conversations between Paul and the clinician. Paul frequently responded by saying, "I can't think of the word I want to say."

Reading and spelling scores were below age level. Reading assessment revealed comprehension skills at the third grade level. Although whole word-recognition skills were slightly higher, Paul's phonic skills were weak; he could not sound out nonsense words and seemed to have no consistent strategy for decoding unfamiliar words. Spelling scores were also between the second and third grade level. Errors revealed little attempt to sound out words.

Similarly, math scores revealed third grade level skills. While Paul was able to carry in addition and simple multiplication problems, he did not know how to borrow or to divide beyond simple two-digit division problems. He could not compute fractions or work problems involving decimals.

Paul was very cooperative during the testing, although he would not attempt difficult problems or tasks. He seemed to have no strategy for solving problems. Paul appeared to be a passive learner with little confidence in his ability to solve problems or successfully complete tasks.

Results of the evaluation revealed that Paul was not eligible for special education placement in a learning disability class, since he scored below average on all tests assessing verbal and nonverbal cognitive abilities. Remediation was recommended, emphasizing a multisensory approach to compensate for generally weak processing skills, and Paul began instruction at the Center for a period of eight two-hour weekly sessions.

Remediation

Remediation objectives were to improve division skills in math, word-attack and comprehension skills in reading and strengthen vocabulary and syntax through written language.

To improve math skills, the clinician used manipulatives and visual cues (a value chart) to reintroduce Paul to concepts of place values and groups. Next, a memory strategy utilizing key sentences (verbal cues) written on small cards (visual cues) helped Paul to master the many steps required in long division. The three cards contained the following key sentences: (1) How many groups of _____ are in _____? (2) ÷, ×, −, compare. (3) Everytime I bring a number down, I _____. After teacher modeling (i.e. working through a problem using the three cards), Paul was instructed to work a problem vocalizing at each step.

Eventually, cards 1 and 3 were removed, but the triple symbols and word *compare* remained for all division problems. If Paul hesitated at a step, an auditory cue such as "Every time..." was provided which enabled Paul to continue successfully. By the end of eight sessions, Paul was able to perform long division problems without the use of phrase cards. Verbal cues, such as vocalizing key phrases, and repeating division procedures were successful strategies to help compensate for weak auditory short-term memory skills.

In the areas of word recognition and reading comprehension, specific objectives were to understand and recall sight words, main ideas and facts related to the content area of social studies. A sorting strategy was used to help Paul memorize oceans and continents. He was given an envelope containing colored word strips naming five oceans, seven continents and the words *land* and *water*. He was told to sort the words in any way that had meaning for him. Finger tracing, naming, cutting shapes of continents and matching the shapes to the globe were used at the beginning of each session to aid in sorting. To help Paul differentiate between main ideas and details, each session Paul and the clinician read material relating to one continent and organized the information by using a mapping strategy, a visual (graphic) representation illustrating the relationship of main ideas to supporting information.

For example, the graphic map depicted the name of each continent enclosed in a box in the center of the paper, with finger-like extensions extending from the box and listing important characteristics particular to each continent. Graphic (semantic) maps have been used successfully to improve comprehension by visually representing the relationships among words (Burns, Roe, and Ross, 1988; Pehrsson and Robinson, 1985). In addition to the mapping strategy, manipulatives and visual cues, such as a globe, flat table map and wall map, helped Paul to understand the relationship of land to water, shapes of continents and relationships of continents and oceans to each other.

While Paul still had difficulty naming all of the continents due to his memory deficit, he was able to perform at a much higher level in the classroom and volunteered in group discussions pertaining to continents and their attributes. Vocabulary increased with regard to words in the social studies unit because of the meaningful multisensory approach (visual, tactile, kinesthetic cues) developed by the clinician.

Finally, a language experience approach, recommended for children with learning difficulties in the upper grades (Burns, Roe, and Ross, 1988), was used to promote a good self-concept as well as to improve written language skills and reinforce learning of social studies content.

First, Paul was asked to visualize a particularly vivid experience, verbally relate that experience to the clinician and then write the experience. Prior to writing, the clinician asked specific questions to help clarify, expand and provide structure for Paul's story. After writing the experience, Paul was asked to proofread his story for capitalization, punctuation and grammar.

Using this strategy to reinforce social studies content, Paul was asked to write a paragraph describing the information contained on the graphic map previously created. Paul verbally related the relationships between main ideas and details depicted on the map prior to writing the paragraph. During initial sessions, the clinician modeled the activity, first summarizing the material organized on the map and then writing a paragraph based on the information. Paul was then encouraged to develop his own paragraph. By incorporating language experiences and writing into reading comprehension activities, such as the social studies unit, concepts became clearer as Paul verbally related main ideas and details and organized them into written form. Additionally, he was quite proud of producing written work, since this was one area both he and the teacher avoided in the classroom.

Concluding Comments

The above strategies, developed to capitalize upon Paul's relative strengths in visual processing areas and compensate for weaknesses in auditory processing abilities, such as memory and thinking skills, demonstrate the effectiveness of basing instruction upon clearly defined objectives and learning strengths and weaknesses. Further, teaching strategies, such as demonstration (modeling), verbal mediation (verbalizing learning processes through problem-solving tasks), providing meaningful experiences (the language experience approach, sorting exercises using a background of prior knowledge) and materials (concrete globes, maps), kinesthetic cues (tracing, writing) and allowing time for repetition and review, were successful tools in improving academic performance and self-concept.

While remediation occurred in a clinical, one-to-one setting, similar strategies can be incorporated in the regular classroom. Chalfant (1985) suggests providing in-services that teach classroom teachers how to analyze a task, develop strategies for individualized instruction, and develop informal methods of assessment. To improve both regular and special education systems, Keogh (1988) recommends more research on individual learning processes within and across groups of mildly handicapped students, such as learning disabled, mentally retarded, and underachievers, to determine if and how these differences relate to instructional approaches.

Further, while curricular modifications, such as transitional rooms (Kirby, 1984) and block planning (Canady and Hotchkiss, 1985), appear to be successful in providing more instructional time for slow learners, Keogh suggests a program's effectiveness should also be evaluated across groups of different learners (LD, underachievers), with more emphasis placed on generalization and maintenance efforts (1988). In other words, educators need to identify programs that provide students with abilities and skills which are maintained and used in subsequent and similar problem-solving situations.

Finally, attention must be focused on providing at-risk young children with effective early learning experiences, such as Feuerstein's MLE (1980), in which parents take an active part in selecting and interpreting environmental stimuli for their children. Like Chalfant's suggestion for effective teacher in-services, schools—preschool and primary—must provide instruction to parents on how to give their children enriching learning experiences that foster active learning and self-confidence. With effective, early intervention, the gray area might be diminished. With appropriate, individualized classroom instruction, gray-area children will achieve.

REFERENCES

Belmont, I. and Belmont, L. (1980). Is the slow learner in the classroom learning disabled? *Journal of Learning Disabilities, 13,* 496–499.

Burns, P., Roe, B. and Ross, E. (1988). *Teaching reading in today's elementary schools* (4th ed.). Boston: Houghton Mifflin, pp. 179, 318.

Canady, R. and Hotchkiss, P. (1985). Scheduling practices and policies associated with increased achievement for low achieving students. *Journal of Negro Education, 54,* 344–355.

Carlson, N. and Winter, P. (1980). General principles of learning and motivation. *Exceptional Children, 12,* 60–62.

Chalfant, J. (1985). Identifying learning disabled students: A summary of the National Task Force Report. *Learning Disabilities Focus, 1,* 9–10.

Cherkes-Julkowski, M., Gertner, N. and Norlander, I. (1986). Differences in cognitive processes among handicapped and average children: a group learning approach. *Journal of Learning Disabilities, 19,* 438–445.

Conant, J. (1961). *Slums and suburbs.* New York: McGraw-Hill, p. 25.

Deshler, D. and Schumaker, J. (1986). Learning strategies: an instructional alternative for low-achieving students. *Exceptional Children, 52,* 583–590.

Dunn, K. and Dunn, R. (1987). Dispelling outmoded beliefs about student learning. *Educational Leadership, 44,* 55–62.

D'Zamko, M. and Hedges, W. (1985). *Helping exceptional students succeed in the regular classroom.* West Nyack, New York: Parker Publishing Company, pp. 226–228.

Epps, S., Ysseldyke, J. and McGue, M. (1984). I know one when I see one: Differentiating LD and non-LD students. *Learning Disability Quarterly, 7,* 89–101.

Feuerstein, R. (1980). *Instrumental Enrichment.* Baltimore: University Park Press, pp. 9, 13, 42, 119, 176, 218.

Fields, M. and Lee, D. (1987). *Let's begin reading right.* Columbus: Merrill.

Gartland, D. and Rosenberg, M. (1987). Managing time in the LD classroom. *LD Forum, 12,* 8–10.

Harris, A. and Sipay, E. (1985). *How to increase reading ability* (8th ed.). New York: Longman.

Hess, A. and Greer, J. (1986). Educational triage and dropout rates. In Phi Delta Kappa Hot Topic Series, *Dropouts, pushouts, and other casualties.* (1987). Bloomington, IN: Phi Delta Kappa, 115–152.

Hodge, H. (1987). I know they can learn because I've taught them. *Educational Leadership, 44*, 3–4.

Inclusion of nonhandicapped low achievers and underachievers in learning disability programs (position statement by Council for Learning Disabilities). (1986). *Learning Disability Quarterly, 9*, 246.

Kaluger, G. and Kolson, C. (1978). *Reading and learning disabilities* (2nd ed.). Columbus: Charles Merrill, p. 16.

Karweit, N. (1984). Time-on-task reconsidered: A synthesis on time and learning. *Educational Leadership, 41*, 33–35.

Keogh, B. (1988). Improving services for problem learners: rethinking and restructuring. *Journal of learning disabilities, 21*, 19–22.

Kilby, G. (1984). Heading off failure before it starts. *Principal, 63*, 29–31.

Kirk, S. and Gallagher, J. (1986). *Educating exceptional children* (5th ed.). Boston: Houghton Mifflin.

Lerner, J. (1985). *Learning disabilities* (4th ed.). Dallas: Houghton Mifflin, p. 187.

Luick, A. and Senf, G. (1979). Where have all the children gone? *Journal of Learning Disabilities, 12*, 5–7.

McDill, E., Natriello, G., and Pallas, A. (1986). The high costs of high standards: school reform and dropouts. In Phi Delta Kappa Hot Topic Series, *Dropouts, pushouts, and other casualties.* (1987). Bloomington, IN: Phi Delta Kappa, 158–174.

Messerer, J., Hunt, E., Meyer, G., and Lerner, J. (1984). Feuerstein's Instrumental Enrichment: a new approach for activating intellectual potential in learning disabled youth. *Journal of Learning Disabilities, 17*, 322–325.

Mink, I., Meyers, C. and Nihira, K. (1984). Taxonomy of family life-styles: homes with slow-learning children. *American Journal Mental Deficiency, 89*, 111–123.

O'Shea, L. and Valcante, G. (1986). A comparison over time of relative discrepancy scores of low achievers. *Exceptional Children, 53*, 253–259.

Pehrsson, R. and Robinson, H. (1985). *The semantic organizer approach to writing and reading instruction.* Rockville, Maryland: Aspen Systems.

Shinn, M., Ysseldyke, J., Deno, S. and Tindal, G. (1986). A comparison of differences between students labeled LD and low achieving on measures of classroom performance. *Journal of Learning Disabilities, 19*, 545–552.

Samuels, S. (1986). Why children fail to learn and what to do about it. *Exceptional Children, 53*, 7–16.

Warner, M., Schumaker, J., Alley, G. and Deshler, D. (1980). Learning disabled adolescents in the public schools: are they different from other low achievers? *Exceptional Education Quarterly, 1*, 22–35.

Weber, K. (1987). Slow learners need a slower and steady pace. *The Education Digest, 52*, 51–53.

Wehlage, G., Rutter, R. and Turnbaugh, A. (1987). A program model for at-risk high school students. *Educational Leadership, 44,* 6.

Ysseldyke, J., Algozzine, B., Shinn, M. and McGue, M. (1982). Similarities and differences between low achievers and students classified as learning disabled. *Journal of Special Education, 6,* 73–85.

CHAPTER 17

HIGHER LEVEL THINKING:
EDUCATIONAL OPPORTUNITY OR EDUCATIONAL
NECESSITY?

SUZANNE WEGENER SOLED

In order for our children to succeed in a constantly changing world, they must possess the ability to do higher-level thinking—to apply, analyze, evaluate and synthesize information and concepts. These abilities are essential in enabling our children to think, to adapt to new learning situations, and to solve problems. Every child may be "at risk" if not provided with educational opportunities which do more than emphasize rote learning, memorization and verbatim recall.

The need for emphasis on higher level thinking during classroom instruction is considerable. This is especially true for our children at risk since they often miss out on these types of educational opportunities, opportunities which would help to insure that they received at least an adequate education. The nature of solving higher level thinking problems and tasks requires the child to become more actively involved in learning which in turn creates interest, enthusiasm and excitement: higher level thinking makes learning come alive. Higher level thinking is remembered and utilized by the learner long after the specifics of the subject area have been forgotten. The abilities involved in higher level thinking are believed to enable the child to see a connection between their own school learning and the everyday problems in their lives.

Unfortunately, there is a persistent and widespread finding that education in schools is primarily concerned only with the acquisition of information. Much of the time spent during classroom instruction is focused on the memorization of facts. One reason for this is that most teachers find this level the easiest at which to teach. Yet, when teachers only emphasize lower level thinking during classroom teaching, children rarely have the opportunity to learn in the classroom from observations, experimentation or firsthand experience. Similarly, when textbook writers develop textbooks that emphasize only the content to be memorized, they do little to provide learning experiences for students to solve real problems. When testing specialists design evaluation instruments for use in the schools, the tests consist largely of questions on factual knowledge and literal interpretation. In the United States, the majority of teaching methods, testing procedures and instructional materials emphasize recall and memorization. It is estimated that over 90 percent of the test questions public school students are asked require little more than information (Bloom, 1984).

The result of teachers teaching primarily facts and things to be memorized is the inability of many of our children to be able to do higher level thinking. The lack of attainment of thinking and problem-solving skills has been pointedly demonstrated by the International Project for the Evaluation of Educational Achievement which showed that in all the countries tested children perform best on lower level objectives requiring acquisition of knowledge, perform less well on objectives requiring interpretation or comprehension and perform least well on higher level objectives involving application and inferences (Bloom, 1974).

In contrast, there are some schools in the world in which school subjects are taught as methods of inquiry, and emphasis is placed on the underlying concepts and principles rather than on only the specific content to be remembered. The teaching and learning processes at such schools emphasize problem solving, application to new situations, analysis of situations, and creativity.

The ability to do higher level thinking or to solve higher level tasks, requiring the mental manipulation of bits of information previously learned to create or support an answer (Winne, 1979), is a desired educational outcome. For as we come to understand more and more about learning, we realize that it is more than the mere regurgitation of facts. And although the ability to analyze and apply knowledge is greatly valued, high levels of achievement in these areas are rarely found in traditional educational settings.

One of the underlying assumptions of many of the classrooms in which we find our at-risk children is that they are incapable of learning how to do higher level thinking. At one time the prevailing belief was that higher level thinking could only be learned by a few capable individuals. Thus, many teachers believed there was no point in teaching higher level thinking—the majority of children couldn't learn it. If higher level thinking were learned, it was assumed to only be by the higher ability children, who learned it on their own.

The construct argued here is that the learning of higher level thinking is not dependent upon the intelligence level nor on the academic achievement of the child. Research has more recently disputed the viewpoint that higher level thinking cannot be taught to all children. Studies have shown that most children can learn how to do problem solving and other types of higher level thinking if it becomes more central in the teaching-learning-testing process (Anania, 1981; Bloom and Broder, 1950; Burke, 1983; Chausow, 1955).

The underlying factor determining higher level thinking and achievement in several research studies is the availability of the opportunity to learn higher level thinking. When insufficient opportunities to learn higher level thinking exist, then low attainment on higher level thinking is expected. When the opportunity to learn higher level thinking is increased, so is the higher level thinking and achievement of the child. Thus, the low attainment of higher level thinking found to persist in school settings throughout the world is in large part due to the lack of opportunities in classrooms to learn and do higher level thinking. However, when children are provided with opportunities to learn higher level thinking, a large proportion of them are likely to learn them.

What kinds of educational opportunities can we provide to help children at risk move into the mainstream of learning so that they can become successful students and citizens? The rest of this chapter suggests some teaching and learning strategies which have been proven effective in increasing both the lower and higher cognitive level thinking skills of children.

Improving the Child's Processing of Instruction

Mastery Learning

One way to improve a child's processing of traditional instruction is by using mastery learning developed by Benjamin S. Bloom (1968). In brief, mastery learning tests the child on what was supposed to be learned to see what has been learned and to see what still needs to be learned. The child is then helped to learn any material not yet mastered (Guskey, 1985).

Although a learning strategy for mastery has historic roots which are centuries old, mastery learning has received a great deal of attention from theoreticians and practitioners in more recent years. Much of this attention is due to worldwide evidence that the use of mastery learning strategies in the classroom has significant positive effects on a variety of student learning outcomes (Block and Burns, 1977).

Central to the mastery learning strategies is the use of feedback-corrective procedures at various stages of the learning process. The use of the feedback and corrective process clearly differentiates mastery learning from more traditional instructional approaches by making part of the learning process individualized. The feedback-corrective process accomplishes this individualization by giving each child precise information on his or her learning process and by then directing the child to specific corrective activities. Successful application of mastery learning usually occurs when the feedback and corrective procedure has been completed.

The purpose of a feedback and corrective procedure is to monitor the child's progress and correct errors and misunderstandings shortly after they have occurred in the learning process. The feedback procedures typically involve brief formative tests at the end of each learning task which provide information about what the child has learned and what the child still needs to learn before attaining mastery. Mastery is typically defined as correctly answering 80 to 85 percent of the items on a criterion-referenced test. The correctives are suggestions and help the children to learn the ideas and material still needed to attain the mastery level of learning.

Similar to traditional classrooms, most classrooms employing mastery learning techniques have children learning the subject matter in a classroom with about thirty children per teacher. However, formative tests are given periodically for the purpose of providing feedback about how well the children have learned the material, rather than for the purpose of grading or judging. These tests help identify the specific learning difficulties a child is having as well as provide individualized information as to what needs to be done for the child to master the material.

Children who have not mastered the material engage in corrective work to learn that material. This typically takes one or two instructional periods to complete. Then a second parallel formative test is given to ensure that they have mastered this material before going on to learn new material.

Children who demonstrate mastery of the material on the first formative test engage in enrichment activities designated to extend their learning of the material or in other learning activities which are challenging and stimulating.

Numerous studies employing this strategy have shown that comparison of children who learn under more traditional conditions with children who learn under mastery learning conditions indicate that virtually all of the children in the mastery learning classrooms will be above the average of the children in the traditional classrooms.

The reason mastery learning appears to be so effective is that the sequence of formative testing and systematic correction of errors in learning provides each and every child with the opportunity to have a more appropriate quality of instruction than is usually available with traditional instruction. Under mastery learning, there is opportunity for all children to learn very well.

Mastery learning techniques have been heavily used to increase lower level thinking and achievement. This emphasis reflects much of current teaching practice where teachers teach mostly at the lower cognitive levels. However, in classrooms where the objective of the learning process is for the children to be able to do higher level thinking, mastery learning feedback-corrective procedures have also been shown to be effective. When the mastery learning strategies include at least one-third higher level problems and tasks, both higher as well as lower level achievement is increased (Soled, 1988). Thus, the best use of mastery learning for children at risk would include both lower and higher level thinking in the feedback-corrective procedures.

Improving the Teaching

Teachers Questioning Behavior

Questions play a major role in teaching. Teachers use questions to stimulate thinking and learning in children and as a tool to evaluate children's learning. Questions are also a major part of examinations and instructional materials.

Research studies have been conducted to specify the impact of teachers' questions on the quality and quantity of student achievement. A small number of studies have attempted to draw conclusions about the effects of particular kinds of questions and questioning strategies. These studies indicate that when teachers use predominately higher cognitive level questions, there is a positive effect on overall student achievement (Redfield and Rousseau, 1981). Other research indicates that when teachers' questions emphasize a particular cognitive level such as application, children's achievement scores at that level will be higher than the scores of children whose teacher did not emphasize questions at that cognitive level (Friedman, 1977). High level questions have also been shown to produce greater high and low level achievement in children than low level questions (Ryan, 1973; Kniep and Grossman, 1979). More specifically, when teachers ask at least one-third of their questions at the higher cognitive level, higher as well as lower level achievement is increased (Soled, 1987).

The importance of emphasizing higher cognitive levels in classroom instruction has become recognized by science teachers in the last twenty years. One result has been a greater emphasis on the development of process skills and on higher levels of thinking rather than on the recall of factual material in school science programs. Research has shown this emphasis has had a positive impact and that children were better able to respond to questions assessing higher levels of thinking and process skills in 1983 than in 1970 (Jacobson and Doran, 1985). Samples of tests items demonstrating improved responses included items requiring interpretation of data, reading and application of data, inferential thinking and analysis of data.

Tutoring

Prior endeavors to foster higher level thinking have been directed to improving the quality of instruction. Burke (1983) used tutoring as the maximal quality of instruction. In one of three studies on tutoring, the tutors were briefed on how to teach higher-level thinking to children. Burke found that the difference in the average higher level achievement between the children taught under traditional instruction and the children taught by tutors was approximately two standard deviations. This means the higher level achievement of the average child tutored in this study was above 95 percent of the students in the traditional classroom.

Cues and Explanations

Other attempts to facilitate higher level thinking have been directed toward the improvement of instructional cues. A study by Tenenbaum (1982) emphasized changing the teacher-student interaction by enhancing cues, participation and reinforcement in combination with mastery learning. Children receiving this type of enhanced instruction achieved above 96 percent of the children learning under traditional instruction. Mevarech (1980) improved instructional cues by teaching specific problem-solving strategies. The average child in this instructional setting was above 73 percent of the children in a traditional setting on higher level achievement.

Improving the Instructional Materials

Textbooks and Instructional Materials

Textbooks and other instructional materials play a major role in school learning. Instructional materials are used by teachers during 90–95 percent of classroom time, of which textbook use reflects 70 percent of that time. Research by the Educational Products Information Exchange (EPIE) Institute (1976) confirm the enormous role textbooks occupy in the teaching-learning process in schools. Instructional materials have been found to comprise 98 percent of the curriculum taught by teachers (Davis, Frymier, and Clinefelter, 1979).

The heavy use of instructional materials in the classroom makes their appropriateness for the learner even more essential. Yet another EPIE study found that instructional materials are frequently not appropriate to the needs of learners. This study found "that a majority of students were able to master 80 percent of the material in some of their subject-matter texts before they had even opened the books. Many books do not challenge the students to whom they are assigned" (National Commission on Educational Excellence, 1983, p. 21).

Textbook publishers frequently refine textbook material. Yet when looking at how textbooks have been improved, very little has been donein terms of helping children to develop higher level thinking skills.

A review by Nicely (1985) of secondary mathematics textbooks printed between 1961 and 1984 revealed that textbooks printed during the 1960s emphasized an average of 84 percent lower level cognitive behaviors and 16 percent higher level cognitive behaviors. During the 1970s the number of higher level behaviors decreased to 7 percent and only a slight increase of 10 percent occurred in the 1980s. This evidence gathered led Nicely to assert that "If our goal is to help students acquire higher-order thinking skills, then teachers, curriculum committees and people responsible for staff development will have to supplement the commercially available textbooks as they plan for effective mathematics instruction" (p.29).

One study did supplement a mostly lower cognitive level textbook with additional instructional material so that students received at least 33 percent higher level illustrations, problems, and tasks (Soled, 1986). Children receiving these improved instructional materials had significantly better achievement on both higher as well as lower level achievement as compared to children who received predominantly lower level materials.

Advanced Organizers

There are a variety of other ways to improve instructional materials. One method is the use of advanced organizers (Ausubel, 1960) where students first read or listen to the advanced organizer passage and then complete the material to be learned. The advanced organizer serves to help interrelate the material the child already knows with what is needed to know to learn the new material. These Ausubelean organizers have been shown to be moderately effective in improving the achievement of children, raising the average achievement of a class from the fiftieth to the fifty-eighth percentile.

Combining Strategies

Achievement may also be increased by combining improved instructional materials with proven methods of increasing achievement. Such combinations appear to have an additive effect. One example is combining the use of advanced organizers with mastery learning techniques (Avalos, 1986). Another example is combining instructional materials which emphasize higher cognitive levels with higher and lower level

questions in the formative testing and in the feedback-corrective procedure (Mevarech, 1980).

Additional Ways to Improve Educational Opportunities

This chapter has addressed the importance of higher level thinking,
and suggested some teaching and learning strategies to increase the
thinking and achievement of children. There are numerous other educational opportunities that can be provided to our children at risk to help
move them into the mainstream of learning. Examples of other educational opportunities that are likely to increase children's higher level
thinking include:

- Using cooperative learning strategies where children work together
  in pairs or small groups to do problem solving.
- Having children create questions requiring higher level thinking.
- Asking children to evaluate or synthesize several different ideas.
- Having children apply knowledge they have learned to new situa-
  tions.
- Insuring that the textbooks and other instructional materials used
  include higher level illustrations, problems and tasks.
- Including higher level thinking in the objectives of the instructional
  curriculum.
- Increasing teachers' expectations that children at risk can learn
  higher level thinking.
- Employing the new science and mathematics curricula which have
  increased emphasis on higher level thinking.
- Using peers or children at upper grade levels to do tutoring of
  children at risk on higher level thinking.
- Increasing children's classroom participation by systematically calling on all children to do higher level thinking, not just the ones who
  raise their hands.
- Waiting for at least thirty seconds to call on a child when a higher
  level problem, task, or question has been posed.

Implementing Educational Opportunities

While many of the teaching and learning strategies discussed here have been proven to be effective, the question arises as to whether they can be implemented by a teacher, school, or school district without difficulty or great cost. Although tutoring is currently regarded as one of the best opportunities for learning, it is not practical for widespread school use where resources and manpower are limited. Yet, it can serve as a yardstick against which to measure the effect of more practical educational opportunities.

The strategies discussed in this chapter may be of particular interest to teachers and schools, since implementation should be relatively easy and not costly. The mastery learning strategy has already been developed to the point where teachers in countries throughout the world teaching in all grade levels are able to attain high levels of achievement. The mastery learning feedback-corrective procedures can even be done by children working on their own, without additional instructional materials being provided by their teacher.

Teachers already know the differences between lower and higher level thinking and are able to ask questions of their students which require either. If teachers increase their use of higher level questioning, they can increase both the lower and higher level thinking of children.

Advanced organizers can be developed by textbook publishers for use in new textbooks. Such texts could be used by teachers without any training or preparation and could be used by children with little explanation from their teacher. Where textbooks and instructional materials are not available, teachers can create their own organizational aids for a topic by introducing important ideas and concepts which interrelate the various components of the subject matter. Students can be asked to note what is already known about new subject matter, what questions they still have, what else they would like to learn about the topic, and to summarize the main ideas they have learned.

Building higher level thinking into the instructional materials and evaluation procedures used in classrooms can be done by teachers with very little training or basic changes in their teaching procedures. Given improved instructional materials and evaluation procedures, many teachers throughout the world should be able to provide a way to improve the thinking of children at risk.

SUMMARY

Children are at risk when they are not provided with educational opportunities which make higher level thinking central in the teaching-learning process. The lack of this type of opportunity is detrimental to these students and ultimately to our nation. Virtually all children are capable of doing higher level thinking; yet in the majority of classrooms we find the emphasis to be on the teaching of things to be remembered for only as long as it takes to use them on an examination.

It is hoped that teachers and schools see the importance of incorporating higher level thinking in instruction and will use the strategies discussed here. It should be realized that there are a number of potential other strategies that also should be explored.

This chapter has addressed the persistent and widespread finding that education is primarily concerned with the acquisition of information. While lower level thinking is of importance, in a rapidly changing world it is likely to be of less significance as compared to higher level thinking. The UNESCO report, *Learning to Be*, implies that a society which cannot master problem solving and inferential thinking will quickly be outmoded.

Teaching-learning strategies can be developed and implemented to enable practically all children to attain higher level thinking. These strategies can be instrumental in moving children at risk into the mainstream of learning so that they can become successful in school and in society. In other words, higher level thinking is more than an educational opportunity, it is an educational necessity.

REFERENCES

Anania, J. (1981). *The effect of quality of instruction on the cognitive and affective learning of students.* Unpublished doctoral dissertation, University of Chicago.

Ausebel, D.P. (1960). The use of advance organizers in the learning and retention of meaningful verbal material. *Journal of Educational Psychology, 51,* 267–272.

Avalos, C.A. (1986). *Improving student learning by using advance organizers and organizers at the middle and end of each textbook chapter.* Unpublished doctoral dissertation, University of Chicago.

Block, J.H. and Burns, R.B. (1977). Mastery Learning. In L. Shulman (Ed.), *Review of research in education* (Vol. 4). Itasca, IL: F.E. Peacock.

Bloom, B.S. (1968). Learning for mastery. *Evaluation Comment* (UCLA–CSIEP), *1*(2), 1–12.

Bloom, B.S. (1974). Implications of the IEA studies for curriculum and instruction. *School Review, 82,* 413–434.

Bloom, B.S. (1984). The 2 sigma problem: The search for methods of group instruction as effective as one-to-one tutoring. *Educational Researcher, 13*(6), 4–16.

Bloom, B.S. and Broder, L.B. (1950). *Problem-solving processes of college students: An exploratory investigation.* Chicago: University of Chicago Press.

Burke, A.J. (1983). *Students' potential for learning contrasted under tutorial and group approaches to instruction.* Unpublished doctoral dissertation, University of Chicago.

Chausow, H.M. (1955). *The organization of learning experiences to achieve more effectively the objective of critical thinking in the general social science course at the junior college level.* Unpublished doctoral dissertation, University of Chicago.

Davis, O.L., Jr., Frymier, J.R. and Clinefelter, D. (1982). Curriculum materials used by eleven-year-old pupils: An analysis using the Annehurst curriculum classification system. *Journal of Educational Research, 75,* 325–332.

EPIE Institute. (1976). Report Number 76, *National study of the nature and the quality of instructional materials most used by teachers and learners.*

Friedman, M. (1977). *Teachers' cognitive emphasis and pupil achievement. Educational Research Quarterly, 2,* 42–47.

Guskey, T.R. (1985). *Implementing mastery learning.* Belmont, CA: Wadsworth.

Jacobson, W.J. and Doran, R.L. (1985). The second international science study: U.S. results. *Phi Delta Kappan, 66,* 414–417.

Kniep, W.M. and Grossman, G. (1979). The effects of high level questions in competitive and cooperative environments on the achievement of selected social studies concepts. *The Journal of Educational Research, 73,* 82–85.

Mevarech, Z.R. (1980). *The role of teaching-learning strategies and feedback-corrective procedures in developing higher cognitive achievement.* Unpublished doctoral dissertation, University of Chicago.

National Commission on Educational Excellence. (1983). *A nation at risk.* Washington, D.C.: U.S. Department of Education.

Nicely, R.F., Jr. (1985). Higher-order thinking skills in mathematics textbooks. *Educational Leadership, 42,* 26–30.

Redfield, D.L. and Rousseau, E.W. (1981). A meta-analysis of experimental research on teacher questioning behavior. *Review of Educational Research, 51,* 237–245.

Ryan, F.L. (1973). Differentiated effects of levels of questioning on student achievement. *Journal of Experimental Education, 41,* 63–67.

Soled, S.W. (1986). *Group methods of instruction which are as effective as one-to-one tutoring in improving higher as well as lower mental processes.* Unpublished doctoral dissertation, University of Chicago.

Soled, S.W. (1987). *Teaching processes to improve both higher as well as lower mental process achievement.* Paper presented at the annual meeting of the American Educational Research Association, Washington, D.C. (Eric Document 287823).

Soled, S.W. (1988). *Does mastery learning improve higher order thinking as well as rote learning?* Paper presented at the annual meeting of the American Educational Research Association, New Orleans.

Tenenbaum, G. (1982). *A method of group instruction which is as effective as one-to-one tutorial instruction.* Unpublished doctoral dissertation, University of Chicago.

Winne, P.H. (1979). Experiments relating teachers' use of higher cognitive questions to student achievement. *Review of Educational Research, 49,* 13–50.

Chapter 18

RISKS TO CHILDREN
RELATED TO
SCHOOL DISTRICT GIFTED PROGRAMS

JUDY W. EBY

A Personal Note:
A Growing Awareness of Children
At Risk in Gifted Education

Since the early 1970s there has been a nationwide interest in gifted education which has resulted in the hasty creation of widely varied gifted programs funded in part by the states and in part by local school districts. I have been actively involved in the field of gifted education since 1978, when I became a gifted program coordinator, and initiated an elementary gifted program in a small Illinois school district. After receiving rudimentary training in the form of a three-semester-hour course and a noncredit workshop in gifted education, I was given total responsibility over the design of the program, including establishing identification procedures to select the gifted children from the rest of the school population and establishing the educational goals and learning experiences which the selected children received. I was also responsible for evaluating the effectiveness of my own program.

From my coursework and readings, I learned the "tricks of the trade" in gifted education. I learned how to efficiently screen children for inclusion in the program on the basis of available standardized test data. I learned how to write my own teacher recommendation checklists based upon "characteristics of the gifted." The accepted practice was (and IS) to create a checklist consisting of twenty items which sounded good to me and to distribute this checklist to classroom teachers asking them to recommend any child in their rooms who match these characteristics.

The collected checklists were scored (5 points per item, a total possible score of 100) and the results were combined with other test data on a matrix. I learned how to manipulate the scores on the matrix by arbitrarily assigning weights to scores so that children could be compared with each other for selection purposes.

The state of Illinois would pay my school district a certain dollar amount for each child in the program up to 5 percent of the total population of the school. I therefore quickly learned how to manipulate the data on the matrix in order to select no more than 5 percent of the population for my new program. These children and their parents received letters from me acknowledging their new status. They were considered to be the "gifted children" in our school, and were now eligible for gifted programming and other services to meet their special needs.

After a year of running such a program, I was horrified by the side effects, which were consequences of *my actions*. Children identified for the program would beg to be released from the program because they didn't want to be different than their friends. Children who were not in the program would come up to me in the hall and beg to be included. Midway through the year, I was teaching a unit on architecture and scale drawing to a group of junior high students. This unit consisted of many rich learning experiences, including a tour of Chicago architecture, a visit to the firm that designed the Sears Tower, interviews with practicing architects and opportunities for children to create and display their own original scale models. A teacher asked me if I was aware that her student, Mark G., spent all his spare time drawing house plans and scale drawings. I wasn't. I had never heard of the child. His test scores had never brought him to my attention and no teacher had ever seen him as outstanding in the twenty gifted characteristics I had selected for my checklist.

Further coursework and gifted conferences gave me many more ideas for programming and further refinements to simplify and document my identification procedures, so that parents who questioned us about their children's candidacy would be satisfied with our statistics. But the ethics of what we were doing was never mentioned, neither was the validity of our methods.

Over the years, I altered my program radically. Between 1978 and 1984, when I left the public schools for college teaching, I became increasingly sensitive and aware of the effects of my (often arbitrary) decisions upon the lives of children. As a result, the gifted program model which evolved under my direction was administered with the guideline borrowed from the field of medicine: "First, do no harm."

In this chapter, I will outline some of the many unnecessary risks affecting children's lives which I have observed in gifted programs over the years. My message to educators involved in gifted education is that we must become more sensitive and aware of the effects of our actions and decisions upon children's lives. We must be aware of and take full responsibility for the administrative decisions we make which cause children to be at risk. At the conclusion, I will describe a gifted program model which eliminates these risks and has the added advantage of a built-in evaluation system to measure the effects of the program in the behavior and the products of the participants.

The Risks to Children Competing for Eligibility

Each morning of the academic year children are waking up, getting dressed, eating their breakfasts (hopefully), and setting off for school. Before they leave home, they gather together their school books and papers, their lunches and jackets, their pencils and crayons. They also bring along their hopes and their fears, their curiosity and their resentments, their diverse cultural backgrounds and physical handicaps, their personalities and their own unique combination of strengths, weaknesses, talents and deficiencies.

Just as children differ in dozens of important ways, so do the schools they attend. In some communities, schools have the resources to provide small classes, well trained support and guidance personnel, a wide diversity of extracurricular activities, and comprehensive gifted programs designed to meet the needs of a wide variety of children with unique talents. In other communities, schools struggle to meet the basic requirements of state mandated programs. There are few resources left over for extras like gifted programs.

Most communities fall somewhere between these two extremes. They establish educational priorities and apportion their resources accordingly. Gifted programs are rarely seen as a high priority, but may frequently be funded at a minimal level by the local district in order to attract the state funds available for such a program. When this happens, the program is usually quite restrictive in terms of numbers of children served. Quotas of 2 to 5 percent of the school population are normally established. With scarce resources and limited access to the program, there is bound to be fierce competition among the children and their parents for the highly prized status and services of the program.

Many of the risks to children could be reduced or eliminated if gifted programming were woven into the regular school programs and curricula. Mainstreaming with appropriate support systems is considered to be in the child's best interests in other types of special education. I believe that to be true in gifted education as well. Curricula can be designed which have built in challenges and opportunities for acceleration without separating and labeling children gifted.

The Risks to Children Labeled Gifted

School districts which limit access to their gifted programs to a quota or percentage of the population do so by identifying this quota and labeling them "gifted children." There is growing awareness that labels are harmful to children whether they connote handicaps or talents. It is becoming well understood that negative, special education labels such as EMH or BD can have serious consequences upon children due to lowered self-concept combined with peer and adult expectations. But what are the risks for a child who is granted the seemingly positive label of gifted child?

In my view, the risks to a child labeled gifted are just as great as to a child labeled a slow learner. Educational psychologist Sylvia Rimm, who specializes in research and clinical practice with children who are gifted underachievers, agrees. In Rimm's experience, labeling a child "gifted" is putting that child at risk. "Any label that unrealistically narrows prospects for performance by a child may be damaging" (Rimm, 1986, p. 84). Peer pressures and resentments occur which may cause the child to cringe and hide from the unwanted notoriety. Even more damaging are the increased risk of unrealistic expectations from parents and teachers which are likely to result from labeling the child gifted.

Haim Ginott (1965) points out that "Direct praise of personality, like sunlight, is uncomfortable and blinding" (p. 41). Children who are labeled "gifted" feel set apart from their peers; they feel guilt and fear when they don't live up to the label. While their parents may relish the label at first, they will find it difficult to explain to other children in the family.

As professional educators, we must also become more sensitive to the effects of labeling upon other nonidentified children. We must recognize and take responsibility for the fact that the remaining 95 percent of the school population are also placed at greater risk in that we are also unwittingly labeling them "nongifted." Being excluded from a gifted program may cause a child to undervalue his or her own talents and abilities to the extent that they remain unrealized throughout his school career.

Labels also cause enormous difficulties in school programs when either a child's performance or the criteria for selection change and children's eligibility for the program changes. It is difficult to explain to parents why a child who was labeled "gifted" in an earlier grade or in a different school district isn't "gifted" anymore. The consequences of such an action can be intensely negative for the affected child.

In concurrence with Rimm and Ginott, I believe that educators must become more conscious of the risks of labeling. We must take responsibility for revising programs established on such a basis or we may find ourselves defending our decisions in a court of law, if the parents of either a labeled, unlabeled or mislabeled child bring suit against us. I recommend a complete cessation of the use of the term "gifted child." It is divisive, psychologically unsound, hurtful and difficult to defend in public education. The field of gifted education may have been initiated by Terman's Stanford-Binet IQ test and his arbitrary label that a child with an IQ above 130 was a gifted child, but in the present day both IQ and the gifted label are oversimplifications of a complex set of talents and motivating forces which may be expressed in an infinite variety of ways depending upon the environment.

The Risks to Children Who Are Culturally Different

An important aspect of the child's environment is the prevailing culture. When children go to their neighborhood school or to the school assigned to them in order to achieve racial integration, they are, quite arbitrarily, either part of the cultural majority or minority. The values and beliefs of the dominant culture tend to prevail over minority cultures in terms of the definitions of giftedness as well as other aspects of life and education.

Students who were raised in homes with cultural heritage that matches the dominant culture of their school are more likely to be identified as gifted or talented than children from culturally different homes. Rimm (1985) suggests that the talents, strengths and gifts of the culturally different children are in many ways "invisible" to the prevailing culture.

When cultural differences extend to language differences, the problems are compounded. Many unusually talented children are overlooked because of their lack of proficiency with the English language. They are given academic tasks which match their English language skills, even though they are capable of doing far more difficult and academically challenging tasks.

In many urban school districts, the percentage of culturally different children is increasing at unprecedented rates. Black and Hispanic children now outnumber Caucasian children in many cities. But the prevailing culture of gifted programs in this country is determined in great part by the tests which are used for identification. These tests were created by highly verbal Caucasians, to reflect their own values and strengths. Indeed, the cultural bias of most verbal tests ensures that the culturally different child will remain invisible.

The Risks to Children With Physical Handicaps

Children with physical handicaps affecting their sight, hearing or motor abilities are seldom included in gifted programs. This is because their handicap is seen as more significant than any other aspect of their personality, including their unrealized talents and gifts. A blind child is educated to compensate for his lack of sight; a hearing impaired child is assisted in learning to cope with her deficiency. Children with bright and inquiring minds trapped inside crippled or spastic bodies are especially vulnerable.

The educational priority for the handicapped child is usually to provide remedial or other support services which will allow the child to be mainstreamed. If children receiving gifted services are "pulled out" of the mainstream then it is unlikely that the handicapped child will receive such services.

The Risks to Learning Disabled Children

Children with perceptual-motor deficits may also have significant talents or academic gifts which are never discovered during his school career. Many dyslexic individuals report that their school experiences caused them to feel stupid or minimally competent, because their considerable talents were masked by their deficits. The current practice of grouping L.D. children with EMH or "slow learners" for remedial services causes even greater harm to the child's self concept. Learning disabled children may have unusual abilities in academic areas such as math or science or in their general abstract thinking abilities. These are frequently overlooked because of poor writing, spelling or other decoding and encoding skills. Poor organizational abilities may also contribute to the child's talents going unnoticed.

Rick Baily, an L.D. specialist in northern Illinois, tells about two students he is currently working with. Terence, age 12, is a sixth grade student who has a significant disability in auditory processing. As a result, he has not yet been able to master phonics. He also possesses a severely limited auditory and visual memory. These disabilities have hampered Terence's ability to learn how to read; his phonics skills are almost nonexistent. As he struggles to decode every reading assignment, it is a painful and difficult experience for him.

But if you didn't know about Terence's disabilities, you would never suspect. His math skills are unusually proficient. He is also a very verbally articulate child with a vast fund of knowledge about the world of science. He appears to be very well-read, though his knowledge comes from public television broadcasts rather than books. Terence was briefly included in his district's gifted program. He was not successful in the program because the learning activities depended upon reading to a great extent. His teacher fears that Terence will become deeply discouraged with all academic work because of its focus on reading, and that he is a child at risk despite his interest in the world and his math and science talents.

Another of Mr. Bailey's students is Alex, a seven year old who has been retained in second grade this year. Alex shows enormous interest in learning. He loves books, thirsts for new knowledge and skills and shows prodigious brain power and speed when answering questions aloud. Alex's motor skills, however, are unusually slow. Writing is a slow, painful process for him. His letter formation is awkward and immature. As a result he experiences enormous frustration when his hand cannot keep up with his quick and active thoughts. Behavior problems result. When he is asked to write, he squirms, talks and gets out of his seat to avoid the painful writing process. His teacher fears that his disability puts him at risk of being seen as a behavior problem rather than as a bright child with no ability to communicate his thoughts.

With the aid of a learning disabilities program, both Terence and Alex may learn to compensate for their disabilities over time. Their teacher fears, however, that with compensation, their performance will be seen as only as average, while their considerable strengths and talents may never be properly addressed.

The Risks to Children From Low Socioeconomic Backgrounds

The abundance or deprivation of the child's home environment has an enormous effect upon the his or her achievement in school. Roy Pellicano, a high school teacher in Brooklyn, sees disadvantaged children as a "domestic third world" (1987, p. 47). They are perceived as being "unproductive, underdeveloped and noncompetitive" when compared to children with greater advantages.

No test can accurately fortell the hidden potential of a child whose verbal skills and experience with the ways of the world have been severely limited in early childhood. Because of their limited experiences, these children are likely to appear low in academic ability. Tests appear to confirm their deficits, and they are rarely looked at again by gifted program personnel. In reality, there may be children from economically deprived environments who are capable of very high achievement, if they are provided with experiences which will make up for their early deficits. Ironically, enriched experiences offered to eligible, identified gifted children (and withheld from others) may be exactly what is needed by impoverished children.

A New Initiative in Gifted Education—Open Access Gifted Programs Designed to Develop Gifted Behaviors in All Children

As described above, current gifted programs which are based upon the notion of identifying and serving a small quota of gifted children may cause more harm than good. Since they are usually evaluated by the personnel who designed the program, the actual effects of such programs may never be known. The accepted practice in gifted program evaluation consists of a survey of satisfaction on the part of *already identified and served children and their parents*. Evaluation in terms of achievement is typically done by a checklist of accomplishments of those in the program which is communicated to the parents at year-end. Those children who succeed in the program are maintained, while those who fail to achieve are "counseled out of the program."

Such rudimentary and self-serving evaluation procedures provide very little real information in terms of actual achievement or growth in any systematic way. They also provide little or no information about the beneficial or harmful effects of the program upon the entire school community.

A new initiative is needed in gifted education—one that creates a positive, growth-oriented achievement motivation on the part of children in a school building. The mission of gifted education has been poorly and inadequately defined. Rather than identifying and serving a tiny minority of children in an isolated environment, the true mission of gifted education could be reevaluated to provide a stimulating challenge to all children to take part in enriched learning and talent developing experiences.

A new initiative is also needed in the evaluation of the effects of gifted programming. There is a critical need in the field of Gifted Education to reach consensus on an operational definition of giftedness such that it encourages greater consistency in pupil selection, programming approaches, curriculum development and evaluation.

Operational Definition of Gifted Behavior

The new initiative which I propose is a model of gifted programming based not upon the exclusive and discriminatory notion of gifted children, but upon the more inclusive notion of encouraging the development of "gifted behavior" in children from all populations.

In order to provide an operational definition of gifted behavior, (i.e., behaviors associated with and related to demonstrations of talents and gifts), I conducted a review of 32 studies of creativity, intelligence, talent development, productivity, inventiveness, achievement and giftedness in 1983–1986 (Eby, 1983, 1985). I synthesized the attributes identified in these studies into the following ten behavioral variables:

- Perceptiveness
- Active Interaction with the Environment
- Reflectiveness
- Persistence
- Independence
- Goal Orientation
- Originality
- Productivity
- Self-Evaluation
- Effective Communication of Findings

The definitions or descriptors of each variable have been fully described and operationalized in a set of instruments called *The Eby Gifted Behavior Index* (GBI) published in 1988. As the sample instrument in Figure 18-1 shows, the behaviors are described in terms of observable behaviors, which can be verified by systematic observations and reports of an individual's actions, processes and products.

The six forms of the GBI allow assessment in six different content or talent areas. The Verbal form assesses a child's performance in literary interpretation, writing and speaking. Other versions of the Index assess a child's performance in Math/Science/Problem Solving; Music; Visual and Spatial Arts; Social/Leadership; and Mechanical/Technical/Inventiveness. The instruments are intended to allow classroom teachers or other observers to evaluate the extent to which these behaviors are used and demonstrated by students in six different content and talent areas.

Assessments of a child's demonstrated gifted behaviors can be used in the process of identifying children for gifted programs. Children from every culture and socioeconomic status can and do show evidence of such behaviors in one or more of the talent areas. Children with learning disabilities and other handicaps can still demonstrate gifted behaviors in the areas of their strengths and talents. By selecting the appropriate form of the GBI, a child's strengths and talents can be assessed independently of his deficiencies.

Gifted Behavior Program Model

Providing an operational definition and assessment of a child's gifted behaviors is only half of the intent of the Gifted Behavior Program Model (Eby, 1983, 1984a, 1985). The next step is the design of curriculum to encourage the development of gifted behaviors. The key to this approach is that each curriculum unit requires the student to create a high quality, original product. Children are highly motivated by a task with a tangible product which they can keep or display or share. The behavioral processes used by the child while he or she is creating the product, as well as the product itself, may be observed and assessed by the teacher in order to evaluate the child's developing levels of gifted behavior.

As behaviors are used and rewarded by the environment, they are developed. Each opportunity given to children to create an original, high quality product calls upon the child to be perceptive, active, reflective, persistent, independent, goal-oriented, original, productive, self-evaluative and to effectively communicate the findings he or she made during the process. The more products created by the child, the greater opportunity for the development of his or her gifted behavior.

The Gifted Behavior Model allows and encourages children throughout the school to be appropriately challenged in a variety of academic

EBY GIFTED BEHAVIOR INDEX
General Checklist
This is a sample document. Gifted Behavior Checklists are available in six forms:
Verbal, Math/Science/Problem-Solving, Social/Leadership, Visual/Spatial, Music, and
Mechanical/Inventiveness
Order From D.O.K. Publications, East Aurora NY

Name_____ Age_____ Date_____

School_____Teacher_____Grade or Year_____

Rated by_____Total Score _____

DIRECTIONS: Please rate this student in terms of the following behavioral descriptors. Circle the numb
which indicates the level or degree of each behavior you have observed .

5=Evidence of this behavior is shown consistently in most activities
4=Evidence of this behavior is shown often in many activities
3=Evidence of this behavior is shown occasionally in some activities
2=Evidence of this behavior is shown infrequently in activities
1=Evidence of this behavior is shown rarely or never

Perceptiveness

1.	Distinguishes between important and unimportant elements, issues and problems	5	4	3	2	1
2.	Perceives and uses subtle and mature patterns, connections and relationships	5	4	3	2	1

Active Interaction with the Environment

3.	Is active rather than passive; Volunteers or chooses to work on self-selected tasks	5	4	3	2	1
4.	Energetically searches for information, ideas and solutions to problems	5	4	3	2	1

Reflectiveness

5.	Shows mature, in-depth understanding of complex ideas in self-selected topics or talent areas	5	4	3	2	1
6.	Works for accuracy; Thinks out the best possible solutions or conclusions	5	4	3	2	1

Persistence

7.	Displays focus, concentration, and absorption on self-selected tasks	5	4	3	2	1
8.	Overcomes problems and difficulties to solve problems and finish products	5	4	3	2	1

EBY GIFTED BEHAVIOR INDEX

General Checklist

Independence

9. Is a self-starter; Works with little or no assistance
    or support   5   4   3   2   1

10. Expresses strong preferences and ideas;
    Redefines goals to fit own interests   5   4   3   2   1

Goal Orientation

11. Has high intrinsic standards; Revises and improves   5   4   3   2   1
    products to meet them

12. Can state and discuss goals and plans to achieve them   5   4   3   2   1

Originality

13. Is a risk-taker; Is willing to experiment with novel ideas
    and forms of expression   5   4   3   2   1

14. Synthesizes elements from many sources into fresh,
    new ideas and products   5   4   3   2   1

Productivity

15. Shows fluency of ideas and/or products; Makes many
    responses to a problem or challents   5   4   3   2   1

16. Works efficiently; Finishes high quality products on or
    before deadline   5   4   3   2   1

Self-Evaluation

17. Knows own strengths and weaknesses; Uses strengths;
    Selects appropriately challenging tasks   5   4   3   2   1

18. Monitors own progress; Knows when to revise and when
    a product is finished   5   4   3   2   1

Effective Communication of Ideas

19. Ideas and purposes are stated with clarity   5   4   3   2   1

20. Uses appropriate methods and styles of communication
    to match purpose (e.g. illustrations, models , graphs)   5   4   3   2   1

Figure 18-1.

and talent areas. While most gifted programs rely upon activities which are highly oriented toward reading for input and writing for output, this model allows children to build upon their strengths and to produce something in their own talent area. Several different learning styles are recognized. Physically handicapped children may express the ten gifted behaviors in verbal products such as stories or poems. For children with disabilities that make verbal production difficult, the behaviors may be expressed through visual/spatial products such as models, drawings, paintings, graphs. Blind children can compose and perform original musical products. Children with learning disabilities can invent machines or draw up blueprints. Children from a variety of cultures can demonstrate extraordinary talents through math and science experiments and products.

The structure of such a gifted program consists of a series of challenging units of study filled with enriched experiences and opportunities for new learning and skill building. The units may be developed around any interesting and stimulating theme or topic, either one related to the regular curriculum or completely different as desired. Designed and taught by classroom teachers, the units are presented to children realistically as challenging work, designed to stretch their abilities. Children who wish to take part in the unit are required to submit a brief "pretask" product to demonstrate their gifted behavior in that subject or talent area (Eby, 1983, 1984).

Units of study may be limited to single academic areas, such as a math unit in probability, algebra or geometry. Other units of study may be cross-disciplinary enrichment opportunities which appeal to children's interests, i.e., dinosaurs for primary children, aviation for middle elementary, heroes for junior high or fashion as a statement of philosophy for high school students. Weaving in strands of literature, primary and secondary research, surveys, graphs and scientific experiments, these units can be powerfully motivating to children. The type of unit offered is limited only by the imagination of the curriculum designer.

This highly motivating program meets the needs of the "invisible" children who would ordinarily be overlooked in traditional identification systems using standardized tests. In the Gifted Behavior Program Model, identification is a natural and flexible part of the learning process. Each unit is offered to children who can satisfactorily meet the pretask requirements regardless of age, sex, learning disability, cultural background or physical handicap.

One of the effects of this programming is a school climate in which teachers are stimulated and challenged to produce and teach units based on their own strengths and interests. In effect, they are modeling the gifted behavior concept for children as they communicate their enthusiasm for the subject or topic they have selected. Children are excited by the prospect of the variety of learning experiences made available to them. Parents enjoy their own involvement with their children's learning. In effect, the entire community is involved with the common goal of developing their gifted behavior in a self-selected unit of study.

Another effect of this program alternative is that children are encouraged to demonstrate their many hidden strengths and talents. Rather than limiting the program to academic (usually highly verbal or mathematical) abilities, the types of units offered are unlimited in subject or talent areas served.

A significant advantage of this program model is that a systematic evaluation of the effects of the program is specified by the operational definition of gifted behavior. If developing the ten gifted behaviors is the goal of the program, then the units of study are designed with the objectives of allowing children to successfully learn to use these behaviors. In fact, the definition can easily be translated into "gifted behavioral objectives." For example, any of the units mentioned above could have as an objective, "The student will perceive the patterns and relationships in (probability; dinosaurs; aviation; heroes; or fashion/philosophy) by creating a chart of (die throws; dinosaur size and food source; airplane engine type and speed; heroic strengths and flaws; hem lengths and political freedom).

In order to evaluate student achievement, the students participate in a joint teacher-student assessment of the extent to which each gifted behavioral objective was met by the student in the unit. By participating in the evaluation procedure, it is assured that the gifted behavioral objective of "self-evaluation" will be met.

In order to evaluate the overall effectiveness of the program, data can be gathered to demonstrate the number of students participating. The goal of this model is to attract and involve the largest possible number of children into the program, rather than the fewest possible as is presently done. It is possible to chart the involvement of certain subgroups of the school population, as desired. Are low SES children being successful in the program? Are physically handicapped children taking part? Are the special needs of any group of children being adequately addressed?

The possibilities for adapting this program to children with special needs are limitless. Units may be designed to attract or meet the needs of a special population. For example, a unit on biomedical engineering might have a special appeal for physically handicapped children, but would also attract science-oriented children from the entire school population.

Finally, let us consider this method of identification in terms of its validity as a means of discovering talented individuals with special gifts, strengths and abilities. Is this method as valid as the other, better known achievement and intelligence assessment devices?

Consider adult applications for prestigious schools, grants for research, tryouts for competitive sports teams, auditions for plays or orchestras and applications for employment with highly regarded companies. What does an editor want to see before awarding a lucrative advance on a book? What does an architect have to do to get a contract? What does an artist show a gallery? Test scores? Hardly.

In real life, the gifted artist is distinguished from his less gifted peers by comparing his paintings with theirs. The musician auditions by playing a sample of his repertoire. The architect provides scale models or drawings to win a contract. The writer provides her editor with a chapter or two of the book she wants to write.

In regard to finding talent, Benjamin Bloom noted that "situational tests in which the examinee attacks real problems are undoubtedly excellent ways of observing and predicting creativity" (1963, p. 260). An educator who specializes in personality and measurement, Fiske remarked that " . . . there is no better way of selecting promising applicants than the properly devised and administered work sample" (1981, p. 4). Renzulli described the need for an identification process consisting of " . . . activities that are conscientiously and systematically designed to develop task commitment and creativity could be viewed as the situations or occasions whereby we can spot examples of gifted behavior" (1981, p. ix).

Present identification systems can be markedly improved by the use of such situational tests, work samples and conscientiously and systematically designed activities which allow children to create original products, give evidence of their talent or otherwise demonstrate their gifts and talents. These performance tasks can be used alone or in combination with other assessment devices to aid in the identification process by allowing children to demonstrate their talents and gifts in a meaningful way. They may be especially valuable in the identification of children with language deficiencies or other cultural or physical differences which invalidate their test scores.

Children with unusual disabilities, deficiencies or disadvantages may also have enormous abilities, talents and advantages. We must discard our present culturally dominant view of giftedness and replace it with a more open, pluralistic definition and system of identification so that the children described in this chapter will be easily spotted and well served by those providing gifted services in their school districts.

REFERENCES

Bloom, B. (1963) Report by the examiner's office of the University of Chicago, in Taylor, C. (ed.) *Scientific Creativity.* New York: John Wiley.

Bloom, B. (1964) *Stability and Change in Human Characteristics.* New York: John Wiley.

Bloom, B. (Ed.) (1985) *Developing Talent in Young People.* New York: Ballantine Books.

Clark, B. (1983) *Growing up Gifted.* Columbus, OH: Charles Merrill.

Cox, J., Daniel, N., and Boston, B. (1985) *Educating Able Learners,* Austin, TX: University of Texas Press.

Eby, J. (1983) Gifted behavior—a non-elitist approach, *Educational Leadership.* 40, 8, pp. 30–36.

Eby, J. (1984) Developing gifted behavior, *Educational Leadership.* 41, 7, pp. 35–43.

Eby, J. (1986) *The Relationship Between Gifted Behavioral Processes Observed in Students and the Quality and Originality of Their Creative Products* Ann Arbor, MI: University Microfilms International.

Feldman, D. (1979) Toward a Non-elitist conception of giftedness. *Phi Delta Kappan,* 60, 660–663.

Fiske, D. (1971) *Measuring the Concepts of Personality.* Chicago: Aldine.

Ginott, H. (1965) *Between Parent and Child.* New York: MacMillan.

Pellicano, R. (1987) At Risk: A view of advantage". *Educational Leadership* 44, 6, pp. 47–49.

Richert, E. S. et al. (1982) *National Report on Identification* Sewell, New Jersey: Educational Improvement Center—South.

Rimm, S. and Davis, G. (1985) *Education of the Gifted and Talented* Englewood Cliffs, NJ: Prentice-Hall.

Rimm, S. (1986) *Underachievement Syndrome: Causes and Cures* Watertown, WI: Apple.

Renzulli, J. (1981) *The Revolving Door Identification Model.* Mansfield Center, CT: Creative Learning Press.

Whitmore, J. (1980) *Giftedness, Conflict and Underachievement.* Boston: Allyn and Bacon.

Chapter 19

CHILDREN AT RISK IN SPORT AND PHYSICAL EDUCATION: IMPLICATIONS FOR THE STRUCTURING OF ATHLETIC ENVIRONMENTS

SHARON R. GUTHRIE

In recent years, concern for children "at risk" has generated much discussion and research within education. The term "children at risk" has been used to describe the following groups of individuals: minority and immigrant children who face discriminatory policies and practices; large numbers of girls and young women who miss out on educational opportunities routinely afforded males; and children with special needs who are unserved, underserved or improperly categorized to their own and the nation's detriment (National Commission, 1983).

Primary energies, thus far, have been directed toward the academic realm, namely identification of potential risk factors and those who are "at risk," as well as strategies for prevention and/or remediation of identified problems. In contrast, this chapter will examine the athletic realm of sport and physical education. These environments also may place children, particularly females, "at risk" in terms of developing their full human potential. In order to understand the potential risk factors, it is necessary to determine the benefits and costs associated with sport and physical education experiences. At the same time, it should be kept in mind that these athletic experiences may include any of the following: (1) highly organized competitive sport (e.g., school athletics); (2) moderately competitive recreational sport (e.g., intramurals); and (3) movement experiences designed to develop movement expertise, efficiency and/or physical fitness (e.g., physical education).

The Athletic Experience

Examination of the potential benefits and costs of athletic experience reveals incongruency among attitudinal and research findings. For instance, some writers have condemned sport as a breeding ground for violence, exploitation and conformity to the status quo (e.g., Hoch, 1972; Leonard, 1973; Ogilvie & Tutko, 1971; Orlick, 1975; Scott, 1973). Others have claimed that sport and physical education make potential contributions, not only to physical health but also to psycho social wellness, development and creativity (Csikszentmihalyi, 1975; Harris, 1974; Michener, 1976; Nielsen, 1983; Ravizza, 1977; Rugg, 1963; Thorton, 1971).

These inconsistencies indicate that athletic participation is not inherently bad or good. More importantly, sport and physical education should not be valued (or devalued) apart from the way in which these settings are structured, as well as the consequences the athletic environment holds for the individual within a context of goals. Despite this reservation, however, there is no doubt that sport and movement experience can enhance the quality of life for both females and males.

While athletic expertise has long been valued by society, historically the world of sport has been considered a male preserve. As a result, females often have been either excluded from athletic activity entirely or have received modified forms of sport and physical education. In addition, they often have encountered psychological barriers to participation due to the negative stereotyping of athletic females. While the Women's Movement and resultant policy changes (e.g., Title IX) have encouraged more egalitarian attitudes toward sporting participation for males and females, stigma surrounding female physicality and athleticism still persists (Gill, 1986). To the extent that sport and physical educators, as well as those who administer such programs, discriminate against females (or males) by allowing them full access to the potential benefits of such programs, then these children are "at risk." Similarly, sport and physical education programs which are structured in a way which maximizes the potential for negative result, place all children "at risk."

Potential Benefits of Sport and Physical Education

Physical fitness and health are the most obvious benefits of sport and physical education experiences and the ones which have received the greatest attention over the years. Research has demonstrated a strong positive relationship between physical fitness and overall health and that these qualities can be achieved through the sporting participation and physical education. Many other benefits, however, may be accrued from such movement experiences.

For centuries, particularly in Far Eastern countries, the benefits to human functioning inherent within sport and movement expertise have been well understood and accepted. Consequently, sport and movement have been utilized to enhance spiritual development through expanding the potential of the mind-body system. Through this process, one is believed to gain self awareness, as well as intuitive knowledge regarding the nature of the universe or reality. Motor skill development and expertise, then, become an outward manifestation or expression of an enlightened state of being (wisdom). Sport and movement, conceptualized and practiced as such, help to shape not only an experience of mind-body unity, but also harmonious integration between the individual and the environment, both of which are considered universal truths. The perception of these truths is considered to be a fundamental ingredient of wisdom. Hence, sport and movement experiences serve as vehicles inspiring the development of spirituality and wisdom.

Sport and movement also have been utilized to encourage philosophical inquiry and development. Linden (1984) has claimed that the body manifests an individual's core philosophical belief system and that changing one's bodily use also changes his or her philosophical stance. More specifically, changing one's bodily use or movement will cause one's experience of life to be different. This altered life experience will give rise to new beliefs and feelings, which in turn may influence the person to move in new and healthier ways. Linden (1981) has further claimed that emotional energy or intention is the motive force underlying all activity. The term "intention" is used to indicate the location where the mind and body interact. As such, emotional energy must be balanced and ordered correctly for the individual to achieve orderly and effective action patterns. Sport and physical education, considered as movement awareness processes, serves as a medium through which individuals may focus, order, as well as learn to control their emotional energies. Through this emotional reordering process, the development of movement efficiency may help children to clarify their visions of and experience in the world by making their physical movement/actions and psychological intentions more congruent.

An additional benefit which may be gained from sport and movement experiences involves creativity. While creativity has been a topic of interest to educational psychologists for years, the fundamental ingredients of this phenomenon have remained elusive. In recent years, however, research in educational psychology and psychotherapy has established the connection between creativity and the intuitive mind. Meditative practices (e.g., Zen) which require a particular attentional focus have been found to enhance the intuitive powers of the mind. Sport and movement may be practiced as a form of meditation and, therefore, hold the potential to motivate intuitive insight, as well as open the doors of creative discovery.

Rugg (1963) also observed the relationship between the intuitive mind and creative discovery, however, he believed that the source of this interaction was movement-related. He has claimed that all cognition has a physiological base and that creativity originates with the (motor) felt-thought of discovery rather than the logical thought of verification. Rugg's ideas have major implications for both education and physical education. In order to provide a completely sound education, learning must be comprised of both motor and verbal components. This means that educational theory and practice must provide a program of designed movement which allows for the development of the gestural symbol as well as the verbal symbol. Rugg has posited that such a movement program (beyond mere training in sport and games) will "force our own felt-thought to profound new depths of creativity" (p. 313).

Rugg's ideas have been supported in recent years by psychologists who have observed a close relationship between the use of body and the deployment of other cognitive powers. As an observer of the mind-body relationship, Gardner (1983) has proposed a theory of multiple intelligences which includes a bodily-kinesthetic component. According to Gardner, bodily intelligence is characterized by the ability to use one's body in highly differentiated and skilled ways, for expressive as well as goal-directed purposes. Also characteristic of this intellectual capacity is the ability to work skillfully with objects, both those which involve the fine motor movements of one's fingers and hands and those that exploit gross motor movements of the body. While Gardner has noted that a given individual may possess only one of these two core elements, he has found it more common for them to operate in conjunction with each other. More importantly, psychologists have found that bodily intelligence does not exist merely at the physical level, but instead encompasses many cognitive processes. Following this line of reasoning, Gardner has stated the following:

> ... the highly skilled performer has evolved a family of procedures for translating intention into action. Knowledge of what is coming next allows that overall smoothness of performance which is virtually the hallmark of expertise. The periods of hovering or halting, which call for keen attention to environmental factors, alternate with periods of seamless fluency, where numerous component parts fall readily into place. Programming of actions at a relatively abstract level allows the choice of those particular units of performance will result in the smoothest possible sequence of activity ... (p. 207) while one's sense of timing may seem a direct consequence of one's bodily intelligence, athletic expertise may well draw on other intellectual strengths. There is the logical ability to plot a good strategy, the capacity to recognize familiar spatial patterns and to exploit them on the spot, and an interpersonal sense of the personality and motivation of other players in a game ... (p. 230–231).

Gardner is suggesting that the development of bodily skill involves the simultaneous development of other forms of intelligence (i.e., logical-mathematical, spatial and interpersonal), each of which is part of his theoretical model. If Gardner's observations are correct, it is quite possible that sporting participation and physical education have the ability to encourage intellectual development beyond the bodily level.

In fact, current research findings have provided beginning support in this regard. In her book, *Overcoming Math Anxiety,* Tobias (1978) has found that female athletes consistently outperform nonathletic males on tests of spatial skills. These spatial skills contribute to mathematical problem-solving, leading Tobias to suggest that girls' poor performance in math may be linked to their lack of athletic experience. This is highly significant in light of the fact that previous research findings have strongly indicated male superiority in spatial ability (Maccoby & Jacklin, 1974). If sport and athletic training do indeed enhance spatial reasoning (i.e., that which relies on the individual's ability to transform objects within the environment and to make his or her way amidst a world of objects in space), then sport and movement experiences should be an important part of every child's education.

Beyond the previously identified benefits associated with sport and physical education, there has been much discussion concerned with the psychological consequences of these athletic experiences. Both research and experience have demonstrated a strong positive relationship between body image and self-concept, as well as between body image and sport and movement expertise. Therefore, when sport and movement experiences serve to enhance a body image, they also appear to contribute to a healthier and more expansive self-concept. For example, many females have experienced a sense of exhilaration and empowerment through integrating their psychophysical energies in the practice of the martial arts (Lenskyj, 1986). Those who have been socialized to view the body as a fragile encumbrance, often develop a style of body use characterized by a lack of fluid and direct motion. This style of movement is commonly observed in both males and females who have not learned correctly how to throw, hit a ball, and run. Females engaged in self-defense and the martial arts have to unlearn this style, as the effectiveness of the techniques is maximized by putting one's whole body into each motion. Through this experience, females develop ease and confidence in their bodies and in their capacity to defend themselves which most males acquire through their early sporting involvement (Young, 1980). This developing consciousness of personal power can be a very radicalizing experience, and one which may have the potential to lessen the imbalance of physical power between the sexes.

Not only may sport participation and physical education alter one's perception of personal power, athleticism also can contribute to the feeling of control over one's life. Psychologists refer to this as "locus of control" (Weiner, 1979). Those with an external locus of control believe that both failure and success in life are determined primarily by sources beyond their own control (e.g., luck, task difficulty, others' actions, God's will). Conversely, individuals with an internal locus of control attribute outcomes to their own actions (e.g., ability, effort). Studies have shown that females, compared to males, tend to have a more external locus of control when accounting for their successes and a more internal locus of control when making attributions for their failures (Feather & Simon, 1975; Nichols, 1975; Taynor & Deaux, 1973). In other words, females are less likely than males to take credit for their own accomplishments and are more likely to blame themselves for their failures.

While these same sex differences have been observed in sport and physical education, athletic females are, nevertheless, more likely to strike a healthy balance between external and internal locus of control perceptions than their nonathletic counterparts (Birrell, 1978; Burke, 1975; McHugh et al., 1978). Females who participate in physical exercise and sport have opportunities to learn that they are not powerless physically and that this sense of personal power can extend beyond the athletic arena (Nielsen, 1983).

There also is evidence that physical exercise alleviates and/or decreases a person's feelings of depression and anxiety. Research has indicated that female sporting participants tend to have higher self-esteem scores and greater feelings of well-being than their nonathletic peers (Harper, 1978; Snyder & Kivlin, 1975). While it is possible to conclude that these girls were self-confident achievers prior to entering sport, research has indicated that regular exercise encourages optimism and self-confidence in females who are depressed and anxious prior to or in the absence of exercise. Whether these psychological changes have a chemical basis (e.g., endorphins, amines) or are due to the sense of satisfaction that accompanies physical fitness and movement efficiency, exercise has been found to play a vital role in alleviating stress and altering negative moods (Bortz, 1982; Buffone, 1984; Harmon, 1978; Sachs, 1984). This finding is particularly significant in light of the fact that many female children and adolescents resort to the use of alcohol, drugs and food to cope with their depressions and lack of self-esteem (Nielsen, 1983).

Beyond these psychological considerations, sport and physical education experiences may well contribute to vocational and professional development. Surveys of successful business women have indicated that participating in competitive sport teaches females the verbal and emotional assertiveness and self-confidence to survive in male-dominated professions as adults. Hennig (1977) and Harragan (1978) both have concluded that girls are deprived of valuable lessons that boys usually master through sporting experience (e.g., how to accept criticism without being emotionally upset; how to achieve personal goals while still serving a group's needs; how to relate to authorities such as coaches and referees; how to sacrifice individual glory for a group's goals; and how to resolve conflicts without feeling personally offended). According to Nielsen (1983), the sense of mastery and competency that young girls derive from sporting participation also can teach them to take more risks, to cooperate with others, to compete without reservations and guilt, to test their physical and mental limits, and to develop self-discipline.

Lever (1976) provided support for these claims when she studied children's play patterns:

> ... differences in leisure patterns of boys and girls lead to the development of particular *social skills* and capacities. These skills, in turn, are important for the performance of different adult roles. Specifically,

I suggest that boys' games may help prepare their players for successful performance in a wide range of work settings in modern society. In
contrast, girls' games may help prepare their players for the private
sphere of the home and their future roles as wives and mothers.

Boys' games provide many valuable lessons . . . they further independence training, encourage the development of organizational skills
necessary to coordinate the activities of numerous and diverse groups
of persons, and offer experience in rule-bounded events and the
abjudication of disputes. Mead offered us the insight that team sports
teach young children to play a role at the same time as they take into
account the roles of other players . . . boys' experience in controlled
and socially approved competitive situations may improve their ability
to deal with interpersonal competition in a forthright manner. And
experience in situations demanding interdependence between teammates should help boys incorporate more general cooperative skills, as
well as giving some team members very specific training in leadership
skills. The social and organizational skills learned in large play groups
may generalize to nonplay situations.

On the other hand, girls' games may provide a training ground for
the development of delicate socioemotional skills. We have seen that
girls' play occurs in small, intimate groups, most often the dyad. It
occurs in private places and often involves mimicking human relationships instead of playing formal games . . . girls' play, to a large extent, is
spontaneous and free of structure and rules; its organization is cooperative more often than competitive (pp. 52–53).

According to Lever, both males and females learn important interpersonal skills through play and games; however, the lessons inherent in
boys' activities are more organizationally relevant.

. . . These interpersonal skills are more instrumental than expressive.
A boy and his best friend often find themselves on opposing teams.
They must learn ways to resolve disputes so that the quarrels do not
become so heated that they rupture friendships. Boys must learn to
"depersonalize the attack." Not only do they learn to compete against
friends, they also learn to cooperate with teammates whom they may or
may not like personally. Such interpersonal skills have obvious value
in organizational milieus. Boys learn to share the limelight, for they
are told that team goals must be put ahead of opportunities for self-
glorification. The lessons in emotional discipline are repeated daily;
boys must restrain their energy, temper, and frustration for the cohe-
siveness of the group. Self-control, rather than self-expression, is valued highly (p. 53).

In contrast, girls' play teaches them interpersonal skills which are
more expressive in nature in that they tend to play in pairs rather than in

larger groups like boys do. According to Simmel (1950), the dyad has a different relation to each of its two elements than larger groups do to their members. The social structure of the dyad depends totally on the other member of the two, and the secession of either eliminates the whole. The dyad, therefore, does not attain "the suprapersonal life which the individual feels to be independent of himself." Following this line of reasoning, Lever has noted the following:

> There can be no shift from the person to the role, let alone from the role to the collectivity, or the dyadic relationship is characterized by the *unique* interaction between two individuals. A girl engaged in pastimes with one of a series of "best friends" may be gaining training appropriate for later dating experiences where sensitivity skills are called for, but she is less likely than her sport-oriented brother to learn organizationally relevant skills. Returning to Meadian terms, boys develop the ability to take the role of the *generalized other*, whereas girls develop empathy to take the role of the *particular other* (p. 53)

Lever's work has profound implications for educational policy and practice in this regard, she has stated the following:

> ...we should support a broadening of physical education programs for girls to include learning opportunities now found primarily in boys' play activities. Since deeply-ingrained patterns are slow to change, alternate opportunities might be developed in nonplay situations—for example, encouraging teachers to design group projects in which girls can gain experience in specialization of labor, coordination of roles, and interdependence of effort. At the same time, males have roles as husbands and fathers as well as occupational roles. A fully considered social policy will have to assess the extent to which emphasis on large-scale, organized sports for boys means systematic underexposure to activities in which delicate socioemotional skills are learned (p. 53).

Sport and physical education, therefore, have the potential to teach children skills (e.g., independence, ambition, assertiveness) which will serve them well in their future vocational and professional roles. In fact, these characteristics often are necessary for financial survival in the adult world. With more and more females entering the work force, either out of need or choice, it is essential that parents and educators structure learning experiences that will foster the development of these vocational/ professional skills. Sport and physical education are environments in which this type of learning may readily occur. Moreover, children who learn to assert themselves through their athletic experiences are develop ing a skill that can serve them equally well in nonathletic domains where assertion is necessary for self-preservation and/or psychological well-being (Nielsen, 1983).

Considering all of the potentially positive outcomes associated with athletic experience, certainly all children can benefit from quality sport and physical education programs. As mentioned earlier in this chapter, however, females are more likely than males to be denied full access to such beneficial experiences. To the extent that educational policy and/or practitioners continue to perpetuate this reality, then female children are "at risk" in terms of developing their full human potential.

While sport and physical education can make many positive contributions to human development, athletic experience also can negatively affect the lives of both male and female children and, thus, place them "at risk." The following discussion focuses on this negative potential.

Risk Factors Associated With Sport and Physical Education

Historically, proponents of athleticism have claimed that sport and physical education promote the development of ethical character and conduct. In fact, moral growth and development often have been cited as one of the primary benefits to be gained from athletic experience. Throughout the years, however, there also have been those who have questioned the moral adequacy of contemporary sport. Most of these concerns have stemmed from the awareness that the reality of the competitive sport ethic (i.e., that which promotes aggression, compulsive competitiveness and dominance) is in direct conflict with the vision of sport fostering prosocial behavior (e.g., cooperation, interdependence and altruism). As long as competition, rather than cooperation and interdependency, is perceived as more important to the development of athletic excellence, as long as success is equated primarily with winning, as long as triumph of self is predicated upon the subjugation of the other, and as long as aggression with the intent to harm is glorified as part of the game as well as winning strategy, then sport and physical education experiences lose much of their potential for facilitating moral development.

While the problem of moral development through sport has not yet been extensively investigated, several studies have indicated that athletic participation has a negative influence on prosocial behaviors and value preferences. Kleiber and Roberts (1961) examined the influence of sport on the prosocial behaviors of cooperation and altruism. They found that sporting experience had a detrimental impact on the occurrence of these behaviors. Moreover, children who were more experienced in competitive sport were significantly less altruistic than those who were less experienced, and boys were less altruistic than girls. Other research has demonstrated that, with age and experience, a progressive change in attitudes toward sport occurs. In a "play orientation," fairness is valued over skill, and skill is more valued than success. In a "professional orientation," the value of fairness becomes increasingly subordinated to competence and winning. This professionalization of values has been found not only to vary with age and sporting experience but also with sex. Males have consistently scored higher on professionalization than females at all levels of athletic involvement (Loy, 1975, Maloney & Petrie, 1974; Mantel & Vander Velden, 1974; Petrie, 1971; Sage, 1980; Webb, 1969). Still other researchers (Brademeier, 1983; Bredemeier & Shields, 1983) have found that reasoning about moral issues in sport is significantly higher for nonathletes than for athletes, and for female athletes than for male athletes. Moreover, reasoning about moral issues in everyday life is significantly higher for athletes than is reasoning about moral life in sport. One finding that is consistent across these studies is that females' value preferences and moral reasoning is different than males.

In recent years, Gilligan (1982) has drawn attention to the existence of gender-related differences in developmental processes. She, as well as others (Belenky et al., 1966; Noddings, 1984), have noted that female experience in the world is fundamentally different than that of males; for this reason, female values, interests and modes of understanding and interpretation often are different as well. By listening to girls and women resolve moral dilemmas in their lives, Gilligan has traced the development of a morality organized around notions of responsibility and care. This conception of morality differs sharply from the morality of "rights," described by Piaget (1932) and Kohlberg (1964), which is based on their studies of moral reasoning in males.

Individuals operating within a "rights" morality—more commonly males—evoke the metaphor of "blind justice" and rely on abstract laws and universal principles to abjudicate disputes between claims. They attempt to achieve resolution impersonally, impartially and fairly. In contrast, individuals operating within a moral system based on responsibility and care—primarily females—reject the strategy of blind impartiality. Instead, they argue for a contextual understanding in making moral decisions, claiming that the needs of individuals cannot always be deduced from general rules and principles. Rather, moral choice must also be determined inductively from the particular experiences each person brings to the situation. They further believe that each person must be understood in his or her own terms and that mutual understanding is likely to promote creative consensus regarding dispute resolution. At the highest ethical level, Gilligan contends that female moral reasoning is guided by the principle of nonviolence. This is considered the equivalent of the justice principle found in Kohlberg's theoretical hierarchy.

These gender-related differences in moral perspective also have been extended to the area of identity development. A "responsibility" orientation has been found to be more central to those whose conceptions of self are rooted in a sense of connection and relatedness to others, whereas a "rights" orientation is more common to those who define themselves in terms of separation and autonomy. Although these differences in self-definition do not necessarily divide along gender lines, researchers have found that many more females than males define themselves in terms of their relationship and connection to others (Noddings, 1984).

If Gilligan is correct, female morality is advanced through experiences which involve personalizing and creating connective bonds with others, developing an ethic of responsibility and care, and searching for ways to avoid harm. The traditional model of competitive sport has not encouraged these processes. Rather, sport often has been an experience in separation not connection. Over time, this experience may actually nurture the tendency to personally detach oneself from moral conflict and to reason only abstractly about moral rights and duties. As a result, sporting participation may be detrimental to the moral development of both males and females (Bredemeier, 1984). Therefore, sport and physical education experiences which are founded on the competitive ethic (i.e., those that reinforce a "win at all costs" attitude) are likely to place all children "at risk."

Still, it is important to remember that sport and movement experiences have the potential to transform children's lives in positive, as well as negative directions. As mentioned earlier, sporting participation is not inherently bad or good. As a social institution and as a personal activity, athletic participation transmits a variety of meanings and values to girls and boys. Therefore, if sport and physical education experiences are to be beneficial for children, they must be structured to achieve these benefits. Ways in which sport and physical education may be structured to achieve positive goals are discussed in the following section.

Structuring Sport and Physical Education to Achieve Benefit and Avoid Risk

Sport, as it is most commonly practiced in Western society, is a social structure which represents and celebrates traditional male (instrumental) value systems. This is not surprising in light of the fact that sport historically has served as a male "rite of passage" and has been used to socialize males into their societal roles. Frequently, claims have been made that "sport builds character." In actuality, this statement has applied to males only. In fact, sporting participation has so efficiently encouraged masculine gender identity, there has been the fear that similar participation among females would masculinize them as well. This fear has been the major reason females have been either discouraged from athletic entirely, or when encouraged, have experienced modified forms of sport and physical education.

Throughout the years, writers have claimed the need for redefining the male model of sport (Boutiller & SanGiovanni, 1983; Felshin, 1974; Sabo & Runfola, 1980) in a more humanistic, androgynous fashion. According to Boutilier and SanGiovanni (1983), sport is androgynous when it incorporates elements of both instrumental and expressivity:

> It is sport that allows for play as well as work, celebrates beauty as well as technique, that stresses the process as well as the end product. It is sport that encourages introspection, sensitivity to others, ethics, and friendship (p. 124) . . . it is this model of sport which comes closest to reflecting women's traditional experience of themselves in the world. It is also a model of sport which will ask that men become more attuned to their expressive qualities and that will give them the chance to have experiences that nourish these qualities. This model of sport will also make it an attractive activity for many men who are also presently alienated from instrumental sport, who find their need and desire for expressive experience severely limited by sport as traditionally conducted (p. 125).

These ideas are consistent with those of Holland and Oglesby (Holland & Oglesby, 1979; Oglesby, 1978) who view sport as an ambiguous contest in which both expressivity and instrumentality should be experienced by participants. They have declared that the instrumental model of competitive sport which males have developed is not only inadequate but also that "a claiming and valuing of the expressive is absolutely necessary if sport is to be salvaged as a developmental cultural product" (p. 86). To accomplish this goal, Oglesby (1984) believes that those in charge of sport programs must go beyond the celebration of expressive activities along with "ordinary sport." Rather, she has proposed the concept of celebrating the expressive *in* sport. To accomplish this, expressive qualities (e.g., passivity, submissiveness, subordination, dependency, cooperation and improvisation) must be taught in conjunction with the teaching of the instrumental qualities that currently dominate sport socialization (e.g., aggressive behavior, domination, risk-taking, compulsive competitiveness). More specifically, she has suggested the following:

> institutions wishing to preserve an expressive orientation in sport may hire expressively oriented women (or men) as coaches or administrators. To assume that all women and only women are expressively oriented is stereotyping and inaccurate. To overvalue the instrumental relative to the expressive is to indirectly practice sexism. To value and search out the expressive leader is what is being recommended. Such measures are only partial and temporary, but they do serve an important purpose. They at least make it possible for children, students, or program participants to experience a reality quite apart from the excessively instrumental, compulsively competitive activity that characterizes sport in its most professional form (p. 396).

Borrowing a term from Boulding (1969), Oglesby has called this other reality "the integry." She has emphasized that "both males and females need the experiences of the integry and males and females alike can and should provide the integry setting" (p. 397).

Gilligan (1962), Haan (1978) and Kohlberg (1964) all agree that the evolution of moral development involves engaging in situations in which real moral decisions and choices must be made. For Gilligan and Haan, careful attention to the needs and interests of all parties must be weighed and coordinated. Concern for the well-being of all must be integrated with a thorough knowledge of the other gained through dialogue and bonds of intimacy. According to Kohlberg, moral growth is the result of "cognitive disequilibrium." Moral lessons in sport are greatest when they provide areas of ambiguity (e.g., sliding into first base) and when the participants experience dissonance (e.g., deciding whether or not to sacrifice a success strategy in favor of a decision guided by moral criteria). According to all of these theorists, however, experiences must be offered in which moral judgment is connected to moral action, with participants perceiving themselves as moral agents, aware of alternative choices of action and cognizant of the possible consequences of these actions (McIntosh, 1979; Park, 1980). Therefore, if sport and physical education experiences are not to place children "at risk" in terms of moral development, they must provide opportunities for such experiences (Bredemeier, 1984).

In this chapter, much discussion has centered on the benefits which can be gained from quality sport and physical education experiences, as well as the fact that children who are not exposed to such opportunities may be "at risk." Designing programs to maximize benefit for all children is an important responsibility of athletic administrators and physical educators. Structuring programs which will enhance participant motivation is an equally important responsibility.

Motivational research has indicated that children participate in athletic activity for a variety of reasons (Gill, Gross & Huddleston, 1981; Griffin, 1980; Robertson, 1981; Skubic, 1956). The most important reasons cited have been improving skills, having fun, being with friends, making new friends, experiencing thrills or excitement, achieving success or winning and developing fitness (Gould and Horn, 1984). Again, sex differences have been identified; namely, female children tend to rate fun and friendship as more important motives for participation than males (Sapp & Haubenstricker, 1978).

While the research on attrition in youth sport (Fry et al., 1981; Gould, Feltz, Horn & Weiss, 1982; Orlick & Botterill, 1975; Pooley, 1981) has indicated that most young athletes drop out of sport due to a conflict of interest, a substantial number of children have been found to drop out because of more negative reasons associated with the athletic environment (e.g., lack of playing time, overemphasis on competition and winning, boredom and lack of fun). In one study (Griffin, 1978) more than 90 percent of the boys stated that they would rather be on a losing team and play than "sit on the bench" on a winning team.

This research has demonstrated that optimal participant motivation occurs when adult leaders understand the young athletes' motives for sport involvement and then structure the athletic environment to fulfill these objectives. Gould and Horn (1984) have suggested the following guidelines for coaches and physical educators who are attempting to build children's athletic motivation: (1) provide opportunities for skill development; (2) use a positive teaching methodology; (3) ensure that the learning environment is fun; (4) provide for affiliation needs; (5) keep practices and games challenging; (6) develop a realistic view of success (i.e., defined according to personal goals and standards rather than winning alone); and (7) provide opportunities for fitness development, as well as knowledge regarding self-assessment and monitoring of fitness levels.

While structuring the athletic environment to enhance the participant motivation of all children is clearly important, more specific attention needs to be directed toward females. A history of sport as male territory, as well as differential socialization practices for males and females make this special focus necessary. In addition, because the dominant model of sport is still founded on male (instrumental) value systems, many females may not feel at home or even attracted to the athletic environment Boutilier & SanGiovanni, 1983).

What, then, can educators and administrators do to help female children overcome the forces which threaten to undermine their active participation in sport and physical education, as well as their commitment to physical exercise? Perhaps the single most influential step is for parents and teachers to provide girls with athletic role models and other females who enjoy exercising their bodies (Nielsen, 1983). Research has demonstrated that females who enjoy physical activity were encouraged to be athletic during their childhood by their parents (Boutilier & SanGiovanni, 1983; Greendorfer, 1978). The overwhelming evidence is that children, especially female children, who have not been encouraged to engage in sport at home will not see this pattern substantially challenged or changed by the elementary school experience (Lewko & Ewing, 1980). Parents and teachers need to strongly encourage female athleticism during grammar school years, because this is when girls are most likely to be physiologically capable of competing successfully with boys in games and sport; hence, elementary school is a prime time for developing a sturdy foundation for body image and self-confidence in the physical realm.

As girls approach adulthood, teachers, friends and female role models become especially important. Therefore, a sound educational curriculum, as well as the support of parents, peers and teachers, have the potential to inspire girls to reap the benefits of physical exercise and organized sport (Nielsen, 1983). Providing more female role models may be accomplished by equalizing the numbers of women and men who teach physical education, coach and have administrative responsibilities. Moreover, the pattern in which males frequently coach females while females rarely coach males needs to change if schools are to avoid the implicit message that sport is a male domain in which males have the expertise (Dillar and Houston, 1983).

Girls are less likely than boys to pick up athletic information without the conscious efforts of adults to assist them. According to Nielsen (1983), "the kind of information that most males accumulate through informal channels like television and older boys in the neighborhood will usually have to be conveyed to girls in a more organized, preplanned fashion by adults" (p. 298). Therefore, a physical education curriculum that provides accurate information about exercise physiology can play an important role in motivating girls to develop their bodily powers. This includes information that contradicts the myths regarding women's bodies and athletic potential (e.g., that exercising builds bulky muscles, decreases femininity, interferes with reproductive capacity, and increases appetite).

Teacher expectations are also important in overcoming the obstacles to female sport and exercise participation. While psychologists do not agree on the extent to which a person's expectations can alter another individual's performance or personality, there is no doubt that prophecies do influence conduct toward other people (Rosenthal & Jacobson, 1968). For example, if teachers and coaches expect females to perform poorly in sport, they will treat these students as though they were weak, incompetent, and uncoordinated. After receiving both verbal and nonverbal messages over a period of time, female children will probably fulfill the prophecy by avoiding sport because they have no athletic self-confidence and no physical skills. While the self-fulfilling prophecy is not limited to females, nor does it always have a negative impact on the individual, most girls do not receive positive expectations regarding their athletic abilities (Nielsen, 1983).

Similarly, physical educators and coaches should be aware that society has instilled in most young girls stereotypical and sexist attitudes regarding their athletic potential. The fact that girls tend to be less assertive, less competitive and less physically self-confident than boys is more a social construction than a biological given. Teachers and coaches, therefore, need to discuss sexism and sex roles with their female students in an effort to counter the messages about "femininity" which undermine the joy of physical activity and athleticism.

Beyond a general awareness and discussion of sexism in society, teachers and coaches also need to be aware of their own sexist behaviors. Griffin's

(1980) examples of teacher-student interactions illustrate ways in which teachers can intervene to counteract sexist stereotypes and discourage sexist language:

Male Student to Another Male Student Who is Crying: "John, if you're going to act like a girl, get off the field."

Teacher: "Tom, anyone, boy or girl, who gets hit and knocked down that hard might cry."

Student: "Why do the girls have to play?"

Teacher: "John, the girls want to play as much as you do. Everyone will have a fair turn to play."

Student: "Mark throws like a girl."

Teacher: "No, Jane, Mark throws like he needs practice throwing. Lots of girls throw well and lots of boys don't."

Another common example of sexist behavior is when male students poach from female students' territory in games and sport (Griffin, 1980). Consider the difference between a teacher who uses a sexist approach: "Susan, if you can't catch it, back off and let Steve get it" and one using a nonsexist approach: "John, that was Susan's ball" or "Don't crowd her out, Dan." These examples further demonstrate how teachers and coaches can take gender into account in order to further sexual equality, as well as prevent sexist bias (Diller & Houston, 1983).

Once teachers are prepared to observe and intervene in sexist interaction, the argument for sex integration becomes stronger (Diller & Houston, 1983). This is so because the interactions in co-ed physical education programs are more likely to reveal sexist attitudes and ideology. An observant teacher can then address prejudice and discrimination more directly. Moreover, according to Nielson (1982), segregating students based on intellectual differences is not motivating to slower students. Similarly, segregating the athletically gifted from the poorly skilled students is a poor strategy for those who have many new skills to learn. Males and females who receive co-ed physical education can share their talents with one another and learn from those whose abilities surpass their own by modeling after them.

Diller and Houston (1983) have stressed the importance of coed physical education, beginning in the elementary school setting:

> In elementary school less reification of gender differences has occurred and the creation of a concrete alternative model of coeducational-physical activities should be relatively successful. Children's concep-

tions about what is and is not sex-role appropriate are still comparatively loose . . . We can, to a great extent, more systematically control the sexism in elementary school through this method than we can later on. But a gender-sensitive perspective for elementary schools would also require us to notice that between the ages of four and twelve, boys usually have a number of outside school advantages, including additional athletic practice, coaching, advice, information about sport, many male role models, and general encouragement for these physical feats. We would recommend, therefore, that in addition to integrated physical education classes and sports there be opportunities for extra activities for girls, such as additional coaching and teaching. This is especially important in elementary school because most sports and physical activities which one engages in as an adolescent or an adult require early development of physical motor skills and build on these (p. 266).

According to Diller and Houston (1983), a "gender-sensitive" perspective on physical education requires the following:

. . . that we be sensitive to what the larger society is teaching that is relevant to its subject matter, what females are learning about their physical selves. It requires that we attend to this learning, recognize its influence upon our goals and find ways of dealing with it that are appropriate to each level of education (p. 267).

While Title IX legislation certainly has helped to enhance gender sensitivity as well as equalize athletic benefits for girls and boys, sexual discrimination still exists (e.g., unequal sport and physical education program expenditures and facilities, far fewer female than male coaches). There is no doubt that more favorable societal attitudes toward female athleticism are a reality today. Still, the majority of girls are being encouraged into sports which are considered socially acceptable for females (e.g., those which are individual rather than team in nature and those that do not require bodily aggression in overcoming an opponent). In addition, a great many females are still exercising primarily to lose weight and to enhance their sexual attractability.

This chapter has highlighted the multiple benefits which children may gain through sport and movement experiences; that is, physical, psychological, intellectual and vocational. Unfortunately, males more often than females are the recipients of such developmental benefits. This should be of great concern to parents, teachers and educational administrators. It is the responsibility of these individuals to prevent and/or eliminate "at-risk" situations within the school setting. To accomplish this within the athletic environment, sport and physical education must be structured to maximize benefit for males and females, as well as to motivate all children to realize their value. Only then will sport and physical education experiences have their greatest positive impact on child development.

REFERENCES

Belenky, M.F., Clinchy, B.M., Goldberger, N.R., and Tarule, J.M. (1986). *Women's ways of knowing*. New York: Basic Books.

Birrell, S. (1978). Achievement related motives and the woman athlete. In C. Oglesby (Ed.), *Women and Sport: From myth to reality*. Philadelphia: Lea & Febiger.

Bortz, W. (1982). The runner's high. *Runner's World*, April, 1982, 58.

Boulding, K. (1969). The grants economy. *Michigan Academician*, 1:3–11.

Boutilier, M.A., and SanGiovanni, L. (1983). *The Sporting Woman*. Champaign, IL: Human Kinetics Publishers.

Bredemeier, B.J. (1983). Athletic aggression: A moral concern. In J. Goldstein (Ed.), *Sports Violence*. New York: Springer-Verlag.

Bredemeier, B.J. (1984). Sport, gender, and moral growth. In J.M. Silva & R.S. Weinberg (Eds.), *Psychological Foundations of Sport*. Champaign, IL: Human Kinetics Publishers.

Bredemeier, B.J., and Shields, D.L. (1983). Body and balance: Developing moral structures through physical education. University of Oregon: Microform Publications.

Buffone, G.W. (1984). Future directions: The potential of exercise as therapy. In M.L. Sachs & G.W. Buffone (Eds.), *Running as therapy: An integrated approach*. Lincoln: University of Nebraska Press.

Burke, E. (1975). Psycho-social parameters in young female long distance runners. Canadian Psycho-motor Learning and Sport Psychology Symposium, Quebec.

Csikszentmihalyi, M. (1975). *Beyond boredom and anxiety*. San Francisco: Jossey-Bass.

Diller, A., and Houston, B. (1983). Women's physical education: A gender-sensitive perspective. In B.C. Postow (Ed.), *Women, philosophy, and sport: A collection of new essays*. Metuchen, N.J.: The Scarecrow Press.

Feather, N., and Simon, J. (1975). Reaction to male and female success and failure. *Journal of Personality and Social Psychology*, 31, 20–31.

Felshin, J. (1974). The triple option . . . For women in sport. *Quest*, 21, 36–40.

Fry, D.A.P., McClements, J.D., and Sefton, J.M. (1981). *A report on participation in the Saskatoon Hockey Association*. Saskatoon, Canada: SASK Sport.

Gardner, H. (1983). *Frames of mind: The theory of multiple intelligences*. New York: Basic Books.

Gill, D.L. (1986). *Psychological dynamics of sport*. Champaign, IL: Human Kinetics Publishers.

Gill, D.L., Gross, J.B., and Huddleston, S. (1981). Participation motivation in youth sports. In G.C. Roberts & D.M. Landers (Eds.), *Psychology of motor behavior and sport—1980*. Champaign, IL: Human Kinetics Publishers.

Gilligan, C. (1982). *In a different voice.* Cambridge: Harvard University Press.

Gould, D., Feltz, D., Horn, T., and Weiss, M. (1982). Reasons for discontinuing involvement in competitive youth swimming. *Journal of Sport Behavior,* 5, 155–165.

Gould, D., and Horn, T. (1984). Participation motivation in young athletes. In J.M. Silva & R.S. Weinberg (Eds.), *Psychological foundations of sport.* Champaign, IL: Human Kinetics Publishers.

Greendorfer, S. (1978). Socialization into sport. In C. Oglesby (Ed.), *Women and sport.* Philadelphia: Lea & Febiger.

Griffin, P.S. (1980). Developing a systematic observation instrument to identify sex role dependent and sex role independent behavior among physical education teachers. Doctoral Dissertation, University of Massachusetts.

Haan, N. (1978). Two moralities in action contexts: Relationship to thought, ego regulation, and development. *Journal of Personality and Social Psychology,* 36, 286–305.

Harman, W.W. (1986). The changing image of man/woman: Signs of a second copernican revolution. In S. Kleinman (Ed.), *Mind and body.* Champaign, IL: Human Kinetics Publishers.

Harmon, L. (1978). And soma. In L. Harmon (Ed.), *Counseling Women.* Monterey, California: Brooks Cole.

Harper, F.D. (1978). Outcomes of jogging: Implications for counseling. *Personnel and Guidance Journal,* 57, 74–78.

Harragan, B. (1978). *Games mother never taught you.* New York: Warner Books.

Harris, D.V. (1974). The sportswoman in our society. In G. Sage (Ed.), *Sport and American society.* Reading, MASS: Wesley Publishing Co.

Hennig, M. (1977). *The managerial women.* New York: Simon and Schuster.

Hock, P. (1972). *Rip off the big game.* New York: Doubleday & Co.

Holland, J. and Oglesby, C. (1979). Women in sport: The synthesis begins. *Annals of the American Academy of Political and Social Science,* 445, 80–90.

Kleiber, D.A. and Roberts, G.C. (1981). The effects of sport experience in the development of social character: An exploratory investigation. *Journal of Sport Psychology,* 3, 114–122.

Kohlberg, L. (1964). Development of moral character and moral ideology. In M.L. Hoffman and L.W. Hoffman (Eds.), *Review of child development research.* New York: Russell Sage Foundation.

Lenskyj, H. (1986). *Out of bounds.* Toronto, Ontario: The Women's Press.

Leonard, G.B. (1973). Winning isn't everything, it's nothing. *Intellectual Digest,* 4(2), 45–46.

Lever, J. (1976). Sex differences in the games children play. In A. Giannakis et al. (Eds.), *Sport sociology: Contemporary themes.* Dubuque, Iowa: Kendall/Hunt.

Lewko, J.H. and Ewing, M.E., (1980). Sex differences and parental influences in sport involvement of children. *Journal of Sport Psychology,* 2, 62–68.

Linden, P.R. (1981). *Physical education activities and their function as art.* Unpublished doctoral dissertation, The Ohio State University.

Linden, P.R. (1984). The art of aikido: Philosophical education in movement. In S. Kleinman (Ed.), *Mind and body.* Champaign, IL: Human Kinetics Publishers.

Loy, J.W. (1975). *The professionalization of attitudes toward play as a function of selected social identities and level of sport participation.* Paper presented at international seminar on Play in Physical Education and Sport, Tel Aviv.

Maccoby, E.E. and Jacklin, C. (1974). *The psychology of sex differences.* Palo Alto, CA: Stanford University Press.

Maloney, T.L. and Petrie, B.M. (1974). Professionalization of attitudes toward play among Canadian school pupils as a function of sex, grade and athletic participation. *Journal of Leisure Research,* 4, 184–195.

Mantel, R.C. and Vander Velden, L. (1974). The relationship between the professionalization of attitude toward play of preadolescent boys and participation in organized sport. In G.E. Sage (Ed.), *Sport and American Society.* Reading, MASS: Addison-Wesley.

McHugh, M.C., Duquin, M., and Frieze, I. (1978). Beliefs about success and failure: Attribution and the female athlete. In C.A. Oglesby (Ed.), *Women and sport: From myth to reality.* Philadelphia: Lea & Febiger.

McIntosh, P. (1979). *Fair play: Ethics in sport and physical education.* London: Heinemann.

Michener, J. (1976). *Sports in America.* New York: Random House.

National Commission on Excellence in Education, (1983). *A nation at risk: The imperative for educational reform.* Washington, D.C.: Department of Education.

Nichols, J. (1975). Causal attribution and other achievement related cognitions. *Journal of Personality and Social Psychology,* 31, 379–89.

Nielsen, L. (1983). Putting away the pom-poms: An educational psychologists' view of females and sports. In B.C. Postow (Ed.), *Women, philosophy and sport: A collection of new essays.* Metuchen, N.J.: The Scarecrow Press.

Noddings, N. (1984). *Caring: A feminine approach to ethics and moral education.* Berkeley, CA: University of California Press.

Ogilvie, B.C. and Tutko, T.A. (1971). Sport: If you want to build character, try something else. *Psychology Today,* 5(5): 61–63.

Oglesby, C.A. (1978). *Women and sport: From myth to reality.* Philadelphia: Lea & Febiger.

Oglesby, C.A. (1984). Interactions between gender identity and sport. In J.M. Silva and R.S. Weinberg (Eds.), *Psychological foundations of sport.* Champaign, IL: Human Kinetics Publishers.

Orlick, T.D. (1973). Children's sports—A revolution is coming. *Canadian Association for Health, Physical Education and Recreation Journal,* Jan./Feb.: 12–14.

Orlick, T.D. (1974). The athletic dropout—a high price of efficiency. *CAHPER Journal,* Nov./Dec., 21–27.

Orlick, T.D. (1975). *In pursuit of excellence.* Champaign, IL: Human Kinetics Publishers.

Orlick, T.D. and Botterill, C. (1975). *Every kid can win.* Chicago: Nelson-Hall.

Park, R.J. (1980). Citius, altius, fortius. *The Academy papers* (No. 14). Reston, VA: American Academy of Physical Education.

Petrie, B.M. (1971). Achievement orientation in adolescent attitudes toward play. *International Review of Sport Sociology,* 6, 89–99.

Piaget, J. (1932). *The moral judgement of the child.* New York: Harcourt & Brace.

Pooley, J.C. (1981). *Drop-outs from sport: A case study of boys' age-group soccer.* Paper presented at AAHPERD Conference, Boston.

Ravizza, K. (1977). Peak experiences in sport. *Journal of Humanistic Psychology,* 17, 35–40.

Robertson, I. (1981). *Children's perceived satisfaction and stresses in sport.* Paper presented at the Australian Conference on Health, Physical Education and Recreation.

Rosenthal, R. and Jacobson, L. (1968). *Pygmalion in the classroom.* New York: Holt & Rinehart.

Rugg, H. (1963). *Imagination.* New York: Harper & Row.

Sabo, D.F. and Runfola, R. (1980). *Jock: Sports and male identity.* Englewood Cliffs, N.J.: Prentice-Hall.

Sachs, M.L. (1984). Psychological well-being and vigorous physical activity. In J.M. Silva and R.S. Weinberg (Eds.), *Psychological foundations of sport.* Champaign, IL: Human Kinetics Publishers.

Sage, G.H. (1980). Orientations toward sport of male and female intercollegiate athletes. *Journal of Sport Psychology,* 2, 355–362.

Sapp, M. and Haubenstricker, J. (1978). *Motivation in joining and reasons for not continuing in youth sports programs in Michigan.* Paper presented at AAHPER Conference, Kansas City, MO.

Scott, J. (1973). Sport and the radical ethic. *Quest,* 19 (Winter), 71–77.

Simmel, G. (1950). *The sociology of Georg Simmel.* New York: Free Press.

Skubic, E. (1956). Studies of Little and Middle League baseball. *Research Quarterly,* 26, 72–80.

Snyder, E.E. and Kivlin, J. (1975). Women athletes and aspects of psychological well-being and body image. *Research Quarterly,* 46, 191–199.

Taynor, J. and Deaux, K. (1973). When women are more deserving than men. *Journal of Personality and Social Psychology,* 28, 360–367.

Thorton, S. (1971). *Labans' theory of movement: A new perspective.* Boston: Plarp, Inc.

Tobias, S. (1978). *Overcoming math anxiety.* New York: Norton.

Webb, H. (1969). Professionalization of attitudes toward play among adolescents. In G.S. Kenyon (Ed.), *Aspects of contemporary sport sociology.* Chicago: The Athletic Institute.

Weiner, B. (1979). A theory of motivation for some classroom experiences. *Journal of Educational Psychology,* 71, 3–25.

Young, I. (1980). Throwing like a girl: A phenomenology of feminine body comportment motility and spatiality. *Human Studies,* 3, 143.

Chapter 20

CHILDREN AT RISK
DUE TO EXPERIENCED TRAUMA AND LOSS

Sheila C. Ribordy

Children exposed to acute or chronic traumatic stress have been found to experience impairment in multiple domains. These negative effects can occur in the areas of emotional and cognitive functioning, physical health and behavior. This chapter will examine children's reactions to psychic trauma by discussing three specific areas: posttraumatic stress reactions, the death of a parent and the loss of the intact family by parental separation or divorce. Particular attention will be given to how children's reactions to these occurrences may be manifested in the school setting.

POSTTRAUMATIC STRESS REACTIONS

The consequences to children of experiencing psychic trauma have only recently been studied as phenomena in their own right. Earlier psychological literature either ignored the possibility that children could be traumatized for more than a brief time ("children bounce back") or assumed that the nature of the traumatic experience was similar to that experienced by adults. Recent examinations of children's reactions to traumatic events have confirmed that some of children's reactions to traumatic stress are similar to adult reactions, but there are also responses specific to children. Most children who have experienced a trauma show these negative effects in the short term, and there are a number of them who continue to evidence reactions for years after a significant trauma.

"Psychic trauma occurs when an individual is exposed to an overwhelming event resulting in helplessness in the face of intolerable danger, anxiety, and instinctual arousal" (Pynoos & Eth, 1985b, p. 38). Common events which have been found to cause psychic trauma are: witnessing traumatic events, especially those involving violence (e.g., murder of a parent, rape of a parent, parental suicide); experiencing violence oneself (e.g., child abuse, being stabbed, being pushed out a window); transportation accidents; natural disasters (e.g., tornadoes, fires, earthquakes); the sudden and/or violent death of a loved one; war and terrorism acts; sexual assault; and kidnappings.

In the psychiatric diagnostic nomenclature, "posttraumatic stress disorder" is a term given to the myriad of reactions which follow the experiencing of a traumatic event. The Diagnostic and Statistical Manual (DSM III–R) of the American Psychiatric Association describes posttraumatic stress disorder as an anxiety disorder involving

> ...the development of characteristic symptoms following a psychologically distressing event that is outside the range of usual human experience (i.e., outside the range of such common experiences as simple bereavement, chronic illness, business losses, and marital conflict). The stressor producing this syndrome would be markedly distressing to almost anyone, and is usually experienced with intense fear, terror, and helplessness (APA, 1987, p. 250).

More specifically, posttraumatic stress occurs when there is an identifiable stressor, there is the reexperiencing of the trauma in a variety of ways once the actual event is over, there is some numbing of responsiveness to or reduced involvement with the external world, and there are a variety of secondary symptoms. Each of these elements will be discussed further.

The identifiable stressor, as mentioned earlier, can have its source in a variety of events. These catastrophic and traumatic events often involve death, mutilation and violence—either experienced directly by the child or witnessed by the child. While the traumatic event can be a one-time occurrence, the trauma can also result from a series of events over time (e.g., physical child abuse, witnessing of spouse battering, incest). The effects of long-lasting, stressful situations have been called "strain trauma" (Green, 1985). Pynoos and Eth (1985a) indicate that stress reactions are more severe and longer-lasting when the stressor event is of "human-design," rather than due to natural disasters or accidents. This is especially the case when there is violence involved. In Los Angeles, it is estimated that almost 20 percent of homicides are witnessed by children, and approximately 10 percent of rapes involve home invasions with children present (Pynoos & Eth, 1985a).

The reexperiencing of the traumatic event can manifest itself in a variety of ways. Common reexperiences for children occur through repetitive dreams, intrusive thoughts, traumatic play (in which elements of the stressor event are acted out), drawings and flashbacks triggered off by stimuli which hold strong associations to the original traumatic event. These recurrent experiences indicate the effects of the trauma are still salient, and the child continues to struggle with psychological mastery of the trauma. The third set of criteria for a posttraumatic stress disorder, that there is some numbing of responsiveness to or reduced involvement with the external world, has been found to vary somewhat for adults and children. It is rare that children are able to numb themselves from their experiences, as adults can do through amnesia and denial. Children do not have cognitive abilities developed to the point where they can easily rationalize or utilize these vehicles of numbing. Instead of having constricted affect, children often experience lability of emotions. These quick mood changes can be very confusing for the adults around the child, as well as for the child. There are, however, some similarities with adult reactions, in that there is often diminished interest in customary activities, especially if places, activities, or persons remind the child of the traumatic event. Social withdrawal is common as the child does not have the energy to play with friends, wants to avoid telling the story repeatedly, and fears embarrassment or shame when facing others. This social isolation may, in fact, allow depression to deepen and be maintained in the long term.

An assortment of secondary symptoms develop as part of the posttraumatic stress disorder. For children these commonly include hyperalertness and super-sensitivity. Whether the stressor event has been a one-time occurrence or has occurred multiple times, it is usual for a child to fear that the catastrophic event will occur again unless he/she is vigilant to prevent it. Startle responses and physical tension are apparent, as these children fight feelings of powerlessness and assume they can ward off further disaster by anticipating it. The original feelings of helplessness experienced in the traumatic event can lead to "a shattered sense of invincibility" and "rob a child of this sense of personal influence" (Terr, 1985). Associated with the helplessness are feelings of intense guilt ("I should have been able to help."). Children often attempt to cope with this helplessness through their play enactments by fantasizing that their new actions lead to a more favorable outcome. A related guilt issue is that children may feel that the trauma was a due punishment for some misbehavior on their part. For example, a child who is struck by a car while crossing the street may feel that the accident was punishment for not looking both ways as the parents had instructed. It is also the case that faulty cause and effect reasoning on the part of the young child may lead to other associations of personal responsibility which are unrealistic. For instance, a boy now compulsively checks all doors and windows before going to bed or fights falling asleep because he feels that if he had checked the doors and windows or been awake, he could have prevented his mother's rape by a home intruder.

Yet another form of guilt is survival guilt, in which the child feels guilty that he/she is still alive or unharmed when a loved one has been injured or has died. This "why not me" experience can be related to low self-esteem and a need later to compensate for the lost life by living one's life for the deceased person. This becomes infinitely more complicated when a sibling dies, as not only is the child suffering a loss, but so are the parents. Thus, the usual primary social supports for the child—the parents—are preoccupied with their own grieving reactions and may not be emotionally available to the child who needs their support. Parents who have lost a child may turn to the surviving children for emotional support (which causes the child to become prematurely adult-like), may pull away emotionally from the surviving child to protect themselves from further trauma should they lose this child also, or may become overly protective of the surviving child in an attempt to keep him/her safe. None of these three reactions are healthy for the surviving child, but do serve to remind those who work with children, how vulnerable and dependent they are to the ineffective functioning of their social support system, especially the parents.

Sleeping disturbances are very common secondary symptoms for children suffering from posttraumatic stress. These can take the form of nightmares, an inability to fall asleep, fear of the dark or sleeping alone, bruxism, sleepwalking and sleeptalking. Eating behavior is also frequently affected, as children develop loss of appetite, become picky eaters, or overeat.

An increased sense of vulnerability on the part of the child can lead to mistrust of others and an assortment of general fears and specific phobias. Fears of things, places, or persons which remind the child of the traumatic event are common. More abstract fears can also develop, such as a child's fear of going to school because he/she is unsure what will happen to the family while he/she is gone. Related to fears are avoidance behaviors, which enable the child to minimize confronting situations which are likely to be anxiety-provoking (e.g., going to school where the kids will ask questions, refusing to ride in a car after a bad accident). Unfortunately, while these avoidance behaviors are effective in controlling anxiety in the short-term, they merely postpone the child's eventual confrontation with and mastery over the fear. Anticipatory anxiety becomes characteristic and eventually may generalize to situations in which the anxiety is inappropriate or unrealistic.

Physiological or somatic reactions are other examples of secondary symptoms in the posttraumatic stress disorder. Stressed children often complain of physical ills and have been found to pay more visits to the school nurse than children who are not under unusual stress. Headaches, upset stomachs and general aches and pains are frequent concerns of children under stress. The somatic reactions are maintained over time as they serve to distract the child from other worries and to elicit sympathy and nurturing from others.

As the child struggles to control his/her reactions to the traumatic event, a considerable amount of psychic energy and attention is required. This leaves less emotional energy and attention available for academic functioning. Besides the specific fears that can develop around going to school, there has been strong documentation that school performance is likely to deteriorate, at least temporarily, for most children who are recovering from a traumatic experience (Green, 1985; Pynoos & Eth, 1985a; Terr, 1983). Concentration and distractibility are often problems, as the intrusive imagery related to the trauma and its consequential affect interfere with attention in the classroom. Many children report that daydreaming increases after they have experienced a traumatic event. It is difficult to achieve scholastically when one is preoccupied with worries. The worries and anxieties also get expressed for some children in restlessness and hyperactivity. The overactivity can be very irritating for teachers who fail to understand what underlies the activity level.

Other cognitive or learning deficiencies develop as well. Especially for younger children, regression is a common stress reaction. This can involve regression in behavior (e.g., going back to sucking thumb, being enuretic) and regression in learning. Thus, a child who was in the process of learning her multiplication tables will "forget" what she has already learned and have to start over. Van Ornum and Mordock (1984) refer to this phenomenon as the child's needing to return to more primitive behavior patterns in order to regain composure. Without an appreciation for the basis of this loss of learning, school personnel may label the child as learning disabled. Gardner (1971) has discussed what he refers to as "nonorganically determined learning neurosis." He feels a major interference in the normal learning process can occur when a child is dealing with a threat in the environment, especially when that threat involves aggression and violence. Curiosity and intrinsic motivation which are critical to learning new things can be greatly diminished as the child deals with a constant state of anxiety. In order to explore and take risks with learning, a child must be free of a sense of helplessness, hopelessness and from expectations of failure, frustration and impotency. The feelings that begin in reaction to a trauma can become generalized to the learning process as well, with dramatic negative effects on learning.

Gardner (1971) discusses four primary defenses that children of trauma use in dealing with the academic environment: (1) withdrawal into fantasy, (2) overactivity, (3) the active seeking for and attending to any external distracting item in the environment, and (4) the active stimulation and utilization of peer group members to effect such distracting events and situations. The end result of the constant use of these defensive reactions is a reduction in ability to concentrate, lowered attention span and lowered desire to deal with novel material.

Because feelings of helplessness and being out of control of one's feelings and external events are acute in children recovering from a trauma, they often resort to exaggerated attempts to control things around them. This can be manifested in obstinency and testing of limits. When control issues are coupled with loss of trust in adults, a myriad of behavioral problems which are defiance-based can occur.

> The child suffering from an emotionally determined learning disability due to an excess of traumatic events—aggression and violence—and negative interpersonal relationships and attitudes in the past, is unable to control his inner fear and unable to accept the outer control of the teacher as anything but aggression (Gardner, 1971, p. 450).

Campos (1987) points out that the fit between the child's efforts to cope and the environment is important. For instance, a child whose reaction to trauma is primarily an externalizing one, in which oppositional behavior and conduct problems develop, is less likely to elicit nurturing and supportive responses from others in the child's environment, compared to another child whose reaction is more internalizing (e.g., sadness, clinginess). When a child is acting-out, whether at home or at school, it is often difficult for others not to react solely to the aversive behavior and thus miss the underlying fear and anxiety. This is especially the case when the adult is uncomfortable and unsure of what to say to the child about the underlying feelings related to the trauma.

Other secondary effects of traumatic reactions which interfere with academic performance are reduced effort and persistence on the part of the child, lowered frustration tolerance, lowered self-confidence, reduced risk-taking, difficulties dealing with changes and transitions, apathy and fatigue (may relate to sleep disturbance and/or depression), cognitive confusion, memory difficulties and rigid thinking. Eth and Pynoos (1985) summarize the effects of trauma reactions on academic performance,

> School and learning problems derive from the intrusion of memories and associations to the violent event, from the retarding effects of a markedly depressed affect, and from the evolution of a cognitive style of forgetting. There also can be multiple, enduring effects on memory, as priority is given to reworking traumatic recollections at the expense of meeting the challenge of other tasks (p. 177).

LOSS FROM PARENTAL DEATH OR DIVORCE/SEPARATION

The sense of loss that follows the death of a parent or a parental separation/divorce can manifest itself in ways similar to posttraumatic stress. Indeed, the death of a parent may be considered "an identifiable stressor" and qualify as a traumatic stressor if the death was sudden and/or by unnatural or violent means. Parental death and divorce/separation are considered separately from posttraumatic stress here, as these loss experiences have been examined very extensively in the psychological literature as phenomena in and of themselves.

Felner, Stolberg and Cowen (1975) found that 20 percent of school referrals of 800 elementary school children to a school mental health program involved either parental death or parental divorce/separation. It was found after examining these children that as a group, the children who had experienced parental death tended to exhibit a somewhat different pattern of school maladaptation than children who had experienced parental divorce/separation. These authors concluded that, "Whereas children who have experienced parental death manifested heightened shyness, timidity and withdrawal, those with histories of parental separation or divorce had elevated acting-out, aggressive, referral patterns" (p. 309). Children of parental death were described as unhappy, depressed and moody; while children of parental divorce/separation were described as showing restlessness, obstinate behavior, disruption of class and impulsiveness. While not all children who have lost a parent through death or divorce/separation will experience this internalizing or externalizing reaction, respectively, these patterns are found frequently enough in the literature to represent some preliminary validity. Each of these two loss experiences will be examined more specifically below.

Parental Death. "A parent's death usually constitutes a massive psychic trauma, because an immature ego cannot sustain the grief process without suffering injury" (Eth & Pynoos, 1985). When there is also a trauma associated with a parental death (e.g., the parent dies violently and suddenly), the child will first concentrate on the elements of the trauma, and only later will engage in mourning. That is, fear and anxiety will be the most salient features initially, and sadness and grief will be delayed. When there is a parental death, members of the child's support system (other members of the family) are also likely to be overwhelmed with grief reactions. Thus, one of the complications to adjustment for children, is the loss of (or ineffective) natural social support. More removed persons, like school personnel, need to provide this support for the child until family members are again able to do so.

Children who are of preschool age often view death as reversible; thus, reunion fantasies are common. Survival guilt and guilt related to the cause of death are not unusual for children of all ages. Children often worry that something they said, did, or felt may have contributed to the parental death. Even if older children know that they did not cause the parent's death, there may be guilt associated with having argued with or disobeyed the parent. Those children who are in accidents in which parents die may feel guilty about having survived. An acute sense of loss and guilt may manifest itself in death/suicide ideation as the child longs for a reunion with parents. For young children, the quality of the nurturance and care given by the substitute caregivers can provide a buffer against overwhelming grief. While young children may attach to these new caretakers rather easily, it does not mean that the sense of loss is any less acute. Instead, it speaks to the great needs of the child to be taken care of during an overwhelming time. Krupnick and Solomon (1987) suggest that children who have experienced the death of a parent will have these primary concerns to deal with: "Did I make this happen?"

"Will the same thing happen to me (or my remaining parent)?" "Who is going to take care of me now?"

The literature on reactions to the death of a parent, suggests that there are a number of mediating variables which determine the severity of a child's reaction to these losses. Besides the quality and availability of social support (particularly from one's family), other mediating factors are: a child's preloss emotional stability, the age and developmental level of the child, a child's willingness and ability to verbalize feelings, the circumstances associated with the loss, the child's relationship with the dead parent and preloss stability of the family. The amount of disruption to the child's life and routine can also exacerbate or minimize negative reactions. Often after the death of a parent (or divorce), a child is moved into a new home, sent to a new school and has to make new friends. While these disruptions are potentially upsetting in and of themselves, when a child has experienced a parental loss, there is little psychic energy left to cope with these additional changes. In fact, even without these numerous transitions, the child's loss will leave him/her diminished in ability to perform academically. Grieving impacts on not only the affective process but also on the cognitive process (Ryan, Giblin, & Schmidt-Janecik, 1986). As with the trauma literature, the parental loss literature indicates there is frequently a temporary (and at times, long-term) decrease in academic functioning caused by distractibility, concentration difficulties, regression in learning, lack of energy for attack skills in learning, diminished motivation, lack of energy for attack skills in learning, diminished motivation, lack of energy and social withdrawal.

Besides interfering with learning, the grief process is sometimes manifested in behavior which can be troublesome for school personnel. Many children whose parents die will show traditional signs of grieving; however, some children will manifest the sadness and guilt as anger and obstinency. Those children who experience the parent's death as an abandonment or rejection will often displace anger onto other family members and authority figures. Since school is an important aspect of a child's life, this hostile reaction can also show itself at school and with the teacher. Testing of limits, aggressive behavior, and hostility may get played out at school. The school setting is viewed as safe to act-out instead of the home, since the child may experience the remaining parent as fragile and vulnerable.

Krupnick and Solomon (1987) summarize the effects of parental death by age levels. Preschoolers often exhibit sleeping and eating disturbances, restlessness, dependency, regression, anxiety and anger. In addition to these reactions, school-age children may develop phobic and hypochondriacal reactions, while adolescents may feel self-conscious about expressing emotions (especially boys). All age groups will commonly show interference with learning processes in the short term, and for some, even over three or four years.

Parental Divorce/Separation. While parents view divorce as the solution to their marital problems, it is rare for a child to feel that the breakup of the intact family is a preferred solution (Van Ornum & Mordock, 1984). Consequently, parental separation/divorce constitutes a very real stressor for children. It is a unique stressor compared to those already discussed in this chapter, in that it is a crisis which unfolds over a long period of time. Prior to the actual point at which one of the parents leaves the family home, there typically will have been a protracted period, often involving years, in which parental conflict has been obvious to the children. This tends also to be so even in those families in which parents try to hide their conflict from the children. Children seem to be very sensitive to the family atmosphere and will have a sense that something is wrong even though it is not overt. Covert tension is sometimes more confusing to children, as they sense something is amiss but are not sure to what to attribute it.

Similar to parental death, divorce and separation are family crises. Because the entire family is experiencing the stress, the natural support system for the child may not be readily available. One of the predictors of a child's reaction to the breakup of the parents' relationship is how the parents themselves are doing (Wallerstein & Kelly, 1980). This is particularly true for the custodial parent, and either of two extreme reactions, from "falling apart" to pretending nothing significant has happened, can make the child's adjustment more difficult. Children who experience the caretaking parent as overwhelmed and fragile, will tend to keep their feelings to themselves and work hard to take care of the parent. In such situations, these pseudo-adult children take on responsibilities and worries inappropriate to their age and postpone their own emotional reactions in order to maintain some stability in the family. The delayed reaction which can come later may be unexpected by both the child and the adults around the child, as the passage of time makes it difficult to associate a later reaction to the initial parental breakup. This pattern of a child's feeling that he/she has to assume a leadership role within the family can be disruptive to the developmental health of the child in another way as well. School-age children are beginning to develop relationships and interests outside the family. This is healthy in terms of developing social relatedness and establishing some identity and autonomy apart from the family. When a child's energies are diverted back into the family during the emotional upset of divorce and separation, the child may interrupt this natural process of relating to others outside the family and establishing preliminary independence. On the other hand, for those children who cannot or do not want to deal with the parental conflict, there may be premature or excessive movement toward the peer culture. Friends and activities outside the family provide a way to escape the overwhelming feelings attached to the parental divorce or separation.

When the parent's reaction is one of pretending that nothing significant has happened ("stiff upper lip"), the child can become confused regarding the appropriateness of his/her feelings and whether it is okay for feelings to be expressed and questions to be asked. Thus, parents who are not openly acknowledging the import of the separation/divorce may inadvertently communicate to the child that he/she should not have any feelings about what is happening. Besides this being very confusing to the child, the child may come to divert his/her emotional reactions into other areas. Psychosomatic concerns, learning problems, and acting-out behaviors are common examples in which diversion of affect has occurred. When the affective realm is not being dealt with, the physical, cognitive and behavioral domains are likely to be affected.

Other predictors of a child's reaction to parental separation and divorce include the availability of an extended support system, the child's predivorce mental health, the extent to which there is ongoing conflict between the parents after the separation (particularly if the child is caught in the midst of this conflict), whether a child blames him/herself for the marital disruption, the degree of preparation for what is happening, the amount of other life disruption that occur as a result of the divorce/separation, and the age and developmental level of the child.

Rohrlich, Ranier, Berg-Cross and Berg-Cross (1977) discuss the effects of divorce on children from a developmental perspective. Children at different age levels tend to react in different ways. Prior to three years, a child's reaction is very strongly connected to the quality of his/her ongoing care. Eating, sleeping and elimination irregularities and irritability are common reactions for this very young child who is responding less to the parental conflict and more to disruptions in the routine and caretaking. The preschool child (3–5) has some limited understanding of what is going on, and he/she now brings his/her own personality and typical coping efforts to deal with this stressor. Eating and sleeping problems, as well as regressive behaviors, are frequently seen initially in these children. Because of the egocentric nature of a child at this age, the child may see him/herself as the cause of the parental rift. These children can evidence sadness, anger, and disbelief as the parental separation unfolds. Reunion fantasies are common and extend into the next age group, the school-age child (6–12).

As mentioned earlier, a danger for the school-age child is that the normal process of getting involved outside the family may be disrupted, thus restricting the development of appropriate autonomy. Of all the age groups, this group was found to feel the most intense sadness. Unlike younger children, these children

> were unable to employ denial and fantasy. They were aware of their suffering but without a means to relieve it. Unable to sublimate their feelings as could older children, they appeared immobilized (Rohrlich et al., 1977, p. 17).

Of particular interest to this chapter, approximately half of these children show a noticeable decline in school performance. Often the decline diminishes after a year, but for about one-fourth with initial learning deficiencies, the academic downturn continues over a longer period. Children this age are particularly vulnerable to ongoing conflict between parents. They want to maintain a relationship with both parents, but often get involved in the ongoing conflict, become pawns of the parents' desire to continue to struggle with the ex-spouse or express loyalty conflicts.

Adolescents are particularly susceptible to becoming pseudo-adults as they take over some of the role responsibilities of the absent parent, parent the younger siblings, and take care of the emotional needs of one or both of the parents. Those teens who already have one foot out the door may accelerate the "leaving home" process and prematurely act adult-like. Sexual acting-out, drinking, smoking and drug-taking are seen as "adult" behaviors that may be tested. Because of the conflict at home, there may be active avoidance of home and increased social activity outside the home. As adolescents are naturally self-conscious and concerned regarding the opinions of peers, shame and embarrassment are often experienced relative to the parental divorce or separation.

More than any other group, adolescents are likely to be open about their anger toward parents for disrupting the family stability. Truancy, diminished interest in school, behavior problems at school, delinquent acts and experimentation with drugs, alcohol and sex become means of acting-out this anger. These problematic behaviors may also increase because rules are no longer being enforced and there are less restraints put on the child by parents who themselves are dealing with a crisis. McCombs, Forehand, Fauber, Brody, Slotkin and Long (1987) found after two years, that teens whose parents divorced were more anxious, had lower grades and had poorer problem-solving skills than teens from intact families. For teens, the predivorce adjustment of the adolescent is very predictive of how they will weather the stress of the parental divorce-separation. Unlike younger children, adolescents have more internal resources and a wider social support network that may aid them in adjusting to this family crisis.

SUMMARY

If we accept that children have a finite amount of psychic energy—energy that is expended on dealing with relationships, learning, changing, etc.—then it is common sense that they would have school difficulties (both in cognitive and behavioral areas) when much of that psychic energy is focused toward dealing with a crisis no matter what its nature. Van Ornum and Mordock (1984) ask their reader to picture being a child experiencing extreme stress and trying to get through a typical school day.

> You are continually bombarded with new challenges, without the energy to face them. You aren't experienced enough to know that the situation will pass or be resolved, *somehow.* In your child's mind, you know only that you feel helpless, caught in the eye of a hurricane. You can't rely on going through the motions as an adult can. Your sense of self has not been fully established, and its wobbly beginnings have collapsed (p. 6).

Whether children have been stressed by a traumatic event, by parental death or by parental separation or divorce, there is abundant evidence that while they are trying to master their personal trauma, their school performance is likely to deteriorate. For some children, this may manifest itself in diminished academic performance and learning problems, while for others, the stress will get expressed through behavior problems. Behavior problems can entail both acting-out problems as well as social withdrawal. Reduced school performance is common in the short-term as children deal with a psychic trauma, and for some, these effects persist over years as the child's personal coping efforts are unsuccessful or the family is unable to reachieve stability.

Schools can be both havens for children from the craziness of the outside world, or the settings in which many unresolved emotions get manifested. Sensitivity on the part of school personnel is needed to support these children through their traumas. Early detection of problems and referral for appropriate remediation or support can prevent or minimize even more serious, long-term effects. The cooperation of and clear communication between families, school personnel, and mental health personnel workers provide the basis for our being able to support these vulnerable children and give them the best opportunity to be psychologically healthy and to be learning up to their potential.

REFERENCES

Linden, P.R. (1984). The art of aikido: Philosophical education in movement. In S. Kleinman (Ed.), *Mind and body*. Champaign, IL: Human Kinetics Publishers.

American Psychiatric Association (1980) *Diagnostic and Statistical Manual of Mental Disorders*, 3rd Edition Revised, Washington, D.C.: American Psychiatric Association.

Compas, B. E. (1987) Coping with stress during childhood and adolescence. *Psychological Bulletin, 101*(3), 393–403.

Eth, S. & Pynoos, R. S. (1985) Interaction of trauma and grief in childhood. In S. Eth & P. S. Pynoos (Eds.) *Post-Traumatic Stress in Children*. Washington, D.C.: American Psychiatric Press, 171–186.

Gardner, G. E. (1971) Aggression and violence — the enemies of precision learning in children. *American Journal of Psychiatry, 128*(4), 445–450.

Felner, R. D., Stolberg, A., and Cowen, E. L. (1975) Crisis events and school mental health referral patterns of young children. *Journal of Consulting and Clinical Psychology, 43*(3), 305–310.

Green, A.H. (1985) Children traumatized by physical abuse. In S. Eth & R. S. Pynoos (Eds.) *Post-Traumatic Stress in Children*. Washington, D.C.: American Psychiatric Press, 135–154.

Krupnick, J. L. and Solomon, F. (1987) Death of a parent or sibling during childhood. In J. Bloom-Feshbach & S. Bloom-Feshbach (Eds.) *The Psychology of Separation and Loss*. San Francisco: Jossey-Bass, 345–371.

McCombs, A., Forehand, R., Fauber, R., Brody, G., Slotkin, J., and Long, N. (1987) Two year assessment of adolescent and maternal adjustment following divorce. Paper presented at the Association for Advancement of Behavior Therapy. Boston, November.

Pynoos, R. S. and Eth, S. (1985a) Children traumatized by witnessing acts of personal violence: Homicides, rape, or suicidal behavior. In S. Eth & R. S. Pynoos (Eds.) *Post-Traumatic Stress in Children.* Washington, D.C.: American Psychiatric Press, Inc., 19–43.

Pynoos, R. S. and Eth, S. (1985b) Developmental perspective on psychic trauma in childhood. In C. R. Figley (Ed.) *Trauma and Its Wake.* New York: Brunner/Mazel, 36–52.

Rohrlich, J. A., Ranier, R., Berg-Cross, L. and Berg-Cross, G. (1977) The effects of divorce: A research review with a developmental perspective. *Journal of Clinical Child Psychology, 6*(2), 15–20.

Ryan, S. F., Giblin, N., and Schmidt-Janecik, W. (1986) Loss: A cognitive and an affective process. *Illinois Association for Counseling and Development Quarterly, 100,* 35–41.

Terr, L. (1983) Chowchilla revisited: The effects of psychic trauma four years after a school-bus kidnapping. *American Journal of Psychiatry, 140*(2), 1543–1550.

Terr, L. (1985) Psychic trauma in children and adolescents. *Psychiatric Clinics of North America, 8*(4), 815–835.

Van Ornum, W. and Mordock, J. B. (1984) *Crisis Counseling with Children and Adults.* New York: Continuum Publishing.

Wallerstein, J. S. and Kelly, J. B. (1980) *Surviving the Breakup: How Children and Parents Cope with Divorce.* New York: Basic Books.

Chapter 21

IDENTIFYING AND HELPING
THE SUBSTANCE ABUSE PRONE CHILD

Margaret Ann Leonard and John R. Taccarino

The consequences of substance abuse (alcohol- and drug-related) problems are obviously of devastating proportions within our culture. We see the effects in adolescence in underachievement patterns, missed opportunities, the death of joy in youth and death itself as seen in substance abuse related suicides, traffic accidents and overdoses. Our beleagured national economy and competitiveness suffers greatly due to reduced productivity, absenteeism and industrial accidents associated with substance abuse. The personal tragedies are huge in terms of destroyed careers, the loss of self-esteem and the crushing effects upon family members and dependents.

Although the great bulk of publicity and research dealing with substance abuse centers on the adolescent and adult, the underlying disposition toward these problems does not begin then. Rather, it has its roots far sooner, perhaps even before birth for some due to possible genetic dispositions. In early, middle and late childhood, tendencies toward substance abuse are being formed and, for some, first manifested. It is here that the chances of helping the child are greatest, that is, in the time before usage either begins or becomes entrenched in the individual's behavior. Thus, it is the purpose of this chapter to explore a technique for identifying substance abuse prone children and to discuss ways of helping these children avoid becoming actual substance abusers as adolescents or adults.

Identification

The early identification of children who are prone to substance abuse is the essential first step in preventing problems of that nature to develop. The authors of this chapter have designed an assessment approach, Leonard and Taccarino (1988), that can be used to help identify substance abuse prone children. It was developed on the basis of research information gathered in the validation of the *Substance Abuse Resistance Scale* of the *SAFE-R* (Taccarino, 1987) and through a review of the research literature that has isolated key factors of environment, behavior and attitudes associated with the manifestation of substance abuse problems. The following is an adaptation of that instrument that can be used by the reader for the purposes of identifying children who are substance abuse prone.

Directions

Try to objectively reflect on the behavior, background and characteristics of the particular child you wish to evaluate. Next, answer each question by writing yes or no on a sheet numbered from one to twenty-four.

THE LEONARD–TACCARINO ANALYSIS OF SUBSTANCE ABUSE PRONENESS

1. Does the child often display rebellious behavior? (1 point)
2. Is he/she a scholastic underachiever? (1 point)
3. Does the child have a generally poor self-concept? (2 points)
4. Does the individual frequently appear depressed? (1 point)
5. Does he/she seem to have more difficulty than most children in dealing with the typical problems of childhood? (1 point)
6. Does the child tend to give up easily when exposed to problems or obstacles in the completion of tasks? (1 point)
7. Is the individual frequently irritable? (1 point)
8. Does he/she tend to avoid difficult or challenging tasks? (1 point)
9. Does the individual tend to become angry more quickly and more frequently than the average child his/her age? (1 point)
10. Does the child lack strong religious beliefs? (1 point)
11. Do either of the child's parents use drugs or drink alcoholic beverages openly in the home? (2 points)

12. Does the child lack close, caring relationships in his/her home? (1 point)
13. Has the child been generally exposed to weak or inconsistent parental control in the home? (2 points)
14. Does the child tend to be a disciplinary problem at home or in the school? (1 point)
15. Do either of the child's parents have difficulty communicating affection toward the child? (1 point)
16. Is the child's home environment often emotionally strained and disruptive? (1 point)
17. Does the child appear to have a sense of personal inferiority or inadequacy? (1 point)
18. Does the child often demonstrate aggressive or belligerent behavior? (2 points)
19. Is the child more of an extrovert than an introvert? (1 point)
20. Does the child live in a home where a sibling is an active substance abuser? (2 points)
21. Does the individual live in a home where at least one parent is an active drug abuser? (2 points)
22. Does the child live in a home where both parents are active drug abusers? (3 points)
23. Has either of the child's parents been treated for alcoholism or consumed six or more alcoholic drinks per day on a regular basis? (4 points)
24. Have both of the child's parents been treated for alcoholism or consumed six or more alcoholic drinks per day on a regular basis? (6 points)

Scoring and Interpretation

Proceeding each question is a number in parentheses which reflects the scoring weight for that item. Add the points for all items answered *yes* and enter the total at the bottom of the answer sheet.

The following ranges of scores indicate the child's risk rating:

(**30–40**) **Very High Risk.** The child has a combination of attitudinal, environmental and perhaps genetic factors which put him/her in very serious risk of developing a substance abuse problem. There is an urgent need for immediate intervention to attempt to change the child's environment, family interactions, perceptions and attitudes. If he/she is in late childhood, there could be a strong possibility that the individual may already be exhibiting active, but undiscovered problems.

(20-29) **High Risk.** There is a significant underlying proneness to substance abuse problems present in the child's personality, family and peer interactions, and attitude formations.

(10-19) **Moderate Risk.** There are some factors in the child's environment, attitudes, perceptions and personality that suggest a possibility of problems, particularly if the individual is influenced by negative role models either in the home or through peer interactions.

(5-9) **Low Risk.** The child has been exposed to the type of home environmental and developmental interactions that has helped him/her to develop a personality, perceptual structure and pattern of attitudes that are useful in helping the individual avoid substance abuse problems.

(4 and below) **Very Low Risk.** The child has the type of attitudes, perceptions, personality and background that will serve him/her extremely well in dealing with alcohol and drug abuse pressures when he/she reaches adolescence.

Helping Strategies

Communicating Risk Level

If a child is seen as falling into the high-risk category, it appears very important to communicate a real and definite concern to the child and his/her parents. The early identification of a proneness toward substance abuse is so important in order that preventive efforts be taken early, rather than waiting until the problem becomes active and entrenched in his/her behavior patterns.

A great problem in dealing with substance abuse prone children and adolescents is that they tend to see the negative consequences of alcohol and drug use as being of harm to others but not themselves. They almost universally believe at the beginning of use that they can handle it. They know they can handle alcohol and drugs; it's just other people that cannot.

Real help in developing a sense of immediate personal danger does not appear to involve what we often see in school-based drug education programs. Halpin and Whiddon (1977) and others have found through their studies that adolescents have a *more* positive attitude toward drug use after they have taken a drug education program or course than before.

What appears to be essential here is that the child begin at an early age to personalize the risk and consequences of drug use. High-risk children must be made aware in gradual, but systematic ways that there is much more danger for them personally than it is for other children. If a child has hemophilia, he/she for self-survival has to realize very early that the risks other children take cannot be theirs. The same concept holds for children who have predispositions that make them prone to substance abuse problems. Drugs and alcohol are what's inside a Pandora's box of their very own. If they can be reasoned with, conditioned or scared into keeping that box closed, they will be able to go through life unscathed by its contents. However, they must be helped to fully understand that if they open it just once, their lives may really never be theirs' again.

It just seems so important that those who really care about high-risk children do all that's possible to keep them from first experimenting with drugs or alcohol. Actually, it probably is a sense of being cared about that helps a child keep a lid on his/her Pandora's box more than anything else.

One of the authors of this chapter had a friend in college who had an alcoholic father who recognized the same predispositions he had within his son. He made his son promise to never take a drink until he was twenty-one. His son kept that promise, but on his twenty-first birthday he took his first drink and kept right on drinking until he died in an accident in which his car plowed into an oncoming car while driving on the wrong side of the road. He took four other people with him, including a young child. Apparently, the fatal glass of beer really was fatal in his case. If he could have been convinced to never take a drink in his life rather than waiting until he was twenty-one, he might still have a life.

Preventing Early Usage of Drugs and Alcohol

In a study in which the authors of this chapter compared a sample of adult substance abusers who were undergoing treatment with a sample of adult non-substance abusers, identified by low-risk ratings in the area of substance abuse behavior via polygraph analysis of self-reports, it was found (see Table 21-1) that 27 percent of the substance abusers had used marijuana before they were thirteen and 45 percent had used it before they were sixteen. In comparison, only 3 percent of the non-substance abuse group had used it before they were sixteen.

Similarly, 41 percent of the substance abusers first began drinking alcoholic beverages before they were sixteen, but only 4 percent of the non-substance abusers had taken their first drink before that age.

Table 21-1.
Comparative Behaviors and Backgrounds of Substance Abusers and Non-substance Abusers

	Substance abusers (n = 212)	Non substance abusers (n = 247)
1. Use of marijuana before 13 years of age	26%	1%
2. Use of marijuana before 16 years of age	45%	3%
3. Use of alcoholic beverages 16 years of age	41%	4%
4. Forbidden by their parents to drink alcoholic beverages while in high school	24%	64%
5. Had mothers who averaged 3 or more alcoholic drinks per day	59%	4%
6. Had fathers who averaged 3 or more alcoholic drinks per day	63%	11%
7. Had mothers who averaged 1 or no alcoholic drinks per day	37%	96%
8. Had strict parents	54%	74%
9. Had close and caring relationships with parents	55%	73%

It was also found (see Table 21-1) that 64 percent of the non-substance abusers had parents who forbade them to drink while they were in high school. On the other hand, only 24 percent of those in the substance abuser group indicated that their parents had sought to prohibit them from drinking while they were in high school.

These findings appear to suggest a strong need for efforts to help prevent the early usage of drugs or alcohol as a means of lowering substance abuse proneness for many individuals. The findings also indicate that the presence of clear parental prohibitions against alcohol usage during adolescence may be an effective preventive barrier in deterring substance abuse problems.

Family Intervention

In many cases it is not just the child who is high risk regarding substance abuse proneness but the family unit as a whole due to factors of genetics, environment, role models and relationships. To change the individual child, change has to occur within the family unit itself in many cases.

Heredity. Although about 2 percent of the population are alcoholics, Fox (1968) found that 52 percent of the alcoholics studied came from families in which one or both of the parents were alcoholics. Later, Goodwin (1979) found that 25 percent of the adopted children studied who had an alcoholic parent also became alcoholics. This does not necessarily prove that a genetic factor causes alcoholism, but it does suggest that for some individuals heredity could play an important part in predisposing an individual to problems dealing with alcohol abuse if that behavior is triggered within the vulnerable person by perceived environmental factors.

Role Models. Substance abuse proneness also appears to be clearly linked with negative role models of alcohol and drug use in the home as exhibited by parents and other siblings. In the previously cited research by the authors (see Table 21-1), it was also found that 59 percent of the mothers and 63 percent of the fathers of the substance abusers had three or more drinks per day. In comparison, only 4 percent of the mothers and 11 percent of the fathers of non-substance abusers had three or more drinks per day.

Further, 96 percent of the mothers of nonsubstance abusers were reported to have averaged one or no drinks per day, but only 37 percent of the substance abusers claimed their mothers had one drink per day or less on the average.

It would appear that if parents are serious about preventing substance abuse problems in their children, they should look into the mirror and observe what type of role model they are presenting. The findings cited clearly indicate that most individuals who ultimately have substance abuse problems had parents who drank fairly heavily or very heavily. Conversely, the presence of parents who abstain or drink very moderately appear to help via their role model to develop a resistance to substance abuse problems.

The parent who drinks often appears to feel that it's okay for his/her adolescent son or daughter to consume alcoholic beverages, because it will provide an acceptable substitute for drug usage. The reverse, however, appears to be true. Research studies (Biddle, Bank and Marin, 1980; Stumphauzer, 1980) have indicated that the link to hard drugs does not begin with marijuana or some other drug but, rather, begins with the early use of cigarettes and alcohol.

It appears that one of the cornerstones of a school-sponsored substance abuse prevention program should be aimed at educating parents with regard to how influential their roles are as behavior models in developing either substance abuse proneness or substance abuse resistance in their children.

Family Relationships

Parental control and the presence of close and caring relationships within the family structure appear to be important in building substance abuse resistance. In the authors' study (see Table 21-1), 74 percent of the non-substance abusers indicated that they were exposed to strong parental control while they were growing up, but 73 percent of these individuals also indicated that they had experienced close and caring relationships with their parents. On the other hand, only 54 percent of the substance abusers reported an exposure to strong parental discipline and 55 percent indicated close, caring relationships with their parents.

Studies by Barnes (1977) and Tudor, Peterson and Elifson (1980) also supported the finding that substance abusers are exposed to less control and less caring relationships within their families. It would thus appear that parents who are trying to build substance abuse resistance in their children need to establish an effective form of caring control that gives the child a sense of limits and boundaries to his/her behavior, but also a sense that the limits are there because the parent cares deeply about his/her welfare.

Developing an Internal Locus of Control

There appears to be a continuum that children proceed along in developing substance abuse resistance. In the first stage of the continuum, they need an external locus of control that clearly gives them guidelines for their behavior. They need to depend upon their parents and teachers to guide them via control that is consistent, rational, protective and caring. However, when they are ready to begin the transition to an internal locus of control, it is extremely important for the parent and teacher to maintain a caring support, but also to gradually reduce external direction and limits when the individual begins to demonstrate an ability to manage his/her behavior independently.

A communication of trust by the parent and the teacher is extremely important as the individual makes the transition, generally at the beginning of adolescence, from an external to an internal locus of control. Trust serves to give the individual support for his/her judgement and reinforces a desire to live up to the confidence placed in him/her. It is ultimately an internal locus of control that is at the foundation of substance abuse resistance. If the individual has values and an independent control of his/her life, peer pressures to conform to a norm of alcohol and drug usage can be effectively resisted.

On the other hand, if the individual begins the transition to an internal locus of control but is systematically blocked by suspicion, distrust and an unwillingness to permit even small areas of personal autonomy and social responsibility by his/her teachers and parents, responses of external rebelliousness or internalized anger, depression and frustration are commonly produced. When this happens the adolescent often seeks out an alternative locus of control.

By blocking a movement to an internal locus of control, the anger and frustration generated tends to discredit teachers and parents. Pursuantly, their power as legitimate control agents diminishes within the adolescent's world view. They now become adversaries whose rules and expectancies are not seen as sources of security and direction but a cage whose bars need to be broken to gain freedom.

As the power of teachers and parents as the adolescent's locus of control weakens, the power of peer opinion and norms increases significantly. Thus, peer pressure and power role models become the dominant locus of control in the individual's life. If the adolescent has not been able to at least form the beginnings of an internal locus of control due to the developmental sabotage of often well-intended, but inflexible teachers and parents, the individual will have now become highly vulnerable if exposed to peer influences to use and often abuse alcohol and drugs. This conclusion is supported by Donovan and Jessor's (1978) study which found that alcohol-dependent adolescents are more influenced by their peers than their parents.

Developing Values and a Sense of Personal Worth

The internalization of values which give purpose and meaning to an individual's life appears to be an important factor in building substance abuse resistance. Burkett (1980), for example, found in a study that adolescent substance abusers tend to have less religious convictions than nonabusers. Obviously, a person's value structure does not have to be based upon religious beliefs to give the individual a sense of life purpose, but the presence of value commitments is linked to an internal locus of control and is an important safeguard against the sense of meaninglessness that so often shapes the lives of substance abusers.

The development of a positive sense of worth and self-esteem appears to be another very important factor in building a child's substance abuse resistance. Conversely, substance abusers tend to be discouraged by life and see themselves as failures. A clear link, for example, appears to be present between academic underachievement and substance abuse proneness (Mitchell, Honig and Corman, 1978). Many substance abusers appear to be so depressed by their feelings of failure and low self-esteem that they use drugs and alcohol as a form of self-destruction, a type of slow suicide.

Pursuantly, to help a child build substance abuse resistance it is important at an early age for parents and teachers to deal with the first signs of depression and feelings of worthlessness. Encouragement, praise, opportunities to experience and be rewarded for success are the obvious antidotes for depression and feelings of worthlessness, unless there is a pathological causation. Communicating a belief in the child and caring in a real, unconditional way can do much to alter the world of a depressed, discouraged child.

Children want to please, but they can easily lose hope and confidence if they fail at even small things. Pursuantly, it is the particularly significant role of educators to help children psychologically when they are down by creating classroom environments that are supportive, caring and emotionally warm places. Teachers can do much to help a discouraged child if they can look beyond the negative behavior and poor performance and find the person within who desperately wants to value and like herself if she could only find a mirror in the eyes of a respected person who believes in her more than she does in herself. She may at first resist the positive image and test the teacher's ability to continue that view despite all behavior and performance to the contrary. However, if the teacher can consistently communicate and encourage this positive belief, the child will generally start believing in it and in herself.

CONCLUSION

Substance abuse is a major problem in our culture but is essentially a solvable problem. The major component of its solution appears to be present in the development of substance abuse resistance in children. This can be done by first identifying substance abuse prone children and then attempting to intervene in building their substance abuse resistance by: communicating the child's level of risk to the individual and his/her parents in an immediate and personal way; preventing the early usage of alcohol and drugs; attempting to treat the role models and interactional relationships within the substance abuse prone family unit; helping the child to move toward the development of an internal locus of control; and helping the child to build a sense of personal worth and meaning.

REFERENCES

Barnes, C.M. The development of adolescent drinking behavior: An evaluative review of the impact of the socialization process within the family. *Adolescence.* 1977, 12, 571–591.

Burkett, S.R. Religiousity, beliefs, normative standards and adolescent drinking. *Journal of Studies on Alcohol,* 1980, 41, 662–671.

Donovan, H.E. and Jessor, R. Adolescent problem drinking— psycholsocial correlates in a national sample study. *Journal of Studies on Alcohol,* 1978, 38, 1506–1523.

Fox, R. Treating the Alcoholic's Family. In J.R. Cantanzaro (Ed.), *Alcoholism — The Total Treatment Approach.* Springfield, Ill.: Charles C Thomas, 1968.

Goodwin, D. *Is Alcoholism Hereditary?* New York: Oxford University Press, 1976.

Halpin, G. and Whiddon, T. Drug education: Solution of problem? *Psychological Reports,* 1977, 40, 373–375.

Leonard, M. and Taccarino, J. *The Leonard-Taccarino Analysis of Substance Abuse Proneness.* Chicago: Psychological Systems International, 1988.

Mitchell, J.E., Honig, N.K. and Corman C. Childhood onset of alcohol abuse. *American Journal of Orthopsychiatry,* 1979, 51, 511–513.

Stumphauser, J.S. Learning to drink: Adolescents and alcohol. *Addictive Behavior,* 1980, 5, 277–283.

Taccarino, J.R. *SAFE-R: Security, Aptitude, Fitness Evaluation— Resistance.* Oak Brook, Ill.: Safe Inc., 1987.

Tudor, C.G., Peterson, D.M., and Elifson, K.W. An examination of the relationship between peer and parental influences and adolescent drug use. *Adolescence,* 1980, 15, 783–797.

Chapter 22

COLLABORATION FOR STUDENTS AT RISK

Nancy A. Evers

Because the problem of high dropout rates threatens the nation's productivity and has many causes, all of those who value education are called to work together to solve this multifaceted problem. Many factors contribute to students being at risk of dropping out of school before their graduation (Hahn, 1987). The causes of this problem are complex and emerge from many segments of the community surrounding the student's life. Similarly, the solutions to the problem are complex and require the involvement of a broad range of institutions and agencies that can influence students. Solutions can be generated out of the collective, focused energies of the community, to support the students in their quest for education. Collaboration among those who can contribute to solving the problem holds great potential for actually saving youth from dropping out of school. In this chapter on collaboration for the students at risk of dropping out of school, a definition of collaboration, a description of the efforts of two urban centers in their collaborative work, and an identification of key characteristics of collaboration for students at risk are presented.

Collaboration

Collaboration is working together to solve problems. The purpose or function of collaboration is to solve problems and thereby accomplish some mutually desired goal. The old adage of "two heads are better than one" and images of one hand upon another hand in solidarity to work together toward a common goal are both expressions of combining resources to accomplish something. The resources may be intellect, skills, values, energy, funds, connections, etc. Tremendous energy is generated through the combined efforts of people working together. When the combined energy is focused upon solving a problem which the participants recognize, it is likely that the effort will be successful.

Collaboration for students at risk, or working together to solve the problem of student dropouts, has been found to be a promising practice in many areas of the nation. At these many sites the function of problem solving is common and varies only in the scope of how it occurs. Some collaboratives raise awareness of the problem, some gather and mobilize resources, some apply resources in solving directly school site problems, and some participate in the full problem-solving process. The forms of these collaboratives are very diverse and occur at the national, regional, state, and local levels. Some collaboratives are between a business and a school or a system, some are among business and local government and the schools within a community, some are among school districts facilitated by a regional service center, some are state task forces composed of many constituencies and typically lead by business leaders, and some are *ad hoc* focus groups convened by the U.S. Department of Education.

Different approaches to collaboration for students at risk are illustrated through some examples of collaboratives. At the national level, the U.S. Department of Education and the Urban Superintendents Network collaborated to produce the report on dropout prevention, *Dealing with Dropouts: The Urban Superintendents' Call to Action* (1988). The report presents six strategies for helping students at risk in school: early intervention, positive school climate, high expectations, teacher selection and development, choices of instructional programs and community collaborative efforts. At the regional level, the Appalachian Regional Commission (1987) identified high school dropouts as a major block to the area's economic growth and developed a regional dropout prevention effort which involved a variety of groups in acquiring and allotting $2.5 million to 46 prevention projects. At the state level, the Commonwealth Futures was an initiative designed to provide services to youth at risk in Massachusetts schools. Through interagency coordination and cooperation, the Futures collaborative resulted in the funding of comprehensive community plans with reallocated state funds (Edna McConnell Clark Foundation, 1987). At the local level, the Valued Youth Partnership program for dropout prevention was developed by the Intercultural Development Research Association, funded by the Coca-Cola Company, and implemented in the Edgewood and South San Antonio school districts in San Antonio, Texas. The program identifies Hispanic junior high and high school students at risk of dropping out and gives them an opportunity to serve as tutors of younger students. Program evaluation results indicate that the program has been successful; both tutors and their students made gains in school (Sosa, 1987).

Collaboration in Two Urban Centers

Particularly noteworthy efforts of collaborative efforts to solve the problem of students at risk have been initiated in Boston, Massachusetts and Cincinnati, Ohio. In each of these urban centers, major segments of the community have combined their resources to focus on the problem and have made significant strides in developing and implementing comprehensive solutions. Because both efforts are so recent, the total impact on youth and their communities has not been determined; however, initial evaluations suggest that there is much hope for reducing the number of students at risk of dropping out.

Boston

Recognizing the increasing demand for skilled workers and a shrinking youth labor market created a sense of urgency among Boston community leaders to do something about the dropout problem in the Boston Public Schools. The public school system, the business community, the universities, cultural organizations and the unions in Boston entered into several agreements called the Boston Compact (Hargraves, 1987).

In 1982, the first agreement was made between the Boston Public School System and 350 Boston businesses. The businesses agreed to provide jobs to high school students and graduates, and the school system agreed to guarantee basic math and reading competencies for all graduates by 1986 and to decrease the high school dropout rate. In 1983, a second agreement was made between the school system and 23 Boston colleges and universities to increase the rate of ninth graders who entered higher education institutions by 25 percent by 1989. In 1985, a third agreement was made between the school system and the trade unions to increase the number of apprenticeships for system graduates.

Four years after the Boston Compact's inception, evidence suggested that progress was being made in accomplishing the compact's goals of jobs and college for high school graduates and basic skills competence in high school graduates; however, no progress was evidenced in reducing the dropout rate.

Concerned about the persisting dropout problem in 1986, the superintendent of the Boston Public School System established a task force of people from the schools, businesses, universities and neighborhood communities to work on solving the dropout problem. The task force developed a long-range prevention strategy. The plan had the two goals of reducing by one-half the annual number of students who dropped out and doubling the number of dropouts who returned to school by 1989. The long-term goals were rooted in the beliefs that the Boston schools should be more effective for all students, that the scope of attention should include the middle school level and that community agencies should be involved in the delivery of services to school children. The plan identified actions to be taken in four areas: school structural issues, basic education, alternative programs and human services.

The Boston experience of uniting a community around solving the problem of school dropouts has resulted in some progress, and Boston holds promise as a model for other communities. The Boston experience also provides those committed to making improvements data for reflection. At present, those involved with Boston's collaborative efforts remain hopeful that they will eventually see a reduction in the dropout rate and continue to apply their collective energy and resources to multidimensional solutions.

Cincinnati

The Cincinnati Public School System recently engaged in two major collaborative efforts to reduce students at risk of dropping out of school. The first was a collaborative long-range planning effort initiated by the school board and involved district administrators, teachers, board members, parents and community representatives. The second is presently in progress and is a collaborative of the school system, private industry, local government and the many social and community groups and agencies having contact with youth.

Believing that broad-based community involvement was critical to realizing the goal of excellence in education for all students, the Cincinnati School Board initiated a long-range planning effort. The purpose of the long-range plan was to set forth a program of actions to be taken by the schools to produce a coherent, high quality educational system which further reduced racial isolation (Cincinnati Public Schools, 1987).

In April, 1986 the board formed a twenty-three-member Long-Range Plan Steering Committee and hired two external consultants to facilitate the process. The Long-Range Plan Steering Committee was composed of community representatives, parents, board members, district administrators, and district teachers. The committee was given the charge to develop a plan of educational excellence for all students and was given a set of questions that the plan needed to address. The committee engaged in an open problem-solving process of: (1) assessing school district needs through meetings with community members and school personnel and through extensive review of school system data; (2) forming initial recommendations; (3) testing the initial recommendations in meetings throughout the community; and (4) forming the final set of recommendations. The final set of interrelated recommendations had major importance for reducing student-at-risk conditions in the district. The plan set direction for the district to: strengthen the neighborhood schools and focus on meeting the needs of students at risk, continue to provide a strong alternative school system, strengthen the education program for early adolescents, provide greater continuity between schools and programs, implement additional ways to reduce racial isolation, strengthen the quality of administrator and teacher leadership and provide an effective vocational program.

In May, 1987 the board approved the set of recommendations for implementation in the schools. The long-range planning was started by the board during the time it was searching for a new superintendent of schools. The new superintendent of schools began October, 1986 and immediately joined in the process. After the board approved the recommendations, the superintendent was given responsibility for implementing the plan in the school system.

Concomitant to the school board's long-range planning effort, a second effort specifically focused on reducing school dropouts and youth unemployment and increasing literacy was initiated (Evers, Faddoul, and Hammel, 1988). Concerned that many young people were not productively entering into and participating in the economic, civic and cultural life of the community, community leaders formed the Cincinnati Youth Collaborative. In December, 1986, the Cincinnati Youth Collaborative was conceived and organized as a "team-oriented, integrated" approach in which collaborative action was valued as the key to fulfilling a clear mission. The fundamental intent was to establish and assure the effective operation of structures and support systems which would lead every youngster to reach his/her potential. The Cincinnati Youth Collaborative holds potential for orchestrating the human and financial resources needed to actually focus on solving the problem.

The collaborative's flexible, dynamic organization facilitates its work. The Cincinnati Youth Collaborative is lead by three cochairpersons who have influence on major dimensions of Cincinnati life: the president of Procter and Gamble, the superintendent of the Cincinnati Public Schools, and an active member of City Council. Midyear 1987, the Collaborative's Steering Committee was formalized. The Steering Committee is presently composed of thirty-two members who represent multiple dimensions of community life: business, social services, community special interests, local government, public schools and institutions of higher education. Subcommittees of the Steering Committee were formed to carry out specific work functions. The subcommittees are: Building Bridges to College; Building Bridges to Jobs; Communications; Community Support; Finance; Development; Instructional Programming; Planning; Preschool; Principal and Teacher Training and Motivation; and Evaluation Task Force. For each of the subcommittees a member of the Steering Committee is chairperson and the membership is composed of other Steering Committee members and invited other community members with expertise and other resources which can be used in accomplishing the work of the subcommittee. At present, the collaborative has approximately 200 people actively engaged in seeking to fulfill the collaborative's mission. Given the extensive nature of the work and numbers of people involved, the collaborative needed a full-time executive director to facilitate the ongoing work.

In January, 1988, the collaborative hired the former president of the College of Mt. St. Joseph in Cincinnati as executive director. The Executive Committee is composed of the three Cochairpersons, the executive director and the subcommittee chairpersons.

At present, the Cincinnati Youth Collaborative is at a readiness stage and beginning to implement solutions. The collaborative has been organized, goals and action plans are being developed and finalized, the community is being mobilized around the mission, financial resources are being acquired from businesses and foundations, budgeting for the next three academic years is underway and evaluation to judge the impact of the collaborative's efforts is being planned. The massive, focused talents and financial resources of the many parties working together to reduce the student dropout rate is likely to enhance the overall quality of life in Cincinnati.

Key Characteristics of Collaboration

Even though there are many different approaches to collaboration for students at risk, there are some identifiable key characteristics of collaborations that contribute to their being successful. For a collaboration to function well, the collaborative must: have clear and commonly valued goals, involve all parties who can contribute to solving the problem, have dynamic and creative leadership, exercise shared decision making, have a flexible organization and have a climate of caring and mutual respect. These key characteristics have been observed in collaborations for students at risk and in other educational collaborations.

Commitment to a clear mission and goals by all of those participating drives the collaborative forward. People involved in collaboration for students at risk respond to the call for reaching out to help youth realize their full potential, knowing that everyone's future depends on developing talent in our youth (Clark, 1985; Ament, 1987). Once multiple dimensions of the community identify with the mission, they are more willing to commit their talent, energy and financial resources to the cause. A multifaceted problem is likely to require a multifaceted solution. There is no single, simple solution to the complex problem of student dropouts. It is likely that the fulfillment of the mission will be long-term (Webb, 1987; Jensen, 1985). It is important that long- and short-range, measurable goals be developed and prioritized (Clark, 1985); by laying out an explicit set of goals, the mission and how it will be accomplished, becomes much more clear to everyone involved. In addition, through this process of clarification, the goals become realistic and participants can begin to understand what resources are needed and how they can contribute (Chalupsky and Peirano-Dalldorf, 1985).

The involvement of all those who can contribute to solving the problem is critical to the success of the collaboration. No one person or organization can solve the problem of students at risk alone; therefore, it takes a broad range of people to work together in lifting our youth (Webb, 1987; Appalachian Regional Commission, 1987; Lewis, 1987; Intriligator, 1986). A student at risk is potentially influenced by home, school, economic opportunity, government and social relationships. The many people and agencies, which have control over how that influence impacts youth, have the potential of solving the problem of student dropouts. Bringing the individual energies of different community groups together in a coordinated fashion creates a synergy necessary to overcome such a large problem. When a community is unified around the belief that "together we can" make a difference for youth and our collective future, enormous potential is realized. When diverse organizations of the community are brought together, recognition of different capacities of and constraints upon each organization is important to the collaborative working well as a team (Clark, 1985). Most frequently, those willing to give to the cause also need to feel that they are receiving. Provision for mutual benefits and reciprocity in giving and receiving resources is important to the well-being of the collaborative (Ament, 1987).

Vital dynamic leadership is essential to collaboration. Inspired leaders of the collaboration can serve as the clarions for mobilizing many aspects of the community around the mission of saving the community's youth and collective future. Effective leaders give themselves to the goals of the collaboration and motivate others to give of themselves. They orchestrate the flow of work within the collaborative, giving recognition to the contributions of those involved (Evers, Faddoul, and Hammel, 1988). Key officials in the organizations participating in the collaborative, for example, corporate executives, superintendents and city councilpersons, hold a unique opportunity for leading (Jensen, 1985). They are usually powerful because they have access to numerous resources which can be focused on students at risk, and they can use their power to benefit the community and students at risk.

In order for collaboration to succeed, participants must exercise shared decision making. Those who are making an investment in collaboration for students at risk need to know that they have an equal opportunity to make decisions which shape the entire effort (Blueprint, 1987; Intriligator, 1986). They need to know that their influence or power is going to make a difference (Clark, 1985). Therefore, the forum for making decisions is the group where every major stakeholder can participate. If the collaborative is large, representative decision groups can be formed for mutually developing policy (Jensen, 1985) and other representative decision groups can be formed for mutually developing programs and operations. Using consensus as the primary mode for shared decision making yields greater commitment by all parties to the decision outcomes and maintains the vested interest of all concerned. Because the problem of students at risk has many possible interrelated solutions, those participating in shared decision making will need to consider many ideas which come from many different perspectives (Ament, 1987). Groups typically make decisions based on information and values. Open, honest communication permits the flow and examination of information and values so important to shared decision making.

A flexible organization facilitates successful collaboration. Flexibility is so important to collaboration for students at risk (Ament, 1987), because control of the structure and resources is shared and does not reside in any one place. Each person and organization participating in the collaborative is usually volunteering time, talent and other resources, each of which is impacted by demands outside of the collaborative, for example, their employment and personal relationships. All persons involved need to be open to possible modifications which can enhance collaboration.

Collaboration in a climate of caring and mutual respect makes the entire effort possible. Successful collaboration for students at risk starts with caring about the welfare of youth and the quality of our collective future; successful collaboration continues with also caring for the others involved in the collaborative (Clark, 1985; Ament, 1987). Many different people and organizations come together in collaboration by respecting and honoring common and divergent perspectives. Having faith in the mission and trust in one another, the collaborative moves forward.

SUMMARY

Part of the solution to the problem of students at risk is how we solve it. Collaboration for students at risk holds great potential for reducing student dropouts and increasing human potential. Working together in solving the problem requires the mobilization of schools, governments, businesses and special-interest groups around the problem of student dropouts and uniting those organizations in applying their collective resources in solving it. Exemplary efforts of collaboration are evidenced at the national, regional, state and local levels. The efforts of Boston and Cincinnati are noteworthy and hold promise of success. The examination of many different collaboratives across the nation indicates that there are some key characteristics of successful collaboration: dedication to clear and commonly valued goals, involvement of all who can contribute to solving the problem, dynamic and creative leadership, shared decision making, flexible organization and a climate of caring and mutual respect. The problem of students at risk can be solved through collaboration.

REFERENCES

Ament, R. R. (1987). *Collaboration in Adult Education; Overview.* Washington, D.C.: Office of Educational Research and Improvement.

Appalachian Regional Commission (1987). *Dropout Prevention in Appalachia: Lessons for the Nation.* Washington, D.C.: Appalachian Regional Commission. (ERIC Document Reproduction Service No. ED 280912.)

Chalupsky, A. B. and Peirano-Dalldorf, M. R. (1985). *Vocational Education — Defense Establishment Collaboration: State-of-the-Practice Report.* Washington, D.C.: Office of Vocational and Adult Education.

Cincinnati Public Schools (1987). *Final Report of the Goals and Long Range Plan Steering Committee.* Cincinnati, Ohio: Author.

Clark, R. J. (1985). *Factors Influencing Success in a School-University-Industry Partnership for Teacher Education.* Amherst, Massachusetts. (ERIC Document Reproduction Service No. ED258955.)

Edna McConnell Clark Foundation (1987). *Commonwealth Futures: Final Report on the Six Month Planning Grant.* New York, N.Y. Edna McConnell Clark Foundation. (ERIC Document Reproduction Service No. ED281928.)

Evers, N. A., Faddoul, S., and Hammel, B. J. (1988). [The Cincinnati Youth Collaborative.] Unpublished raw data.

Hahn, A. (1987). Reaching Out to America's Dropouts: What to Do? *Phi Delta Kappan, 69,* 256–263.

Hargroves, J. S. (1987). The Boston Compact: Facing the Challenge of School Dropouts. *Education and Urban Society, 19,* 303–310.

Intrilligator, B. A. (1986). *Collaborating with the Schools: A Strategy for School Improvement.* (From ERIC Abstracts, 1987, No. ED277089.)

Jensen, M. C. (1985, September). Salem Program Demonstrates Five Keys to a Successful Business—School Partnership. *OSSC Bulletin, 29.*

Lewis, A. C. (1987). Partnerships: Connecting School and Community. (From ERIC Abstracts, 1987, No. ED283247.)

Office of Educational Research and Improvement. (1988). *Dealing with Dropouts: The Urban Superintendents' Call to Action.* Washington, D.C.: U.S. Government Printing Office.

Packard, B. (1987). *Arizona's Blueprints for Building Partnerships.* Phoenix, Arizona. Arizona State Department of Education. (ERIC Document Reproduction Service No. ED281016.)

Sosa, A. S. (1986, November). Valued Youth Partnership Program: Dropout Prevention Through Cross-Age Tutoring. *Intercultural Development Research Association Newsletter,* 6–8.

Webb, M.B. (1987). *Notes Concerning Dropout Prevention in New York State.* Buffalo, New York. (ERIC Document Reproduction Service No. ED280907)

A Blueprint for Success: Operation Rescue (1987). Washington, D.C. (ERIC Document Reproduction Service No. ED274093).

Chapter 23

DEMYTHOLOGIZING SCHOOLS: EDUCATORS AND THE SOCIAL ORDER

J. HARRY WRAY

On March 24, 1988, the *Chicago Tribune* carried a front-page story that illuminates a fundamental issue in American education. It was a story about U.S. Education Secretary William Bennett's visit to the Chicago public school system the previous day. Secretary Bennett, who enjoyed a reputation as a controversial and pugnacious critic of U.S. education, had outraged some elements of the Chicago education establishment the previous November by calling Chicago schools the worst in the country. Jacqueline Vaughn, president of the Chicago Teachers' Union, responded to Mr. Bennett's charge by inviting him to visit two nonmagnet Chicago schools on his next trip to Chicago. Mr. Bennett agreed and, although he found the two schools he visited to be "above average," he remained unconvinced that he should retract his previous statements about Chicago schools. Citing high dropout rates and low standardized achievement scores, he argued that "Two schools do not a system make."

This controversy highlights two obvious components of the current conventional wisdom regarding U.S. education. The first is that American schools are in serious trouble. Although in the immediate case it was Chicago schools that were the focus of Mr. Bennett's ire, anyone following his tenure as Education Secretary knows he is severely critical of the state of public education generally. Nor can these criticisms be dismissed as the hysterical musings of an eccentric crank. Similar charges echo throughout the education establishment, in government assessments, in academic studies, and in foundation reports. Almost no one has anything good to say about public schools these days. On the contrary, there is a consensus of belief that schools are not doing their job, although this consensus begins to weaken when critics seek to define precisely the meaning of "job" in this context.

A second component of the current conventional wisdom is also revealed by this incident. It is that schools can do a significantly better job than they are doing, *however* that job is defined. Ms. Vaughn argued that if schools had more money, their performance would improve; Mr. Bennett used the two schools to argue that other Chicago schools could do better at their current level of funding. Neither quarrelled with the notion that schools both could and ought to be doing better. Indeed, most of the essays in this book develop arguments purporting to demonstrate how schools can do a better job educating students.

I have opened this essay with the Bennett/Vaughn dispute to make a less obvious point, however. Their argument illustrates the narrowness of the parameters within which the debate on educational enhancement usually occurs. It is assumed by both liberals and conservatives that good education is precisely and solely a function of what happens in schools. In part, this is a natural consequence of the disputants typically associated with educational issues. Overwhelmingly, they tend to be educators, people who by training and often by personal experience are lead to believe in the potential efficacy of the educational system. In the parlance of functionalist theory, when the "output" of the schools is unsatisfactory, we tend to look at some deficiency in the school "system."

The purpose of this essay is not to disagree with the notion that improved schools can make a difference in the education of our children. Rather, it is to suggest that, to the extent that our goal is a well-educated citizenry, our vision is often too constricted. Additionally, we attempt to explain why this is the case. Finally, we shall argue that educators and others concerned about genuine educational improvement have a particular intellectual and moral obligation to expand the parameters of the current great education debate.

One cannot understand the way Americans typically think about schools without identifying at least some core cultural beliefs or myths. Cultural myths exist in all societies. They vary, of course, and they are not impervious to change, but they tend to be durable because they exist beyond reason. They are affirmations born of our limited ability to apprehend. Rather than contradicting reason, myths typically support it, providing structures within which to locate and identify "facts." In short, myths structure our vision of reality, causing us to "see" the world in certain ways. Cultural myths are relevant to schools, first because all social institutions connect to these myths in some way, and second because schools, as major agents of socialization, help extend these myths.

One of the central governing myths of our cultural tradition has been individualism. Since Toqueville, through Bryce, Bellah and Wills, thoughtful analysts have noted the extent to which individualism is ingrained in the American consciousness. The absence of a feudal tradition meant that the oppressiveness of social class was not as keenly felt here as in other industrializing nations. The Protestant religious tradition, so influential among the early nation builders, also contributed substantially to our individualist tradition. By emphasizing both a personal relationship with God and individual responsibility for one's destiny, early Protestantism added the substantial weight of religious authority to the building of this myth.

To these can be added the factor of geography. The historic presence of a vast frontier and an underpopulated continent has made an independent contribution to individualism. For most of our history the idea of starting over was not an ideological abstraction but a real possibility. On this underpopulated, seemingly limitless continent, individual destinies appeared unusually open in comparison to the European experience. It is hardly surprising that capitalism became so firmly rooted here. In this fertile soil, it grew and, by generating such popular spokespersons as Horatio Alger, Oliver Optic and Andrew Carnegie, managed to replenish the soil of individualism in which it was planted.

A deeply ingrained spirit of individualism in American culture has important implications for the establishment of social institutions. With regards to schools, there are at least three important consequences. First, by definition, an individualist vision has a minimalist view of social barriers to accomplishment. Thus, while everyone recognizes that some children, through no fault of their own, may have inherited social disadvantages—such as poverty or race—the significance of these is often downplayed. School is seen as the egalitarian starting place that evens out such disadvantages. This intuitively implausible notion is reductionist in the extreme, and it is contradicted by substantial empirical investigation (Coleman, 1966; Jencks, 1972; Bowles and Gintis, 1976). Despite this, public discourse on schools is dominated by the individualist vision, and people continue to respond to it as if it were a reality (Weikart, 1987).

Second, there is an inherent tension between the individualist spirit and schools. As public institutions, schools are necessarily collectivist in intent. The very existence of public schools is testimony to the belief that something must be done with our children and that what is done is not merely a private individual concern. A major impetus for the establishment of U.S. public schools was the desire by the dominant social class to instill proper values in the surging tide of immigrant Catholic workers (Nasau, 1979; Katz, 1976).

Thus, to some extent, individualism came to be seen as a problem. Today, similar controversies persist as, on the one hand, business leaders complain about an improperly trained work force and, on the other, parents criticize schools for trying to instill an alien "secular humanist" ideology in their children. We have sanctioned the operation of schools, but they operate in a milieu that continues to invoke suspicion. The public realm exists in a perpetual state of tension with our individualist ethos.

At a more broadly philosophical level, individualism encourages intellectual segmentation. Whereas a communitarian vision of society encourages one to see the interrelatedness of things, individualism encourages the opposite. Thus, what happens at school is thought to be largely unrelated to what is happening at home or in the work place, and vice versa. In such a view, the existence of ignorant children means *simply* that schools have failed.

These various currents, which at times seem to swirl unpredictably, have led to significant ambiguity with respect to schools. No nation comes close to the U.S. in the amount of money spent on public education. We spend so much because we expect so much from our schools. We expect not only well-educated children but well-trained ones as well. We expect them to have decent values that are also largely inoffensive. Most of all, we expect the schools to ratify perhaps our most central social myth: individualism. No matter what the social circumstances, and despite *changing* social circumstances, schools are supposed to redeem the American Dream—that individual initiative is the linchpin of success and that schools are adequate to summon forth that initiative from students.

Elizabeth Janeway (Janeway, 1971) has written revealingly of the dilemmas of being a housewife, arguing that the job ultimately is unrewarding because it is so open-ended. In the traditional family, the husband's job is to bring home the paycheck, while the wife's job is to create the good life. There is always more that a housewife can do in family settings, and, therefore, when something goes wrong, she is the one who usually must shoulder the blame. The same can be said about the social role of our schools. It is no wonder that they have become society's punching bag. There is a persistent tendency to hold schools accountable for social failure. School of Education academics, who ought to help clarify the untenable situation of schools, have all too often joined this endeavor, thus adding to it a patina of scholarly respect.

Are schools worse today than they were thirty years ago? The recent tide of criticism of schools is such that even to raise this question is to invite disdain. Certainly, external barometers such as falling scores on standardized tests are not hopeful. Nor does the recent easing of this trend offer much solace. Responding to the pressures such tests create, district after district has come to regard these tests, not as measures of performance, but as ends in themselves. Increasingly, our children are learning that the point of education is to enable one to perform on multiple-choice tests. As training for these tests becomes the core of curricula, of course scores will improve. Anyone who has spent time reading essays written by college freshmen, however, understands that our nation's children are receiving a woefully inadequate education.

Perhaps the quality of our teachers has declined. It has been argued, for example, that thirty years ago gender discrimination kept many very bright women in the teaching profession because jobs in other areas simply were unavailable to them. As this discrimination has ebbed, the most talented women have been drawn into more prestigious professions.

Allan Bloom's recent diatribe against schools (Bloom, 1987) identifies yet a different reason for the indifferent results of schooling: the curriculum. Children no longer are instructed according to an external and absolute moral code, argues Bloom. Relativism has reared its ugly head, and the student, not knowing what to learn, doesn't bother to learn anything.

Such observations notwithstanding, the notion that schools are growing worse is implausible. Studies that have looked carefully at our teaching core cite an abundance of dedicated teachers, although many feel unappreciated (Sizer, 1985). And, surely, education research has exerted at least some marginally positive impact over the last thirty years. It is important to recall that schools are convenient targets. As ubiquitous public institutions they are highly visible. Moreover, they are supposed to open unlimited vistas for the nation's children. When they fail to do this, resentment ensues and talk about school reform boils anew.

It is always important to think about how schools can do their job better, but it is also important to see clearly how schools connect to larger social currents. There is the possibility that a major portion of the declining performance of children in schools has nothing to do with schools at all. Consider Professor Bloom's lament. He is probably correct in his assertion (Frances Fitzgerald documents it far more clearly than he [Fitzgerald, 1979]) that high school curriculum is increasingly contentless, but this is not because teachers love relativism, as he assumes. It is because of cultural fragmentation. To say children ought to be taught to respect decent values is fine as an abstraction, and it could be done in times like the fifties, when there was a consensus on what those values were. Professor Bloom believes he knows which values are the right ones, but today there are many who do not share his white-anglo-male, America-first, last and only vision of the ideal state—even as *he* excoriates ex-sixties radicals. Given this fragmented vision of national purpose, it is hardly surprising that teachers seek to remain above the fray by avoiding it altogether. High school students are spoon-fed innocuous pabulum in the social sciences and humanities, in part because it is so difficult to teach anything important that is also not controversial.

This is only one example of how our social fabric defines the limits of what can happen in the classroom. Other social changes carry far more important implications for schooling. Consider the typical student in 1989 with his or her counterpart twenty years earlier. The earlier student is far less likely to come from a single-parent home, far more likely to come from an English-speaking background, less likely to be economically impoverished, and likely to be significantly less afflicted by America's national disease—watching television. Scores of studies confirm what is intuitively obvious: that these social factors have a serious effect upon educational achievement.

None of the social factors here mentioned have anything to do with schools, but they have a great deal to do with education, as any educator knows. It is quite possible, within the limits of what they can do, that the schools are doing a better job than ever and that declining educational achievement is largely a function of factors outside the school.

Forecasting in the social sciences is often hazardous. Predicting "national moods" or presidential outcomes is highly problematic. Projecting the composition of schools, however, is much easier. Fertility rates of various social groups, immigration patterns, children already born, all ease the difficulty of projections with respect to schools. Although statisticians might quarrel over the precise numbers, it is very clear that the proportion of children-at-risk in public schools will increase substantially by the year 2000.

If the eighties can be characterized educationally, it would surely be as the decade of reports on education. Driven by the twin engines of declining educational achievement and a falling economic status, there seemed to be a limitless supply of organizations and individuals willing to suggest what was wrong with education in America. Overwhelmingly, these reports focused upon the institutional school. Typically, there was not even a bow in the direction of exogenous factors. The litany of solutions is by now quite familiar: longer school days, longer school years, back to the basics, school vouchers, higher teacher pay, and merit pay.

Such issues are worth considering, but to suggest that they define the bounds of thinkable thought with respect to the improvement of educational achievement is to be simpleminded in the extreme. It is to perpetuate that aspect of our social mythology that is less and less able to withstand scrutiny. In short, there is an ironic component to these reports. They add to the myth of schools even as they attack schooling. One waggish critic of a series of 1983 reports on schools writes that they blame schools for not solving "The Toyota Problem" (Cohen, 1984). But the Toyota problem is not the schools' to solve and the suggestion that it is unduly, distorts what schools can do. Even as they are attacked, the vision of what schools can do is inflated. Serious thinking about education might substantially benefit from a demythologizing of schools. We need to face the reality of what schools *cannot* do if we are to understand how education might be improved.

In the fall of 1987, a bitter teachers' strike closed the Chicago public schools for a month. Some of the parents of the school attended by my children organized an *ad hoc* education program to help students and to relieve other parents of a substantial burden. As a participant in this program, I taught ten children in my home one day a week. Two of the children came from a single-parent, relatively poor Hispanic family. As I worked with these two children, I became aware of several things. I learned that they were bright, that they were not doing well in school and that their mother, who loved the children dearly, used the television a great deal to help take care of them. After working all day as a beautician and then coming home to her usual domestic chores, she found it difficult to give much of herself to her children. Although our school has a quite active parents organization, this mother has not had the time nor the resources to attend meetings, nor has she ever spoken to school authorities on behalf of her children. If not these particular children, we know what is going to happen to kids like these. They will fall further behind in school; they will be identified as "dumb" and they will disappear. There is no one to speak on their behalf.

Public school personnel are in a unique social position. They comprise a well-educated segment of the middle class that also has regular contact with the tangible effects of social disintegration and poverty. The vast majority of middle-class and upper-class Americans know little of the effects of poverty on children. To them, poverty is either an abstraction or an occasional wrong turn off the freeway.

Teachers (at least collectively) regularly encounter a broad cross section of society and they daily experience the effects on education of the social forces about which we've been writing. While it is important for them to consider how they can best serve their diverse clientele, it is also essential that they identify the limits of what can be done by schools and that they raise these matters judiciously and publicly. If educational achievement is to be a central concern (and what modern society can afford not to make it one), teachers must show others *their* responsibilities. For purposes of illustration, let us consider how two seemingly exogenous factors impinge directly on the education experience and how educators ought therefore to respond to them.

Developmental psychologists have clearly demonstrated that the quality of the affective bond established between child and caregiver in the first year or two of life has a dramatic effect upon cognitive growth and emotional development. Sroufe and Cooper catalogue a vast array of research on the effects of attachment to later development (Sroufe and Cooper, 1988). A nice summary of this research was offered in the extensive testimony of David Hamburg, the president of the Carnegie Corporation, in his appearance before a joint committee of Congress in September, 1987. Hamburg identified numerous studies that showed children who are strongly attached to the caregiver early in life are more positively oriented towards their peers, are more interested in engaging the world, are more exploratory, experience more extensive language development, and do better in school than their less well-attached counterparts. Attachment also has an important impact upon prosocial behavior. To quote Doctor Hamburg's testimony (Hamburg, 1987, pp. 14–16):

This work can be related to another body of inquiry dealing with the effects of the family on the development of prosocial behavior. In this work, both direct family observations and experimental studies have examined the effects of a model on later prosocial or antisocial behavior. The results are clear. Children exposed to such models, when compared to similar children in control groups, tend to show the behavior manifested by the models: whether it be honesty, generosity, helping or rescuing behavior.

Many laboratory and clinical studies of social learning indicate that certain factors enhance the impact of a model for the child: (1) the adult's power; (2) the adult's perceived competence; (3) the adult's long-term nurturance of the child. All this puts securely attached children in a strong position to adopt salient patterns of behavior through observational learning of their parents and other family members. That is, the combination of early attachment plus abundant modeling over the years of growth and development can lead to prosocial behavior that becomes firmly established and may be highly adaptive. The prosocial behavior is particularly significant in adaptation because it is likely to open up new opportunities for the growing child, strengthen additional human relationships, and contribute to the building of self-esteem.

In the context of secure attachment and valued adult models—*provided by either a cohesive family or a more extended social support network* —certain norms are established early in life in the context of a modicum of warmth and trust: (1) taking turns; (2) sharing with others; (3) cooperating, especially in learning and problem solving; (4) helping others, especially in times of stress. These norms, though established on a simple basis in the first few years of life, open the way to much more complex and beneficial human relationships that have significance throughout the life span. They tend to earn respect, provide gratification, and amplify the effectiveness of anything the individual could do alone. Therefore, as a practical matter, it appears that early intervention programs need to take account of the factors that influence the development of attachment and prosocial behavior. (emphasis added)

This extensive research has corroborated what many teachers have known at a visceral and less systematic level for years. Kids who feel loved have major advantages over those who do not. If this research resonates with the experience of teachers, then they must assist in bringing it to public attention. Historically, of course, attachment has occurred in the context of the family. As a matter of policy, we need to think along two dimensions. The first is how to help families in this process. In some cases this may involve parental training. Some evidence suggests that parents who are young or who were not themselves strongly attached as children can profit enormously by a relatively simple education program.

We must also consider carefully both the recent efforts to require poor mothers to work and more flexible hours for those who do work. Furthermore, it has been more than fifty years since a reduction of the work week. In fact, full-time workers are spending *more* time on the job in recent years. Reducing the work week ought at least to be the subject of an extensive public hearing. Finally, an extensive public day-care system staffed by an imaginative combination of professionals and our most wasted public resource, senior citizens, could be of major assistance in promoting attachment and thereby improving education.

Educators tend not to respond to such issues collectively. Operating in the intellectually segmented manner described earlier, their organizations typically only take stands on a much narrower range of issues. "Out of school, out of mind" seems to be the governing assumption. These narrower stands, such as teacher pay, may be viewed by others as simply self-serving. The broader issues pertaining to attachment provide the opportunity to speak about educational improvement in ways that are clearly not self-serving. This would add a special legitimacy to their argument.

Perhaps the most broadly accepted definition of politics is that it is the authoritative allocation of values for society. Politics is the process through which people come to accept a given distribution of both tangible and intangible goods as legitimate. Since values in the political realm are typically either scarce or contentious, any given outcome benefits some people even as it harms others.

This understanding of politics sheds some interesting light on the question of poverty, for it suggests that poverty is the result of social decisions we have made. It is not typically viewed as such. On the contrary, poverty is characteristically viewed as an extremely complex and implacable phenomenon that is probably related to a flaw in human nature (or at least the nature of some humans), the consequences of which are universally harmful. These notions fit comfortably within the individualist cultural values we described earlier.

The American vision of poverty has two important consequences. The first is that it leads to what has been called the therapeutic approach to welfare (Polsky, 1983). Welfare is not seen as a matter of right or social membership. Rather, it is seen as an attempt to correct those deficiencies in people that have made them poor. The poor must be constantly monitored and prodded. When they fail to work themselves out of poverty in sufficient numbers to satisfy our individualist mythology, they are attacked for not having the right character and are prodded more vigorously. If the poor are seen as having character flaws, the question of why we refuse to allocate goods more equitably, as does virtually every other industrialized nation in the world, need never be asked.

The second consequence, following from the view of poverty as an unmitigated evil, is that there is a unified interest in its elimination. Poverty has no public friends. If poverty is the result of social decisions, however, it follows from our definition of politics that some people benefit from it. The poor, for example, benefit the rich in a number of ways. They are a ready army of cheap labor willing to provide services. Domestic labor is only the most obvious example. They also create a generally depressive effect upon the wages of workers and encourage workers to be more compliant. Labor loses some of its bargaining power when there are lots of people anxious for work under almost any circumstances.

Any deliberations about children at risk must inevitably come to terms with the question of poverty. While not all children at risk live in poverty, a disproportionate number of them do, and current trends suggest poor children will populate our public schools in unprecedented numbers. Poverty is an important issue in education because it generates a number of effects that hinder learning. These effects are physical, psychological, and social, and they ultimately relate to the question of citizenship.

The physical effects of poverty are well-documented. They begin in utero with malnourishment and continue through development. Infant mortality rates are substantially higher among poor children, and these children are more likely to be born with physical and mental handicaps. Malnutrition is a continuing problem among poor youth. They are more likely to be sick, they are more likely to become seriously ill, and they visit the doctor less often (Walzer, 1983).

As Bellah argues (Bellah, 1975, p. 135), poverty is not bad merely because it means material deprivation. It is a social and political status involving vulnerability. It is bad because it is a condition of powerlessness. Poverty exacts a psychological toll as well. It is possible to be "poor and proud," but our culture makes this a difficult option. Studies show that poor people have significantly less self-esteem and that family tension increases with poverty (Schlozman and Verba, 1979). This lack of self-esteem begins quite early, as Erikson has shown in his studies of self-portraits of kindergarten children (Erikson, 1964).

The dropout rate for the poor is staggering. Nationwide, 25 percent of all poor children drop out of school, and the dropout rate for black and Hispanic poor exceeds 50 percent (Shalala, 1986). Within the school the poor confront serious problems. They are often less adept socially than their middle-class peers. They are constantly reminded, in school and on television, of the things they do not have. Disproportionately, they either vent their anger by acting out, thus becoming "problem children," or they become resigned to their fate and psychologically disappear. And far too often the presence of poor children in school is little more than a physical phenomenon. Many sense that what happens there has no consequence for them whatsoever. Ted Sizer reports, of his wide-ranging visits to high schools across America (Sizer, 1985), that he was surprised at how similar our high schools are. There was one exception— the economic level of the students. After a few weeks, Sizer was able to predict accurately the economic level of the children in the school by simply spending a few hours in classrooms.

The adjustments that the education system has made to poverty have been almost exclusively internal, when they are made at all. The best educators ask how, with their limited resources, they might serve poor students better. This book represents an attempt to raise such questions. But we must also realize that as educators we have a social and moral responsibility to call attention to the *limits* of what we can do and to the tragic social and economic waste that results from widespread poverty. We have this responsibility, because we are the ones who see this toll being exacted daily in our nation's classrooms.

Americans consistently underestimate the extent to which poverty is simply a function of social rules and social organization. The Reagan Administration came to Washington with a supposedly new idea, labelled supply-side economics. Simply put, this idea was that poor people could be helped by giving rich people a larger proportion of our economic pie. By providing the rich with a huge tax cut in 1981 and cutting social welfare programs aimed at the poor, we were simultaneously supposed to promote economic growth and give the poor, in George Gilder's famous phrase, "the spur of their poverty" (Gilder, 1981, p. 118). We can now see the devastating results of that program. The number of poor has grown and so has the intensity of their poverty.

In 1986 (Greenstein, 1987a), four years into an economic recovery, 13.6 percent of all Americans were poor, living below the poverty line of $11,203 for a family of four. The poverty rates for children were much higher. More than one child in five was classified by the Census Bureau as poor in 1986. A decade earlier the poverty rate stood at 11.6 percent and included eight million fewer Americans. Not only has the eighties seen an increase in poverty, but the poor have grown poorer. In 1986 the poverty gap (the amount by which the incomes of the poor fell below the poverty line) was $49.2 billion, compared to $32.1 billion a decade earlier.

Perhaps the most striking of the 1986 census data pertain to income division. The gap between the rich and the poor, and also between the rich and the middle class, hit its widest point since the Census Bureau began collecting such data in 1947. In 1986 the wealthiest 20 percent of U.S. families received 43.7 percent of the national family income, the highest percentage ever recorded. The poorest *40 percent* of U.S. families received 15.4 percent of national family income, the lowest ever recorded. The 20 percent of U.S. families right in the middle of the income spectrum received their lowest share of national family income (16.8%) since 1947. This is not because the rich have worked harder than middle and lower income Americans. It is because the distributional rules have been altered.

As bad as things were, President Reagan worked hard to make things worse for low-income Americans. After six years of cutting programs aimed at poor people, and in the face of their deteriorating circumstances, the president requested Congress to go further. In his fiscal year 1988 budget report, one-third of his proposed reductions came out of programs targeted at low-income Americans, despite the fact that these programs constituted only one-ninth of the federal budget (Greenstein, 1987b).

In economic theory there is a dilemma that occasionally finds its way into economic textbooks called the Tragedy of the Commons. It is used to illustrate the limitations of highly individualized, self-interested market choices. In that dilemma, there is a common pasture wherein farmers can graze sheep. Each farmer starts with the same number of sheep and the pasture is sufficient to feed them all. The farmers, however, in order to maximize their personal returns from the common ground, add to the size of their herds. Moreover, all realize that if they do *not* add to the size of their herds, the others will, and the prudent will end up being losers. As the herds grow, of course, the commons is wiped out and *all* the farmers lose.

There is no way to resolve this dilemma within a highly individualized market system. What is necessary is the public recognition of common interest and a decision to limit market choices. As Michael Walzer has convincingly shown (Walzer, 1983, Ch. 4), the market is fine within its sphere, but it has a tendency to exceed that sphere. In many areas of public policy people often react in ways characteristic of the farmers in the Tragedy of the Commons. Spurred by an intensely individualist ethos, social policy is often seen *merely* as a zero-sum game in which one wins only by extracting concessions from others. Because they have relatively little political power, the poor lose far more often than they win.

But to calculate wins and losses so narrowly is folly, for we are far more interdependent than is generally recognized. We do not "win" when children go hungry or when they struggle to raise themselves, even though we may pay a little less in taxes. Any society's most important investments are the ones it makes in its children. These are indeed social investments, for it is our children, *all* our children, to whom power and responsibility will inexorably pass.

The surging number of children at risk is shocking enough, but in a curious way to conceive of the problem in this way is a palliative. The term "children" conveys a sense of dependence, of innocence, finally, of harmlessness. It is understandable that the issue should take this form, because it is thoughtful educators who are identifying the problem. That educators are beginning to think seriously about it can be a source of pride for the profession, but it is crucial that the problem be accurately framed.

First, it is not *merely* children who are at risk; it is the social fabric of society. Second, although schools might do somewhat better with children at risk than they are at present, this problem is not, finally, an educational one. We do the nation a disservice if we help perpetuate the myth that schools are an effective counterbalance to social inequity and neglect. This myth pleases the economically powerful who too often are content simply to maintain their dominance. It also may flatter some educators who enjoy the image of educational institutions as socially redemptive. But the myth ill-serves society, and it is urgent that we convey this message. A mature society must not shunt aside its social problems. It must face them shorn of illusion.

There are clear advantages to seeing *schools* as the ultimate institutions that will eradicate poverty. They certainly conform to the therapeutic model of social welfare and they have a strong sense of legitimacy. The notion that schools can somehow significantly reduce poverty persists in the face of substantial social science research to the contrary (Coleman, 1966; Jencks, 1972). Isolated cases of "successful" schools in poverty areas are given national attention. Presidents visit them. Their leaders appear on "60 Minutes" and testify before congressional committees (Weiskart, 1987). Instead of marvelling at how a particular school was able to overcome incredible odds, these schools are used to blame ordinary schools and to justify the status quo. None of this should surprise historians of education. Public schools were established, not to question the existing order, but to justify and reproduce it. They are primary agents of socialization, and socialization is inculcation into the existing order.

And yet to say only this about schools is to say too little, for institutions often outgrow their original purposes. At this point the dynamic between schools as agents of domestication in an individualist society takes a curious turn. No decent teacher is willing to settle for schools that only ratify the status quo. They desire to awaken and nurture in students something else—a critical capacity, independence of thought, a sense of social responsibility and so forth. The practical result of this is that some students come to be critical of some institutions or social relationships. Most of the time teachers fail in this undertaking. Given the inertia of the status quo, it is quite ambitious. But there are enough successes to keep this ideal alive.

It is possible that the contradiction between schools as agents of socialization and as trainers of sharp-brained analytical thinkers can be eliminated, but this would require significant changes both within the school and in the society. Within the school there must be education, both in form and content, that takes seriously the notion of human dignity. And in society at large we would need to accept the notion of constant renewal, of assessing our institutions as honestly and as clearly as we can. Only a society that is unafraid of itself can do that, but it is also the only society befitting our best selves and, therefore, the only society worth struggling for.

Any discussion of poverty must move beyond therapeutic solutions if it is to be considered within the context of educational enhancement. At this nexus of history, we need to think less about changing the character of students and more about changing the character of our social system to make it more inclusive and fair. The will to ignorance is not sewn in human nature. It is something that is learned, and it comes at a terrible price. When people are made to feel that they matter, they look towards the future; they aspire, and they learn. Schools cannot teach children that they matter if everything outside the schoolyard contradicts this teaching. The *first* step in enhancing our educational experience should be to rethink our social contract, the nature of our interdependence, what we therefore owe to one another, and what we ought to guarantee everyone by virtue of their membership in society.

I am well aware of the fact that this is not the type of discussion that typically finds its way into books targeted for current and potential educators. And yet the relevance of these questions to our enterprise seems manifest. If one begins with a democratic theory of education and takes the logic of that theory seriously, eventually the question of widespread poverty must be addressed. If economists can discuss publicly what they think are the economic consequences of poverty and economic inequality, if Catholic bishops can publicly discuss their moral consequences, and political scientists their effects upon democracy, then certainly educators can publicly discuss their effects on education.

Individualism is an important value, but it cannot be the primary value of a society. It cannot inform the dominant myth of a society, for it is inadequate to express the common needs that everywhere bind humans into groups. We live together because we need each other. Everywhere lives intermingle and fates overlap. If the problem of children at risk is as serious as suggested by various contributors to this volume, it will take all the wit and wisdom we can muster to resolve it. We cannot be content to turn inward, speaking only to each other. We must draw upon our expertise and state what our experience in our professions has taught us. But our actions must be directed outwards, towards the community. We must speak not as professionals but as citizens.

REFERENCES

Bellah, Robert, *The Broken Covenant.* New York: Seabury, 1975.

Bloom, Allan, *The Closing of the American Mind.* New York: Simon and Schuster, 1987.

Bowles, Samuel and Gintis, Herbert, *Schooling in Capitalist America.* New York: Basic, 1972.

Cohen, David, "The Conditions of Teachers' Work." *Harvard Educational Review* 54, No. 1 (February, 1984).

Coleman, James, *Equality of Educational Opportunity Report* U.S. Dept. of HEW, U.S. Government Printing Office, 1966.

Erikson, Erik, *Childhood and Society.* New York: Norton, 1964.

Fitzgerald, Frances, *America Revised.* Boston: Little Brown, 1979.

Gilder, George, *Wealth and Poverty.* New York: Basic, 1981.

a Greenstein, Robert, "Gap Between Rich and Poor Widest Ever Recorded." Washington, D.C.: Center on Budget and Policy Priorities, Aug. 17, 1987.

b Greenstein, Robert, "FY 1988 President's Request." Center on Budget and Policy Priorities, Jan. 5, 1987.

Hamburg, David, Testimony before Senate Committee on Labor and Human Welfare and House Committee on Education and Labor, Sept. 9, 1987.

Janeway, Elizabeth, *Man's World, Woman's Place.* New York: Morrow, 1971.

Jencks, Christopher, *Inequality; a Reassessment of the Effect of Family and Schooling in America.* New York: Basic, 1972.

Katz, Michael, *School Reform, Past and Present.* Boston: Little, Brown, 1971.

Nasau, David, *Schooled to Order.* New York: Oxford University Press, 1979.

Polsky, Andrew, "Welfare Policy: Why the Past Has No Future." *Democracy* Vol. 3 No. 1 (Winter, 1983).

Schlozman, Kay and Verba, Sidney, *Injury to Insult.* Cambridge: Harvard University Press, 1979.

Shalala, Donna, "It Just Makes Sense to Help Poor People." *Chronicle of Higher Education,* October 28, 1986, p. 96.

Sizer, Theodore, *Horace's Compromise.* Boston: Houghton, Mifflin, 1985.

Sroufe, Alan and Cooper, Robert, *Child Development.* New York: Alfred A. Knopf, 1988.

Walzer, Michael, *Spheres of Justice.* New York: Basic Books, 1983.

Weikart, David P. Testimony before Senate Committee on Labor and Human Welfare and House Committee on Education and Labor, September 9, 1987.

INDEX